Stages and Pathways of Drug Involvement

Examining the Gateway Hypothesis

This book represents the first systematic discussion of the Gateway Hypothesis, a developmental hypothesis formulated to model how adolescents initiate and progress in the use of various drugs. In the United States, this progression proceeds from the use of tobacco or alcohol to the use of marijuana and other illicit drugs. This volume presents a critical overview of what is currently known about the Gateway Hypothesis. The authors of the chapters explore the hypothesis from various perspectives ranging from developmental social psychology to prevention and intervention science, animal models, neurobiology, and analytical methodology. This book is original and unique in its purview, covering a broad view of the Gateway Hypothesis. The juxtaposition of epidemiological, intervention, animal, and neurobiological studies represents a new stage in the evolution of drug research, in which epidemiology and biology inform one another in the understanding of drug abuse.

Denise B. Kandel is Professor of Public Health and Psychiatry at the College of Physicians and Surgeons of Columbia University and Chief of the Department of the Epidemiology of Substance Abuse at the New York State Psychiatric Institute. She has published numerous articles in *Science*, the *American Journal of Public Health, Drug and Alcohol Dependence, Archives of General Psychiatry*, the *Journal of the Academy of Child and Adolescent Psychiatry*, the *American Journal of Sociology*, and the *American Sociological Review*.

Stages and Pathways of Drug Involvement

Examining the Gateway Hypothesis

Edited by

Denise B. Kandel
Columbia University

CAMBRIDGE
UNIVERSITY PRESS

PUBLISHED BY THE PRESS SYNDICATE OF THE UNIVERSITY OF CAMBRIDGE
The Pitt Building, Trumpington Street, Cambridge, United Kingdom

CAMBRIDGE UNIVERSITY PRESS
The Edinburgh Building, Cambridge CB2 2RU, UK
40 West 20th Street, New York, NY 10011-4211, USA
477 Williamstown Road, Port Melbourne, VIC 3207, Australia
Ruiz de Alarcón 13, 28014 Madrid, Spain
Dock House, The Waterfront, Cape Town 8001, South Africa

http://www.cambridge.org

First published 2002

Printed in the United States of America

Typeface Ehrhardt 11/13 pt.   *System* QuarkXPress™[KW]

A catalog record for this book is available from the British Library.

Library of Congress Cataloging in Publication Data

Stages and pathways of drug involvement : examining the gateway hypothesis/edited by
Denise B. Kandel.
p. cm.
Includes bibliographical references and index.
ISBN 0-521-78349-6 – ISBN 0-521-78969-9 (pb.)
1. Drug abuse. 2. Substance abuse. I. Kandel, Denise Bystryn.
HV5801 .S733 2001
362.29 – dc21   2001018457

ISBN   0 521 78349 6 hardback
ISBN   0 521 78969 9 paperback

Contents

Contributors

Sara R. Battin-Pearson, Research Consultant, Social Development Research Group, School of Social Work, University of Washington, Seattle, Washington

Peter M. Bentler, Professor of Psychology and Statistics, and Chair, Department of Psychology, University of California, Los Angeles, California

Anthony Biglan, Senior Scientist, Oregon Research Institute, Eugene, Oregon

Gilbert J. Botvin, Professor and Director, Institute for Prevention Research, Weill Medical College of Cornell University, New York, New York

Linda M. Collins, Director, The Methodology Center, The College of Health and Human Development, Pennsylvania State University, University Park, Pennsylvania

Martha M. Faraday, Assistant Professor of Medical and Clinical Psychology, Medical and Clinical Psychology Department, Uniformed Services University of the Health Services, Bethesda, Maryland

Andrew Golub, National Development and Research Institute, Inc., New York, New York

Kenneth W. Griffin, Assistant Professor, Weill Medical College of Cornell University, New York, New York

Neil E. Grunberg, Professor of Medical and Clinical Psychology and Neuroscience, Medical and Clinical Psychology Department, Uniformed Services University of the Health Services, Bethesda, Maryland

Jie Guo, Analyst, Social Development Research Group, School of Social Work, University of Washington, Seattle, Washington

J. David Hawkins, Director and Professor, Social Development Research Group, School of Social Work, University of Washington, Seattle, Washington

Karl G. Hill, Project Director, Social Development Research Group, School of Social Work, University of Washington, Seattle, Washington

Richard Jessor, Director, Institute of Behavioral Science, and Professor of Psychology, University of Colorado, Boulder, Colorado

Bruce D. Johnson, Director, Institute for Special Populations Research, National Development and Research Institute, Inc., New York, New York

Denise B. Kandel, Professor of Public Health in Psychiatry, Columbia University, and Chief, Department of the Epidemiology of Substance Abuse, New York State Psychiatric Institute, New York, New York

George F. Koob, Professor, Department of Neuropharmacology, The Scripps Research Institute, La Jolla, California

Erich Labouvie, Professor, Center of Alcohol Studies, Rutgers University, Piscataway, New Jersey

Chaoyang Li, Research Assistant, Department of Preventive Medicine, University of Southern California, Los Angeles, California

Michael D. Newcomb, Professor and Chair, Division of Counseling Psychology, Rossier School of Education, University of Southern California, Los Angeles, California

Mary Ann Pentz, Professor, Department of Preventive Medicine, University of Southern California, Los Angeles, California

Lawrence M. Scheier, Associate Professor of Psychology, Weill Medical College of Cornell University, New York, New York

Susan Schenk, Associate Professor, Department of Psychology, Texas A&M University, College Station, Texas

Keith Smolkowski, Research Analyst, Oregon Research Institute, Eugene, Oregon

Helene R. White, Professor, Center of Alcohol Studies, Rutgers University, Piscataway, New Jersey

Kazuo Yamaguchi, Professor of Sociology, University of Chicago and National Opinion Research Center, Chicago, Illinois

Marc A. Zimmerman, Associate Professor of Health Behavior and Health Education, and Psychology, University of Michigan, Ann Arbor, Michigan

Foreword

Alan I. Leshner
National Institute on Drug Abuse

A key element to thoughtful discussions on this topic is alluded to in the title of this book, *Stages and Pathways of Drug Involvement: Examining the Gateway Hypothesis.* Dr. Kandel and her colleagues do an excellent job of presenting what science has to offer on this subject. Although the verdict is still out on whether or not the Gateway Hypothesis represents a true causal progression, one point is certain: There is nothing inevitable about drug progression from alcohol and/or nicotine to drugs such as cocaine and heroin.

This notion of inevitability creates a problem in the way the Gateway Hypothesis has been used in policy formation. There is a connotation associated with this concept that the original researchers who coined the phrase probably never intended. Most of the world has interpreted the pattern or sequence of drug use as a pathway, whereas at best it is more like a funnel. According to this metaphor, everyone who has ever tried or used drugs is at the large end of the funnel, and, although events may foster more drug use for some individuals, there remains only a small subset of users who actually go on to become addicts at the other end of the funnel. Why is this? I believe a key part of the answer to questions about drug use patterns and behaviors lies in increasing our understanding of the neurobiological basis of addiction, specifically the brain mechanisms involved in the transition to addiction and of how the brain is sensitized to or cross-sensitized by various drugs.

Over the past two decades our understanding of drug abuse has grown tremendously, including our knowledge of both the neurobiology of addiction and the factors that increase the risk that an individual will initiate drug use or will escalate to a level of drug addiction or a substance abuse disorder. Studies dating back to the 1970s suggest that adolescents tend to use alcohol and/or tobacco before marijuana, and marijuana and alcohol before other illicit drugs, such as cocaine and/or heroin. Research conducted by many of the authors assembled in this book has shown that there does appear to be an agreed-upon model of sequential stages of involvement with substances, which typically begins with beer and wine. Although there appears to be some variation in the model, each stage seems to play some kind of important role in the movement to the next stage, although this kind of staged progression is not a pre-requisite for drug addiction. In fact, the majority of individuals at one stage do not progress to another stage. National drug use and behavior studies show that although a great many, perhaps even a majority of, adolescents have some experiences with alcohol and/or tobacco, most do not go on to become drug addicts. But the other side of the coin is clear: The majority of the nation's heaviest drug users did use tobacco and/or alcohol before using drugs like heroin or cocaine.

There is also new research emerging that shows that use of cigarettes, alcohol, marijuana, and illicit drugs may be related to later psychiatric disorders. This finding adds yet another wrinkle to the drug use pattern dilemma. Not only do we have to consider that use of nicotine and alcohol may be a precursor to later drug abuse, but they may also open the door for later psychopathologies as well. Thus it is more critical than ever that prevention efforts be targeted to preteens and adolescents. It is also crucial that we keep our public health priorities in perspective and do not underestimate the health consequences associated with alcohol and tobacco use. They are major problems in their own way.

This book is not the final chapter on the question of gateways or pathways to drug use. But it is an excellent beginning of the next chapter. We now know there is no single factor that determines whether a person might abuse a substance; instead, substance abuse develops from the interaction of complex biological, psychological, and social/environmental determinants. We as a society urgently need the research community to sort this all out further as quickly and as clearly as possible.

Preface

The notion that use of certain drugs is a precursor to the use of other drugs was first proposed in the 1970s. The notion derived from the empirical observation that young people progressed from the use of legal drugs, such as tobacco or alcohol, to the use of illicit drugs, such as marijuana, cocaine, and heroin. In the 1980s, the term *Gateway drug* was introduced and it was emphasized that certain drugs serve as gateways for other substances. Because of the theoretical and public policy implications of the Gateway Hypothesis for understanding the progression of adolescent drug use and for formulating prevention and intervention programs, a conference was organized to examine the hypothesis critically. That conference, Stages and Pathways of Drug Involvement: Examining the Gateway Hypothesis, was held in Los Angeles on June 27–30, 1998. This book derives from the conference.

To evaluate current thinking and the strengths and weaknesses of various aspects of the Gateway Hypothesis, a multidisciplinary group of scientists was brought together, representing the disciplines of sociology, psychology, epidemiology, statistics, animal behavior, molecular biology, and prevention. In addition to the authors of the chapters in this volume, several senior scholars attended the conference: Lee Robins of Washington University in St. Louis, Klaus Hurrelmann of the University of Bielefeld of the Federal Republic of Germany, David Huizinga of the Institute of Behavioral Research of the University of Colorado, Charles O'Brien of the University of Pennsylvania, James D. Colliver and Lucinda L. Miner of the National Institute on Drug Abuse, Vivian Faden of the National Institute on Alcohol Abuse and Alcoholism, and Herbert Simpson of the Traffic Injury Research Foundation.

Each participant was asked to consider three broad issues: the nature of the pathways into drug abuse, the risk and protective factors that predict progression along the pathways, and the policy implications of the Gateway Hypothesis. Within these three areas, specific questions were highlighted. These are presented in Chapter 1.

Richard Jessor, Director of the Institute of Behavioral Science of the University of Colorado at Boulder, invited me to organize the conference. The conference was sponsored by the Youth Enhancement Service, a division of the Brain Information Service of the University of California at Los Angeles, directed by Michael Chase. Richard Jessor and Michael Chase were closely involved in planning the conference. Their contributions helped make it a successful forum for a stimulating and critical interchange of ideas. Michael Chase and his staff, especially Jena Miller, provided exceptional administrative support and contributed immeasurably to the success of the meeting. Funding for the conference was provided to the Youth Enhancement Service by the Anheuser-Busch Foundation, whose support is greatly appreciated. My work on this volume was supported by a Research Scientist Award (K05 DA00081) from the National Institute on Drug Abuse, for which I am most appreciative. I am particularly grateful for the contributions of the participants, which form the body of this volume.

Many of the ideas developed in the concluding chapter incorporate issues and points raised by the participants at the conference and in the chapters of this volume. Many ideas derive from my long-standing collaboration with Kazuo Yamaguchi on the study of stages of drug involvement. Many issues were clarified by the conference. But many remain unresolved and much remains to be done.

Part I

Overview

1

Examining the Gateway Hypothesis

Stages and Pathways of Drug Involvement

Denise B. Kandel

The notion that there are developmental stages and sequences of involvement in drugs was first advanced a quarter of a century ago (Hamburg, Kraemer, & Jahnke, 1975; Kandel, 1975). According to this notion, there is a progressive and hierarchical sequence of stages of drug use that begins with tobacco or alcohol, two classes of drugs that are legal, and proceeds to marijuana, and from marijuana to other illicit drugs, such as cocaine, metamphetamines, and heroin. The basic premise of the developmental stage hypothesis is that involvement in various classes of drugs is not opportunistic but follows definite pathways; an individual who participates in one drug behavior is at risk of progressing to another. The notion of developmental stages in drug behavior does not imply, however, that these stages are either obligatory or universal, nor that all persons must progress through each in turn.

In the early 1980s, the term *Gateway drug* began to be used to refer to alcohol and cigarettes, the drugs that are used prior to the use of illicit drugs. Soon, the usage was extended to include the use of marijuana as a precursor to the use of other illicit drugs, such as cocaine or heroin, and more rarely even to cocaine as a precursor to heroin. It is not clear how the term *Gateway drug* originated and I could not locate any relevant literature. Robert Dupont seems to have coined this term when he was director of the National Institute on Drug Abuse, and Dupont certainly was responsible for later popularizing its use (Dupont, 1984) and for connecting it with the stage hypothesis. The Gateway Hypothesis is implicit in the Gateway term and in the concept that certain drugs serve as gateways for the use of other drugs.

Validity of the Gateway Hypothesis is based on two criteria: sequencing of initiation of use between drug classes, and association in the use of drugs, such that use of a drug lower in the sequence increases the risk of using drugs higher in the sequence. Ultimately, association implies causation if all possibilities for spurious associations have been eliminated. Given the difficulties of establishing true causality in the social sciences, the term *association* rather than *causation* is emphasized in most of the chapters. Because of the theoretical and policy implications of the Gateway Hypothesis for understanding adolescent development and the formulation of prevention and intervention programs, a critical examination of the hypothesis is warranted. That is the purpose of the volume.

Although the Gateway Hypothesis had its origins in the mid-1970s, the concept of progression in drug use has a long history. It was first promulgated in the 1930s as the Stepping-Stone Theory (Etz, Robertson, Glanz, & Colliver, 1999; Goode, 1974). However, there is a crucial difference between the two concepts. The Stepping-Stone Theory considered the progression in drug involvement to be inexorable, with the use of marijuana invariably leading to heroin addiction. This position derived from an erroneous interpretation of data from clinical samples of treated heroin addicts. In these samples, most clients reported that the first drug they used prior to heroin was marijuana. From these selected samples, the investigators concluded that all those who used marijuana would eventually also use heroin. The subsequent prospective naturalistic studies of general population samples documented that in fact this was not the case. The Gateway Hypothesis, which emerged from this modern epidemiological tradition, emphasizes that although the use of certain drugs precedes the use of other classes, progression is not inevitable. Rather, the phases in drug behavior are facilitative. Entry into a particular stage is a common and perhaps even a necessary step but is not a sufficient prerequisite for entry into the next higher stage. Many youths stop at a particular stage without progressing further. In 1998, over 90% of young adults 20 to 30 years old in the United States had followed the assumed sequence. Of those who had used alcohol or tobacco, 49% proceeded to use one or more illicit drugs. Although steps in regression have been little studied, one early study reported that the same steps appeared in regression as in progression (Kandel & Faust, 1975).

Whereas much work has been done to identify the stages themselves, much less work has been carried out to identify the risk and protective factors underlying progression from one drug to another or the factors responsible for progression to heavier use of the same drug. A full accounting of developmental processes regarding drug use would also need to consider the place of drug use among a wider range of other problem behaviors in adolescence, including violence, delinquency, early sexual experimentation, premarital pregnancy, depression, suicide, dropping out of school, eating disorders, and even poor driving (see Dryfoos, 1990). These developmental progressions are not dealt with in this volume. The primary focus here is on progression through the use of different classes of drugs.

Numerous cross-sectional and longitudinal investigations have documented regular sequences of progression from legal to illegal drugs among adolescents and young adults of both sexes, irrespective of the age of first initiation into drugs, among different ethnic groups, in different countries, and at different historical periods spanning a 20-year interval. (For a review, see Kandel & Yamaguchi, 1999.) The sequence has been observed in countries other than the United States: in France, Israel, Australia, Japan, Spain, and Scotland (Adler & Kandel, 1981; Blaze-Temple & Lo, 1992; Oh, Yamazaki, & Kawata, 1998; Adrados, 1995; Morrison & Plant, 1991).

One group of cross-sectional studies does not take temporal order into account. An order has been inferred in the absence of information about timing of the onset of drug use. Evidence includes cross-sectional analyses based on Guttman scaling, a method that identifies unidimensional cumulative features of attributes (Adler & Kandel, 1981; Blaze-Temple & Lo, 1992; Brook, Hamburg, Balka, & Wynn, 1992; Brook, Whiteman, & Gordon, 1983; Donovan & Jessor, 1983; Kandel, 1975; Merrill, Kleber, Schwartz, Liv, & Lewis, 1999; Mills & Noyes, 1984; Single, Kandel, & Faust, 1974; Sorenson & Brownfield, 1989; Welte & Barnes, 1985; Yu & Williford, 1992). Other evidence derives from structural equation models based on cross-sectional data (Free, 1993; Hays et al., 1986; 1987; Huba & Bentler, 1982; Huba, Wingard, & Bentler, 1981; Marcos & Bahr, 1995; Martin, 1982; Potvin & Lee, 1980; Windle, Barnes, & Welte, 1989); latent class models (Sorenson & Brownfield, 1989); and log linear models (Miller, 1994). Historically, Guttman scaling has been the most frequently used method. Guttman scaling based on cross-sectional patterns of use reflects a hierarchical and unidimensional order of use, which, in the absence of age of onset or longitudinal data, does not necessarily reflect an order of initiation.

A second group of studies documents an order by taking timing into account. These include studies based on age of initiation of the use of various classes of drugs (Fleming, Leventhal, Glynn, & Ershler, 1989; Golub & Johnson, 1994; Hamburg, Kraemer, & Jahnke, 1975; Johnson, 1973; O'Donnell & Clayton, 1982; Voss & Clayton, 1987; Welte & Barnes, 1985); cross-tabulations of use patterns at different point in time (Elliott, Huizinga, & Menard, 1989); modified log linear Guttman scale analysis (Ellickson, Hays, & Bell, 1992; Gould, Berberian, Kasl, Thompson, & Kleber, 1977); path or structural equation models of panel data (e.g., Kaplan, Martin, & Robbins, 1984; Osgood, Johnston, O'Malley, & Bachman, 1988); latent transition analysis (Collins, Graham, Long, & Hansen, 1994; Collins & Wugalter, 1992; Graham, Collins, Wugalter, Chung, & Hansen, 1991); event history and parametric event sequence analysis (Yamaguchi & Kandel, 1984a; 1996); and extensions of log linear models (Kandel, Yamaguchi, & Chen, 1992). Some investigators have combined an initial Guttman scale analysis of cross-sectional data with an examination of patterns of subsequent transitions (Andrews, Hops, Ary, Lichtenstein, & Tildesley, 1991; Fleming, Leventhal, Glynn, & Ershler, 1989; Kandel & Faust, 1975).

Although illicit drugs other than marijuana are usually aggregated in a single group, several investigators have examined the order among specific illicit drugs other than marijuana (Ellickson, Hays, & Bell, 1992; Newcomb & Bentler, 1986; Mills & Noyes, 1984; Single, Kandel, & Faust, 1974; Sorenson & Brownfield, 1989; Welte & Barnes, 1985). Distinctions are usually made among pills (e.g., barbiturates, stimulants), cocaine, hallucinogens, and heroin. The greater the number of drugs to be ordered, the poorer the fit. There is much similarity across studies in the order: marijuana, pills, cocaine, heroin. The position of hallucinogens is the most unstable; it preceded cocaine in the New York state sample studied in 1971 (Single, Kandel, & Faust, 1974) but followed cocaine in samples of Maryland high school students surveyed in 1978–1981 (Mills & Noyes, 1984) or White males surveyed in Seattle in 1980 (Mills & Noyes, 1984). Sorenson and Brownfield (1989), who conducted systematic analyses based on Guttman scaling and latent structure analyses, found that the most unscalable scale types resulted from an assumed order between cocaine and hallucinogens. Heroin was not included among the drugs scaled. Hays et al. (1987) and Windle, Barnes, and Welte (1989) differentiated illicit drugs other than marijuana into enhancers and dampeners but could not successfully identify a sequential order for these two classes.

Sequences of involvement can also be distinguished within specific classes of drugs, involving shifts from initiation, to experimentation, casual use, regular use, abuse, and dependence (Clayton, 1992; Glantz & Pickens, 1992; Werch & Anzalone, 1995). With the exception of early discussions of heroin (Robins, 1979), most of this work has focused on cigarette smoking (e.g., Chassin, Presson, & Sherman, 1984; Flay, 1993; Leventhal & Cleary, 1980; Werch & Anzalone, 1995) and alcohol (Tarter & Vanyukov, 1994; Zucker, Fitzgerald, & Moses, 1995). Stages of involvement within a particular drug class may provide important specifications of progressions across classes of drugs. For example, Donovan and Jessor (1983) identified problem drinking as intervening between the use of marijuana and the use of other illicit drugs. Similarly, Collins and her colleagues (Collins, 1991; Collins et al., 1994; Graham et al., 1991) emphasized the role of drunkenness as a stage between the use of alcohol and tobacco and advanced drug use. In general, increasing involvement within a particular drug class precedes progression to the next stage (Ellickson, Hays, & Bell, 1992; Kandel & Faust, 1975; Yamaguchi & Kandel, 1984b).

Issues Underlying the Gateway Hypothesis

There has been a resurgence of interest in the Gateway Hypothesis as a framework for understanding adolescent drug involvement. This interest has been fueled, in part, by the national concern with adolescent smoking, by the role of tobacco in the progression into drug use, by the increase in the use of marijuana by adolescents during the last decade, and by recent reports pointing to a potentially common biological basis underlying addiction to different substances. However, the Gateway Hypothesis is not universally accepted. Showing that there is a sequence of initiation is not the same as showing that there is a causal link in the use of different drugs. Furthermore, as noted earlier, many users of a particular drug do not progress to the use of other drugs.

To evaluate properly the Gateway Hypothesis, several important issues need to be resolved. These include not only conceptual issues but also issues of substance, methods, underlying mechanisms, and policy.

The notion of a Gateway drug itself is vague. What makes a drug a Gateway drug? Is it any lower-ranked drug whose use precedes the use of a higher-ranked substance? As noted earlier, the most common hierarchy assigns alcohol and cigarettes to the initial stage, followed by marijuana, and by other illicit drugs; an order among illicit drugs other than marijuana has been difficult to establish. Even this general ordering has been challenged. Furthermore, the basis underlying any obtained ordering remains to be elucidated. Is the ordering the result of cultural definitions for normative behavior, psychological traits related to deviancy, differential availability, or the commonality of biological processes underlying addictive behaviors? Should one not refer to "Gateway use" of a drug rather than to a "Gateway drug"?

A fundamental issue pertains to the nature of the sequences themselves. What specific developmental stages and pathways of drug involvement can be identified currently among young people in the United States? Does the basic sequence from legal to illegal drugs characterize the general population and subgroups within it? Are there regular patterns of regression as well as progression? How do these pathways vary for different subgroups in the population, especially those distinguished by age, gender, or ethnicity, and for general population versus selected samples of heavy drug users? Have there been historical changes in the patterns? Are there identifiable pathways across drug use and other adolescent behaviors?

Another crucial issue pertains to the causal role of the use of one drug on initiation of another. The existence of sequential stages of progression does not necessarily imply causal linkages among different drugs. The observed sequences could simply reflect the association of each class of drugs with different ages of onset or individual attributes rather than the specific effects of the use of one class of drug on the use of another.

The evidence that addresses these questions derives mainly from naturalistic observational studies of a population. Two additional sources of data have been little utilized: programs implemented among youth to prevent or reduce drug use and animal experiments in which the drug seeking and behaviors of animals primed with specific drug classes can be observed. The implementation of drug prevention programs provides an imperfect substitution for an unrealizable social experiment in which adolescents would be randomly assigned to initiate the use of different drugs. Much can be learned, however, from prevention programs that have attempted to delay onset of the use of specific drug classes and to reduce levels of use among those who start. To test the Gateway Hypothesis, such programs would ideally focus on single drug classes to monitor more precisely the effect of the program on progression to higher-stage drugs. As we will see, in reality, very few such programs have been implemented. Most target several drug classes simultaneously. Animal models provide a test of progression in which the drug seeking of animals can be observed in relation to well defined prior experiences with specific drugs and independently of any social, legal, or moral definitions regarding the use of various substances.

Another set of issues pertains to the explanation of progression among classes of drugs and a specification of the risk and protective factors that predict transitions through the pathways. What are the biological, psychological, interpersonal, community, and cultural factors that promote or constrain progression? How do these factors vary by users' characteristics and by stage of drug use? Can one develop animal models to examine the nature of sequences and the predictors of progression, including factors that promote and those that inhibit progression? What explanatory insights can be provided by the new understanding of the biology of addiction?

There are methodological issues. How good is the statistical evidence for the existence of pathways and predictors of progression or regression? The identification of pathways and predictors of progression depends on the adequacy of the statistical evidence. The methodological approaches best suited to identify potential pathways, their risk and protective factors, the advantages and disadvantages of alternate approaches need to be evaluated. True sequential patterns need to be distinguished from chance occurrences. Association and causation need to be documented in addition to sequencing. Indeed, timing and sequence are not sufficient criteria for establishing developmental linkages. It is necessary to assess the extent to which the use of a drug at a particular stage actually determines initiation of the use of a drug at a higher stage.

There are also important policy issues. One set of issues pertains to the implications of findings from research on the Gateway Hypothesis for the development and implementation of prevention and treatment programs. The Gateway Hypothesis provides a useful organizing framework around which to develop specific theories of initiation, progression, and regression in drug use and specific intervention strategies to deal with the various stages of participation in drug behaviors. The hypothesis provides for an optimal specification of the periods in the life span when intervention efforts should be initiated, the types of drugs to be targeted, and the individuals who should be the target of the intervention. Ultimately it will help identify the characteristics of population groups at a particular stage who are most at risk for progression to the next stage or stages. By isolating populations at risk for progression from one drug stage to the next, it becomes possible to identify more accurately the factors that impact on those transitions.

Another set of policy issues pertains to the research that needs to be carried out to advance knowledge in the field. The work reported in this volume makes it clear that a transdisciplinary approach that cuts across the traditional disciplines of sociology, psychology, epidemiology, and biology will be essential for further advances in the field. The study of drug abuse in general and of the Gateway Hypothesis in particular provides unique opportunities for bridging meaningfully the social and psychological influences on drug seeking behavior with the molecular underpinnings of the reward system of the brain.

Organization of the Volume

The volume is organized into six parts. Following an overview in Part I, Part II presents empirical evidence regarding developmental pathways of drug involvement in different groups in the United States and selected risk and protective factors underlying the observed progressions. Several studies are based on prospective longitudinal follow-ups (Labouvie & White, Chapter 2; Hawkins, Hill, Guo, & Battin-Pearson, Chapter 3); others are based on retrospective reports of ages of onset into various substances (Kandel & Yamaguchi, Chapter 4; Golub & Johnson, Chapter 5). The prospective studies are based on adolescents; the retrospective studies are based on adults. Golub and Johnson's study is unusual because it deals with a group of hard core users and attempts to identify a comparison group of minority subjects drawn from national surveys.

Part III documents the impact of drug prevention programs on youths' subsequent drug progressions. These programs include a school-based prevention intervention targeting tobacco, alcohol, and marijuana in urban schools, based on the Life Skills program, now widely used throughout the United States (Botvin, Griffin, & Scheier, Chapter 6); an ambitious community wide effort that engages the efforts of relevant community groups and institutions, including parents, schools, mass media, local groups, and health policymakers (Pentz & Li, Chapter 7); and a school-based intervention specifically targeted to smoking in eight western communities in the United States (Biglan & Smolkowski, Chapter 8). This is the first time that drug prevention programs have examined the impact they have had on drug progression and the relevance of the intervention for evaluating the Gateway Hypothesis.

Part IV presents descriptions and applications of three major statistical approaches to the study of developmental pathways, including log linear methods (Yamaguchi & Kandel, Chapter 9); a modified version of structural equation modeling (Bentler, Newcomb, & Zimmerman, Chapter 10); and latent transition analysis (Collins, Chapter 11). These chapters discuss specific methodological approaches and present important substantive findings. In the last chapter in this section, Yamaguchi (Chapter 12) provides an integrated discussion of the advantages and disadvantages provided by each approach; he identifies aspects of the Gateway Hypothesis that each method can best illuminate and aspects that each is less suited for.

Part V focuses on biological approaches. Two of the chapters describe work based on animal experiments and discuss animal models of relevance to the Gateway Hypothesis (Grunberg & Faraday, Chapter 13; Schenk, Chapter 14). Koob (Chapter 15) summarizes what is presently known about the molecular biology of drug behavior and addiction.

In Part VI, in a concluding chapter (Chapter 16), Kandel and Jessor integrate the major findings presented in the volume, emphasize what is known and what remains to be learned, and suggest further lines of inquiry.

A unique contribution of this volume is the juxtaposition of epidemiological, intervention, animal, and neurobiological studies. This juxtaposition represents a new stage in the evolution of drug research, an evolution in which epidemiology and biology inform one another in the understanding of drug abuse.

References

Adler, I., & Kandel, D. B. (1981). Cross-cultural perspectives on developmental stages in adolescent drug use. *Journal of Studies on Alcohol, 42*, 701–715.

Adrados, J. L. (1995). The influence of family, school, and peers on adolescent drug misuse. *International Journal of the Addictions, 30*, 1407–1423.

Andrews, J. A., Hops, H., Ary, D., Lichtenstein, E., & Tildesley, E. (1991). The construction, validation and use of a Guttman scale of adolescent substance use: An investigation of family relationships. *Journal of Drug Issues, 21*, 557–572.

Blaze-Temple, D., & Lo, S. K. (1992). Stages of drug use: A community survey of Perth teenagers. *British Journal of Addictions, 87*, 215–225.

Brook, J. S., Hamburg, B. A., Balka, E. B., & Wynn, P. S. (1992). Sequences of drug involvement in African-American and Puerto Rican adolescents. *Psychological Reports, 71*, 179–182.

Brook, J. S., Whiteman, M., & Gordon, A. S. (1983). Stages of drug use in adolescence: Personality, peer, and family correlates. *Developmental Psychology, 19*, 269–277.

Chassin, L., Presson, C., & Sherman, S. (1984). Cigarette smoking and adolescent development. *Basic and Applied Social Psychology, 5*, 295–315.

Clayton, R. R. (1992). Transitions in drug use: risk and protective factors. In M. Glantz & R. Pickens (Eds.), *Vulnerability to drug abuse* (pp. 15–51). Washington, DC: American Psychological Association.

Collins, L. M. (1991). Measurement in longitudinal research. In L. M. Collins & J. L. Horn (Eds.), *Best methods for the analysis of change: Recent advances, unanswered questions, future directions* (pp. 137–148). Washington, DC: American Psychological Association.

Collins, L. M., Graham, J. W., Long, J. D., & Hansen, W. B. (1994). Cross-validation of latent class models of early substance use onset. *Multivariate Behavior Research, 29*, 165–183.

Collins, L. M., & Wugalter, S. E. (1992). Latent class models for stage-sequential dynamic latent variables. *Multivariate Behavior Research, 27*, 131–157.

Donovan, J. E., & Jessor, R. (1983). Problem drinking and the dimension of involvement with drugs: A Guttman scalogram analysis of adolescent drug use. *American Journal of Public Health, 73*, 543–552.

Dryfoos, J. G. (1990). *Adolescents at risk*. London: Oxford University Press.

Dupont, R. L. (1984). *Getting tough on gateway drugs: A guide for the family*. Washington, DC: American Psychiatric Press.

Ellickson, P. L., Hays, R. D., & Bell, R. M. (1992). Stepping through the drug use sequence: Longitudinal scalogram analysis of initiation and regular use. *Journal of Abnormal Psychology, 101*, 441–451.

Elliott, D. S., Huizinga, D., & Menard, S. (1989). *Multiple problem youth*. New York: Springer-Verlag.

Etz, K. E., Robertson, E. R., Glantz, M. D., & Colliver, J. (1999). History of the Gateway Theory. Poster presented at the biennial meetings of the Society for Research on Child Development, Albuquerque, NM.

Flay, B. R. (1993). Youth tobacco use: Risks, patterns, and control. In J. Slade & C. T. Orleans (Eds.), *Nicotine addiction: Principles and management* (pp. 365–384). New York: Oxford University Press.

Fleming, R., Leventhal, H., Glynn, K., & Ershler, J. (1989). The role of cigarettes in the initiation and progression of early substance use. *Addictive Behavior, 14*, 261–272.

Free, M. D. (1993). Stages of drug use: A social control perspective. *Youth and Society, 25*, 251–271.

Glantz, M., & Pickens, R. (Eds.) (1992). *Vulnerability to drug abuse*. Washington, DC: American Psychological Association.

Golub, A., & Johnson, B. (1994). The shifting importance of alcohol and marijuana as gateway substances among serious drug abusers. *Journal of Studies on Alcohol, 55*, 607–614.

Goode, E. (1974). Marijuana use and the progression to dangerous drugs. In L. L. Miller (Ed.), *Marijuana effects on human behavior* (pp. 303–338). New York: Academic Press.

Gould, L. C., Berberian, R. M., Kasl, S. V., Thompson, W. D., & Kleber, H. D. (1977). Sequential patterns of multiple-drug use among high school students. *Archives of General Psychiatry, 34,* 216–226.

Graham, J. W., Collins, L. M., Wugalter, S. W., Chung, N. K., & Hansen, W. B. (1991). Modeling transitions in latent stage-sequential processes: A substance use prevention example. *Journal of Consulting and Clinical Psychology, 59,* 48–57.

Hamburg, B. A., Kraemer, H. C., & Jahnke, W. (1975). A hierarchy of drug use in adolescence: Behavioral and attitudinal correlates of substantial drug use. *American Journal of Psychiatry, 132,* 1155–1163.

Hays, R. D., Stacy, A. W., Widaman, K. F., DiMatteo, M. R., & Downey, R. (1986). Multistage path models of adolescent alcohol and drug use: A reanalysis. *The Journal of Drug Issues, 16,* 357–369.

Hays, R. D., Widaman, K. F., DiMatteo, M. R., & Stacy, A. W. (1987). Structural-equation models of current drug use: Are appropriate models so simple(x)? *Journal of Personality and Social Psychology, 52,* 134–144.

Huba, G. J., & Bentler, P. M. (1982). On the usefulness of latent variable causal modeling in testing theories of naturally occurring events. *Journal of Personality and Social Psychology, 43,* 604–611.

Huba, G. J., Wingard, J. A., & Bentler, P. M. (1981). A comparison of two latent variable causal models for adolescent drug use. *Journal of Personality and Social Psychology, 40,* 180–193.

Johnson, B. D. (1973). *Marihuana users and drug subcultures.* New York: John Wiley & Sons.

Kandel, D. B. (1975). Stages in adolescent involvement in drug use. *Science, 190,* 912–914.

Kandel, D. B., & Faust, R. (1975). Sequence and stages in patterns of adolescent drug use. *Archives of General Psychiatry, 32,* 923–932.

Kandel, D. B., & Yamaguchi, K. (1999). Developmental stages of involvement in substance use. In R. E. Tarter, R. J. Ammerman, & P. J. Ott (Eds.), *Sourcebook on substance abuse: Etiology, assessment and treatment* (pp. 50–70). Needham Heights, MA: Allyn & Bacon.

Kandel, D. B., Yamaguchi, K., & Chen, K. (1992). Stages of progression in drug involvement from adolescence to adulthood: Further evidence for the gateway theory. *Journal of Studies on Alcohol, 53,* 447–457.

Kaplan, H. B., Martin, S. S., & Robbins, C. (1984). Pathways to adolescent drug use: Self-derogation, peer influence, weakening of social controls, and early substance use. *Journal of Health and Social Behavior, 25,* 270–289.

Leventhal, H., & Cleary, P. (1980). The smoking problem: A review of the research and theory in behavioral risk modification. *Psychological Bulletin, 88,* 370–405.

Marcos, A. C., & Bahr, S. J. (1995). Drug progression model: A social control test. *The International Journal of the Addictions, 30,* 1383–1405.

Martin, J. A. (1982). Application of structural modeling with latent variables to adolescent drug use: A reply to Huba, Wingard, and Bentler. *Journal of Personality and Social Psychology, 43,* 598–603.

Merrill, J. C., Kleber, H. D., Shwartz, M., Liu, H., & Lewis, S. R. (1999). Cigarettes, alcohol, marijuana, other risk behaviors, and American youth. *Drug and Alcohol Dependence, 56,* 205–212.

Miller, T. Q. (1994). A test of alternative explanations for the stage-like progression of adolescent substance use in four national samples. *Addictive Behaviors, 19,* 287–293.

Mills, C. J., & Noyes, H. L. (1984). Patterns and correlates of initial and subsequent drug use among adolescents. *Journal of Consulting and Clinical Psychology, 52,* 231–243.

Morrison, V., & Plant, M. (1991). Licit and illicit drug initiations and alcohol-related problems amongst illicit drug users in Edinburgh. *Drug and Alcohol Dependence, 27,* 19–27.

Newcomb, M. D., & Bentler, P. M. (1986). Frequency and sequence of drug use: A longitudinal study from early adolescence to young adulthood. *Journal of Drug Education, 16,* 101–120.

O'Donnell, J. A., & Clayton, R. (1982). The stepping-stone hypothesis: Marijuana, heroin and causality. *Chemical Dependence, 4,* 229–241.

Oh, H., Yamazaki, Y., & Kawata, C. (1998). Prevalence and a drug use development model for the study of adolescent drug use in Japan. *Japanese Journal of Public Health, 45,* 870–882.

Osgood, D. W., Johnston, L. D., O'Malley, P. M., & Bachman, J. G. (1988). The generality of deviance in late adolescence and early adulthood. *American Sociological Review, 53,* 81–93.

Potvin, R. H., & Lee, C. (1980). Multistage path models of adolescent alcohol and drug use. *Journal of Studies on Alcohol, 41,* 531–542.

Robins, L. N. (1979). Addict careers. In R. Dupont, A. Goldstein, & J. O'Donnel (Eds.), *Handbook on Drug Abuse* (pp. 325–355). Washington, DC: National Institute on Drug Abuse and Office of Drug Abuse Policy.

Single, E., Kandel, D. B., & Faust, R. (1974). Patterns of multiple drug use in high school. *Journal of Health and Social Behavior, 15,* 344–357.

Sorenson, A. M., & Brownfield, D. (1989). Patterns of adolescent drug use: Inferences from latent structure analysis. *Social Science Research, 18,* 271–290.

Tarter, R. E., & Vanyukov, M. M. (1994). Stepwise development model of alcoholism etiology. In R. Zucker, G. Boyd, & J. Howard (Eds.), *Development of alcohol problems: Exploring the biopsychosocial matrix of risk.* NIAAA Monograph 26. Bethesda, MD.

Voss, H. L., & Clayton, R. R. (1987). Stages in involvement with drugs. *Pediatrician, 14*, 25–31.

Welte, J. W., & Barnes, G. M. (1985). Alcohol: The gateway to other drug use among secondary-school students. *Journal of Youth and Adolescence, 14*, 487–498.

Werch, C. E., & Anzalone, D. A. (1995). Stage theory and research on tobacco, alcohol, and other drug use. *Journal of Drug Education, 25*, 81–98.

Windle, M., Barnes, G. M., & Welte, J. (1989). Causal models of adolescent substance use: An examination of gender differences using distribution-free estimators. *Journal of Personality and Social Psychology, 56*, 132–142.

Yamaguchi, K., & Kandel, D. B. (1984a). Patterns of drug use from adolescence to early adulthood. II. Sequences of progression. *American Journal of Public Health, 74*, 668–672.

Yamaguchi, K., & Kandel, D. B. (1984b). Patterns of drug use from adolescence to early adulthood. III. Predictors of progression. *American Journal of Public Health, 74*, 673–681.

Yamaguchi, K., & Kandel, D. B. (1996). Parametric event sequence analysis: An application to an analysis of gender and racial/ethnic differences in patterns of drug-use progression. *Journal of the American Statistical Association, 91*, 1388–1399.

Yu, J., & Williford, W. (1992). The analysis of drug use progression of young adults in New York state. *The International Journal of the Addictions, 27*, 1313–1323.

Zucker, R. A., Fitzgerald, H. E., & Moses, H. D. (1995). Emergence of alcohol problems and the several alcoholisms: A developmental perspective on etiologic theory and life course trajectory. In D. Cicchetti & D. J. Cohen (Eds.), *Developmental psychopathology. Vol. 2. Risk, disorder, and adaptation* (pp. 677–711). New York: John Wiley & Sons.

Part II

Recent Substantive Findings

What Do We Know About Stages of Drug Use, Risks, and Protective Factors?

2

Drug Sequences, Age of Onset, and Use Trajectories as Predictors of Drug Abuse/Dependence in Young Adulthood

Erich Labouvie and Helene R. White

According to Wohlwill (1973), developmental trajectories can be described in terms of a variety of parameters indicating presence of change; direction of change; shape of trajectory; values of maxima, minima, or terminal levels; sequencing of events; timing of events; and/or age corresponding to specified values of any of those characteristics. The sheer number of possible parameters serves as a reminder that whichever one is used in empirical studies can only provide a very incomplete picture of individual differences in developmental trajectories. The empirical study of such parameters can be aimed at two somewhat different objectives. First, researchers may be interested in identifying the factors and mechanisms that produce individual differences in a parameter of interest. Second, it is also desirable and useful to examine whether differences in a given parameter predict differences in relevant developmental outcomes at a later point in time. In this chapter, we are primarily concerned with the second objective. Ideally, the two approaches complement each other by focusing on the same or similar parameters. Unfortunately, however, theories of substance abuse and dependence provide little guidance as to which of the many available parameters are more or less useful for an understanding of the development of abuse and dependence in young adulthood. In spite of, or perhaps because of, this lack of theoretical guidance, empirical studies of the initiation and development of substance use in adolescence and early adulthood have primarily focused on the sequencing of

Preparation of this chapter was supported in part by grants from the National Institute on Drug Abuse (#DA/AA-03395) and the Robert Wood Johnson Foundation (#03295).

drug use and ages of onset as the parameters that are presumably of critical importance.

A number of general population studies have replicated a similar sequence of drug use progression, which, for the majority of individuals, starts with alcohol/cigarettes and proceeds to marijuana and then to other illicit drugs (Kandel & Yamaguchi, 1999). This progression has been found in general population samples of adolescents and adults in the United States as well as other countries (Kandel, Yamaguchi, & Chen, 1992). Not surprisingly, this consistency in findings has led to the claim that alcohol, cigarettes, and even marijuana serve as Gateway drugs for other illicit drug use. According to the Gateway Hypothesis, it is assumed that individuals progress from a lower-stage drug to the next higher-stage drug in a sequence. A person is unlikely to proceed to a drug stage without having first tried a lower-stage drug. However, most individuals are likely to stop at an early stage without progressing through the whole sequence. The Gateway Hypothesis implies that the sequence of drug use onsets is universal and that the most important individual differences are differences in the end stage that is reached by different persons.

A good deal of empirical evidence provides limited support for the validity and generality of the Gateway Hypothesis (e.g., Peele & Brodsky, 1997) and points to the need to consider differences in other features of individual use histories. Consistent with the hypothesis, a majority of drug users in general population samples are only experimental users and relatively few individuals proceed to the regular use of hard drugs such as cocaine or heroin (Golub & Johnson, 1994; see also Golub & Johnson, Chapter 5). However, when studies have focused on heavy and/or drug dependent users (e.g., Golub & Johnson, 1994; Mackesy-Amiti, Fendrich, & Goldstein, 1997), it has been found that the typical sequence is relatively rare. In a study of inner-city, predominantly lower-class New York City heavy drug users, Mackesy-Amiti and colleagues (1997) found that only 33% of drug users followed the conventional alcohol–marijuana–hard drugs progression. Only about 60% of the users initiated marijuana use prior to hard drug use as compared to 90–95% of users in general population samples.

Similarly, Golub, and Johnson (1994) found that, in a sample of serious drug users in New York City, alcohol was less salient for progression to serious drug use than was marijuana. Further, in contrast to general population samples, more individuals had smoked marijuana (91%) than had used alcohol (75%), thus indicating that a substantial minority of the sample deviated from the conventional sequence. Golub and Johnson (1994) concluded that marijuana rather than alcohol serves as a "gateway"drug for serious drug use (see also Golub & Johnson, Chapter 5). It should be noted, however, that both studies did not assess cigarette use and thus may underestimate the extent to which onset of licit use preceded that of marijuana and other illicit drugs.

Historical changes in licit and illicit drug use also suggest that a description of the development of substance use solely in terms of onset sequences may provide an overly simplistic view that ignores other potentially important individual differences in use histories. Since the late 1960s there have been numerous shifts in the prevalence and age of onset of illicit drug use, even though these behaviors have remained relatively constant for alcohol use and prevalence of cigarette use has declined since the mid-1970s followed by a slight increase in recent years (Blane & Hewitt, 1977; Johnston, Bachman, & O'Malley, 1998). According to Hawkins, Hill, Guo, and Battin-Pearson (Chapter 3) sequences of drug use vary with historical time because of changes in societal norms and in availability of various substances. Golub and Johnson (1994) found that a greater proportion of older (born before 1953) as compared to younger (born after 1962) serious drug users began their use with alcohol. The same authors (Golub & Johnson, this volume) also report that more individuals in the younger than older cohorts began their use with marijuana (see also Mackesy-Amiti, Fendrich, & Goldstein, 1997; Holland & Griffin, 1984). Finally, the fact that many individuals try or use illicit drugs for only a limited period and then stop (e.g., Labouvie, 1996; Bachman, Wadsworth, O'Malley, Johnston, & Schulenberg, 1997) also suggests that the developmental description of substance use trajectories requires elaboration of differences that go beyond those emphasized by the Gateway Hypothesis.

Kandel and colleagues (1992, p. 453) were careful to stress that use at one stage does not invariably lead to use at the next stage. Instead, entry into one stage may only be a necessary but not a sufficient prerequisite for progression to the next stage. Although it has been argued that initiation of use of various drugs can be predicted by a common set of risk factors (Jessor, Donovan, & Costa, 1991; Hawkins, Catalano, & Miller, 1992), we agree with Kandel, Yamaguchi, and Chen (1992) that a stage model is advantageous because such a description of use histories makes it possible to identify specific risk factors that can explain movement from one stage to the next. However, as stated at the outset, the developmental study of alcohol and other drug use is not only concerned with investigations of differences in the initiation of use. If, instead, one is interested in the prediction of abuse and/or dependence in young adulthood, differences in onset sequences may be of little usefulness.

Much of the research on drug sequences has been based on reported ages of first use, which have also been studied by themselves as predictors of subsequent alcohol and other drug involvement and problems (Robins & Pryzbeck, 1985). For example, in a large national epidemiological survey, Grant and Dawson (1997) found age of first use of alcohol to be a strong predictor of lifetime alcohol abuse and dependence, although the relationship was not completely linear. In a large national study of individuals 18 years and older, Chou and Pickering (1992) found that the earlier a person started drinking, the greater the number of alcohol dependence symptoms manifested at a later time. However, those starting before age 12 had a lower likelihood of experiencing three or more symptoms than those who began between 12 and 17 years of age. In a more recent study, Hawkins and colleagues (1997) found that the earlier individuals began drinking alcohol, the greater their level of alcohol misuse at age 17–18. Pedersen and Skrondal (1998) also found that age of onset of alcohol use was an important predictor of heavy alcohol use during adolescence and of alcohol problems in late adolescence. These authors, however, raised the possibility that the role of age of onset may be overestimated whenever common risk factors predicting both onset and consumption are not measured and left out of empirical analyses. They also argued that it is important to distinguish between "normal" early onset and "problem-prone" early onset (see also Weber, Graham, Flay, & Johnson, 1989) .

When Labouvie, Bates, and Pandina (1997) controlled for age of illicit drug use, age at onset of licit drug use no longer predicted alcohol or illicit drug use in late adolescence (age 20). Further, neither ages of licit or illicit drug use onset were significant predictors of use intensity or use consequences at age 30. Finally, in a sample of clients in treatment for drug abuse, Holland and Griffin (1984) found age of onset was not significantly related to addiction liability nor to prior treatment history. Taken together, these findings suggest that age of onset has predictive utility that varies both with the type (e.g., use intensity, abuse/dependence) and the temporal distance (e.g., proximal, distal) of use outcomes that are being considered.

Abuse/dependence presupposes the presence of heavier consumption levels during and/or before the period when it manifests itself (Skinner, 1990). Thus, when one is interested in the prediction of abuse and/or dependence in young adulthood, it would seem reasonable to expect that differences and changes in use intensity following the onset of use are features of individual use histories that provide substantial predictive utility. Only to the extent that age of onset can be shown to be strongly correlated with subsequent differences in levels of intensity over time should the former be expected to provide a useful predictor of later abuse or dependence. Similarly, only to the extent that different sequences of onset of drug use can be shown to be strongly correlated with differences in intensity and persistence of use over time do such sequences provide shortcut indicators of individual use histories with predictive utility.

As previous research (Bachman, Wadsworth, O'Malley, Johnston, & Schulenberg, 1997; Yamaguchi & Kandel, 1985; Labouvie, 1996; White, Bates, & Labouvie, 1998) suggests, many individuals stop using drugs prior to entry into adult roles. Therefore, escalation of drug use during adolescence does not necessarily predict continuation of use or later drug problems or problems in other life areas in adulthood. Ages of onset and/or sequences of drug use onset are parameters that fail to distinguish between adolescence-limited patterns of drug use on the one hand and patterns of use that persist into adulthood on the other (see also Schulenberg, O'Malley, Bachman, & Wadsworth, 1996; Jessor, Donovan, & Costa, 1991). Therefore, we propose that individual differences in ages of onset and sequencing of drug use must be considered in conjunction with intraindividual changes in use intensity and individual differences in those changes.

In this study we compare three models describing drug use histories in terms of (1) ages of onset, (2) sequencing of initiation, and (3) trajectories based on the joint considerations of ages of onset and intensity of drug use across several points in time. Inclusion of use intensity at several points in time provides information about individual differences in intraindividual changes in use (including cessation of use). Specifically, we assess the relative utility of each of the three models in predicting abuse and dependence outcomes in young adulthood with the aim of identifying one of the models as having substantially better predictive utility. We then assess whether and to what extent the predictive utility of that model is possibly reduced when proximal risk factors in adulthood are simultaneously taken into account. Finally, we also examine risk factors in middle adolescence as predictors of individual differences in use histories as described by the best model.

Method

Design and Sample

Eligible adolescents were recruited through a random sampling of telephone numbers covering all but the five counties of New Jersey most distant from the test site. The procedure was estimated to reach 95% of all households in the specified geographic area. Between 1979 and 1981 successive rounds of telephone calls were carried out to fill specified quotas of 200–225 males and females aged 12, 15, or 18. An initial anonymous telephone interview served to identify households with eligible adolescents and to obtain demographic information. Following the telephone survey, field interviewers visited prospective subjects at their homes to gather additional demographic information and obtain informed consent.

Demographic comparisons of nonparticipants and participants on variables obtained in the initial telephone interview indicated that higher levels of family income and parental education are somewhat overrepresented among the sample of participants as compared to those who refused. In spite of these initial biases, the sample was heterogeneous and similar to the population of the state of New Jersey at that time in terms of family income and religion (Bureau of Census, 1981). This sample is most representative of white working- and middle-class youth living in a metropolitan area of the eastern United States. (For more detail on sample and design, see Pandina, Labouvie, & White, 1984.) Patterns of drug use in this sample are comparable to those reported in national representative samples for same age peers living in the Northeast region of the United States (Johnston, Bachman, & O'Malley, 1998).

Participants were tested initially between 1979 and 1981 (Time 1, T1) at the ages of 12, 15, and 18, representing the young, middle, and old cohorts, respectively ($N = 1,380$). They returned 3 years later in 1982–1984 (Time 2, T2), again in 1985–1987 (Time 3, T3), and finally in 1992–1994 (Time 4, T4). Ninety-one percent of the original participants returned at T4. A comparison of those subjects who were retested and those who dropped out indicated minimal differences in the extent of substance use at T1. A total of 1,201 participants were tested at all four points in time and are included in the analyses reported in the discussion that follows.

Measures

Age of Onset. For each of 14 substances (beer, wine, hard liquor, cigarettes, marijuana, cocaine, psychedelics, heroin, inhalants, phenyl-cyclohexyl-piperidine [PCP], and nonprescription use of sedatives, tranquilizers, stimulants, and analgesics) we assessed self-reported age of first use. For alcohol, it was defined as the minimum age of first use of beer, wine, or hard liquor outside a family gathering. For hard drugs, age of first use was the minimum age reported for nine drugs other than marijuana. We also distinguished between age of first licit use (the minimum age for alcohol and cigarettes) and age of first illicit use (the minimum for marijuana and hard drugs). For analytical purposes, age of onset was converted into time since onset, defined as the difference between individuals' age at T4 and age of onset. Individuals who had never tried a drug were given a score of zero on that variable.

Drug Use Intensity. At T1, individuals reported the total number of times they had ever used each of the 14 substances. At T2, T3, and T4 they reported the total number of times they had used each substance during the past 3 years. For alcohol we chose the maximum number reported for beer, wine, and hard liquor; for hard drugs we chose the maximum number reported for nine drug categories at each point in time.

Drug Use Sequence. For descriptive purposes, all empirically observed sequences among the four drugs were considered, yielding a total of 88 different sequences. However, in order to obtain groups of sufficient size, drug sequence was defined only in terms of the age of onset of licit versus illicit substances in the predictive analyses and did not include further drug distinctions within each of those two categories. A total of six possible sequences were defined: no onset of any substance, licit only, illicit only, licit before illicit, illicit before licit, and onset of licit and illicit substance use in the same year.

Drug Abuse / Dependence at T4. Current drug abuse/dependence for the 3-year period preceding T4 was measured by a self-report inventory of negative consequences and symptoms associated with alcohol, marijuana, cocaine, and other drug use. Items were selected to operationalize the four abuse and seven dependence criteria defined in DSM-IV (American Psychiatric Association, 1994; Muthen, Grant, & Hasin, 1993; Woody, Cottler, & Cacciola, 1993). Individuals who scored positively on one or more of the four criteria for abuse were diagnosed with abuse. Individuals who scored positive on three or more dependence criteria were diagnosed as dependent on alcohol, marijuana, and/or other drugs (a diagnosis based on the maximum number of symptoms for cocaine and other drugs). Strictly speaking, a DSM-IV diagnosis of dependence requires the occurrence of three or more dependence symptoms within a 12-month rather than a 3-year period. In light of this discrepancy in time frames, we decided to combine abuse and dependence into a single dichotomous variable for alcohol, marijuana, and hard drugs.

Rates of abuse/dependence at T4 for participants who reported onset of at least one substance ($N = 1,185$) were 36.7% for alcohol, 11.7% for marijuana, and 5.7% for hard drugs. Of these users, 59.7% did not meet criteria for any abuse/dependence diagnosis, 29.4% met abuse/dependence criteria for a single substance, 7.8% for two substances, and 3.0% for three substances.

Adolescent Risk Factors at Age 15. Table 2.1 presents a description of the risk variables included in the analyses as potential predictors of differences in individual use histories. The list of variables includes both social (peer-related) risks and personal risks (negative affect, impulsivity/ undercontrol, and unconventionality/deviance). Because the oldest cohort was only assessed at age 18 and later, it is not included in those analyses that examine adolescent risk factors.

Adult Risk Factors at T4. We also wanted to assess whether descriptors of use histories continue to be significant predictors of abuse/ dependence at T4 when proximal risk factors are taken into account. Although measures administered at T4 were formally different from those administered at age 15, the list of T4 proximal risks was chosen to parallel, at least in terms of content domains, the list of adolescent risk variables (see Table 2.1). Previous analyses (Bates & Labouvie, 1998) indicated that the 11 T4 risk variables could be reduced to three risk factors that accounted for 55.4% of the variance. The first factor captures primarily differences in social risks, the second factor marks differences in negative affect, and the third factor indicates differences in self-control and disinhibition. Individual scores on the three risk factors were used in subsequent analyses.

Results

Ages of Onset and Sequencing

First we present some descriptive results concerning ages of onset, escalation, and sequencing. Average age of onset increases from alcohol/ cigarettes to marijuana and to hard drugs (Table 2.2). In addition, the likelihood of onset, the likelihoods of escalation (having used a substance 20 or more times during at least one of the four periods), and persistence

Table 2.1. *Adolescent and Adult Risk Variables*

Variable	Description
Adolescence: Age 15	
Personal risks	
Impulsivity	impulsivity + play – harm avoidance – cognitive structure (Personality Research Form, Jackson, 1974) + disinhibition (Sensation Seeking Scale, Zuckerman, 1979)
Negative affect	anxiety + depression + hostility (SCL-90R, Derogatis, 1977)
Delinquency	sum of the frequencies of 14 behaviors ranging from evasion of payment to armed robbery
Social risks	
Friends' alcohol use	number of friends who have tried alcohol (maximum reported for beer, wine, and hard liquor)
Friends' cigarette use	number of friends who have tried cigarettes
Friends' marijuana use	number of friends who have tried marijuana
Friends' hard drug use	number of friends who have tried hard drugs (maximum reported for nine drug categories)
Adulthood: T4	
Social risks	
Friends' alcohol use	number of friends who drink alcohol
Friends' marijuana use	number of friends who smoke marijuana
Friends' tolerance of deviant activities	8 items; alpha = .84
Personal risks	
Loneliness	8 items; alpha = .92 (Russell, Peplau, & Cutrona, 1980)
Optimism	9 items; alpha = .89 (Scheier & Carver, 1987)
Self-esteem	8 items; alpha = .84 (Rosenberg, 1965)
Self-sentiment	16PF Q3 scale (Cattell, Eber, & Tatsuoka, 1970)
Thrill seeking	5 items; alpha = .88 (Cloninger, 1987)
Delinquency	sum of the frequencies of 30 behaviors
Mental disorganization	8 items; alpha = .82 (Dorner, Kreuzig, Reither, & Staudel, 1983)
Financial strain	6 items; alpha = .88

(having used 10 or more times during at least three of the four periods) all decrease from alcohol to hard drugs. Furthermore, correlations between age of onset and intensity of use of the four substances are all moderate in size at the first three occasions followed by a drop-off

Table 2.2. *Onset and Escalation of Use (Total* N = *1,201)*

Substance	N	%	Use Onset Age M (sd)	Percentage of Users Escalation[a]	Percentage of Users Persistence[b]
None	16	1.3	—	—	—
Alcohol	1,182	98.4	13.56 (2.67)	92.2	67.4
Cigarettes	932	77.6	12.90 (3.46)	72.0	39.8
Marijuana	958	79.8	14.85 (2.63)	55.6	23.7
Hard drugs	670	55.8	16.91 (2.63)	41.5	9.3

Notes: [a] Used 20 or more times during at least one of the four periods. [b] Used 10 or more times during at least three of the four periods.

Table 2.3. *Correlations Between Age of Onset and Use Intensity at Four Points in Time*

Substance	N	Time (Mean Age) T1 (15)	Time (Mean Age) T2 (18)	Time (Mean Age) T3 (21)	Time (Mean Age) T4 (28)
Alcohol	1,181	− .26*	− .34*	− .35*	− .21*
Cigarettes	931	− .42*	− .36*	− .26*	− .09
Marijuana	957	− .45*	− .49*	− .37*	− .17*
Hard drugs	670	− .44*	− .40*	− .36*	− .11

Note: * $p < .001$.

thereafter (Table 2.3). Overall, these findings indicate that onset of use is not invariably followed by intensification or persistence of use and that differences in onset age are, at best, moderately related to differences in intensity of use.

Table 2.4 presents the distribution of individuals across different sequences together with ages of onset as well as results of configural frequency analyses (von Eye, 1990). Given a set of events, configural frequency analysis allows one to examine the frequency with which each of several possible configurations or patterns of events has occurred in a given sample of subjects. In the present case, the set of events includes onset of licit and illicit use. The six possible configurations are defined in terms of both the occurrence and the sequence of these two events. Onset of licit use before illicit use is the predominant type (i.e., observed frequency is significantly greater than expected frequency, with 66.7% of the participants exhibiting that sequence. In comparison, onset of illicit

Table 2.4. *Onset Sequences* (N = *1,201*)

| Sequence | O | E | T/A | Onset Age | |
				Licit Use M (sd)	Illicit Use M (sd)
None	16	2.90	T	—	—
Licit only	207	220.5		14.7 (3.2)	—
Licit < illicit	801	321.6	T	11.6 (2.6)	15.3 (2.6)
Licit = illicit	128	321.6	A	13.6 (2.4)	13.6 (2.4)
Illicit < licit	49	321.6	A	14.2 (2.4)	11.7 (2.6)
Illicit only	0	12.7	A		

Notes: O = observed frequency; E = expected frequency (independence model); T = type (O is significantly larger than E); A = antitype (O is significantly smaller than E).

use before licit use is an antitype (i.e., observed frequency is significantly smaller than expected frequency), with only 4.1% of participants reporting that sequence. Representing neither a type nor an antitype, another 207 individuals initiated only licit use. Thus, 85.1% of those who began any use proceeded in a sequence that is consistent with the Gateway Hypothesis. Individuals who ever tried both an licit and an illicit drug reported the earliest onset age irrespective of sequential order (age 11.6 years for those who used licit drugs first; age 11.7 years for those who used illicit drugs first), whereas those who reported onset of both in the same year began, on average, at age 13.6. However, the delay between the first and the second stage of the sequence is shorter for those who began with illicit use (2.5 years) than for those who started with licit use (3.7 years).

Developmental Trajectories Based on Ages of Onset and Intensity

One of our goals was to obtain a more complete description of individual use trajectories based simultaneously on ages of onset and use intensities assessed at all four points in time. Because we were interested in combining two different features (age of onset and intensity) and because we expected many trajectories to be nonlinear and nonmonotonic in shape, latent growth curve analysis was deemed too cumbersome. Instead, in order to obtain a simultaneous analysis of both cross-sectional and longitudinal relationships, we decided to conduct a combined R-technique/ T-technique factor analysis. The well-known R-technique factor analysis is based on cross-sectional covariations between variables and is used to identify variable dimensions. In comparison, T-technique factor analysis is based on longitudinal covariations between occasions and is used to identify occasion dimensions (Cattell, 1978; Nesselroade, 1970). A combination of both techniques can be used to identify dimensions in terms of both variables and occasions. We computed a principal components analysis (with Varimax rotation) that included the following 20 variables: times since onset and number of times used at T1, T2, T3, and T4 (four intensity levels) for alcohol, cigarettes, marijuana, and hard drugs. T4 intensity levels were included for two reasons. First, abuse and/or dependence, which is assessed here in reference to a specified interval (i.e., the 3-year interval preceding T4), presupposes consumption during that same interval (Skinner, 1990). In other words, use intensity is a necessary, though not sufficient, formal cause (Reese & Overton, 1970) for abuse and/or dependence. Second, decreases in use, if they occur, become clearly evident only after age 25. Thus, an omission of T4 use levels would make it impossible to distinguish between time limited use patterns and those exhibiting persistence into adulthood.

Because the analysis is based on cross-sectional and longitudinal data, the resulting components represent occasion dimensions, that is, longitudinal trajectories of use of one or more substances. Each component describes a prototypical use trajectory. The loading pattern indicates which of the original variables and occasions should be viewed as its distinguishing features. Individuals' manifest use trajectories are obtained as weighted combinations of the prototypes, with individuals' scores on the components representing the weights and, thus, the degree to which each prototype is expressed in their observed use trajectories. Furthermore, given that the components are derived from a correlation matrix, individual differences need to be interpreted as deviations from normative (average) use trajectories for the sample as a whole.

Four components (with eigenvalues larger than 1) accounted for 68.2% of the variance and are shown in Table 2.5. Measurement errors in the manifest variables are assumed to constitute most of the variance that remains unaccounted for. The distinguishing features of the first component (loadings larger than .45) are the four ages of onset and the four T1 and three of the T2 use intensities. This component captures differences in trajectories describing adolescence limited use (AL) of all substances. A high score on this component (and average or below average on the other three) indicates a trajectory characterized by earlier than average onset and above average use of all substances in adolescence followed by average levels of substance use after the age of 21.

Table 2.5. *Varimax Rotated Trajectory Components*

Variable		AL	HC	HA	HD
			Trajectory Component		
Time since onset of	alcohol use	.67		.48	
	cigarette use	.45	.64		
	marijuana use	.66	.31	.31	.21
	hard drug use	.69	.17		.49
Alcohol use intensity	T1	.76		.38	
	T2	.57		.62	
	T3	.20		.79	.18
	T4			.67	.30
Cigarette use intensity	T1	.66	.53		
	T2	.32	.81		
	T3		.89		
	T4		.80		.25
Marijuana use intensity	T1	.86			
	T2	.68	.22	.15	.39
	T3	.29	.25	.24	.69
	T4			.15	.77
Hard drug use intensity	T1	.69			.15
	T2	.74			.37
	T3	.48	.20		.60
	T4				.72

Notes: Loadings absolutely smaller than .15 are omitted. AL = adolescence limited use; HC = cigarette use; HA = alcohol use; HD = drug use.

The remaining three components are substance-specific in their distinguishing features. A high score on the second component indicates a trajectory characterized by earlier than average onset and subsequent persistence of heavier (above average) cigarette use into adulthood (HC). A high score on the third component indicates a trajectory characterized by an earlier than average onset and persistence of above average levels of alcohol use from adolescence into adulthood (HA). The fourth component represents illicit drug use trajectories (HD). A high score reflects an earlier than average onset of hard drug use followed by an escalation of marijuana and hard drug use from below average levels at T1 to above average levels at T3 and T4. The fact that individuals' scores on the four components are uncorrelated allows for a considerable variety of individual use trajectories. For instance, some individuals may have low scores on all four components, indicating little or no use of all substances across the full period studied. Other individuals may have high scores on the first two components (AL and HC), indicating that their earlier than average onset of use of all substances is followed by a decline in alcohol, marijuana, and hard drug use but a persistence of heavy cigarette use. Yet other individuals may have high scores on the second and third components (HC and HA), indicating that their earlier than average onset of alcohol and cigarette use is followed by persistence of heavy use of both substances with little or no use of marijuana and hard drugs during that same time.

Predicting Adult Drug Abuse/Dependence From Trajectory Characteristics

To compare the predictive utility of the three descriptions of use histories (i.e., age of onset, onset sequences, and trajectories), we computed logistic regression analyses predicting T4 alcohol, marijuana, and hard drug abuse/dependence from three sets of predictors: (1) ages of onset for alcohol, cigarettes, marijuana, and hard drugs (entered as times since onset); (2) onset sequences (entered as a set of dummy variables); and (3) scores on the four trajectory components. Also entered in these analyses were sex and age (the latter as two dummy variables with the middle cohort as the reference group). Ages of onset and onset sequences clearly precede T4 abuse/dependence. In addition, as indicated by the factor loading pattern in Table 2.5, none of the four trajectory components is defined solely in terms of T4 use intensities. Consequently, individuals' scores on those trajectories indicate use intensities that are maintained across extended intervals. In each case, those extended intervals precede, either completely or partially, the T4 period.

The results of the three sets of logistic regressions are summarized in Table 2.6 by the generalized R-square (Cox & Snell, 1989) for each. Onset sequences account for the smallest proportions of variance. That result was expected, given that a substantial majority of the sample exhibited the same sequence (resulting in a predictor variable with relatively little variance). The largest proportions of variance are accounted for by the trajectory components. This finding is not surprising given that individual differences in component scores provide a more complete description of individual use histories in terms of both age of onset and use intensity across time.

Table 2.6. *Prediction of T4 Abuse / Dependence: Generalized R-Squares*

	Predictor Set		
Substance	Ages of Onset	Onset Sequences	Trajectory Components
Alcohol	.13	.12	.27
Marijuana	.14	.05	.31
Hard drugs	.08	.01	.18

Predicting T4 Abuse/Dependence From Trajectories and T4 Risk Factors

Although a description of trajectories in terms of age of onset and use intensities provides significantly better predictive utility than descriptions based on either ages of onset or onset sequences, knowledge of individuals' use histories may be of little predictive utility once proximal risk factors are taken into account. We replicated the third set of logistic regression analyses with the four trajectory scores as predictors of abuse/dependence by also including the three T4 risk components as predictors. Results of these analyses in terms of odds ratios are presented in Table 2.7. (These analyses were also computed with marital and parental status included; however, no significant effect was obtained for either variable.)

Comparison of R-squares in Table 2.7 with the corresponding ones in Table 2.6 shows that the inclusion of T4 risk components provides only a slight improvement in the accuracy of prediction. As expected, proximal risks are significant predictors. Higher levels of T4 social risks predict a greater likelihood of alcohol and marijuana abuse/dependence. Higher levels of T4 personal risks, involving lack of self-control and lack of mental organization, contribute to a greater likelihood of alcohol and hard drug abuse/dependence. However, contrary to expectation, differences in T4 negative affect do not make a difference.

Importantly, knowledge of individuals' use histories remains relevant for predicting T4 abuse/dependence outcomes. Differences in adolescence limited trajectories and cigarette use trajectories are unrelated to abuse/dependence regardless of substance category. However, differences in the escalation and maintenance of marijuana and hard drug use from late adolescence into adulthood predict abuse/dependence for all three substance categories. For every 1-point increase in drug use trajectory

Table 2.7. *Prediction of T4 Abuse/Dependence: Odds Ratios* (N = *1,159*)

Predictor	Substance		
	Alcohol	Marijuana	Hard Drugs
Male	2.0		
Younger			
Older			
Adolescence limited use (AL)			
Cigarette use (HC)			
Alcohol use (HA)	2.6		
Drug use (HD)	1.2	6.9	6.8
T4 Social risks	1.6	1.9	
T4 Negative affect			
T4 Undercontrol	1.4		1.6
Generalized R-square	.30	.32	.19

Note: Nonsignificant ($p > .01$) odds ratios are omitted.

score, individuals become 1.2 times more likely to exhibit alcohol abuse/ dependence and nearly 7 times more likely to exhibit marijuana and hard drug abuse/dependence. In addition, differences in alcohol use trajectories contribute to the prediction of alcohol abuse/dependence though not marijuana or hard drug abuse/dependence.

Adolescent Predictors of Use Trajectories

Conventional regression analyses were computed to examine the extent to which adolescent risk factors assessed at age 15 could predict differences in use trajectories (Table 2.8). Consistent with the previous findings, differences in negative affect are not significantly related to any differences in use histories of any substance. Somewhat surprisingly, delinquency at age 15 is only predictive of differences in adolescence limited use of all substances (AL), suggesting that the structure of problem behaviors as a syndrome may be largely an adolescence limited phenomenon. Higher levels of impulsivity and disinhibition predict earlier onset and persistence of higher levels of alcohol use (HA) and earlier onset of hard drug use and its escalation to above average levels in adulthood (HD). This finding is consistent with the fact that T4 differences in self-control and mental organization were found to predict alcohol and hard drug abuse/dependence. Social risks at age 15 predict differences in adolescence limited, cigarette, and alcohol use trajectories

Table 2.8. *Adolescent Predictors of Use Trajectories: Standardized Regression Weights* (N = *808*)

Predictor	AL	HC	HA	HD
		Trajectory Component		
Male		−.17	.14	.12
Age	.49		.28	−.19
Impulsivity			.22	.21
Negative affect				
Delinquency	.14			
Friends' alcohol use			.34	
Friends' cigarette use		.33		
Friends' marijuana use	.26			
Friends' hard drug use	.12			
R-square	.56	.21	.28	.14

Notes: Nonsignificant regression weights ($p > .01$) are omitted. AL = adolescence limited use; HC = cigarette use; HA = alcohol use; HD = drug use.

but not in illicit drug use trajectories. Again, this finding parallels, in part, the finding that proximal social risks at T4 were predictive of alcohol and marijuana abuse/dependence but not hard drug abuse/dependence. Finally, males are less likely to initiate early and continue heavy smoking and more likely to initiate early and continue heavier drinking and illicit drug use. The role of age as a predictor primarily stems from the fact that the two age cohorts were followed over two only partially overlapping age periods: from ages 12 to 25 and from ages 15 to 28, respectively. Given that the distinction between persistence of and reduction in use becomes more evident with increasing age beyond 25, it is not surprising that both adolescence limited use (AL) and persistence of alcohol use (HA) are more clearly evident in the older age cohort. At the same time, however, early onset of hard drug use with subsequent escalation into adulthood is more pronounced in the younger age cohort, suggesting either a historical difference between the two age cohorts or the possibility of an adulthood limited pattern of drug use with decreases in use not becoming evident until the late 20s or early 30s.

Discussion

This study sought to evaluate the comparative utility of three different descriptions of use histories for predicting abuse/dependence outcomes in young adulthood. The study offers several advantages. Data were based on a longitudinal prospective follow-up of individuals from adolescence into young adulthood. Information about use intensity was obtained at four points in time. Ages of onset were recalled at times relatively close to the actual onset of events. The sample was not selected on any particular characteristic, allowing generalization of our findings to nonclinical populations of adolescents and young adults. However, these advantages also present limitations. Because this is a normal community sample, it is not made up of many heavy drug users. Observed findings reflect normative use patterns of a mostly white, middle- and working-class sample in one state and may not be generalizable to minority populations, more serious drug users, or persons living in other parts of the country. Furthermore, although the data are prospective, the oldest cohort was first interviewed at age 18. Therefore, the reported age of onset for alcohol and cigarette use is, for most of these individuals, based on retrospective recall. Finally, if two or more drugs were initiated at the same age (measured in years), we could not determine the order in which they were initiated.

Overall, the findings from the present study suggest the following conclusions:

1. *It is important to distinguish between early onset that is followed by an adolescence limited pattern of use and early onset that is followed by a persistent pattern of chronically higher levels of use.* That distinction is consistent with the distinction between "normal" early onset and "problem-prone" early onset proposed by Pedersen and Skrondal (1998) and the corresponding distinction between Type I and Type II adolescents suggested by Weber et al. (1989). Our findings suggest that early onset followed by a pattern of adolescence limited use of licit and illicit drugs is only linked to social risk factors that may be encountered by normally socialized (Type I) adolescents. In contrast, early onset followed by a pattern of persistent use of alcohol and/or illicit drugs is linked not only to social risks but also to personal risks (e.g., impulsivity and undercontrol) and is more likely to be exhibited by problem-prone (Type II) adolescents.

2. *A description of individual use histories in terms of trajectories based on ages of onset and use intensities is preferable to descriptions based only on ages of onset or onset sequences for predicting*

abuse/dependence in young adulthood. Following from point (1) and consistent with prior findings (Labouvie, Butes, & Pandina, 1997), ages of onset and sequences of onset of use do not provide sufficient information about the subsequent escalation, persistence, or decrease in drug use across relatively lengthy periods. Therefore, ages of onset and onset sequences (i.e., licit before illicit, illicit before licit) are, by themselves, of limited utility in predicting abuse/dependence outcomes in young adulthood. The transition from adolescence to adulthood, more often than not, is accompanied by substantial changes in use. It should come as no surprise that a description of use histories that takes information about longitudinal patterns of intensity of use into account yields considerably better predictive accuracy.

3. *There is little support for the notion that onset of alcohol or cigarette use serves as a gateway or marker for the development of marijuana or hard drug abuse/dependence in young adulthood.* Trajectories of cigarette use did not predict any abuse/dependence at T4, and trajectories of alcohol use only predicted alcohol abuse/dependence at T4. In contrast, trajectories of marijuana/hard drug use predicted both alcohol abuse/dependence as well as marijuana and hard drug abuse/dependence. Thus, earlier onset of hard drug use and subsequent escalation to above average levels of marijuana and hard drug use in young adulthood were more likely to be associated with the manifestation of abuse/dependence of both alcohol and illicit substances during that period of the life span.

4. *Not only is it useful to distinguish between onset sequences and use stages, but the concept of stage of use can be meaningfully applied without reference to the concept of sequence of onset. Onset sequence* refers to the ordering of initiation of various drugs (e.g., alcohol first, followed by marijuana and then hard drugs). *Stages of use,* on the other hand, indicate the highest level of drug that has been initiated. According to the Gateway Hypothesis, a *higher-use stage* is defined as a stage with a normatively later onset in a fairly universal onset sequence (e.g., alcohol/cigarette use only versus alcohol/cigarette *and* marijuana use versus alcohol/cigarettes, marijuana *and* hard drug use). It is also possible to define stages of use simply in

terms of the "most severe" substance an individual has used irrespective of sequence of onset (e.g., alcohol/cigarettes versus marijuana versus hard drugs). Our findings suggest that sequences of initiation are less useful than stages of use as predictors of later drug problems. That is, individuals who are in the highest or most severe stage (i.e., hard drug use), irrespective of sequence, compared to those who are at a lower or less severe stage are more likely to develop problems with hard and softer drugs.

In sum, the present findings, together with other available evidence, suggest that the usefulness of age of onset and onset sequences depends on the time scale that one applies to the study of use histories. These parameters are more useful within a short-term, adolescence focused time perspective. However, as one moves toward a longer term, life span oriented perspective, they become less useful as adequate descriptors of differences in individual use histories. Finally, differences in the time scales that are applied to the study of drug use histories will have a bearing on how different researchers conceptualize the Gateway Hypothesis.

References

American Psychiatric Association. (1994). *DSM-IV diagnostic and statistical manual of mental disorders* (4th ed.) Washington, DC: American Psychiatric Association.

Bachman, J. G., Wadsworth, K. N., O'Malley, P. M., Johnston, L. D., & Schulenberg, J. E. (1997). *Smoking, drinking, and drug use in young adulthood.* Mahwah, NJ: Erlbaum.

Bates, M. E., & Labouvie, E. W. (1998, June). The structure of alcohol and marijuana use in young adulthood. Paper presented at the 6th Annual Meeting of the Society for Prevention Research, Park City, UT.

Blane, H. T., & Hewitt, L. E. (1977). *Alcohol and youth: An analysis of the literature 1960–1975.* Washington, DC: National Technical Information Service.

Bureau of Census. (1981). *Current population survey: Money, income and poverty status of families and persons in the United States, 1980.* Current population reports, Series P-60, No. 127. Washington, DC: U.S. Government Printing Office.

Cattell, R. B. (1978). *The scientific use of factor analysis in behavioral and life sciences.* New York: Plenum Press.

Cattell, R. B., Eber, H. W., & Tatsuoka, M. M. (1970). *Handbook for the Sixteen Personality Factor Questionnaire (16PF)*. Champaign, IL: Institute for Personality and Ability Testing.

Chou, S. P., & Pickering, R. P. (1992). Early onset of drinking as a risk factor for lifetime alcohol-related problems. *British Journal of Addiction, 87,* 1199–1204.

Cloninger, C. R. (1987). *Tridimensional Personality Questionnaire (Version 4)*. Unpublished manuscript.

Cox, D. R., & Snell, E. J. (1989). *The analysis of binary data* (2nd ed.). London: Chapman and Hall.

Derogatis, L. R. (1977). *SCL-90-R (questionnaire form): Administration, scoring and procedures manual* (Vol. 1). Baltimore: Johns Hopkins University, School of Medicine.

Dorner, D., Kreuzig, H. W., Reither, F., & Staudel, T. (1983). *Lohhausen. Vom Umgang mit Unbestimmtheit und Komplexitat*. Bern: H. Huber.

Golub, A., & Johnson, B. D. (1994). The shifting importance of alcohol and marijuana as gateway substances among serious drug abusers. *Journal of Studies on Alcohol, 55,* 607–614.

Grant, B. F., & Dawson, D. A. (1997). Age at onset of alcohol use and its association with DSM-IV alcohol abuse and dependence: Results from the National Longitudinal Alcohol Epidemiologic Survey. *Journal of Substance Abuse, 9,* 103–110.

Hawkins, J. D., Catalano, R. F., & Miller, J. Y. (1992). Risk and protective factors for alcohol and other drug problems in adolescence and early adulthood: Implications for substance abuse prevention. *Psychological Bulletin, 112,* 64–105.

Hawkins, J. D., Graham, J. W., Maguin, E., Abbott, R., Hill, K. G., & Catalano, R. F. (1997). Exploring the effects of age of alcohol use initiation and psychosocial risk factors on subsequent alcohol misuse. *Journal of Studies on Alcohol, 58,* 280–290.

Holland, S., & Griffin, A. (1984). Adolescent and adult drug treatment clients: Patterns and consequences of use. *Journal of Psychoactive Drugs, 16,* 79–89.

Jackson, D. N. (1974). *Personality research form manual*. Goshen, NY: Research Psychologists Press.

Jessor, R., Donovan, J. E., & Costa, F. M. (1991). *Beyond adolescence: Problem behavior and young adult development*. New York: Cambridge University Press.

Johnston, L. D., Bachman, J. G., & O'Malley, P. M. (1998). *National survey results on drug use* (Vol. 1). Rockville, MD: National Institute on Drug Abuse.

Kandel, D. B., & Yamaguchi, K. (1999). Developmental stages of involvement in substance use. In R. E. Tarter, R. J. Ammerman, & P. J. Ott (Eds.), *Sourcebook on substance abuse: Etiology, assessment and treatment* (pp. 50–74). New York: Allyn & Bacon.

Kandel, D. B., Yamaguchi, K., & Chen, K. (1992). Stages of progression in drug involvement from adolescence to adulthood: Further evidence for the gateway theory. *Journal of Studies on Alcohol, 53,* 447–457.

Labouvie, E. (1996). Maturing out of substance use: Selection and self-correction. *Journal of Drug Issues, 26,* 455–474.

Labouvie, E., Bates, M. E., & Pandina, R. J. (1997). Age of first use: Its reliability and predictive utility. *Journal of Studies on Alcohol, 58,* 638–643.

Mackesy-Amiti, M. E., Fendrich, M., & Goldstein, P. J. (1997). Sequence of drug use among serious drug users: Typical vs atypical progression. *Drug and Alcohol Dependence, 45,* 185–196.

Muthen, B. O., Grant, B., & Hasin, D. (1993). The dimensionality of alcohol abuse and dependence: Factor analysis of DSM-III-R and proposed DSM-IV criteria in the 1988 National Health Interview Survey. *Addiction, 88,* 1079–1090.

Nesselroade, J. R. (1970). Application of multivariate strategies to problems of measuring and structuring long-term change. In L. R. Goulet & P. B. Baltes (Eds.), *Life-span developmental psychology: Research and theory* (pp. 193–207). New York: Academic Press.

Newcomb, M. D., & Bentler, P. M. (1986). Frequency and sequence of drug use: A longitudinal study from early adolescence to young adulthood. *Journal of Drug Education, 16,* 101–120.

Pandina, R. J., Labouvie, E. W., & White, H. R. (1984). Potential contributions of the life span developmental approach to the study of adolescent alcohol and drug use: The Rutgers Health and Human Development Project, a working model. *Journal of Drug Issues, 14,* 253–268.

Pedersen, W., & Skrondal, A. (1998). Alcohol consumption debut: Predictors and consequences. *Journal of Studies on Alcohol, 59,* 32–42.

Peele, S., & Brodsky, A. (1997). Gateway to nowhere: How alcohol came to be scapegoated for drug abuse. *Addiction Research, 5,* 419–426.

Reese, H. W., & Overton, W. F. (1970). Models of development and theories of development. In L. R. Goulet & P. B. Baltes (Eds.), *Life-span developmental psychology: Research and theory* (pp. 116–145). New York: Academic Press.

Robins, L. N., & Przybeck, T. R. (1985). Age of onset of drug use as a factor in drug and other disorders. In C. L. Jones & R. J. Battjes (Eds.), *Etiology of drug abuse: Implications for prevention* (pp. 178–192). Washington, DC: Government Printing Office.

Rosenberg, M. (1965). *Society and the adolescent self image.* Princeton, NJ: Princeton University Press.

Russell, D., Peplau, L. A., & Cutrona, C. E. (1980). The revised UCLA Loneliness Scale: Concurrent and discriminant validity evidence. *Journal of Personality and Social Psychology, 39,* 472–480.

Scheier, M. F., & Carver, C. S. (1987). Dispositional optimism and physical well-being: The influence of generalized outcome expectancies on health.

Special issue: Personality and physical health. *Journal of Personality, 55,* 169–210.

Schulenberg, J., O'Malley, P. M., Bachman, J. G., Wadsworth, K. N., & Johnston, L. D. (1996). Getting drunk and growing up: Trajectories of frequent binge drinking during the transition to young adulthood. *Journal of Studies on Alcohol, 57,* 289–304.

Skinner, H. A. (1990). Spectrum of drinkers and intervention opportunities. *Canadian Medical Association Journal, 143,* 17–22.

von Eye, A. (1990). *Introduction to configural frequency analysis.* New York: Cambridge University Press.

Weber, M. D., Graham, J. W., Hansen, W. B., Flay, B. R., & Johnson, C. A. (1989). Evidence for two paths of alcohol use onset in adolescents. *Addictive Behavior, 14,* 399–408.

Welte, J. W., & Barnes, G. M. (1985). Alcohol: The gateway to other drug use among secondary-school students. *Journal of Youth and Adolescence, 48,* 329–336.

White, H. R., Bates, M. E., & Labouvie, E. W. (1998). Adult outcomes of adolescent drug use: A comparison of process-oriented and incremental analyses. In R. Jessor (Ed.), *New perspectives on adolescent risk behavior* (pp. 150–181). Cambridge: Cambridge University Press.

Wohlwill, J. F. (1973). *The study of behavioral development.* New York: Academic Press.

Woody, G. E., Cottler, L. B., & Cacciola, J. (1993). Severity of dependence: Data from the DSM-IV field trials. *Addiction, 88,* 1573–1579.

Yamaguchi, K., & Kandel, D. B. (1985). On the resolution of role incompatibility: Life event history analysis of family roles and marijuana use. *American Journal of Sociology, 90,* 1284–1325.

Zuckerman, M. (1979). *Sensation seeking: Beyond the optimal level of arousal.* Hillsdale, NJ: Erlbaum.

3

Substance Use Norms and Transitions in Substance Use

Implications for the Gateway Hypothesis

*J. David Hawkins, Karl G. Hill, Jie Guo,
and Sara R. Battin-Pearson*

Specific progressions or stages of drug initiation in adolescence have been identified (Collins, Graham, Rousculp, Fidler, Pan, & Hansen, 1994; Kandel, Kessler, & Margulies, 1978; Kandel & Davies, 1992; for a review, see Kandel, Yamaguchi, & Chen, 1992). The typical sequence begins with either alcohol or tobacco, followed by marijuana, which is followed by other illicit drugs. This sequence is relatively robust and has been replicated in retrospective data (Kandel et al., 1992), prospective data (Collins et al., 1994), and in international data (Adler & Kandel, 1981).

However, the determinants of this sequence are less clear. Why does the sequence begin with alcohol or tobacco? Why does marijuana initiation follow, rather than the initiation of other illicit drugs? We hypothesize that this progression reflects the normative social definitions of specific drugs in the community. Substances that are more *socially acceptable*, or viewed as *less harmful*, are more likely to be initiated first. The progression is not immutable. It reflects the norms of the society regarding the relative acceptability of different substances. Social norms of acceptability and perceived harm have frequently been cited as likely determinants in substance initiation (Bachman, Johnston, & O'Malley, 1998; Johnston, 1985; Johnston, O'Malley, & Bachman, 1994). However, the extent to which differences in the norms regarding specific substances determine the sequence of substance initiation has not been examined.

This research was supported by Research Grant #1R01DA09679 from the National Institute on Drug Abuse, Grant #2158 from the Office of Juvenile Justice and Delinquency Prevention (OJJDP), Grant #1R24MH56587 from the National Institute of Mental Health, and Grant #21548 from the Robert Wood Johnson Foundation.

Furthermore, among youths who initiate the "gateway" substances alcohol and/or tobacco, not all go on to initiate marijuana use, and fewer still go on to initiate use of other illicit drugs. What contributes to progression along the pathway after initiation of a prior substance? The social norm hypothesis suggests that it is individual variability in substance use norms. In sum, we hypothesize that aggregate social norms regarding which substances are viewed as more socially acceptable and less harmful determine the sequence of drug use initiation and that youths' individual norms regarding the acceptability and harmfulness of specific drugs predict the extent to which they progress along the pathway.

This study assesses empirical support for this hypothesis by examining the relationship between aggregate social norms for the use of specific substances and the sequence of initiation of these substances and the contribution of individual norms to subsequent substance initiation, once prior substance use and other predictors have been controlled.

Method and Results

The Seattle Study Sample

The Seattle Social Development Project (SSDP) is a longitudinal prospective panel study guided by the Social Development Model (Catalano & Hawkins, 1996). The target study population included all fifth-grade students in 18 Seattle elementary schools in the fall of 1985 ($N = 1,053$) that overrepresented students from high-crime neighborhoods. From this population, 808 students (77%) consented to participate in the longitudinal study and constitute the total sample. Subjects were interviewed nine times over the ensuing 11½ years. Retention rates for the sample have remained above 94% since 1989, when subjects were 14 years old, and approximately 91% ($n = 735$) of the original fifth-grade sample was present for at least seven of the nine data assessment waves. At the most recent data collection (age 21) 765 (95%) of the original fifth-grade sample were interviewed.

Data collection for these analyses began in the fall of 1985, when most subjects were approximately 10½ years old, and occurred in the spring of each succeeding year through 1991, when most respondents were 16 years old. Study subjects were again interviewed in the spring of 1993, when most respondents were 18 years old, and again in 1996 at age 21 (ages reported are the median ages of respondents at each data collection point). Subjects were asked for their confidential responses to a wide range of questions concerning family, community, school, and peers, as well as their attitudes toward and experiences with alcohol, drugs, and delinquency. Early in the study, subjects received a small incentive for their participation (e.g., an audio cassette tape); later they received a small monetary compensation.

The SSDP sample consists of nearly equal numbers of males ($N = 412$) and females ($N = 396$). Slightly less than half identified themselves as European Americans (46%), about one fourth (24%) as African Americans, and 21% as Asian Americans. The remaining youth were Native American (5%) or of other ethnic groups (3%). A substantial proportion of subjects were from low-income households. Median annual family income in 1985 was approximately $25,000. Forty-six percent of parents reported a maximum family income below $20,000 per year, and over half of the student sample (52%) had participated in the National School Lunch/School Breakfast Program at some point in the fifth, sixth, or seventh grade, indicating that they were members of families living in poverty. Forty-two percent of the sample reported only one parent present in the home in 1985.

Method Overview

This study examines the extent to which youths' norms regarding specific substances influence their initiation and progression through stages of drug use by using three complementary methods. In Part 1 we examine the relative norms for alcohol, tobacco, and marijuana use among adolescents developmentally from age 11 to age 18. This part seeks to determine whether youths report, on average, more favorable norms for one substance compared to another, and how these norms change developmentally (Guo et al., 2000). Part 2 employs Latent Transition Analysis (see Collins, Chapter 11) to determine common substance use statuses at three periods (elementary school, middle school, and high school) and examines the sequence of transitions between these statuses. The most common transition sequence between alcohol, tobacco, marijuana, and hard drug initiation is then compared to the normative findings in Part 1. Part 3 employs survival analysis to examine the contribution of substance use norms to the initiation of alcohol, tobacco, and marijuana use, controlling for other likely confounds (ethnicity, gender, family predictors, and peer predictors). The specific measures, procedures, and results for each of theses analyses are presented in the three sections that follow.

Missing Data Procedures

Because listwise deletion often omits a large number of cases, resulting in bias, this study used recently developed methods for handling missing data that make use of all available variables and cases, thereby reducing bias (Graham, Hofer, & Piccinin, 1994; Little & Rubin, 1987; Rubin, 1987). In order to obtain maximally unbiased parameter estimates and reasonable standard errors, NORM, a data imputation program based on an expectation-maximization (EM) algorithm (Graham & Hofer, 1993; Graham, Hofer, & Piccinin, 1994), was used to create analysis data sets. The imputation was based on the longitudinal patterns of responses to items where data were present. Following a procedure outlined by Graham, Hofer, Donaldson, MacKinnon and Schafer (1997), each data set was imputed six times, analyzed independently, and the analysis results (parameters and standard errors) were pooled to determine final results. Across all variables, persons, and years in Parts 1 and 2, 5.4% of the total number of data points were missing, ranging from less than 1% to 8% per variable. Of the total number of data points (year by subject by variable) in the predictors in Part 3, less than 8.4% were missing. In reporting sample sizes for analyses employing multiple imputation, Graham and Hofer (2000) suggest using the formula $N' = N(1 - \text{totpmiss})$ where totpmiss is the total proportion of missing data values from the $N * k$ data matrix. This procedure yields the estimates of maximum $N = 764$ (95% of the original 808) for Parts 1 and 2 and $N = 740$ (92% of the original 808) for Part 3. Because youths who have already initiated a substance are not included in its survival analysis (they are "left censored"), the actual N may be smaller than 740, as indicated in the results tables.

Missing data are almost exclusively due to nonparticipation at a given wave rather than failure to answer. However, missing data due to attrition were relatively few; nearly 94% of the original fifth-grade sample were interviewed at age 18. Furthermore, nonparticipation at each of the assessment waves was not related to gender or to age 10 lifetime use of tobacco, alcohol, and participation in delinquency; nor was it consistently related to ethnicity.

Part 1: Substance Use Norms From Late Childhood to Late Adolescence

Procedures and Measures. The first step of this analysis compared norms in the sample about specific substances across time. Two dimensions of substance use norms, social acceptability and perceived harm, were used to assess the consistency in the development of the normative climate pertaining to the use of cigarettes, alcohol, and marijuana between the ages of 11 and 18. Substance use norms regarding other illicit drugs (cocaine, heroin, amphetamines, etc.) were not assessed in this data set. Social Acceptability was measured by three questions pertaining to overall use of certain substances: "Do you think it's ok for someone your age to smoke cigarettes?" "Do you think it's ok for someone your age to drink alcohol?" and "Do you think it's ok for someone your age to smoke marijuana?" Perceived Harm was measured by three questions that reflected perceptions of harm pertaining to heavy use of a substance: "Do you think it hurts people if they smoke one or more packs of cigarettes per day?" "Do you think it hurts people if they take one or two drinks nearly every day?" and "Do you think it hurts people if they smoke marijuana regularly?" Each question was assessed annually and coded so that the higher value reflected more favorable norms toward the particular substance. (Thus, Perceived Harm was reversed to be coded as Perceived Harmlessness.) These two measures were combined to form an overall measure of the normative status of each of the three substances.

Results for Part 1. The mean levels of favorable drug use attitudes for each substance for each year are shown in Figure 3.1. The combined measure of favorability toward all substances increased over time. All nonsuperscripted mean norm levels were significantly different at the .05 level or better. Alcohol was perceived as significantly more favorable than either cigarettes or marijuana at every point across time, and cigarettes were perceived as significantly more favorable than marijuana at every point except age 11.

This normative sequence reflects the findings of the Monitoring the Future (MTF) study of high school students (Johnston et al., 1994), which found acceptability to decrease from alcohol to tobacco, to marijuana. Further, the MTF study found that attitudes toward other illicit (hard) drugs (not assessed in the present study) were the least favorable.

Part 2: Latent Transition Analysis of Substance Use Onset

The examination of the normative structure of these substances in Part 1, in conjunction with the findings on hard drug norms from the MTF

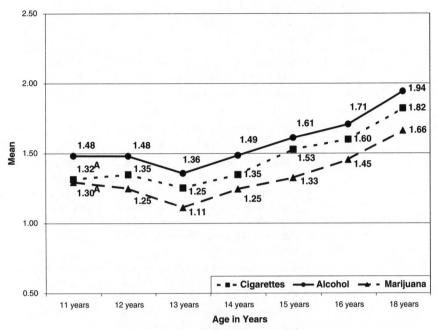

Figure 3.1. Mean level of norms favoring cigarette, alcohol, and marijuana use across time ($N = 764$). All nonsuperscripted mean norm levels were significantly different at the .05 level or better.

study, indicate that alcohol is viewed most favorably, then cigarettes, then marijuana, then hard drugs. If substance use norms are related to initiation, we would predict certain patterns in the statuses and sequences of substance use initiation.

1. The most common initiation sequence should be alcohol, then cigarettes, then marijuana, then hard drugs.
2. We are more likely to find youths who use alcohol only than those who use cigarettes only, and we should find very few or none who initiate marijuana only, or hard drugs only.
3. Youths having initiated cigarettes and marijuana without having first tried alcohol should be rare. The norms indicate alcohol would be tried first.
4. Cigarettes could be added to alcohol use without also adding marijuana; thus youths having initiated both alcohol and cigarettes should be present.

Table 3.1. *Measures for Assessment of Substance Initiation Status*

Substance	Item
Alcohol	Other than a sip or two, have you ever drunk beer, wine, wine coolers, whiskey, gin, or other hard liquor?
Tobacco	Have you ever smoked cigarettes?
Marijuana	Have you ever smoked marijuana?
Hard drugs	Have you ever used crack or rock cocaine?
	Have you ever used cocaine in forms other than crack?
	Doctors sometimes give people pills called amphetamines to help them lose weight or gain energy. These pills are sometimes called uppers, ups, crank, ice, speed, dexies, and pep pills. Have you ever taken amphetamines on your own – that is, without a doctor's telling you to take them? (Do not include over-the-counter drugs like Vivarin or Nō Dōz.)
	Doctors sometimes give people pills called tranquilizers to help them calm down, quiet their nerves, or relax their muscles. Librium, Valium, and Miltown are all tranquilizers. Have you ever taken tranquilizers on your own – that is, without a doctor telling you to take them?
	Doctors sometimes give people pills called sedatives to help them relax or get to sleep. Barbiturates and Quaaludes are both sedatives. They are sometimes called downs, goofballs, yellows, reds, blues, rainbows, quads, soapers, methaqualone. Have you ever taken sedatives on your own – that is, without a doctor telling you to take them?
	Have you ever used psychedelics like LSD ("acid"), mescaline, peyote, psilocybin, mushrooms, ecstasy, and PCP?
	There are a number of narcotics, such as heroin, methadone, opium, morphine, codeine, Demerol, Paragoric, Talwin, laudanum. These are sometimes prescribed by doctors. Have you ever taken narcotics on your own – that is, without a doctor telling you to take them?

Measures for Part 2. The dynamic latent variable of substance use was measured by four manifest indicators of initiation of alcohol, tobacco, marijuana, and hard drugs (use of crack or rock cocaine, cocaine in forms other than crack, or psychedelics, or nonprescription use of amphetamines, tranquilizers, sedatives, or narcotics). Table 3.1 shows the variables that were used to construct the manifest indicators. If an individual responded yes to any of these questions, he or she was coded as a yes on

Table 3.2. *Predicted Prevalence of Each Latent Substance Use Status in Three Periods* (N = 764)

Latent Status		Period	
	Elementary School	Middle School	High School
NONE	0.42	0.23	0.10
A	0.26	0.26	0.15
T	0.05	0.03	0.02
M —	0.00	0.00	0.00
H —	0.01	0.01	0.00
AT	0.15	0.22	0.18
AM	0.01	0.02	0.04
AH —	0.01	0.02	0.01
TM —	0.00	0.00	0.00
TH —	0.00	0.00	0.00
MH —	0.00	0.00	0.00
ATM	0.06	0.10	0.20
ATH	0.01	0.03	0.03
AMH —	0.00	0.00	0.01
TMH —	0.00	0.00	0.00
ATMH	0.02	0.07	0.25

Notes: A = alcohol; T = tobacco; M = marijuana; H = hard drugs; — = status that never achieved more than 2% of the sample.

the substance initiation indicator; otherwise, he or she was coded no. These four types of substances were coded for each of three periods: elementary school (ages 10–12), middle school (ages 13–14), and high school (ages 15–18). Since we were studying initiation, once a subject reported a yes, he or she was coded as having initiated that substance for subsequent periods. Desistance was not studied.

Latent Transition Analysis (LTA) Procedures for Part 2. The latent transition analysis (LTA) used three periods and two transitions run simultaneously (Elementary to Middle and Middle to High School). Responses to initiation questions (Yes and No) for substances were constrained to have equal loadings within a substance, and across latent statuses and periods. Impossible transitions (in addition to desistance) were set to zero. A model involving all possible substance use statuses was tested to determine the accuracy of the predictions from Part 1. These possible statuses are listed in the left column of Table 3.2.

Results for Part 2. Table 3.2 presents the predicted prevalences at each period in all possible latent statuses. Those statuses that never achieved more than 2% predicted prevalence are indicated with a minus.

As predicted from their relative norms, a significant proportion of youths initiated alcohol use without adding other substances (A = 26%, 26%, and 15% in elementary, middle, and high school, respectively), and a smaller proportion initiated tobacco use only (T = 5%, 3%, and 2%, respectively). Virtually none initiated marijuana (M) or hard drug (H) use without having first used alcohol or tobacco. The next most prevalent status was to have initiated both alcohol and tobacco (AT = 15%, 22%, and 18% in elementary, middle, and high school, respectively). Alcohol and marijuana use only (AM) or alcohol and hard drug use only (AH) was rare, and tobacco and marijuana use only (TM) or tobacco and hard drug use only (TH) was nonexistent. The next most common statuses were to have added either marijuana to alcohol and tobacco use (ATM = 6%, 10%, and 20% in the three periods) or to have initiated all four substances (ATMH = 2%, 7%, and 25%, respectively). Note the increasing prevalence of these polydrug use statuses from elementary to high school, as expected.

Thus, overall, the distribution of youths into different substance use statuses in late childhood and adolescence is consistent with the hypothesis that the ordering of substances in the gateway sequence reflects their normative status in the community. Although it is useful to know the distributions of youths into substance use statuses at a given point in time, it is also important to examine transition patterns from one status to another across time: for example, what proportion of youths remain in the alcohol use only status in the transition to high school, and what proportion transition to multiple-substance use statuses? Table 3.3 presents the substance use transitions from elementary to middle school, and Table 3.4 presents the transitions from middle to high school. To simplify the presentation, those initial statuses that never achieved more than 2% of the sample in Table 3.2 are not included in these tables, although the LTA was run on all 16 statuses. These results represent 98% of the sample. The initial prevalence for each latent status is also included in Tables 3.3 and 3.4 to allow their transition probabilities to be seen in the context of the proportion of the sample undergoing that transition.

An examination of these two tables indicates that the transitions one would expect from their relative norms in Part 1 are the most common. For example, the most common first substance initiated was alcohol

Table 3.3. *Transition Probabilities Between Latent Substance Use Statuses: Elementary to Middle School* (N = 764)

	ELEM PREV	NONE	A	T	AT	AM	ATM	ATH	ATMH
NONE	0.42	0.55	0.19	0.03	0.12	0.01	0.05	0.01	0.01
A	0.26	—	0.68	—	0.16	0.04	0.04	0.02	0.04
T	0.05	—	—	0.33	0.51	—	0.12	0.02	0.02
AT	0.15	—	—	—	0.71	—	0.14	0.06	0.09
AM	0.01	—	—	—	—	0.46	0.39	—	0.04
ATM	0.06	—	—	—	—	—	0.64	—	0.36
ATH	0.01	—	—	—	—	—	—	0.71	0.29
ATMH	0.02	—	—	—	—	—	—	—	1.00

Notes: To simplify the presentation, those initial statuses that *never* achieved more than 2% of the sample in Table 3.2 are not included in this table, although the LTA was run on all 16 statuses. The results represent 98% of the sample. A = alcohol; T = tobacco; M = marijuana; H = hard drugs; — = fixed to zero.

Table 3.4. *Transition Probabilities Between Latent Substance Use Statuses: Middle to High School* (N = 764)

	MIDD PREV	NONE	A	T	AT	AM	ATM	ATH	ATMH
NONE	0.23	0.41	0.19	0.06	0.12	0.03	0.08	0.01	0.07
A	0.26	—	0.44	—	0.19	0.09	0.15	0.02	0.10
T	0.03	—	—	0.22	0.51	—	0.22	0.00	0.04
AT	0.22	—	—	—	0.42	—	0.36	0.03	0.19
AM	0.02	—	—	—	—	0.43	0.27	—	0.27
ATM	0.10	—	—	—	—	—	0.54	—	0.46
ATH	0.03	—	—	—	—	—	—	0.31	0.69
ATMH	0.07	—	—	—	—	—	—	—	1.00

Notes: To simplify the presentation, those initial statuses that *never* achieved more than 2% of the sample in Table 3.2 are not included in this table, although the LTA was run on all 16 statuses. The results represent 98% of the sample. A = alcohol; T = tobacco; M = marijuana; H = hard drugs; — = fixed to zero.

(from None to Alcohol, N → A, 19% in both tables), and fewer initiated tobacco first (N → T, 3% from elementary to middle, and 6% from middle to high school). After alcohol use had been initiated, the next most likely substance added was tobacco (A → AT, 16% from elementary to middle, and 19% from middle to high school). Having initiated both alcohol and tobacco, youths were most likely next to add marijuana (AT → ATM, 14% from elementary to middle and 36% from middle to high school). Finally, having initiated alcohol, tobacco, and marijuana, from about a third to a half went on to initiate other illicit drugs in the next period (ATM → ATMH, 36% from elementary to middle, and 46% from middle to high school). Taken together, these results indicate the most common transition sequence to be from alcohol to tobacco to marijuana to other illicit drugs, a sequence that reflects the relative aggregate norms regarding these substances in the sample.

Part 3: Survival Analysis of Alcohol, Tobacco, and Marijuana Initiation

The most common sequence of substance initiation in the sample is consistent with the aggregate social norms of the sample. To what extent do norms explain why individuals initiate drug use and progress to different degrees through the sequence of initiation? To examine this question we considered the impact of individuals' norms regarding a particular substance in one year on the likelihood of their initiating that substance in the following year, controlling for the use of prior substances in the sequence and other possible predictors of initiation. Thus, Part 3 examined the effects of norms on initiation net of other influences.

One possible method to examine this question would be to incorporate the latent classes pro- and antisubstance norms into the LTA analyses to see whether the prevalences and transition patterns differed for youths holding different norms. However, this method allows the examination of only one independent variable at a time and would not allow for controls of a variety of possible confounding variables. Thus, Part 3 examined the predictive capacity of substance use norms in determining alcohol, tobacco, and marijuana use onset, controlling for other likely confounds by using survival analysis.

Method for Part 3

Measures for Part 3
Initiation. Alcohol, tobacco, and marijuana initiation were assessed by using the same items presented in Table 3.1 across all waves of assessment from age 10 to age 18 and were coded as the first point at which a participant responded affirmatively to the item.

Predictors. Time varying covariates were constructed to reflect likely predictors of initiation other than substance use norms. The following predictors were measured with the same items at each wave of data collection. Items were combined into scales by adding item responses and calculating the mean.

Parents' perceived proactive family management combined six items assessing participants' reports of their parents' monitoring, rules, discipline, and reward practices. Higher scores indicated that parents were more likely to know their children's whereabouts, have clear rules, discuss misbehavior, and notice and praise good behavior.

Parents' perceived substance use norms combined two items regarding parents' permissiveness and rules about alcohol, tobacco, and marijuana, along with participants' perceived likelihood of being caught and punished for drinking alcohol or smoking marijuana. To ensure consistency with norm analyses from Part 1, items were coded such that higher scores indicated parental norms more favorable toward substance use and child's lower perception of being caught and punished for using each substance. Three different measures were created, one each for alcohol, tobacco, and marijuana use.

Bonding to mother combined two items about sharing thoughts and feelings with one's mother and desiring to be the kind of person one's mother is. (Higher scores indicated more sharing and desire to emulate.)

Peer perceived substance use was measured with two different scales, one for alcohol use and one for marijuana use. (Peer use of tobacco was not assessed across all years.) *Alcohol use* items (three items) referred to peer use (whether or not one's friends had tried alcohol, whether or not the friend had been drunk, etc.). *Marijuana use* combined two items that asked about knowing acquaintances who used, along with items about sibling use. (Higher scores indicated more use by peers and siblings.)

Participants' substance use norms combined the same two items used in Part 1 of this study (social acceptability and perceived harmlessness). Again, three different measures were created, one specific to norms about alcohol, one for norms about tobacco, and one for norms about marijuana. Higher scores indicated more favorable norms for the substance.

Procedures for Part 3. Since most of the measurements of drug use initiation were available on an annual basis, there were many ties in terms of the number of individuals initiating one particular substance at each time point, a situation not handled well in traditional continuous time survival models. Therefore, a discrete time model of survival analysis, specifically, a complementary log log model (Allison, 1995; Yamaguchi, 1991), was used to estimate the effects of a set of predictors on initiation ($\log [-\log (1 - P_u)] = \alpha_t + \beta_t X_u$) where P_u is the discrete time analog of the hazard rate in a continuous time model, α_t is a set of constants representing the baseline hazard rates by time, and β_t is the coefficient vector. The covariate matrix x_u included the initiations of two other substances, subjects' substance use norms, and a group of other important predictors of drug initiation.

Multivariate survival analyses were conducted hierarchically, permitting assessment of the unique contributions of each block of predictors. Each survival analysis began by entering the demographic predictors of gender and ethnicity. The second block examined the contribution of prior initiation of other substances, the third block examined the contribution of parental influences, the next block examined peer influences, and the final block examined the contribution of the youth's substance use norms once all these factors had been controlled.

Results for Part 3

Cumulative Initiation and Hazard Rates. Figure 3.2 presents the cumulative initiation plot for use of alcohol, tobacco, and marijuana. Before age 10–11, 25%, 13%, and 3% of the participants had ever used alcohol, tobacco, or marijuana, respectively. By age 18, the cumulative percentage of initiation increased to 88%, 68%, and 50%, respectively, for alcohol, tobacco, and marijuana use. This cumulative initiation plot again reflects the sequence of initiation of alcohol followed by tobacco then marijuana.

In order to reflect the risk of initiation, the hazard rates of alcohol, tobacco, and marijuana initiation were calculated from a model in which the hazard rate varied in each time interval but did not depend on any other predictors. These results are plotted in Figure 3.3. Note that at any age, the hazard of alcohol initiation was always higher than that of tobacco or marijuana initiation. For the most part, the hazard of marijuana initiation was the lowest among the three substances. However, the risk of marijuana initiation increased faster than that of tobacco initiation; as a result, by age 17 the risk of marijuana initiation was comparable to the risk of tobacco initiation if subjects had abstained from these substances until then. Kandel and Logan (1984) showed similar patterns in hazard rates for alcohol, tobacco, and marijuana initiation in their

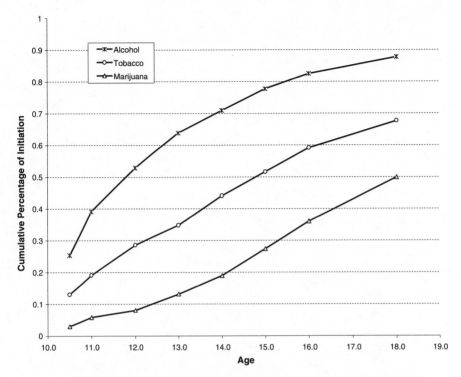

Figure 3.2. Cumulative percentage of alcohol, tobacco, and marijuana initiation by age for full sample ($N = 764$).

study. Finally, it is noteworthy that the differences in initiation risk of alcohol, tobacco, and marijuana were very similar to the differences in norms of alcohol, tobacco, and marijuana use shown in Figure 3.1.

The Initiation of Alcohol Use. There was no effect of gender, but there was a relatively large negative effect of Asian American ethnicity (versus Caucasian American) on alcohol initiation (Step 1, Table 3.5). The effects of gender and ethnicity did not change very much in subsequent steps when other predictors were added. Prior tobacco use was significantly associated with a higher hazard of initiation of alcohol use in the following year (Step 2, Table 3.5). After accounting for the demographic and initiation effects, parents' proactive family management still made a significant contribution (Step 3), reducing the risk of alcohol initiation. In the next step, however, family management was no longer significant when parents' norms about teen alcohol use were added. Parental norms favorable to alcohol use increased the risk of alcohol initiation, even

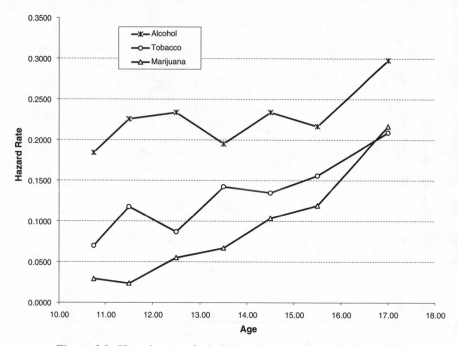

Figure 3.3. Hazard rate of alcohol, tobacco, and marijuana initiation
(*N* = 764). *Note:* The hazard rates cover the intervals between two adjacent
surveys, and the midpoints of the intervals are used in the plot.

when bonding to mother, peer alcohol use, and subjects' alcohol use
norms were included in the models. Bonding to mother, however, had
little effect on alcohol initiation. Peer alcohol use was significantly associated with the risk of alcohol initiation. After controlling for all the
factors described, participants' norms about alcohol use had little effect
on alcohol initiation. Finally, to determine whether perceived parental
norms and peer alcohol use had reduced the effect of participants' alcohol norms, a model omitting perceived parental norms and peer alcohol
use was examined, but participants' alcohol norms remained nonsignificant (results not tabled).

The Initiation of Tobacco Use. There was no effect of gender on
tobacco initiation, but there was a relatively large effect of Asian American
ethnicity (versus Caucasian American) (Step 1, Table 3.6). Asian Americans
were significantly less likely to initiate tobacco use compared to
Caucasian Americans. The effects of gender and ethnicity did not change
very much in subsequent steps when other predictors were added. Prior

Table 3.5. *Discrete Time Survival Analysis of Alcohol Initiation*

Predictors	Step 1 b	(se)	Step 2 b	(se)	Step 3 b	(se)	Step 4 b	(se)	Step 5 b	(se)	Step 6 b	(se)	Step 7 b	(se)
Gender (male)	.10	(.09)	.09	(.09)	.07	(.09)	.09	(.09)	.08	(.09)	.10	(.09)	.09	(.09)
African American (vs. Caucasian American)	.16	(.10)	.16	(.10)	.17[+]	(.10)	.14	(.10)	.13	(.10)	.10	(.10)	.10	(.10)
Asian American (vs. Caucasian American)	-.46***	(.10)	-.42***	(.10)	-.44***	(.10)	-.41***	(.10)	-.42***	(.10)	-.37***	(.10)	-.37***	(.10)
Native American (vs. Caucasian American)	.17	(.16)	.05	(.16)	.04	(.16)	.06	(.16)	.06	(.16)	.05	(.16)	.05	(.16)
Other ethnicities (vs. Caucasian American)	-.07	(.22)	.02	(.22)	.04	(.22)	.04	(.22)	.04	(.22)	.03	(.22)	.02	(.22)
Tobacco initiation			.73***	(.12)	.72***	(.12)	.72***	(.12)	.72***	(.12)	.62***	(.12)	.62***	(.12)
Parents' proactive family management					-.14*	(.06)	.07	(.08)	.12	(.10)	.11	(.10)	.11	(.10)
Parents' alcohol use norms							.27***	(.07)	.26***	(.07)	.25***	(.07)	.25***	(.07)
Bonding to mother									-.08	(.07)	-.07	(.07)	-.07	(.07)
Peer alcohol use											.40***	(.07)	.40***	(.07)
Subjects' alcohol use norms													.05	(.08)
-2 log likelihood	2379.38		2346.73		2341.79		2327.88		2326.72		2295.96		2295.60	
Δ -2 log likelihood	40.05***		32.65***		4.94*		13.92***		1.16		30.76***		.36	

Notes: Those initiating alcohol use before age 10½ were invalid for complementary log-log regression analysis. Analysis $N = 603$ throughout.
[+] $p < .10$. * $p < .05$. ** $p < .01$. *** $p < .001$.

Table 3.6. *Discrete Time Survival Analysis of Tobacco Initiation*

Predictors	Step 1		Step 2		Step 3		Step 4		Step 5	
	b	(se)	b	(se)	b	(se)	b	(se)	b	(se)
Gender (male)	−.04	(.10)	−.06	(.10)	−.07	(.10)	−.08	(.10)	−.10	(.10)
African American (vs. Caucasian American)	.01	(.10)	−.01	(.10)	−.01	(.10)	−.01	(.10)	−.02	(.10)
Asian American (vs. Caucasian American)	−.59***	(.12)	−.48***	(.12)	−.50***	(.12)	−.51***	(.12)	−.52***	(.12)
Native American (vs. Caucasian American)	.27	(.17)	.24	(.17)	.25	(.17)	.27	(.17)	.27	(.17)
Other ethnicities (vs. Caucasian American)	.13	(.21)	.13	(.21)	.13	(.21)	.13	(.21)	.12	(.21)
Alcohol Initiation			.58***	(.11)	.56***	(.11)	.55***	(.11)	.55***	(.11)
Parents' proactive family management					−.15+	(.08)	.03	(.09)	.05	(.10)
Bonding to mother							−.25**	(.08)	−.24**	(.08)
Subjects' tobacco use norms									.31***	(.09)
−2 log likelihood	2597.08		2565.60		2562.03		2552.11		2541.33	
Δ − 2 log likelihood	310.93***		31.48***		3.57+		9.92**		10.78***	

Notes: Those initiating tobacco use prior to age 10½ were invalid for complementary log-log regression analysis. Analysis $N = 703$ throughout. Parents' tobacco use norms and peers' tobacco use were not available.
$^+ p < .10.$ $^* p < .05.$ $^{**} p < .01.$ $^{***} p < .001.$

alcohol use was significantly associated with a higher hazard of initiation of tobacco use in the following year (Step 2, Table 3.6). After accounting for the demographic and initiation effects, proactive family management was marginally significant in predicting tobacco initiation. In the next step, however, the effect of family management was no longer significant when bonding to mother was added. Although bonding to mother had little effect on alcohol initiation, it was an important predictor of tobacco initiation. Stronger bonding to mother was associated with lower risk of tobacco initiation. Finally, after controlling for all the factors described, participants' norms about tobacco use were significantly associated with tobacco initiation. The more favorable the youth's norms were toward tobacco, the more likely was he or she to initiate tobacco use in the following year even after controlling for all other blocks of predictors.

The Effect of Norms on Marijuana Initiation. Unlike for alcohol and tobacco initiations, gender was significantly associated with the risk of marijuana initiation (Table 3.7). Boys had a significantly higher risk of initiating marijuana use than girls, even when other predictors were included in the models. Compared to Caucasian Americans, Asian Americans were much less likely to initiate marijuana use, but African Americans were more likely to initiate marijuana use. These results held when other predictors were added into the models. Native Americans had a higher hazard of initiating marijuana use than Caucasian Americans in Step 1, but that effect gradually decreased when other predictors were added.

Both alcohol and tobacco initiation had strong and significant effects on the risk of marijuana initiation (Step 2, Table 3.7). Use of alcohol or tobacco in the preceding year increased the risk of marijuana initiation, although the effect of tobacco initiation appeared to be stronger than that of alcohol initiation. This result remained after other predictors were entered in the models. Proactive family management significantly reduced the hazard of marijuana initiation, even when other predictors were accounted for. However, parents' marijuana use norms and bonding to mother were not significantly associated with the likelihood of marijuana initiation. Marijuana use by peers and siblings was positively associated with the risk of marijuana initiation. Finally, as with tobacco initiation, participants' own norms favorable to marijuana use predicted increased risk of marijuana initiation in the next period even after all the other factors had been considered.

Table 3.7. Discrete Time Survival Analysis of Marijuana Initiation

Predictors	Step 1		Step 2		Step 3		Step 4		Step 5		Step 6		Step 7	
	b	(se)	b	(se)	b	(se)	b	(se)	b	(se)	b	(se)	b	(se)
Gender (male)	.30**	(.10)	.29**	(.10)	.27**	(.10)	.27*	(.11)	.25*	(.11)	.28*	(.11)	.24*	(.11)
African American (vs. Caucasian American)	.32**	(.11)	.35***	(.11)	.34**	(.11)	.34**	(.11)	.33*	(.11)	.30**	(.11)	.28*	(.11)
Asian American (vs. Caucasian American)	−1.00***	(.15)	−.81***	(.15)	−.87***	(.15)	−.87***	(.15)	−.87***	(.15)	−.73***	(.15)	−.74***	(.15)
Native American (vs. Caucasian American)	.44*	(.18)	.32+	(.18)	.33+	(.18)	.33+	(.18)	.34+	(.18)	.29	(.18)	.27	(.18)
Other ethnicities (vs. Caucasian American)	.08	(.23)	.06	(.23)	.11	(.23)	.12	(.23)	.11	(.23)	.07	(.23)	.10	(.23)
Alcohol initiation			.66***	(.15)	.61***	(.15)	.60***	(.15)	.60***	(.15)	.51***	(.15)	.47**	(.15)
Tobacco initiation			1.00***	(.11)	.96***	(.11)	.97***	(.11)	.96***	(.11)	.85***	(.11)	.83***	(.12)
Parents' proactive family management					−.40***	(.08)	−.35***	(.10)	−.27*	(.11)	−.24*	(.11)	−.24*	(.11)
Parents' marijuana use norms							.07	(.07)	.06	(.07)	.08	(.07)	.07	(.07)
Bonding to mother									−.13	(.08)	−.09	(.08)	−.08	(.08)
Peer and sibling marijuana use											.36***	(.06)	.33***	(.06)
Subjects' marijuana use norms													.41***	(.09)
−2 log likelihood	2369.58		2228.64		2206.46		2205.29		2202.88		2161.76		2142.50	
Δ −2 log likelihood	76.77***		140.94***		22.18***		1.17		2.41		41.12***		19.26***	

Notes: Those initiating marijuana use before age 10½ were invalid for complementary log–log regression analysis. Analysis $N = 740$ throughout.
$^+$ $< .10.$ * $p < .05.$ ** $p < .01.$ *** $p < .001.$

60

Conclusion and Discussion

Results of this study are consistent with the Gateway Hypothesis for substance initiation. The initiation of alcohol significantly increased the risk of tobacco use, and vice versa, and both were predictors of marijuana initiation. Along with the results from the LTA presented earlier, these findings are consistent with those of other studies (see Kandel et al., 1992; Kandel and Yamaguchi, 1999, for detailed reviews).

Although a developmental sequence in drug involvement has been identified, the use of a particular drug does not always lead to the use of other drugs later in the sequence (Kandel et al., 1992). As can be seen by the relatively large diagonal elements of the LTA transition matrices, many adolescents stopped at a particular stage and progressed no further. Many factors beyond age and the use of other drugs had significant effects on the progression of drug use. One of these factors, substance use norms, was examined in detail in the present study.

The effects of an individual's norms in shaping future behavior may depend on the normative context itself. Individual norms about alcohol did not predict alcohol initiation in the next year after controlling for other influences, including parental norms about alcohol and peer alcohol use. Perhaps if a substance is widely used, as is alcohol in this sample, being surrounded by social influences of parents and peers that counter the predominant pattern of behavior may be more important in inhibiting use of that substance than the individual's own views that the substance is unacceptable. These views may be quite malleable in the face of increasingly prevalent alcohol use if not supported by parents and peers. These results suggest that parents can reduce the likelihood that their children will initiate alcohol use in adolescence by communicating that alcohol use in the elementary to high school years is not acceptable and by encouraging their children to associate with others who do not drink.

However, individual norms about the acceptability and harm associated with tobacco use and marijuana use predicted whether youths in this sample would initiate tobacco and marijuana in the next year, even after controlling for other influences, including parental and peer norms. These results suggest that when substances are less widely accepted, encouraging adolescents to perceive the substance as harmful and use as unacceptable should reduce the initiation of that substance in the following year. These findings support the emphasis on developing norms against the use of tobacco and marijuana in school-based preventive interventions seeking to prevent tobacco and marijuana initiation (Hansen & Graham, 1991).

It is interesting that proactive family management did not delay alcohol initiation. This may reflect the ambivalence among adults about adolescent drinking. Some parents who set clear rules and monitor their children also condone drinking. Hence, it was parental norms about alcohol use by teens rather than family management practices that influenced alcohol initiation in adolescence. In contrast, proactive family management was a strong deterrent to marijuana initiation, whereas parental norms about marijuana were not independently predictive of marijuana initiation by their children. This finding may reflect the greater normative consensus among parents about marijuana use by adolescents. Parents in this sample generally expressed the view that marijuana use by adolescents was unacceptable. In the presence of a shared norm among parents, those who set clear expectations and monitored their children would be expected to be more effective in inhibiting rule violating behavior such as marijuana use. Although consistent with the data, these ideas require more exploration. Nevertheless, the results show that parents can prevent their children from initiating marijuana use by providing effective monitoring and supervision through the high school years.

Also interesting is the finding that bonding to mother was not independently predictive of either alcohol or marijuana use initiation, though it did inhibit tobacco initiation. These findings require more investigation. However, it is possible that during adolescence when parents set clear standards opposing adolescent alcohol use and monitor their children, adolescents feel less bonded to their parents, refraining from sharing thoughts and feelings, for example. Adolescents may not like their parents for being strict at the time, but these results indicate that setting a clear policy against teen drinking and monitoring and managing the family effectively are more important than feeling close during the adolescent years in inhibiting adolescent drinking and marijuana use.

The data presented here are consistent with the hypothesis that broad social definitions of the acceptability of the use of specific substances and proscriptive norms in the adolescent's immediate social environment affect the sequencing of drugs in the gateway progression of substance use. The sequencing of initiation of alcohol, tobacco, and marijuana use in the SSDP sample was consistent with the sample's social norms regarding each substance. However, with respect to individual norms, the normative social context matters. In a social world where alcohol use is increasingly common with age, individual norms may be less important than social influences, parental norms, and peer influences in the decision to initiate alcohol use. In a social world where there is less overall approval and use of marijuana and other illicit drugs, individual norms against use may be important in halting the progression to marijuana use after alcohol initiation.

References

Adler, I., & Kandel, D. B. (1981). Cross-cultural perspectives on developmental stages in adolescent drug use. *Journal of Studies on Alcohol, 42,* 701–715.

Allison, P. D. (1995). *Survival analysis using the SAS System: A practical guide.* Cary, NC: SAS Institute.

Bachman, J. G., Johnston, L. D., & O'Malley P. M. (1998). Explaining recent increases in students' marijuana use: Impacts of perceived risks and disapproval, 1976 through 1996. *American Journal of Public Health, 88,* 887–892.

Catalano, R. F., & Hawkins, J. D. (1996). The social development model: A theory of antisocial behavior. In J. D. Hawkins (Ed.), *Delinquency and crime: Current theories* (pp. 149–197). New York: Cambridge University Press.

Collins, L. M., Graham, J. W., Rousculp, S. S., Fidler, P. L., Pan, J., & Hansen, W. B. (1994). Latent transition analysis and how it can address prevention research questions. In L. M. Collins & L. Seitz (Eds.), *NIDA Research Monograph No. 142. Advances in data analysis for prevention research* (pp. 81–111). Washington, DC: U.S. Government Printing Office.

Graham, J. W., & Hofer, S. M. (1993). *EMCOV.EXE users guide.* University Park, PA: Department of Biobehavioral Health, Pennsylvania State University.

Graham, J. W., & Hofer, S. M. (2000). Multiple imputation in multivariate research. In T. D. Little, K. U. Schnabel, & J. Baumert (Eds.), *Modeling longitudinal and multiple-group data: Practical issues, applied approaches, and specific examples* (pp. 201–218, 269–281). Hillsdale, NJ: Erlbaum.

Graham, J. W., Hofer, S. M., Donaldson, S. I., MacKinnon, D. P., & Schafer, J. L. (1997). Analysis with missing data in prevention research. In K. Bryant, M. Windle, & S. West (Eds.), *The science of prevention: Methodological advances from alcohol and substance abuse research* (pp. 325–366). Washington, DC: American Psychological Association.

Graham, J. W., Hofer, S. M., & Piccinin, A. M. (1994). Analysis with missing data in drug prevention research. In L. M. Collins & L. A. Seitz (Eds.), *NIDA Research Monograph No. 108. Advances in data analysis for prevention intervention research* (pp. 13–63). Washington, DC: U.S. Government Printing Office.

Guo, J., Collins, L. M., Hill, K. G., & Hawkins, J. D. (2000). Developmental pathways to alcohol abuse and dependence in young adulthood. *Journal of Studies on Alcohol, 61,* 799–808.

Hansen, W. B., & Graham, J. W. (1991). Preventing alcohol, marijuana, and cigarette use among adolescents: Peer pressure resistance training versus establishing conservative norms. *Preventive Medicine, 20*, 414–430.

Johnston, L. D. (1985). The etiology and prevention of substance use: What can we learn from recent historical changes? In C. L. Jones & R. J. Battjes (Eds.), *NIDA Research Monograph No. 56. Etiology of drug abuse: Implications for prevention* (pp. 155–177). Washington, DC: U.S. Government Printing Office.

Johnston, L. D., O'Malley, P. M., & Bachman, J. G. (1994). *National survey results of drug use from the Monitoring the Future Study, 1975–1993* (Vols. 1 & 2). Rockville, MD: National Institute on Drug Abuse.

Kandel, D. B., & Davies, M. (1992). Progression to regular marijuana involvement: phenomenology and risk factors for near-daily use. In M. Glantz & R. Pickens (Eds.), *Vulnerability to abuse* (pp. 211–253). Washington, DC: American Psychological Association.

Kandel, D. B., Kessler, R. C., & Margulies, R. Z. (1978). Antecedents of adolescent initiation into stages of drug use: A developmental analysis. *Journal of Youth and Adolescence, 7*, 13–40.

Kandel, D. B., & Logan, J. A. (1984). Patterns of drug use from adolescence to young adulthood. I. Periods of risk for initiation, continued use, and discontinuation. *American Journal of Public Health, 74*, 660–666.

Kandel, D. B., & Yamaguchi, K. (1999). Developmental stages of involvement in substance use. In R. E. Tarter, R. J. Amerman, & P. J. Ott (Eds.), *Sourcebook on substance abuse: Etiology, assessment and treatment* (pp. 50–74). Boston: Allyn & Bacon.

Kandel, D. B., Yamaguchi, K., & Chen, K. (1992). Stages of progression in drug involvement from adolescence to adulthood: Further evidence for the gateway theory. *Journal of Studies on Alcohol, 53*, 447–457.

Little, R. J. A., & Rubin, D. B. (1987). *Statistical analysis with missing data.* New York: Wiley.

Rubin, D. B. (1987). *Multiple imputations for nonresponse in surveys.* New York: Wiley & Sons.

Yamaguchi, K. (1991). *Event history analysis: Applied social research method series.* Newbury Park, CA: Sage.

4

Stages of Drug Involvement in the U.S. Population

Denise B. Kandel and Kazuo Yamaguchi

The preceding chapters have described developmental patterns of use in different populations, as well as risk and protective factors for progression to various stages of use. With the exception of the research of Golub and Johnson, the studies are based on representative longitudinal school or community samples of adolescents and young adults selected from different regions or cities in the United States. The representative samples do not extend through the entire period of risk for initiation of illicit drugs. The older sample described by Golub and Johnson in Chapter 5 is of particular interest because it consists of deviant individuals. It is not clear, however, to what extent the patterns observed in that sample are affected by factors that determine criminal behavior and apprehension by the police. In all the studies, the conceptualization of stages is characterized by two features. All illicit drugs other than marijuana are aggregated into a single class and no attempt is made to determine an order among these drugs. Furthermore, with the exception of the chapter by Labouvie and White (Chapter 2), the focus is mostly on progression from one class of drugs to another; no attention is paid to progressive involvement within a particular drug class.

We take advantage of a large national data set to explore previously unexplored substantive and methodological issues related to drug use

Work on this manuscript was partially supported by Grant DA09110 and a Senior Scientist Award (K05DA00081) to Denise Kandel, from the National Institute on Drug Abuse. Partial support for computer costs was provided by Mental Health and Clinical Research Center Grant MH30906 from the National Institute on Mental Health (NIMH) to the New York State Psychiatric Institute. The research assistance of Christine Schaffran is gratefully acknowledged.

progression. The data, from the National Household Survey on Drug Abuse, have several advantages as well as disadvantages over other data sets. The advantages are that the sample is representative of the United States population; because of the entire age range of the population, individuals can be studied past the period of risk for involvement in illicit drugs; the large sample makes it possible to consider progression through specific illicit drug classes beyond marijuana, in particular heroin, and ethnic comparisons in patterns of progression; the inclusion of criteria for drug dependence makes it possible to relate progression through classes of drugs to substance use dependence. We have taken advantage of these features to examine the role of heroin in the sequence of drug involvement and the relationship between stage of drug use and drug dependence. The former has not previously been examined in a general population sample, and the latter has not previously been examined, either in the general population or in clinical samples.

However, as will become apparent, the data set has major limitations. Because these are cross-sectional surveys, the information on age of onset is based on retrospective reports, with the biases that these reports entail. In addition, the data are not well suited to investigating risk and protective factors related to progression. Not only are the data cross-sectional, but they contain almost no information about individuals other than their drug behavior and demographic characteristics. Thus, our presentation focuses mainly on describing the phenomenology of drug progression and subgroup differences in the progression.

The statistical techniques that were used in the analyses are discussed in detail by Yamaguchi and Kandel in Chapter 9.

We address four themes:

- The nature of developmental stages and pathways of involvement in the use of different classes of drugs in the United States population

- Gender and ethnic patterns in the pathways

- Behavioral features of drug histories associated with progression through the stages

- The relationship between stage of drug use and dependence

In addressing these themes, we specify three aspects of drug use progression: (a) the nature of pathways of progression across multiple drug classes; (b) the sequencing tendency from one class to another for a pair of drugs; and (c) the strength of the association in the initiation of use between two drug classes. The combination of sequences between two drugs produces pathways and trajectories of progression across classes of drugs. Sequencing and assoication are used to clarify gender and ethnic group differences in the nature of the pathways.

The analyses reflect an advance in the conceptualization and identification of stages of drug use progression. Although for most individuals the use of one class of drugs, such as a licit drug, precedes the use of another drug, such as marijuana, the sequencing tendency from the use of one drug to use of another and the association of the initiation of two drugs may still be significantly stronger in one group than in another. This may occur primarily because a greater proportion of one group than the other falls into certain random progression patterns rather than because different groups vary systematically in their patterns of progression. For example, although we hypothesize, on the basis of our previous research, that marijuana use will precede the initiation of cocaine and heroin use for all groups, the extent to which such an order holds may still depend on ethnicity, because a greater proportion of minorities than Whites may have random patterns of progression.

The nature of the pathways is the most fundamental feature of the identification of developmental patterns of progression, and all other features depend upon dealing with it first. Other features besides sequencing tendency and strength of association of use can and should be investigated. For instance, rate of progression from one drug class to another is another crucial feature, which we do not consider here. In addition, we introduce limited control for spuriousness of association.

The National Household Survey on Drug Abuse

The data are drawn from the National Household Survey on Drug Abuse (NHSDA), a national survey of the population 12 and over, conducted by the Substance Abuse and Mental Health Services Administration (1996, 1997) on an annual basis.

Sample

The universe for the NHSDA sample is the civilian noninstitutionalized population of the United States, including those living in noninstitutional group quarters, such as homeless shelters, rooming houses, and college dormitories. The household population represents over 98% of the total U.S. population. Young persons 12–34 years old and minorities have been oversampled. The analyses are based on the 1994B–1995 surveys (Substance Abuse and Mental Health Services Administration, 1996, 1997), the most current available data at the time the analyses were undertaken. Completion rates were 78% or above. Although the rates of drug use in the NHSDA are probably biased downward because of the omission of groups at highest risk for using drugs, such as the homeless or those in institutions, the survey has the advantage that it includes school dropouts. The self-acknowledged heroin users are from the general population and not from a treatment program or the criminal justice system.

We present data for men and women 18 to 40 years of age ($N = 21,000$) from the aggregated 1994B–1995 surveys (Substance Abuse and Mental Health Services Administration, 1996, 1997). We restricted the analyses to persons aged 18 to 40 because these ages include periods in the life span when the use of illicit drugs is most prevalent (ages 18–24) and by age 30 the risk period for initiation of all drug classes is terminated.

The data are collected through anonymous personal household interviews that include self-administered drug use modules. Separate modules ask about patterns and age of first use of tobacco and 11 other drug classes, as well as about symptoms of dependence and problems experienced with each drug class. These items were designed to approximate most of the criteria specified by the American Psychiatric Association (DSM-IV) to identify individuals with substance use disorders. We defined dependence on four drug classes: nicotine, alcohol, marijuana, and cocaine (Kandel, Chen, Warner, Kessler, & Grant, 1997).

Developmental Aspects of Drug Involvement

Identification of Models of Progression: Conceptual Considerations and Statistical Approaches

The identification of developmental stages and pathways of drug use was based on self-reported ages of onset in each of five classes of drugs. In the first part of the analyses, we identify sequential patterns of progression. In the second part, we examine sequential tendencies and the strength of association of lifetime use between two drugs to explain group differences in patterns of progression. A unique feature of our approach is that it can identify major *trajectories* in drug involvement, as well as significant deviations in these trajectories.

Two conditions must be met for a stage of drug use progression to be established. The first condition is that a sequential order of initiation between a lower-stage drug (e.g., A) and a higher-stage drug (e.g., D) must be satisfied by *all systematic pathways* of drug use progression, other than random patterns, involving all drugs A through D; no reverse order of initiation is allowed. The second condition specifies two requirements: (2a) being in stage A must indicate a significantly higher risk of progression into stage D compared with being in any stage still lower than stage A; and (2b) this higher risk of progression must not be due to the spurious effect of common antecedents. Conditions 2a and 2b are necessary because a sequential order between stages A and D can be established without there being a causal relation between the two. However, the exclusion of spurious effects is more difficult to establish than the significance of the risk of progression itself.

Two classes of log linear models were applied to address these issues, as is explained by Yamaguchi and Kandel in greater detail in Chapter 9. *Pathways of progression* were identified through a log linear quasi-independence model that hypothesizes that there is a latent group of individuals in the population who follow one among several specified pathways of drug use progression and a latent group for whom the sequencing of drug use initiations depends only on random nonequal probabilities of initiating various drugs independently. This model identifies nonrandom patterns of drug use progression and the proportion of nonrandom and random progression types in each gender and racial/ethnic group. Differences in *sequencing tendency* and the *strength of the association* in the lifetime use of different drug classes underlying group differences in patterns of progression were identified through log linear models for parametric event sequence analysis (Yamaguchi & Kandel, 1996). These analyses are complementary: whereas the first model identifies pathways of drug use progression for each group separately, the second model identifies the extent of difference in sequential ordering and in the strength of association in the lifetime use of various drug classes among different gender and racial/ethnic groups. The methods and models employed in the present analysis are powerful for examining pathways and progression; they are limited for controlling for population heterogeneity and spurious effects. In particular, the log linear quasi-independence model developed to date does not allow the inclusion of covariates. As we have noted, although the same pathways of progressions may hold for different groups, the groups may still differ in the extent to which a sequential order holds between two drugs. Groups may differ in the latent proportion of persons who do not progress systematically and in

Table 4.1. *Mean Age of Onset Into Five Drug Classes by Gender and Ethnicity (NHSDA 1994B–1995, Ages 18–40)*

	Cigarettes M Age	Alcohol M Age	Marijuana M Age	Cocaine M Age	Heroin M Age
Total	14.3	16.2	16.6	20.2	20.1
Total N	(15,402)	(17,962)	(9,471)	(3,642)	(319)
Men	14.7	15.6	16.5	20.3	20.1
Total N	(7,041)	(8,042)	(4,552)	(1,910)	(199)
Women	15.2	16.8	16.8	20.0	20.2
Total N	(8,361)	(9,920)	(4,919)	(1,732)	(120)
White	14.6	15.8	16.5	20.0	20.0
Total N	(8,217)	(9,310)	(5,797)	(2,318)	(165)
African American	16.0	17.3	17.1	21.9	21.5
Total N	(3,202)	(3,822)	(1,867)	(558)	(72)
Hispanic	15.9	17.1	16.8	20.4	19.3
Total N	(3,641)	(4,404)	(1,632)	(706)	(75)

the extent to which the pathways of drug use progression reflect an order between two drugs.

Basic Model of Progression

We considered five classes of drugs: alcohol, cigarettes, marijuana, cocaine/crack, and heroin. The lifetime prevalence of the use of each class of drugs in the sample was 89.6% for alcohol, 74.6% for cigarettes, 49.3% for marijuana, 18.7% for cocaine/crack, and 1.4% for heroin.

The ages of drug use onset provided a good indication of potential stages in use. In the U.S. population 18 to 40 years old in 1994–1995, the mean age of smoking onset was 14.9 years for cigarettes, more than 1 year later for alcohol (age 16.2), slightly later for marijuana (16.6 years), and more than 3 years later for cocaine (age 20.2) and heroin (age 20.1) (see Table 4.1). Using the data on ages of onset and the two log linear models, we identified major pathways of progression among adults aged 18 to 40 for men and women and for each of the three major ethnic groups, namely, (non-Hispanic) Whites, African Americans, and Hispanics. Men start the use of drugs earlier than women, and Whites initiate earlier than minorities. Hispanics start slightly earlier than African Americans (Table 4.1).

Various hierarchical models were specified and their goodness of fit compared to that of the saturated model that reproduced the observed frequencies (see Chapter 9). The identification of the best model was based on a series of tests that examined whether each particular sequence was a necessary step in the progression, except for those who progressed randomly without a systematic order. We started from a test of the basic model that hypothesized the sequences found in our previous research (Yamaguchi & Kandel, 1984; 1985; Kandel et al., 1992; Kandel & Yamaguchi, 1993). The model hypothesizes that (1) use of at least one licit drug, alcohol or cigarettes, precedes marijuana use; and (2) marijuana use precedes the use of other illicit drugs. We did not previously analyze the progression to heroin use. We tested various hypotheses that modified the sequences in the model between the use of each separate licit drug and each of the three illicit drugs, between the use of marijuana and the use of two other illicit drugs (cocaine and heroin), and between cocaine use and heroin use, in order to determine whether these modifications improved the fit of the basic model. For instance, we tested whether cigarettes must precede marijuana as well as cocaine and heroin; whether marijuana must precede both cocaine and heroin; and so on. In Chapter 9, we discuss in detail the specific models and modifications that were tested. Here, we focus on the substantive results and present the best fitting final model.

We have found that the same overall stage model of progression applies to men and women alike, and to each ethnic group. However, there are differences in the fit of the model, the extent to which drug users in various subgroups follow the sequence, and the actual proportions of each group that attain each stage.

The best fitting common stage model specifies the following three conditions:

1. Either alcohol or cigarettes precede marijuana
2. Alcohol and marijuana precede cocaine
3. Alcohol, cigarettes, and marijuana precede heroin

The detailed pathways of progression that meet these conditions are displayed in Figure 4.1. The relative importance of the various sequences is indicated approximately with variations in the thickness of the lines.

The first stage represents the use of cigarettes and alcohol. A higher number of individuals start their drug use with alcohol than with cigarettes. However, although only a minority of those who start with alcohol go on to smoke, the large majority of those who start with cigarettes go on to drink alcohol. The next stage is that of marijuana use. Although only one licit drug is required to make the progression to marijuana use, the overwhelming majority use marijuana after initiating both alcohol

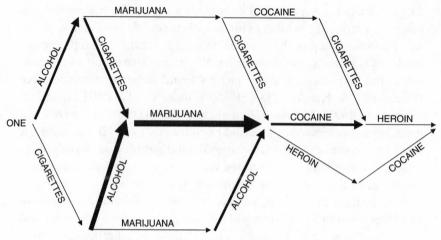

Figure 4.1. Pathways of drug involvement.

and cigarettes. The third stage is that of cocaine use. Although smoking is not a prior requirement to cocaine use, the large majority of cocaine users still progress to cocaine use after using cigarettes as well as alcohol and marijuana, which are required precursors.

In a small proportion of cases, cocaine use is followed by the use of heroin. A less frequent pathway involves the use of heroin directly after marijuana, followed by cocaine. The majority of heroin users used cocaine first. Although only a fraction of those who initiate cocaine go on to use heroin, all those who initiate heroin immediately after marijuana go on to using cocaine.

Thus, either heroin use or cocaine use represents the last stage in the developmental sequence of drug involvement.

In summary, individuals are unlikely to experiment with marijuana without prior experimentation with an alcoholic beverage or with cigarettes; very few try cocaine without prior use of marijuana. A small number of individuals use heroin directly after marijuana without prior use of cocaine. All these heroin users go on to use cocaine subsequently.

With one exception, 95% of any one group fall into one of the hierarchical scale types, 90% not by chance. The proportions are slightly lower among African Americans. The percentages classified in one of the scale types are 94.8% for men (89.5% not by chance); 95.6% for women (90.5% not by chance); 95.5% for Whites (90.7% not by chance); 92.8%

for African Americans (84.0% not by chance); and 95.2% for Hispanics (89.6% not by chance).

A stronger sequential order is consistently observed between marijuana and other illicit drugs than between the legal drugs and marijuana (Table 4.2). For instance, close to 70% of those who used cigarettes and marijuana clearly started cigarettes before marijuana and close to 20% started at the same age. The order is slightly clearer for cigarettes than for alcohol.

The timing is even clearer for cocaine than for marijuana. Over 90% of cocaine users started using cigarettes, alcohol, and marijuana before using cocaine. Fewer than 4% initiated the use of cocaine prior to use of a legal drug; 1% initiated the use of marijuana before cocaine. There are many fewer ties involving onset of the use of legal drugs with cocaine than with marijuana. Among heroin users who also used cocaine, 23.8% started heroin first.

Gender Differences in Sequences of Progression

The same overall model fits men and women; the scale-type patterns of progression are identical for both genders (Table 4.3). However, more men than women reached the highest stages in the sequence. The gender differences increase with each succeeding step. About 40% of men and 45% of women did not proceed beyond using alcohol and/or cigarettes; less than one third stopped at marijuana. Of men 1% and of women 0.5% reached the heroin stage after having proceeded through each of the preceding stages in the sequence. Overall, 17.5% of men and 12.7% of women proceeded through the three developmental stages of drug use involving a legal drug, marijuana, and cocaine. All these differences are statistically significant.

However, there are significant gender differences in the proportions who follow specific sequences. As regards the progression from legal drugs to marijuana, three patterns are more prevalent for women than for men: the use of alcohol with no further drug use (16.4% versus 12.4%, $p < .001$); the use of cigarettes followed by alcohol, with no use of any other drug (18.6% versus 16.1%, $p < .001$); and the use of cigarettes first, marijuana second, and alcohol third, with no use of any other drug class (5.2% versus 4.0%, $p < .001$). Initial use of cigarettes rather than alcohol is a better indicator of further drug use progression for women than for men.

Table 4.2. *Sequential Order of Initiation of Cigarettes and Alcohol With Marijuana and Cocaine and Among Illicit Drugs (NHSDA 1994B–1995, ages 18-40)*

Onset Order	Percentage					
Drug A	Cigarettes	Alcohol	Any Legal	Cigarettes	Alcohol	Marijuana	Cocaine/Crack
Drug B	Marijuana	Marijuana	Marijuana	Cocaine/Crack	Cocaine/Crack	Cocaine/Crack	Heroin
Drug A first	67.6	56.9	77.4	92.8	93.7	89.3	56.0
Ties	18.9	25.4	17.4	3.8	4.4	9.2	20.2
Drug B first	13.5	17.7	5.3	3.4	1.9	1.5	23.8
Total *N*	(8,899)	(9,345)	(9,445)	(4,384)	(4,601)	(3,519)	(318)

Table 4.3. *Distribution of Sequential Stages of Drug Use Among Men and Women (NHSDA 1994B–1995, Ages 18–40)*

Sequential Stages	Percentage		
	Men	Women	Total
None	5.6	9.8	7.7
Alcohol/Cigarettes	40.0	45.0	42.5
Marijuana	30.0	27.3	28.6
Cocaine/Crack	17.5	12.7	15.1
Heroin	1.5	0.7	1.1
From heroin to cocaine	.4	.2	.3
Errors	4.8	4.3	4.5
Total *N*	(11,959)	(12,369)	(24,328)

The parametric sequence analyses confirm gender differences in the more important role of tobacco cigarettes among women than among men in the progression into marijuana use, and the more important role of alcohol among men. However, for cigarettes both sequencing and association of use are significantly stronger for women than for men, whereas for alcohol sequencing is stronger for men than for women, with no gender difference for association. The odds of sequencing from cigarette smoking to marijuana use (versus the reverse sequence) are 1.23 [= exp(2 × 0.144)] times as high for women as for men, whereas the odds of sequencing from alcohol drinking to marijuana use (versus the reverse sequence) are 0.74 [= exp(2 × −0.150)] time as high for women as for men. There is also a strong significant gender effect on the association between the initiations of cigarette smoking and of marijuana use, reflected in an odds ratio that is 1.78 [= exp(4 × 0.144)] times higher for women than for men. By contrast the gender effect on the association between the initiation of alcohol drinking and marijuana use is not significant.

In summary, cigarette use is a better precursor of marijuana initiation for women than for men not only because the sequence of initiation between cigarette smoking and marijuana use is better established for women than for men, but because cigarette smoking predicts higher odds of marijuana use for women than for men. On the other hand, although the alcohol–marijuana sequence is less well established for women than for men, the association between alcohol drinking and marijuana use does not differ between men and women.

As regards the progression among illicit drugs, gender differences appear with respect to the progression from cocaine to heroin but not from marijuana to cocaine or heroin. The sequencing from cocaine use to heroin use is weaker for women than for men (odds ratio = .54). However, once use of cocaine has been initiated, the risk of progression to heroin is the same for both genders.

Ethnic Differences in Sequences of Progression

The same sequential model of drug progression characterizes all three ethnic groups. However, the distribution of each group among the stages and the proportions of individuals who fall into the scale types differ significantly by ethnicity (Table 4.4).

Two trends should be noted. First, the proportions who have not used any drugs are larger among minorities than among Whites, and the proportions who have progressed sequentially to cocaine and heroin are smaller. Second, among users of illicit drugs, the proportion who have followed the scale-type pattern of progression from a legal drug to marijuana to cocaine or heroin is significantly higher among Whites than among minorities. Among cocaine users, 92.3% of Whites have followed the major sequential pattern compared with 83.3% of African Americans and 81.8% of Hispanics. Among heroin users, 93.3%, 25%, and 80.6%, respectively, have done so.

There are strong significant racial/ethnic effects both on sequencing and on the association of use between each legal drug and marijuana use. For African Americans, the sequencing tendency from cigarette smoking to marijuana use and the association between the initiation of each legal drug and marijuana are significantly weaker than for Whites. For example, the association (in odds ratio) between the lifetime use of cigarette smoking and marijuana use is 0.60 time [= $\exp(4 \times -0.128)$] as high for African Americans as for Whites. Alcohol and cigarettes are weaker precursors of marijuana use initiation for African Americans than for Whites, because the sequencing between each licit drug and marijuana use is much less well established, and initiation of a licit drug is a weaker predictor of the risk of initiating marijuana use for African Americans than for Whites.

The patterns for Hispanics are more complex than for African Americans. The *sequencing* between cigarettes and marijuana and the *association of lifetime use* between alcohol and marijuana are significantly weaker

Table 4.4. *Distribution of Sequential Stages of Drug Use Among Three Ethnic Groups (NHSDA 1994B–1995, Ages 18–40)*

Sequential Stages	Percentage		
	White	African American	Hispanic
None	4.4	14.8	15.9
Alcohol/Cigarettes	39.3	46.7	54.8
Marijuana	32.6	23.1	15.4
Cocaine/Crack	18.1	7.2	8.2
Heroin	1.1	.9	.8
From heroin to cocaine	.3	.4	.2
Errors	4.2	6.1	4.7
Total N	(17,404)	(3,004)	(2,850)

Note: Based on results of logistic models.

for Hispanics than for Whites. Whereas cigarette smoking is as strong a predictor of marijuana initiation for Hispanics as for Whites, the tendency for cigarette smoking to precede marijuana use is weaker for Hispanics. On the other hand, although alcohol is a weaker predictor of marijuana use initiation for Hispanics than for Whites, the tendency for alcohol drinking to precede marijuana use does not differ between the two groups. Since the association between alcohol drinking and cigarette smoking is stronger for Hispanics than for Whites, the use of both substances is an effective, if weaker, precursor of marijuana initiation for Hispanics than for Whites.

Ethnic differences also appear in patterns of progression from marijuana to cocaine use but not between cocaine and heroin use. Both the sequencing tendency and the strength of association of lifetime marijuana use with cocaine and heroin are lower among minorities than among Whites. For instance, the odds of sequencing from marijuana use to cocaine use are 0.31 time as high for African Americans compared with Whites. Marijuana use is a weaker precursor of cocaine use initiation for African Americans and Hispanics than for Whites not only because the sequencing between the initiations of marijuana use and cocaine use is much less established for African Americans and Hispanics than for Whites, but also because marijuana use is not as effective a predictor of the risk of cocaine use initiation for African Americans and Hispanics as for Whites. The sequencing tendency and the extent of association of lifetime use between cocaine and heroin do not differ significantly among racial/ethnic groups.

No systematic deviation from the modal pattern in trajectories could be identified among minorities. A higher proportion of African Americans initiated their drug use with marijuana, without having used alcohol or cigarettes (6.2% versus 3.8% for Whites, and 3.2% for Hispanics, $p < .001$). A higher proportion also initiated cocaine prior to marijuana (1.3% versus .5% for whites, and .8% for Hispanics, $p < .001$).

These results suggest that drug use progressions are somewhat more difficult to predict for African Americans and Hispanics than for Whites. Use of a lower-stage drug is a weaker indicator of the higher risk of further progression into drug use for minorities than for Whites. However, it is the case that the majority of users in all ethnic groups follow the modal pattern of progression.

The lower proportion of minorities than of Whites at each sequential stage is due to several factors. Smaller proportions of minorities than Whites report having ever used each of the drugs. Smaller relative proportions fall into each of the scale types. Ethnic differences in ages of onset into the different drug classes may also contribute to the poorer fit of the overall model for minorities, especially African Americans, than for Whites.

Behavioral Features of Drug Histories Associated With Progression

Given the fact that there are stages of drug use, what are some of the predictors of movement from one stage to another? Because the NHSDA is a cross-sectional survey with very limited information on individuals aside from their drug use, it does not lend itself to identifying risk and protective factors for progression into various stages of drug use. The only variables that can be examined describe behavioral features of drug behavior, and only one of these can be clearly timed to progression.

Two behavioral features of a person's drug history are strongly associated with stage of drug involvement: (a) age of onset into an earlier stage drug; and (b) degree of involvement in a prior drug.

Age of Onset

A particularly crucial factor is early age of onset. Earlier onset into the use of a lower-stage drug is associated with greater involvement in the use of higher-stage drugs. Individuals who progressed to using heroin

Table 4.5. *Mean Age of First Use of Cigarettes, Alcohol, and Marijuana by Lifetime Stage of Lifetime Drug Use (NHSDA 1994B–1995, Ages 18–40)*

Age of Onset of Use	Lifetime Sequential Stage			
	Alcohol/ Cigarettes	Marijuana	Cocaine/Crack	Heroin
Cigarettes				
Mean age	15.8	14.6	14.0	12.6
S.D.	4.2	3.4	3.4	3.2
Total *N*	(6,826)	(6,911)	(3,914)	(312)
Alcohol				
Mean age	17.4	15.6	14.6	12.8
S.D.	3.5	2.9	2.8	3.1
Total *N*	(9,734)	(7,412)	(4,108)	(316)
Marijuana				
Mean age	—	17.2	15.7	13.9
S.D.	—	3.0	2.7	2.6
Total *N*		(7,475)	(4,124)	(317)

began using each of the drugs at the preceding stages, that is, cigarettes, alcoholic beverages, and marijuana, several years earlier than users of each of these substances who did not go on using any higher-stage substance (Table 4.5). They started using cigarettes and marijuana more than 3 years earlier, and alcohol more than 4.5 years earlier. Those who used cocaine started slightly more than a year and a half earlier. Those who did not progress beyond marijuana started more than a year earlier. Thus, heroin users started smoking at age 12.6 on average, compared with age 14.0 for smokers who used cocaine but no heroin, 14.6 years for smokers who used marijuana but no other illicit drug, and age 15.8 years for smokers who may have also drunk an alcoholic beverage but did not go on to using any illicit drug.

Frequency of Drug Use

Furthermore, progression to a higher-ranked drug is positively associated with frequency of use at the prior stage drug. Over 71% of those who ever used marijuana more than 300 times in their lives ever used cocaine compared with 38.7% or less of those who ever used marijuana 12 to 100 times or 12.8% of those who only tried marijuana once or twice. It is crucial to keep in mind that since this is a cross-sectional association, it is not clear to what extent it represents the progression to cocaine of frequent marijuana users rather than increases in marijuana use following cocaine involvement. However, similar trends are found in longitudinal studies in which the timing between frequency of marijuana use and subsequent use of an illegal drug can be clearly established (Kandel & Faust, 1975). In a longitudinal cohort of young adults, only 6% of men who had never used marijuana by age 24–25 initiated the use of an illicit by age 28–29 compared with 77% of those who had used marijuana at least 100 times.

Stage of Drug Use and Dependence

Most models of drug use progression focus on progression through classes of drugs and, by and large, ignore progressive involvement within individual drug classes. The NHSDA provides a unique opportunity to examine substance use dependence as a function of stage of drug involvement. Although the cross-sectional nature of the survey precludes a true developmental analysis of the relationship between stage of drug use and drug dependence, it makes possible an analysis of that association.

On the basis of data about symptoms of dependence and problems experienced from using each drug class in the last year, we identified individuals who met criteria for nicotine, alcohol, and marijuana dependence (Kandel et al., 1997). We examined the proportions of individuals at each stage of drug use within the last year who also met criteria for dependence within the last year on each of the three drugs.

For each lower drug class, the highest rates of dependence were observed among those who had reached the highest cumulative stage of drug use involving use of a legal drug, marijuana, and cocaine. We categorized drug users in two hierarchical and cumulative classifications of drug use that alternately included cigarettes or alcohol as the legal drug consumed. The first classification distinguished those who reported having used only cigarettes within the last year; cigarettes and alcohol; cigarettes and marijuana; and cigarettes, marijuana, and cocaine or heroin (Table 4.6).

For nicotine dependence, 55.6% of those who were in the highest stage of cocaine and/or heroin use met criteria for nicotine dependence in the last year preceding the survey compared with 48.2% of those who had not used an illicit drug other than marijuana or 36.0% of those who

Table 4.6. *Last Year Dependence on Nicotine, Alcohol, and Marijuana by Last Year Stage of Drug Use (NHSDA 1994B–1995, Ages 18–40)*

| | Last Year Stage of Drug Use, Percentage | | | | |
Dependence on	Cigarettes Only	Cigarettes/ Alcohol	Cigarettes/ Marijuana	Legal/ Marijuana Cocaine/ Heroin	Errors
Nicotine	36.0	31.2	48.2	55.6	49.2
Total N	(1,059)	(5,895)	(1,896)	(534)	(113)
Alcohol	3.7	10.5	22.9	37.4	32.5
Total N	(9,479)	(5,895)	(2,706)	(620)	(162)
Marijuana	—	—	11.3	30.4	28.0
Total N			(2,764)	(633)	(21)

had only smoked. For alcohol dependence, the association between stage of drug use and dependence was completely linear; each successive higher stage of a drug was associated with a 50% to 100% increase in the proportion of those currently dependent on alcohol. For marijuana dependence, almost three times as many were dependent among last year users of cocaine or heroin as among those who were exclusive marijuana users. Those who were classified as representing error patterns had rates of dependence that were almost as high as those observed among those who had reached the highest stage of drug involvement in an orderly sequence.

Individuals at a particular stage of drug use were heavy users of lower-stage drugs and started using these drugs at an earlier age. To control for the possibility that the association of stage of drug use with dependence on a lower-stage drug may be due to extensiveness of consumption and earlier age of onset of lower-stage substances, logistic regressions predicting dependence were estimated. Degree of use and age of onset of the lower-stage drug were entered in the models together with stage of drug use and age (Tables 4.7–4.9). Although both extensiveness of use and age of onset had a significant effect on dependence, stage of drug use retained a highly statistically significant unique effect of its own on dependence on lower-stage drug(s). The adjusted odds ratios were not much different from the odds ratios unadjusted for age of onset and frequency of use of the lower-stage drug.

The effect of stage position is stronger on alcohol than on nicotine dependence. The odds of being dependent on nicotine are 2.3 times

Table 4.7. *Logistic Regressions Predicting Last Year Dependence on Nicotine by Stage of Drug Use Among Last Year Smokers (NHSDA 1994B–1995, Ages 18–40)*

Predictors	OR	AOR
Male (vs. female)	.83***	.70***
Age (years)	.99	.98***
Drug stage last year (vs. used cigarettes only)		
Cigarettes and alcohol	.81**	.86*
Cigarettes and marijuana	1.66***	1.79***
Cigarettes, marijuana, and cocaine/heroin	2.22***	2.27***
Errors	1.72***	1.97**
No cigarettes per day last month	1.06***	1.07***
Age of onset	.95***	.99
Constant		−.20
Total *N*	(9,692)	(9,692)

Notes: OR = odds ratios; AOR = adjusted odds ratios. * $p < .05$. *** $p < .001$.

higher among those who have used an illicit drug within the last year than among those who only smoked cigarettes (Table 4.7). The adjusted odds of being dependent on alcohol (versus not being dependent) are more than 8 times higher among those at the cocaine stage than among those who used only alcohol (Table 4.8). The odds of being dependent on marijuana among those who have used cocaine/heroin are more than twice as high as among those who have only used marijuana and legal drugs (Table 4.9).

Experience with higher-stage drugs and the multiple use of different drug classes increase the liability for dependence on a lower-stage substance, over and beyond the degree of involvement in the lower-stage drug. There appear to be strong additive effects. These may be partially explained by commonalities in neurophysiological processes underlying the addictive properties of different drug classes.

Implications

Among the implications of these data, we focus on two.

The earlier the age of onset into a lower-stage drug, the higher the risk of progression to a higher stage and the higher the risk of becoming a heavy user. Early onset into the use of alcohol and cigarettes is emerging as a consistently crucial marker and risk factor for progression to the use of illicit

Table 4.8. *Logistic Regressions Predicting Dependence on Alcohol by Stage of Drug Use Among Last Year Drinkers (NHSDA 1994B–1995, Ages 18–40)*

Predictors	OR	AOR
Male (vs. female)	2.08***	1.40***
Age (years)	.95***	.97***
Drug stage last year (vs. used alcohol only)		
Alcohol and cigarettes	3.07***	2.49***
Alcohol and marijuana	7.75***	4.91***
Alcohol, marijuana, and cocaine/heroin	15.60***	8.85***
Errors	12.61***	10.39***
No drinks per day last month	1.22***	1.14***
Age of onset	.87***	.94***
Constant		−.54**
Total N	(14,942)	(14,942)

Notes: OR = odds ratios; AOR = adjusted odds ratios. ** $p < .01$. *** $p < .001$.

Table 4.9. *Logistic Regressions Predicting Dependence on Marijuana by Stage of Drug Use Among Last Year Marijuana Users, NHSDA 1994B–1995, Ages 18–40*

Predictors	OR	AOR
Male (vs. female)	1.46***	1.30***
Age (years)	.96***	.92***
Drug stage last year (vs. used cigarettes only)		
Legal, marijuana, cocaine/heroin	2.00**	2.47***
Errors	0.01	4.83***
No days used marijuana last year	1.03***	1.01***
Age of onset	.94***	.95*
Constant		.87*
Total N	(3,207)	(3,207)

Notes: OR = odds ratios; AOR = adjusted odds ratios. * $p < .05$. *** $p < .001$.

drugs, and early onset into marijuana is a crucial marker for progression to the use of illicit drugs other than marijuana. Prevention and educational efforts must be initiated in early adolescence and be targeted toward preventing initiation into the use of alcohol and cigarettes, drugs that are legal and commonly used for recreational purposes by adults in our society. Further interventions in middle adolescence should be targeted toward preventing experimentation with marijuana.

Postponement of initiation itself can have beneficial effects other than reducing progression to other drugs by reducing the time in a formative period of the life span when an individual experiences the effects of drugs. An analogy with early teenage pregnancy may be illuminating. Simply postponing the timing of the first birth greatly improves the life chances of young women by eliminating the burden on a teenager created by raising a child.

However, there is an important factor to consider, namely, that of self-selection into drugs. As noted by Lee Robins (Robins & Przybeck, 1985), early initiators self-select into early use and are already different from their peers at the time of initiation. One cannot naively assume that by postponing initiation into drugs one will simultaneously change adolescents in such a way that their chances of subsequent involvement in other drugs will be substantially reduced. One may simply shortcut a process in which risk-taking and nonconforming tendencies will express themselves eventually in the use of drugs other than marijuana or in other ways.

Frequency of a lower-stage drug is related to degree of involvement in a higher-stage drug. The associations between increasing frequency of use of cigarettes and alcohol with marijuana use and of increasing frequency of marijuana use with increasing use of other drugs are of special public health concern in view of the recent increases in the use of cigarettes and of marijuana by young people.

Indeed, epidemiological data reveal that the proportion of frequent and heavy marijuana users does not represent a consistent fraction of the marijuana using adolescent population. The trends, whether increases or decreases, are accentuated with respect to extent of use compared with lifetime prevalence of use. Concurrently with the decline in the overall rates of lifetime experimentation with marijuana observed in the late 1980s, there were even more striking declines in the proportions of daily users among lifetime users. Correlatively, as the proportions of lifetime experimenters started to increase again from 1993, the proportions of daily users among marijuana users increased even more sharply.

This is illustrated by trend data provided nationally for high school students by *Monitoring the Future* (Johnston, O'Malley, & Bachman, 1998) (Figure 4.2). At the height of the marijuana epidemic in 1978, when 60% of high school seniors reported that they had ever used marijuana, almost one in five of the users was a daily user. At the lowest levels of use

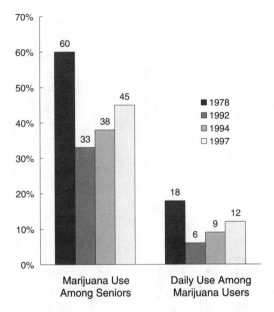

Figure 4.2. Prevalence of lifetime marijuana use among all seniors and daily use among marijuana users in 1978, 1992, 1994, and 1997. Based on data from *Monitoring the Future* (Johnston, O'Malley, & Bachman, 1998).

observed in 1992, when a third had ever used marijuana, only 1 in 20 users was a daily user. In 1997, when 45% reported having ever used marijuana, slightly over 1 in 10 users was a daily user. Thus, although the proportions of high school seniors who ever tried marijuana declined by almost half in 1992 from its peak period of use in the years 1978–1979, the proportion of daily marijuana users among the users declined by 300 percent, or three times as much, in the same period. As the proportion of marijuana users among high school seniors increased by more than a third from 1992 to 1997, the proportion of daily users among all seniors doubled in that same period.

During a period of increase in use in the nation, there are not only increases in the proportion of adolescents who ever experimented with marijuana but even more important increases in the proportions of frequent regular users, those who can be expected to progress to other illicit drugs and experience the most severe negative health and social consequences of their drug use. These are important trends because the adolescent years represent a period of major risk for involvement in

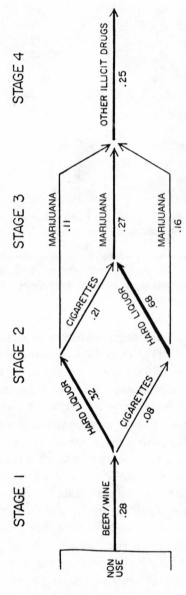

Figure 4.3. Major stages of adolescent involvement in drug use. Probabilities of moving from one stage to another are based on changes between fall 1971 and spring 1972 in a cohort of New York State high school students, 14 to 18 years old. Youths who started using more than one drug within the follow-up interval were distributed in a sequential order that reproduced the proportions of known exclusive starters of each drug. Reprinted from Kandel (1975).

86

drugs, and involvement in marijuana use is a precursor of cocaine use, which itself is a precursor of heroin use.

The behavior of users within a society is determined in part by broader social–cultural factors, and in particular by the overall pervasiveness of the use of drugs in that society. The changing proportions of heavy users in the drug using population suggest that heavy use results in part from a process of social contagion.

The present results reflect striking similarity and consistency of patterns across historical time. We first presented the stage model of drug involvement more than 20 years ago. The model published in *Science* in 1975 (Kandel, 1975) based on a New York state survey (Figure 4.3) shows exactly the same pathways observed in the United States in 1994–1995. More adolescents start with alcohol than with cigarettes. Many more of those who start with cigarettes proceed to use alcohol than those who start with alcohol proceed to smoke. Then, as now, the highest rates of progression were observed for those who had tried both legal drugs.

The sources of these patterns replicated across different historical times and among different groups in the population remain to be understood. In addition to psychosocial characteristics of users, commonalities in the neurophysiological basis of addiction (e.g., de Fonseca, 1997; Tanda et al., 1997) might partially account for the developmental progressions that we observed. Use of marijuana, a lower-stage drug, may prime the brain for use and dependence on higher-stage substances, such as cocaine and opiates. The underlying mechanism appears to be a surge in dopamine release through neurophysiological processes common across drugs.

A complete explanation of drug consumption requires understanding of the biological as well as the sociological and psychological factors underlying drug use and addiction.

References

De Fonseca, F. R., Carrera, M.R.A., Navarro, M., Koob, G., & Weiss, F. (1997). Activation of corticotropin-releasing factor in the limbic system during cannabinoid withdrawal. *Science, 276*, 2050–2054.

Epstein, J. F., & Gfroerer, J. C. (1997). Heroin abuse in the United States. Substance Abuse and Mental Health Services Administration, Office of Applied Studies Working Paper, Rockville, MD.

Johnston, L. D., O'Malley, P. M., & Bachman, J. G. (1998). *National survey results on drug use from Monitoring the Future Study, 1975–1997.* The University of Michigan Institute for Social Research. National Institute on Drug Abuse. Rockville, MD: U.S. Department of Health and Human Services.

Kandel, D. B. (1975). Stages in adolescent involvement in drug use. *Science, 190*, 912–914.

Kandel, D. B., Chen, K., Warner, L., Kessler, R., & Grant, B. (1997). Prevalence and demographic correlates of symptoms of dependence on cigarettes, alcohol, marijuana and cocaine in the U.S. population. *Drug and Alcohol Dependence, 44*, 11–29.

Kandel, D. B., & Faust, R. (1975). Sequence and stages in patterns of adolescent drug use. *Archives of General Psychiatry, 32*, 923–932.

Kandel, D. B., & Yamaguchi, K. (1985). Development patterns of the use of legal, illegal and medically prescribed psychotropic drugs from adolescence to young adulthood. In C. L. Jones & R. Battjes (Eds.), *Etiology of drug abuse: Implications for prevention*. NIDA Research Monograph 56. National Institute on Drug Abuse. Rockville, MD: U.S. Department of Health and Human Services.

Kandel, D. B., & Yamaguchi, K. (1993). From beer to crack: Developmental patterns of involvement in drugs. *American Journal of Public Health, 83*, 851–855.

Kandel, D. B., & Yamaguchi, K. (1999). Developmental stages of involvement in substance use. In R. E. Tarter, R. J. Ammerman, & P. J. Ott (Eds.), *Sourcebook on substance abuse: Etiology, assessment and treatment* (pp. 50–74). New York: Allyn & Bacon.

Kandel, D. B., Yamaguchi, K., & Chen, K. (1992). Stages of progression in drug involvement from adolescence to adulthood: Further evidence for the Gateway Theory. *Journal of Studies on Alcohol, 53*, 447–457.

Koob, G. F. (1996). Drug addiction: The yin and yang of hedonic homeostasis. *Neuron, 16*, 893–896.

Robins, L. N., & Przybeck, T. R. (1985). Age of onset of drug use as a factor in drug and other disorders. In C. L. Jones & R. J. Battjes (Eds.), *Etiology of drug abuse: Implications for prevention* (pp. 178–192). Rockville, MD: NIDA, 1985.

Substance Abuse and Mental Health Services Administration (1996). *National household survey on drug abuse: Main findings 1994*. Rockville, MD: U.S. Department of Health and Human Services.

Substance Abuse and Mental Health Services Administration (1997). *National household survey on drug abuse: Main findings 1995*. Rockville, MD: U.S. Department of Health and Human Services.

Tanda, G., Pontieri, F. E., & DiChaira, G. (1997). Cannabinoid and heroin activation of mesolimbic dopamine transmission by a common μ_1 opioid receptor mechanism. *Science, 276*, 2048–2050.

Turner, C. F., Ku, L., Rogers, S. M., Lindberg, L. D., Pleck, J. H., & Sonenstein, F. L. (1998). Adolescent sexual behavior, drug use, and violence: Increased reporting with computer survey technology. *Science, 280*, 867–873.

Yamaguchi, K., & Kandel, D. B. (1984). Patterns of drug use from adolescence to young adulthood. 2. Sequences of progression. *American Journal of Public Health, 74,* 668–672.

Yamaguchi, K., & Kandel, D. B. (1996). Parametric event sequence analysis: An application to an analysis of gender and racial/ethnic differences in patterns of drug-use progression. *Journal of the American Statistical Association, 91,* 1388–1399.

5

Substance Use Progression and Hard Drug Use in Inner-City New York

Andrew Golub and Bruce D. Johnson

The Gateway Hypothesis holds that substance use typically follows a series of stages from nonuse of any substance as a child to use of alcohol and/or tobacco in early adolescence, potentially followed by use of marijuana and then hard drugs. Not all users of substances at one stage progress to the next. Most importantly, however, individuals who do not use substances at one stage rarely use any of the substances associated with later stages. This theory was first stated in its current form and supported by empirical evidence by Denise Kandel (1975) in the 1970s and has been confirmed widely since (as documented elsewhere in this volume).

It is quite remarkable that this simple sequence has so often emerged, given the wide variation in factors that have been found to affect youthful substance use. In particular, the attitudes, values, and opportunities available to youths have distinct roots that are historical, geographical, religious, and ethnocultural (Schulenberg, Maggs, & Hurrelman, 1997). Each individual's characteristics and family experiences have a role in defining her or his behavior within this larger context. Brown, Dolcini, & Leventhal (1997) describe how this person–context interaction may be reciprocal, particularly with regard to adolescent peer groups, further complicating matters. They found that youths both form or join groups partially based on common substance use patterns and that groups pressure individuals to use (or not use) various substances.

Preparation of this chapter was partially supported by a grant from the Robert Wood Johnson Foundation's Substance Abuse Policy Research Program. Additional support was provided by National Development and Research Institutes, Inc. Points of view and opinions expressed do not necessarily reflect the positions of the Robert Wood Johnson Foundation, nor of the National Development and Research Institutes.

The meaning of substance use is not the same for all youths; rather it must be understood as embedded in a developmental process. Nurmi (1997) describes one such process, "the failure trap syndrome," in which progressively more serious substance use is part of a downward spiral. Nurmi (1997, pp. 405–406) explains that "[some] young people use dysfunctional strategies in managing major developmental transitions.... Due to low self-esteem, they expect failure. Because they believe this expected outcome to be beyond their control, they turn to task-irrelevant and blunting behavior, perhaps to reduce their anxiety." This nonproductive behavior can lead an individual to "accumulat[e] negative developmental markers such as low self-esteem, depression, dysfunctional strategies, lack of self-protecting attributional bias, problem behavior and subsequent mental health problems," which can lead to the use and abuse of more serious substances (Nurmi, 1997, p. 411). Other research findings suggest that increased substance use can be part of a more positive developmental path. Eccles and coworkers (1997, p. 310) found that "among the low achieving adolescents, those whose self-esteem increased during the transition to junior high school reported the most frequent use of alcohol and drugs in 12th grade.... This group of students may represent those who place more value on the increased social network of the junior high experience, gain feelings of self-worth more from these affiliations than from school, and become the 'partiers' of the school."

Most of the research on substance use progression has focused on the sequences prevailing in the general population. However, individuals who develop serious drug abuse problems are relatively rare in general populations. It is possible that the sheer volume of less serious users may potentially mask different sequences followed by youths who do become serious drug abusers.

Two prior studies provide partial support for this hypothesis. Golub and Johnson (1994a) examined the sequences of substances reported by 994 serious drug abusers (primarily crack abusers) recruited from the streets of inner-city Manhattan. That study found that about equal numbers had started their substance use with marijuana and with alcohol. Among the younger drug abusers, almost twice as many had started with marijuana as alcohol. Unfortunately, the study had not asked about tobacco use, precluding a test of whether these persons had used tobacco before progressing to marijuana use. Mackesy-Amiti, Fendrich, and Goldstein (1997) examined substance use sequences through alcohol, marijuana, and "other" drugs, among 233 drug users from the Lower

East Side of Manhattan. Again, respondents were not asked about tobacco use. Only a third of the sample followed the strict Gateway sequence from alcohol to marijuana to other drugs. Close to one quarter reported starting with other drugs such as cocaine, heroin, amphetamines, hallucinogens, and inhalants. The authors note that the prevalence of early "other" use was most likely influenced by inclusion of inhalants in this category.

The present study further explored the sequences of substance use progression prevailing in inner-city New York by using two data sets: a household survey and a survey of arrestees. Unlike in the previous studies, tobacco use was included in the analysis. The researchers hypothesized the following:

> **Hypothesis 1:** Inner-city New York residents were substantially more likely to deviate from the Gateway sequence than youths in the general population.

The popularity of specific drugs shifts over time. Golub and Johnson (1999) identified three distinct generations among Manhattan arrestees: the Heroin Injection Generation (born 1945–1954), the Cocaine/Crack Generation (born 1955–1969), and the Marijuana/Blunts Generation (born since 1970). Since the 1960s, marijuana use has become widespread and popular among youths (Johnson & Gerstein, 1997). In the 1990s, high school seniors perceived marijuana use to be about as dangerous as use of alcohol and tobacco (Johnston, O'Malley, & Bachman, 1999). Regarding substance use progression, there was a further hypothesis:

> **Hypothesis II:** Inner-city New York residents born more recently were more likely to use marijuana prior to alcohol or tobacco than individuals born earlier.

Both the hypothesized variations, across locations and across birth cohorts, are consistent with a broader hypothesis that there is a strong cultural influence on the sequence of substances through which youths tend to progress, if at all.

Methods

This study examined substance use sequences prevailing in two data sets: (1) the 1991–1993 surveys of low-socioeconomic status (low-SES) New York City neighborhoods conducted as part of the National Household Survey on Drug Abuse (NHSDA), substance

Abuse and Mental Health Services Administration (SAMHSA) (1993, 1994, 1995), and (2) the 1989–1997 survey of Manhattan arrestees conducted by the Arrestee Drug Abuse Monitoring (ADAM) Program. Findings with two additional NHSDA samples are also presented to allow for important comparisons: (3) the 1991–1993 NHSDA national sample and (4) the subsample of inner-city New York respondents to the 1991–1993 NHSDA survey who had used *hard drugs* (operationally defined as cocaine powder, crack, or heroin) (SAMHSA, 1993, 1994, 1995). The NHSDA subsample provides information about individuals from a crime- and drug-ridden area. As a result of the nexus of poverty, crime, drugs, and other social problems, the ADAM-Manhattan arrestees tend to come from many of these same neighborhoods. This section describes the strengths and limitations of these data sets and the use of transition diagrams to analyze substance use sequences.

The National Household Survey on Drug Abuse

Since 1971, the NHSDA has measured the prevalence of use of illicit drugs, alcohol, and tobacco in the United States (Substance Abuse and Mental Health Services Administration, 1999). Data collection procedures include personally visiting each residence, administering questionnaires, and providing self-administered answer sheets for sensitive information. The complex selection procedure includes unequal selection probabilities, stratification, and clustering. To account for this non-proportional sampling, the NHSDA program constructs a sample weight for each respondent proportional to her or his probability of inclusion. These weights were used in this study to obtain unbiased estimates. (Because of the complexity of the analysis, the conventional formula for standard errors, which does not account for design effects, was employed.)

From 1991 to 1993, the NHSDA oversampled individuals from six metropolitan areas and oversampled residents of low-SES neighborhoods within each (SAMHSA, 1993, 1994, 1995). This low-SES criterion was used as an operational definition of inner-city for this study. A modest proportion of respondents (12%, 441 of 3,700) reported ever using a hard drug. The demographic characteristics of this sample are discussed later.

Those cases missing information on birth year, age at first use, or lifetime use for any substance were excluded from the study. A small proportion of NHSDA cases from the inner-city New York subsample (2.7%) and the national sample (3.1%) lacked information, yielding final samples of 3,601 and 85,171 cases, respectively. Logistic regression was used to identify appropriate adjustments to the sample weights to account for variation in the probability of inclusion systematically associated with substances ever used, region, urbanicity, population density, demographic characteristics, and educational attainment.

The Arrestee Drug Abuse Monitoring Program

Since 1987 the ADAM Program (formerly known as the Drug Use Forecasting [DUF] Program) has interviewed arrestees about their drug use at police booking facilities across the United States quarterly (National Institute of Justice, 1999). This study examined the subsample recruited in Manhattan from 1989 to 1997 who had used hard drugs. Of the 12,022 ADAM–Manhattan arrestees, a substantial proportion (35%) reported no lifetime use of hard drugs, leaving 7,815 cases. A few (1%) were excluded from the analyses for lack of information about age at first use of the substances studied, yielding 7,713 respondents.

Sample Characteristics

Table 5.1 presents the demographic characteristics of the New York inner-city NHSDA and ADAM–Manhattan samples. Table 5.2 presents the substance use of each sample.

In comparison to the national sample, larger proportions of the New York inner-city NHSDA respondents were Black and Hispanic. These persons were less likely to have achieved mainstream statuses: fewer were married; fewer had graduated from high school or college; and slightly fewer were employed. Surprisingly, fewer reported having ever been arrested or having ever used any substances. Small percentages of both NHSDA samples reported having ever used hard drugs. Only 4% of the sample reported *daily use* (defined as use on 25 of the last 30 days) of alcohol, and 1% reported daily use of any illicit drug. Only 9 of the 3,700 New York inner-city NHSDA respondents reported daily use of cocaine, crack, or heroin. Thus, even this household survey oversample from communities where drug abuse was commonplace failed to access persons or obtain self-disclosures of regular hard drug use or arrest.

Compared to the NHSDA inner-city New York hard drug users, the ADAM–Manhattan hard drug users were much more likely to report daily use of hard drugs. Only 1% of the NHSDA hard drug users reported daily cocaine use; none reported daily heroin use. In stark

Table 5.1. *Demographic Profile of NHSDA, U.S., and Inner-City New York Residents, 1991–1993, and of ADAM-Manhattan Hard Drug Using Arrestees, 1989–1997*

| | U.S. Sample | NHSDA Inner-City New York | | ADAM |
		All Residents	Hard Drug Users	Hard Drug Users
Sample size	87,915	3,700	441	7,713
Typical S.E.[a]	0.2%	0.8%	2.4%	0.6%
Male	48%	43%	55%	67%
Race/ethnicity				
White	77%	28%	30%	15%
Black	11%	32%	33%	57%
Hispanic	8%	34%	36%	26%
Marital status				
Single	23%	32%	47%	74%
Separated/ widowed/ divorced	16%	22%	23%	15%
Married	56%	40%	29%	11%
Education attained				
No high school degree	8%	23%	24%	38%
In school	21%	20%	12%	1%
High school graduate	31%	31%	32%	36%
Some college	20%	14%	15%	15%
College graduate	20%	12%	17%	7%
Employment status				
Work full-time	46%	40%	53%	19%
Work part-time	12%	7%	10%	5%
Unemployed	5%	9%	17%	—[b]
Other	36%	44%	20%	55%
Missing	0%	0%	0%	22%
Ever arrested	9%	3%	17%	100%[c]
Average age in years	40.9	40.4	33.7	32.7
(Standard error)	(0.1)	(0.3)	(0.5)	(0.1)

Notes: [a] Standard error for a prevalence rate of 50%. [b] — Question not asked. [c] By design, all ADAM respondents are arrestees.

Table 5.2. *Substance Use Profile of NHSDA US., and Inner-City New York Residents, 1991-1993, and of ADAM-Manhattan Hard Drug Using Arrestees, 1989-1997*

		NHSDA Inner-City New York		ADAM
	U.S. Sample	All Residents	Hard Drug Users	Hard Drug Users
Sample size	87,915	3,700	441	7.713
Typical S.E.[a]	0.2%	0.8%	2.4%	0.6%
Ever used				
Alcohol	84%	71%	97%	90%
Tobacco	72%	48%	84%	85%
Marijuana	33%	26%	93%	81%
Hard drugs	11%	10%	100%	100%
Any substance	88%	77%	100%	100%
Use daily				
Alcohol	4%	4%	12%	18%
Tobacco	—[c]	—[c]	—[c]	75%
Marijuana	0%	1%	4%	7%
Cocaine	0%	0%	1%	11%
Crack[b]	0%[b]	0%[b]	0%[b]	24%
Heroin	0%	0%	0%	25%
Any hard drug	0%	0%	1%	41%

Notes: [a] Standard error for a prevalence rate of 50%. [b] Past 30 day use is indicated in number of vials, not days of use. It was assumed that individuals who consumed at least 30 vials were daily users. [c] — Question not asked.

contrast, 41% of the ADAM sample reported daily use of either cocaine, crack, or heroin. These individuals were also substantially less likely to have attained mainstream statuses than were the NHSDA hard drug users: far fewer were married; fewer had graduated from high school or college; far fewer had a full-time job; and all (by sample definition) had been recently arrested.

Of the 441 NHSDA inner-city New York residents who had used hard drugs, surprisingly, more of them had completed college. The comparison of employment statuses yielded mixed findings. More of the hard drug users reported having jobs, but more of them also reported being unemployed. Fewer of them reported holding "other" positions such as full-time student or homemaker. These higher rates of employment and reported unemployment may be associated with the higher proportion of males, lower proportion of married respondents, and lower proportion of full-time students in this subsample. About the same proportion of hard drug users were non–White as in the full inner-city New York subsample. The hard drug users were much more likely to have used alcohol, tobacco, and marijuana, but few reported using any substance daily.

Transition Diagrams

Transition diagrams were used to analyze the progression through use of alcohol, tobacco, and marijuana prior to use of hard drugs by youths in inner-city New York. Transition diagrams are widely used by operations researchers and were previously used to study substance use progression by the authors (Golub & Johnson, 1994a; 1994b). Most of the published research on the Gateway Hypothesis employed Guttman scalograms deductively to confirm whether a prespecified sequence matches those prevailing in a data set. Typically, different scales are tried until a reasonable fit is obtained.

In contrast, the transition diagram works inductively by characterizing each respondent's substance use history as a sequence of transitions between states, creating a summary diagram of these sequences, then determining which patterns are most common. For this analysis, a *state* was defined as the collection of substances tried up to a given time. All individuals start as nonusers of any substance at birth. A *transition* was defined as the initiation of one or more of the following substances: alcohol, tobacco, marijuana, or hard drugs. Transitions were inferred from reported age at first use of each substance. This resulted in some ambiguity regarding the exact sequence of substances used in the case of ties. For example, an individual who used both alcohol and tobacco at age 13 may have progressed from alcohol to tobacco, or vice versa.

The analyses are accurate only to the extent that respondents provided accurate information retrospectively. One concern is whether individuals will even disclose use of a substance. Indeed, several studies suggest that individuals often underreport whether they had used a substance, thus potentially affecting any study of self-report data (General Accounting Office, 1993; Harrison & Hughes, 1997). Several factors suggest that the impact of nondisclosure on this study was minimal: (1) the analysis focused on lifetime use as opposed to recent use, individuals might feel less threatened about disclosing use that occurred well in the past as opposed to current use (Turner, Lessler, & Gfroerer, 1992); and (2) the analysis focused on the implied sequences of substances, which might still be representative as long as respondents who reported use followed sequences similar sequences to those followed by respondents who did not report their use.

Another problem is that self-reports of age at first use tend to be inaccurate. A vast psychological literature suggests that as events become more distant in time, individuals tend to discount how long it has been since their occurrence (Eisenhower, Mathiowetz, & Morganstein, 1991). As a result, individuals appear to inflate how old they were at first use of any particular substance as they age – a recall phenomenon referred to as *forward telescoping*. Golub, Labouvie, & Johnson (2000) examined how this inaccuracy affected the reliability of inferred sequences of substance use with a sample of 892 youths interviewed on two occasions separated by 3 years. The sequencing of tobacco and alcohol was highly unreliable; barely half the sequences matched. However, the sequencing of alcohol/tobacco (whichever occurred first) and marijuana was reliable, especially if ties were evaluated as ambiguous but not inconsistent with either possible ordering (94% concordance).

Results

This section first examines overall sequences and then explores variations in first substance used and age at first substance use.

Pathways to Hard Drug Use

Figures 5.1 through 5.4 examine transition diagrams of substance use sequences with four nested samples: (1) the population of the United States, (2) inner-city New York residents, (3) inner-city New York residents who had used hard drugs, and (4) ADAM-Manhattan hard drug using arrestees. The typical Gateway sequence is represented as the horizontal sequence of transitions from nonuse to use of alcohol/tobacco, potentially followed by use of marijuana and then hard drugs. Figure 5.1 indicates that most (88%) individuals reported some substance use; conversely, 12% reported never using any substances. Nearly all substance users nationwide (82% of 88%) started with alcohol/tobacco. Slightly more than a quarter (26%) proceeded to marijuana and one tenth proceeded to hard drugs. These percentages do not necessarily represent the true probabilities of transitions for numerous reasons, including that youthful respondents may have not yet progressed to further stages and

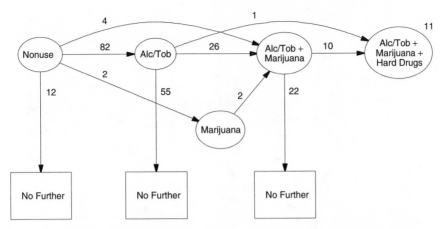

Figure 5.1. Substance use sequences among U.S. respondents, NHSDA 1991–1993 (N = 83,962). *Note:* In this and all subsequent figures, numbers on arrows indicate the percentage of all respondents' sequences in which transition appears.

the NHSDA household sample excludes many hard core drug users (Golub & Johnson, 2001).

Figure 5.1 also indicates that some individuals passed through two stages in a single year. Four percent of the sample went from nonuse to use of alcohol/tobacco and marijuana in a single year. It is not known whether these persons used alcohol/tobacco before marijuana, or vice versa. These transitions were classified as being consistent with the Gateway model (at least not clearly inconsistent). Similarly, the transition from alcohol/tobacco to alcohol/tobacco + marijuana + hard drugs, which skips the intermediate state of alcohol/tobacco + marijuana, was classified as being consistent with the Gateway model. Thus, nationwide very few substance use sequences were clearly inconsistent with the Gateway model. Two percent of NHSDA respondents started with marijuana; these individuals subsequently initiated use of alcohol/tobacco. The chapter by Kandel and Yamaguchi (Chapter 4) provides a complementary analysis with national data from the NHSDA 1994–1995 surveys.

The sequences reported by inner-city New York residents (Figure 5.2) conformed somewhat less to the Gateway model than those of the national sample (Figure 5.1). A comparable analysis, not presented here, with the NHSDA subsample of all New York residents provided similar results, suggesting that the difference is associated with the metropolitan area

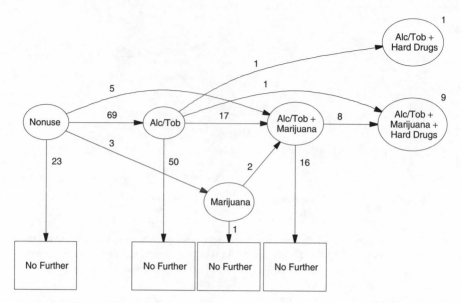

Figure 5.2. Substance use sequences among inner-city New York residents, NHSDA 1991–1993 ($N = 3,535$).

and is not unique to the inner-city residents from low-SES neighborhoods. Somewhat fewer respondents (77%) reported any substance use. Of those who did, 3% started with marijuana. Additionally, some alcohol/tobacco users (1%) initiated use of hard drugs without having used marijuana. This latter group comprised a barely discernible portion (1%) of the population surveyed. However, they comprised a noticeable portion (1 of 10, or 10%) of those individuals who reported ever using hard drugs.

There was even more deviation from the Gateway sequence among those individuals who became hard drug users both among hard drug users from the NHSDA sample of inner-city New York (Figure 5.3) and among ADAM-Manhattan arrestees (Figure 5.4). Fewer of these persons started with alcohol/tobacco exclusively (only 71% and 58% in Figures 5.3 and 5.4, respectively). A noticeable proportion started exclusively with marijuana (7% and 10%, respectively). Indeed, not all of these persons had used both alcohol/tobacco and marijuana by the time they initiated use of hard drugs (89% and 74%, respectively, had). A few skipped both alcohol/tobacco and marijuana (1% and 4%, respectively). Some skipped marijuana only (8% and 21%, respectively), and a few skipped alcohol/tobacco only (2% of each sample).

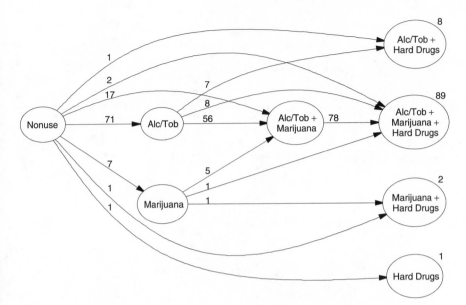

Figure 5.3. Substance use sequences among inner-city New York hard drug-using residents, NHSDA 1991–1993 (*N* = 418).

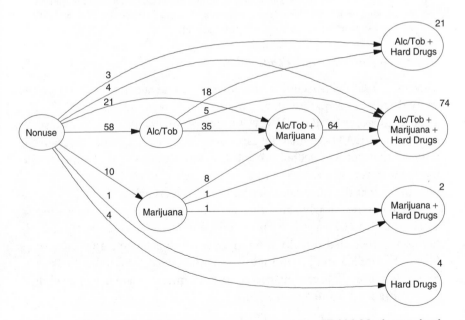

Figure 5.4. Substance use sequences among ADAM-Manhattan hard drug-using arrestees, 1989–1997 (*N* = 7,713).

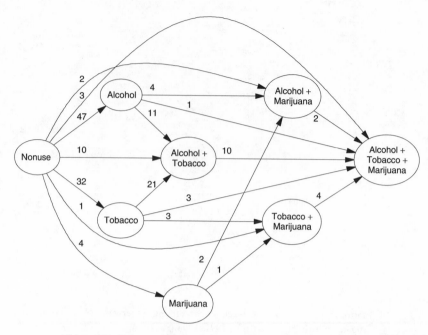

Figure 5.5. Substance use sequences through alcohol, tobacco, and marijuana among inner-city New York residents, NHSDA 1991–1993 ($N = 2,508$ respondents who reported any substance use).

Ordering of Alcohol and Tobacco Use

Figures 5.5 and 5.6 examine the importance of alcohol and tobacco individually as separate steps, instead of as a single step (i.e., alcohol/tobacco) for the NHSDA sample of inner-city New York residents and ADAM-Manhattan arrestees, respectively. Both diagrams indicate that neither alcohol nor tobacco was always the first substance used. However, the interpretation of this result is confounded by the possibility that the inferred ordering may not be reliable.

The diagrams clearly show that neither alcohol use nor tobacco use alone appears to be a necessary prerequisite to marijuana use. Many alcohol users proceeded directly to marijuana without having used tobacco (4% in Figure 5.5 and 7% in Figure 5.6). Somewhat fewer tobacco users proceeded directly to marijuana use without intermediate use of alcohol (3% in Figure 5.5 and 5% in Figure 5.6).

Historical Variation in First Substance Used

Table 5.3 indicates how the proportion of individuals who started with each substance changed across successive birth cohorts for three

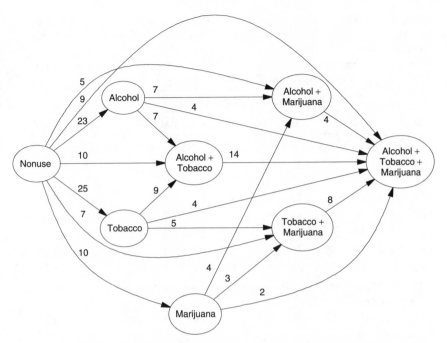

Figure 5.6. Substance use sequences through alcohol, tobacco, and marijuana among ADAM-Manhattan hard drug-using arrestees, 1989–1997 ($N = 7,713$).

populations: all New York inner-city residents, New York inner-city residents who had used hard drugs, and ADAM-Manhattan arrestees who had used hard drugs. The columns indicate the percentage of individuals who started with alcohol, tobacco, marijuana, and hard drugs. (Nonusers of any substance were excluded from this analysis.) For each substance, there are two columns: exclusive use and any use (including ties). The rows indicate the respondents' birth year. Hence, variation down any column identifies the extent to which a substance's popularity as the first substance used shifted across successive birth cohorts. (The identification of this cohort effect is potentially confounded by migration: older respondents from inner-city New York may not have grown up there.)

Inner-city New York residents born prior to 1945 typically started with alcohol. Over half (53%) reported exclusive use of alcohol in the first year of any substance use and two thirds (68%) reported any use. Thus, somewhere between 53% and 68% started with alcohol. Many (30% to 44%) started their substance use progressions with tobacco, but few with marijuana (2% to 4%). Compared to earlier birth cohorts,

Table 5.3. *Variation in First Substance Used Across Birth Cohorts, NHSDA, Inner-City New York Residents, 1991–1993, and ADAM-Manhattan Hard Drug Using Arrestees, 1989–1997*

Birth cohort	Percentage Using Substance in First Year								Sample Size	% S.E.[a]
	Alcohol		Tobacco		Marijuana		Hard Drugs			
	Exc	Any	Exc	Any	Exc	Any	Exc	Any		
NHSDA 1991–1993, Inner-City New York respondents aged 21+[b]										
1900–1944	53	68	30	44	2	4	0	0	389	2.5
1945–1949	45	55	43	54	1	4	0	0	132	4.4
1950–1954	45	54	39	48	5	11	1	1	163	3.9
1955–1959	36	55	39	56	4	13	0	1	390	2.5
1960–1964	44	62	28	45	7	20	0	1	413	2.5
1965–1969	40	59	29	47	9	21	0	2	420	2.4
Total	46	62	33	48	4	10	0	1	1907	1.1
NHSDA 1991–1993, hard drug using, Inner-City New York respondents aged 21+										
1900–1944	35	63	30	62	4	23	0	0	24	10.2
1945–1949	39	45	49	61	0	10	0	0	17	12.1
1950–1954	25	61	27	54	5	27	5	5	34	8.6
1955–1959	20	43	48	68	6	22	1	3	98	5.1
1960–1964	30	54	34	54	5	29	1	4	113	4.7
1965–1969	16	42	32	58	16	41	0	9	78	5.7
Total	26	51	37	60	6	26	1	4	364	2.6
ADAM-Manhattan hard drug using arrestees, 1989–1997, aged 21+										
1900–1944	28	57	31	61	5	21	3	8	261	3.1
1945–1949	26	59	24	55	6	24	6	14	389	2.5
1950–1954	21	50	28	59	8	30	5	15	1014	1.6
1955–1959	24	53	25	57	9	33	3	11	1646	1.2
1960–1964	23	52	23	53	12	38	4	8	2080	1.1
1965–1969	23	51	24	55	12	39	3	9	1535	1.3
1970–1974	20	52	23	56	11	43	3	12	366	2.6
Total	23	52	25	56	10	35	4	11	7291	0.6

Notes: [a] Standard error for prevalence rate of 50%. Exc = exclusive use in first year of substance use.

persons born just after World War II (1945–1949) were slightly less likely to have started with alcohol (45% to 55%) and slightly more likely to have started with tobacco (43% to 54%). From then on, the proportion starting with alcohol held relatively steady, and the proportion starting with tobacco declined. The proportion starting with marijuana increased from a negligible amount (2% to 4%) for the 1900–1944 cohort up to a fairly sizable proportion (9% to 21%) for the 1965–1969 cohort.

The identification of trends among inner-city New York residents who reported any hard drug use was less reliable. The variations over time associated with alcohol and tobacco were neither consistent nor statistically significant. Even the increase in any marijuana use from 23% among the 1900–1944 cohort to 41% among the 1965–1969 cohort was not significant at the $\alpha = .05$ level. (As a result of the small sample sizes within cohorts, the standard errors of the estimates were on the order of 5 to 10 percentage points.) However, the overall proportion of respondents who started with any marijuana use among the NHSDA inner-city sample of hard drug users (26%) was substantially higher than among the complete inner-city New York sample (10%) and was significant at the $\alpha = .01$ level.

Among ADAM-Manhattan arrestees, the proportion starting with any marijuana use increased substantially and significantly from 21% among the 1900–1944 cohort to 43% among the 1970–1974 cohort. The proportion of individuals who started with alcohol and tobacco remained about the same across cohorts. The modest declines in rates from 1900–1944 to 1970–1974 were consistent, some were barely significant at the $\alpha = .05$ level, but none was significant at the more rigorous $\alpha = .01$ level.

Historical Variations in Age at First Use

A series of regression analyses examined variations in age at first use of alcohol, tobacco, marijuana, and hard drugs across birth cohorts, in order to understand recent trends in adolescent substance use more fully. Race/ethnicity and gender were also included as control variables. To prevent a potential censoring bias, only those individuals who both were aged 21 and above at the time of their NHSDA or ADAM interview and reported initiation of use by age 21 were included in each ordinary least-squares regression analysis. (Individuals are effectively "observed" up until their age at interview. Older respondents can potentially report later ages at initiation, possibly biasing the analysis.) The sample sizes varied across the analyses since not all respondents reported use of each substance.

The independent variables were coded as series of dummy variables. The constant estimated for each regression model represents the average age at first use among members of the *base case*: White males, born 1965–1969. The average age at first use for individuals who differ from the base case can be determined by adding the coefficients associated with the individual's characteristics to the constant. The amount of variation explained by each attribute was assessed by estimating a submodel excluding the dummy variables associated with an attribute. The difference in the sum-of-the-squared variation explained by the full model versus the submodel was credited to inclusion of the attribute.

Table 5.4 presents the results of the regression analyses for ADAM-Manhattan hard drug using arrestees and Table 5.5 for the NHSDA respondents from inner-city New York. The high standard deviations (2 to 3 years) and the low R^2's (10% or less) for each model attest to wide variation in age at first use of each substance across individuals, variation that cannot be explained by a few basic demographic characteristics. Still, each data set did identify systematic variations in the age at first use across birth cohorts.

The variation among ADAM-Manhattan arrestees was most pronounced (Table 5.4). The average age at first use of marijuana among the base population – White, male arrestees, born 1965–1969 – was 14.1 years, only slightly higher than the average ages at first use of alcohol (13.4 years) and tobacco (13.8 years). This nearness in age could possibly have been caused by a belief among these persons that alcohol, tobacco, and marijuana are similarly dangerous (or nondangerous) and is consistent with the findings that similar proportions started their substance use with alcohol as with tobacco and also that a moderate proportion started with marijuana (see Table 5.3).

In contrast, there was greater difference in age at first use across substances among arrestees born 1900–1944 and many fewer of them started their substance use with marijuana (see Table 5.3). The average ages at first use were 14.2 years (13.4 + 0.8) for alcohol, 16.0 years for marijuana, and 13.6 years for tobacco (the variation in age at first tobacco use was not statistically significant). The average ages at first use of alcohol and tobacco were about 2 years younger than the average age at first use of marijuana.

Among NHSDA respondents from inner-city New York (Table 5.5), the average ages at first use declined by about 2 years for marijuana, 1.6 years for tobacco, and just under 1 year for alcohol between the 1900–1944 and the 1965–1969 birth cohorts. Among persons born 1900–1944, the average ages at first use of alcohol (15.8) and marijuana (16.5) differed by 1.7 years. This gap decreased to 0.7 year among the 1965–1969 cohort (15.7–15.0). The difference in average ages at first use of tobacco and marijuana, however, held relatively constant at about 1.5 years. This helps

Table 5.4. *Covariates of Age at First Use by Substance, ADAM–Manhattan Hard Drug Using Arrestees, 1989–1997, Aged 21+, Who Reported Use by Age 21)*

		Variation in Age at First Use (OLS Results)			
Attribute	Levels	Alcohol	Tobacco	Marijuana	Hard Drugs
Race/ethnicity (contrast with White)	(*effect*)	(0.7%)**	(0.4%)**	(0.2%)**	(0.6%)**
	Black	0.5	0.5	0.3	0.3
	Hispanic	0.8	0.4	0.2	−0.2
	Other/Missing	0.9	0.5	0.3	0.2
Gender (contrast with Male)	(*effect*)	(0.4%)**	(0.1%)*	(0.0%)	(0.0%)
	Female	0.4	−0.2	0.0	0.0
Birth cohort (contrast with 1965–1969)	(*effect*)	(0.7%)**	(0.1%)*	(4.1%)**	(1.3%)**
	Born 1900–1944	0.8	0.2	1.9	0.0
	Born 1945–1949	0.6	0.1	1.6	−0.2
	Born 1950–1954	0.7	0.2	1.2	−0.7
	Born 1955–1959	0.4	0.1	0.9	−0.3
	Born 1960–1964	0.1	0.0	0.3	0.1
	Born 1970–1975	−0.1	−0.2	−0.2	−0.5
	Constant	13.4	13.6	14.1	17.2
	R^2	1.6%	0.7%	4.4%	1.9%
	s	3.1	2.8	2.6	2.5
	Sample Size	6,304	5,924	5,683	5,016

Notes: Standard errors for individual coefficient estimates were typically around 0.15. * Significant at the $\alpha = .05$ level, based on an F-test. ** Significant at the $\alpha = .01$ level, based on an F-test.

Table 5.5. *Covariates of Age at First Use by Substance, NHSDA, Inner-City New York Residents, 1991–1993, Aged 21+, Who Reported Use by Age 21*

Attribute	Levels	Variation in Age at First Use (OLS Results)			
		Alcohol	Tobacco	Marijuana	Hard Drugs
Race/ethnicity (contrast with White)	(*effect*)	(1.4%)*	(2.7%)**	(1.2%)	(3.1%)
	Black	0.5	−0.8	−0.1	−0.8
	Hispanic	0.5	0.4	−0.2	−0.8
	Other/Missing	1.3	0.5	1.3	−1.9
Gender (contrast with Male)	(*effect*)	(3.5%)**	(1.2%)*	(0.0%)	(0.0%)
	Female	1.0	0.7	0.1	0.1
Birth cohort (contrast with 1965–1969)	(*effect*)	(1.5%)	(4.0%)**	(8.6%)**	(4.0%)
	Born 1900–1944	0.8	1.6	1.8	−0.2
	Born 1945–1949	0.9	0.5	2.1	1.8
	Born 1950–1954	0.1	0.9	0.9	0.5
	Born 1955–1959	0.3	0.5	0.5	0.3
	Born 1960–1964	0.2	0.2	0.4	0.7
	Constant	15.0	14.4	15.7	17.8
	R^2	6.0%	7.8%	10.4%	7.8%
	s	2.6	2.9	2.3	2.1
	Sample size	1,620	1,238	761	283

Notes: Standard errors for individual coefficient estimates were typically around 0.15. * Significant at the $\alpha = .05$ level, based on an F-test. ** Significant at the $\alpha = .01$ level, based on an F-test.

account for the continually high proportions of inner-city New York residents who started with tobacco (Table 5.3).

Conclusion

This study empirically confirmed that the Gateway theory quite accurately summarizes the substance use sequences typically prevailing in the general population of the United States. Youths tend to progress from no substance use to alcohol/tobacco use and then potentially to marijuana and hard drug use. The data suggested that either alcohol or tobacco could serve as a first stage and that neither alcohol use nor tobacco use was a necessary prerequisite to further progression. From a biochemical perspective, it seems unlikely that alcohol could substitute for tobacco, or vice versa: They are consumed very differently and have very different effects. It would appear that the Gateway sequence is strongly influenced by the social environment: Both alcohol and tobacco are legally available and commonly used by adults in the United States. The distinction between a biochemical and a social basis is important. To the extent that the Gateway sequence is a social phenomenon, cultural and subcultural changes could lead to shifts in substance use sequences.

This study also examined the extent to which the Gateway Hypothesis describes the developmental experiences of youths growing up in inner-city New York, a particularly harsh social environment. In this environment, drug abuse both is caused by and contributes to a whole constellation of problems, including poverty, lack of economic opportunity, crime, violence, dissolution of the family, insufficient housing, poor education, and overall despair (Bourgois, 1996; Crocket, 1997; Johnson & Muffler, 1997). Contrary to the Gateway theory, a substantial and growing proportion of inner-city New York residents and arrestees used marijuana before either alcohol or tobacco and a few proceeded to hard drug use without any prior use of marijuana.

These findings are consistent with our broader hypothesis that the Gateway sequence reflects age-graded perceptions of the seriousness and acceptability of using various substances. These perceptions and the resulting conduct norms change as an individual ages and are specific to a place and time. The Gateway sequence suggests use of alcohol and of tobacco is comparably serious, as perceived by youths; marijuana (an illegal drug) is somewhat more serious; and use of cocaine powder, crack, and heroin is even more serious. The widespread use of marijuana since the 1960s could have fueled a growing sense among youths that marijuana is about as dangerous as alcohol or tobacco and about as easy to obtain, despite the fact that it is illegal (Johnston et al., 1999).

This mutability of the developmental sequence suggests that increased efforts to control youths' access to alcohol, tobacco, and marijuana, even if effective, will not necessarily reduce subsequent hard drug abuse. Youths could potentially substitute any one of these substances for another as a first step toward hard drug use, on the basis of availability. If all three substances were completely unavailable, youths might start directly with hard drugs or find some other readily available substance to use, such as inhalants.

This variation also suggests that the recent increases in youthful marijuana use may not foretell as dire a future as predicted by some (Office of National Drug Control Policy, 1997; Gfroerer & Epstein, 1999). If marijuana is now perceived by youths as less serious, perhaps many fewer of the marijuana users in the 1990s will progress to hard drug use and abuse. It is essential both to continue to track prevailing trends in youthful substance use progression over time and across locations as well as to study what use at each stage means to the youths themselves.

References

Bourgois, P. (1996). *In search of respect: Selling crack in El Barrio*. Cambridge: Cambridge University Press.

Brown, B. B., Dolcini, M. D., & Leventhal, A. (1997). Transformations in peer relationships at adolescence: Implications for health-related behavior. In J. Schulenberg, J. L. Maggs, & K. Hurrelmann (Eds.), *Health risks and developmental transitions during adolescence* (pp. 161–189). Cambridge: Cambridge University Press.

Crocket, L. J. (1997). Cultural, historical, and subcultural contexts of adolescence: Implications for health and development. In J. Schulenberg, J. L. Maggs, & K. Hurrelmann (Eds.), *Health risks and developmental transitions during adolescence*. Cambridge: Cambridge University Press.

Eccles, J. S., Lord, S. E., Roeser, R. W., Barber, B. L., & Jozefowicz, D. M. H. (1997). The association of school transitions in early adolescence with developmental trajectories through high school. In J. Schulenberg, J. L., Maggs, & K. Hurrelmann (Eds.), *Health risks and developmental transitions during adolescence*. Cambridge: Cambridge University Press.

Eisenhower, D., Mathiowetz, N. A., & Morganstein, D. (1991). Recall error: Sources and bias reduction techniques. In P. P. Biemer, R. M. Groves, L. E. Lyberg, N. A. Mathiowetz, & S. Sudman (Eds.), *Measurement errors in surveys* (pp. 127–144). New York: Wiley.

General Accounting Office. (1993). *Drug use measurement: Strengths, limitations and recommendations for improvement*, GAO/PEMD-93-18, Washington, DC: U.S. Government Printing Office.

Gfroerer, J. C., & Epstein, J. F. (1999). Marijuana initiates and their impact on future drug abuse treatment need. *Drug and Alcohol Dependence, 54*, 229–237.

Golub, A., & Johnson, B. D. (1994a). The shifting importance of alcohol and marijuana as gateway substances among serious drug abusers. *Journal of Studies on Alcohol, 55*(5), 607–614.

Golub, A., & Johnson, B. D. (1994b). Cohort differences in drug use pathways to crack among current crack abusers in New York City. *Criminal Justice and Behavior 21*(4), 403–422.

Golub, A., & Johnson, B. D. (1999). Cohort changes in illegal drug use among arrestees in Manhattan: From the heroin injection generation to the blunts generation. *Substance Use and Misuse, 34*(13), 1733–1763.

Golub, A., & Johnson, B. D. (2001). Variation in youthful risk of progression from alcohol/tobacco to marijuana and hard drugs across generations. *American Journal of Public Health, 91*(2), 225–232.

Golub, A. L., Labouvie, E., & Johnson, B. D. (2000). Response reliability and the study of adolescent substance use progression. *Journal of Drug Issues, 30*(1), 103–118.

Harrison, L., & Hughes, A. (1997). Validity of self-reported drug use: Improving the accuracy of survey estimates (pp. 59–80). NIDA Research Monograph 167, NIH Publication No. 97-4147.

Johnson, B. D., & Muffler, J. (1997). Sociocultural determinants and perpetuators of substance abuse. In J. H. Lowinson, P. Ruiz, R. B. Millman, & J. G. Langrod (Eds.), *Substance abuse: A comprehensive textbook* (3rd ed.). (pp. 107–117). Baltimore: Williams & Wilkins.

Johnson, R. A., & Gerstein, D. R. (1997). Initiation of use of alcohol, cigarettes, marijuana, cocaine and other drugs in U.S. birth cohorts since 1919. *American Journal of Public Health 88*(1), 27–33.

Johnston, L. D., O'Malley, P. M., & Bachman, J. G. (1999). National survey results on drugs use from the monitoring the future study, 1975–1998. (Vol. 1). NIH Publication No. 99-4660.

Kandel, D. B. (1975). Stages in adolescent involvement in drug use. *Science 190*, 912–914.

Mackesy-Amiti, M. E., Fendrich, M., & Goldstein, P. J. (1997). Sequence of drug use among serious drug users: Typical vs. atypical progression. *Drug and Alcohol Dependence 45*, 185–196.

National Institute of Justice. (1999). *1998 Annual report on drug use among adult and juvenile arrestees*. Publication No. NCJ 175656.

Nurmi, J. E. (1997). Self-definition and mental health during adolescence and young adulthood. In J. Schulenberg, J. L. Maggs, & K. Hurrelmann (Eds.), *Health risks and developmental transitions during adolescence*. Cambridge: Cambridge University Press.

Office of National Drug Control Policy. (1997). The National Drug Control Strategy: 1997. Publication No. NCJ 160086, Washington, DC: U.S. Government Printing Office.

Schulenberg, J., Maggs, J. L., & Hurrelmann, K. (1997). Negotiating developmental transitions during adolescence and young adulthood: Health risks and opportunities. In J. Schulenberg, J. L. Maggs, & K. Hurrelmann (Eds.), *Health risks and developmental transitions during adolescence.* Cambridge: Cambridge University Press.

Substance Abuse and Mental Health Services Administration. (1993). National Household Survey on Drug Abuse: Public Release Codebook 1991. (ICPSR 6128) Obtained from http://lion.icpsr.umich.edu/.

Substance Abuse and Mental Health Services Administration. (1994). National Household Survey on Drug Abuse: Public Release Codebook 1992. (ICPSR 6887) Obtained from http://lion.icpsr.umich.edu/.

Substance Abuse and Mental Health Services Administration. (1995). National Household Survey on Drug Abuse: Public Release Codebook 1993. (ICPSR 6852) Obtained from http://lion.icpsr.umich.edu/.

Substance Abuse and Mental Health Services Administration. (1999). Summary of Findings from the 1998 National Household Survey on Drug Abuse. US Department of Health and Human Services. Rockville, Md.

Turner, C., Lessler, J., & Gfroerer, J. (1992). *Survey measurement of drug use: Methodological studies.* Rockville, MD: National Institute on Drug Abuse.

Impact of Prevention Interventions
A Test of the Progression Hypothesis

6

Preventing the Onset and Developmental Progression of Adolescent Drug Use

Implications for the Gateway Hypothesis

Gilbert J. Botvin, Lawrence M. Scheier,
and Kenneth W. Griffin

Efforts to combat the problem of drug abuse have involved a combination of strategies including education, treatment, law enforcement, and mass media campaigns. Among these, approaches intended to prevent the onset and developmental progression of drug use among adolescents have received considerable attention in recent years. A particularly fruitful area of research has involved the development and testing of school-based prevention approaches targeting youth during the early adolescent years. This research has demonstrated that at least some approaches to drug abuse prevention can produce substantial reductions in the incidence and prevalence of adolescent drug use. Moreover, this research clearly indicates that ongoing intervention during junior high school can result in durable prevention effects that last at least until the end of high school. Finally, the effectiveness of school-based prevention approaches has been demonstrated for a relatively broad range of students including White, suburban youth, and inner-city minority youth.

A necessary precondition for the development of effective prevention approaches is an understanding of both the causes of drug use and its developmental progression. Together they provide essential information concerning the nature and timing of preventive interventions. Research delineating the etiologic determinants of adolescent drug use has highlighted the importance of an array of interpersonal and intrapersonal factors for promoting and sustaining drug use and has provided guidance to program developers concerning the appropriate focus of preventive interventions. The growing body of etiologic evidence deriving from longitudinal research has led to a realignment of prevention objectives, away from an emphasis on knowledge concerning the adverse consequences of drug use and toward a focus on social and psychological factors. Similarly, research concerning the developmental progression of drug use indicates that it proceeds from the use of legal and widely available substances to the use of illegal substances. As a consequence, prevention approaches have generally targeted the use of tobacco and alcohol, two substances whose use is identified as occurring at the beginning of this progression. An implicit assumption of contemporary prevention approaches is that if they are successful, they will not only reduce the initiation of drug use but will also disrupt its developmental progression.

The purpose of this chapter is to summarize nearly two decades of research with a school-based approach to drug abuse prevention called *Life Skills Training* (LST) and examine the extent to which it not only prevents drug use but disrupts its developmental progression. Within the context of a broader discussion of the impact of this prevention approach on the initiation and developmental progression of drug use, special attention is given to the implications of this research for the Gateway Hypothesis. The chapter begins with a discussion of perspectives on the developmental progression of adolescent drug use, describes the LST prevention program, summarizes research testing the efficacy of the LST prevention approach with respect to its impact on the initiation and developmental progression of drug use, and ends with implications for the Gateway Hypothesis and future prevention efforts.

Perspectives on the Developmental Progression of Drug Use

Progression as a Multidimensional Process

The initiation and early stages of drug use typically occur at the beginning of adolescence, escalating from the onset of drug-taking behavior to progressively more serious involvement with drugs. However, whereas the general developmental trajectory of drug use is relatively well understood, what appears to be a simple progression from nonuse to use of one or more substances is more complex than is readily apparent. One source of this complexity is that the developmental course of adolescent drug use is multidimensional. These dimensions include the frequency of drug use, consumption or amount of a drug or drugs used per drug-taking occasion, use of single versus multiple substances, use of licit versus illicit drugs, and use of specific drugs or classes of drugs.

Frequency and Amount. Frequency of drug use progresses from nonuse to initial use, to occasional (annual or monthly) use, and to more frequent (weekly and daily) patterns of use along with an escalation of the amount used. The amount of a given drug used on each drug-taking occasion escalates along a continuum ranging from light to heavy use. With dependency-producing drugs, this escalation in both the frequency and amount of use typically eventuates in the development of tolerance (as larger and/or more frequent administrations of the drug are required to produce the same psychoactive effect) and in both physical and psychological dependence.

Single Versus Multiple Substances. Another way in which drug use can develop is through progression from the use of a single substance to the use of two or more substances. Individuals typically start with the use of a single substance. As frequency and amount of drug use escalate, the likelihood increases that they will proceed to use a second or a third substance.

Licit Versus Illicit Substances. Drug use also tends to progress from the use of legal substances to the use of illegal substances. For example, individuals may progress from the use of substances that are legal for adults (tobacco and/or alcohol) to the use of substances that are illegal (marijuana, cocaine, heroin, hallucinogens, and so on).

Substance-Specific Progression. The other way the sequence of drug use appears to progress is in terms of the type of drug or drugs used. The notion that the development of drug-taking behavior involves progression through a series of stages based on the use of specific substances has been a source of controversy for many years. Still, it is based on empirical evidence indicating that for most individuals alcohol and tobacco are the first substances used. Because of their availability, inhalants may also be among the first used. Individuals may later progress to the use of marijuana.

The use of tobacco, alcohol, inhalants, and marijuana provides adolescents with an introduction to the world of drugs. For some individuals, the use of these drugs may lead to the use of stimulants, opiates, hallucinogens, cocaine, and other illicit drugs. The probability of using any substance in this developmental progression increases significantly with the use of one or more drugs earlier in the progression. The use of tobacco, alcohol, and inhalants significantly increases the risk of use of marijuana, and the use of marijuana significantly increases the risk of use of illicit drugs other than marijuana. The Gateway Hypothesis and the evidence supporting it are discussed more fully in the following section as well as throughout this volume.

Stage Sequence for Specific Substances: The Gateway Hypothesis

Models of the developmental progression of drug use invariably suggest that early-stage drug use begins with alcohol and progresses to more involved and varied use of other drugs (e.g., cigarettes, marijuana, and other illicit drugs). Over 20 years of longitudinal research suggests that a succession of developmental stages ordered in a progressive sequence characterizes the earliest stages of drug involvement (Kandel, 1975; Kandel & Faust, 1975; Kandel, Treiman, Faust, & Single, 1976; Single, Kandel, & Faust, 1974). On the basis of findings obtained from cross-sectional and longitudinal studies of high school students, Kandel and colleagues outlined a specific developmental sequence that begins with alcohol (beer and wine), followed by cigarettes or hard liquor, marijuana, then other illicit drugs, including pills, heroin, cocaine, and hallucinogens.

The underlying notion that early-stage drug use proceeds in a stage-like manner has been important to both etiologic knowledge as well as prevention science. From a prevention standpoint, there are many bene-fits to knowing that patterns of early-stage adolescent drug use follow a fairly invariant pathway. First, if efficacious prevention efforts can be targeted to one or more of the drugs that are involved in the early-onset years, a potential benefit of these efforts is to reduce the likelihood of advancing or progressing to more involved and deleterious stages of drug use. Not only are there anticipated health benefits that result from achieving significant reductions in youthful cigarette smoking, for exam-ple, but there also may be substantial gains both to society and to the individual if prevention efforts can reduce the likelihood that early-onset cigarette smokers will advance to marijuana or other illicit drug use.

In addition, knowledge that the early stages of drug use proceeds in an orderly stepwise fashion can help focus prevention efforts to identify and ameliorate those risk factors associated with the earliest exposure to the Gateway substances and increase the probability of reducing vulnerability to later and more deleterious substances, such as heroin. Changing certain behaviors at one stage can avert later, more advanced, and possibly more harmful behaviors.

Evidence for a Developmental Sequence

Despite a wealth of information based on epidemiologic and etiological studies (see review by Kandel & Yamaguchi, 1999), only a handful of studies have applied tests of stage theory within a prevention framework (Collins, Graham, Rousculp, & Hansen, 1997; Collins et al., 1994; Graham, Collins, Wugalter, Chung, & Hansen, 1991). Graham et al. (1991), for example, examined one-year prevention effects on transitions between latent statuses of drug use including cigarettes, alcohol, and marijuana. Latent transition analysis (LTA) showed that a normative education intervention designed to modify perceptions regarding the prevalence and social acceptability of drug use by peers and adults was effective in reducing the probability of moving from a lower-ranked class of drug use (e.g., alcohol) to a higher-ranked class (e.g., alcohol and tobacco). Examination of transitional probabilities showed that students exposed to the intervention were more likely to remain nonusers in the eighth grade than the untreated control group. Among those reporting some use of alcohol at the outset of the study, treated youth were more likely to remain in this status than control youth, who were more likely to transition to more involved drug use (alcohol and tobacco).

In summary, prior research has helped develop a growing understanding of the early stages of drug use. Alcohol is known to play a key role in promoting further and more varied drug use; however, several studies also have highlighted the role of cigarettes and problem alcohol use (e.g., binge drinking and drunkenness) as key risk factors in promoting the transition to problem drug (including marijuana) use. Information from these and related studies has helped to shape primary prevention efforts and may be largely responsible for the emphasis of many current prevention programs on reducing Gateway drug use. However, there is a paucity of research from prevention studies examining the validity of the Gateway Hypothesis. One reason for this is that most prevention programs target multiple drugs, making it difficult to determine whether preventing the use of one drug necessarily deters progression to others.

Approaches for Preventing Onset and Developmental Progression

Focus of Prevention Efforts

According to the Gateway Hypothesis, any level of drug use (even trying a drug just once) can increase the risk of developing drug-related problems. From this perspective, occasional drug use is a risk factor for drug abuse and other drug-related problems. For this reason, drug abuse prevention programs targeting youth have focused on preventing the early stages of drug involvement as a method of reducing drug abuse risk. For middle or junior high school students, this might involve attempting to prevent onset or occasional (annual or monthly) use. For high school students, it might involve attempting to deter more serious levels of drug involvement (e.g., weekly or daily use of a single drug, use of multiple drugs, or "heavy" use) as well as preventing drug-related problems such as accidents or violence.

More specifically related to the Gateway Hypothesis is the notion that use of drugs that are legal for adults (tobacco and alcohol) and/or use of marijuana will eventuate in the use of illicit drugs such as heroin and cocaine. Although this is often used as the rationale for focusing on the prevention of tobacco, alcohol, and marijuana, prevention studies have generally not addressed the crucial issue of whether preventing Gateway drug use is an effective strategy for preventing the use of illicit drugs other than marijuana.

Both because mortality and morbidity are associated with tobacco and alcohol and because the use of marijuana increases the risk of using other illicit substances, drug abuse prevention programs have usually focused primarily on preventing the use of tobacco, alcohol, and marijuana. Moreover, because there is a direct relationship between the age of onset and the subsequent development of serious drug-related problems, prevention programs are likely to be valuable even if they merely delay drug use initiation or prevent the transition from occasional use to more serious levels of drug involvement.

Approaches to Prevention

Over the past 20 years, considerable attention has been given to the identification and testing of intervention approaches offering the potential of preventing the initiation and early stages of drug use. A variety of approaches have been tested, including public information campaigns, school-based approaches, family interventions, and community-based prevention approaches. Perusal of the growing prevention literature indicates that most prevention research has been conducted with approaches designed to be implemented in school settings. One reason is that schools are a natural site for implementing and testing prevention programs targeting children and adolescents. Schools not only provide easy access to the appropriate target populations for these interventions, but also offer the kind of well-structured setting that is necessary for conducting rigorous evaluation research. This research has proceeded from small-scale pilot studies assessing the feasibility, acceptability, and preliminary efficacy of promising prevention approaches to large-scale randomized, controlled trials.

Early efforts to develop effective prevention approaches were generally based on the assumption that individuals who used drugs did so largely because they were unaware of the deleterious effects of drug abuse (Goodstadt, 1986). It was therefore assumed that providing information about the dangers of drug use would serve as an effective deterrent. Unfortunately, countless literature reviews have highlighted the ineffectiveness of such approaches to prevention (e.g., Botvin, 1999; Botvin & Botvin, 1992; Schinke, Botvin, & Orlandi, 1991).

As etiologic evidence has emerged, it has become increasingly clear that there is no single factor or single pathway that serves as a necessary and sufficient condition leading to drug abuse. Rather, drug abuse is the result of a multivariate mix of factors (Hawkins, Catalano, & Miller, 1992; Newcomb & Bentler, 1989). Some of these etiologic factors increase risk for drug involvement, whereas other (protective) factors decrease the potential for involvement. Conceptualized very broadly, the process of becoming a drug abuser involves the dynamic interaction of an individual and his or her environment. Social influences to use drugs (along with the availability of drugs) interact with individual vulnerability. The media portrayal of drug use (TV shows and movies glamorizing drug use or suggesting that drug use is normal or socially acceptable, as well as advertising efforts promoting the sale of alcohol and tobacco products) plays a major role in promoting drug use. Another important social influence is that of family members who either use drugs or express pro-drug-use attitudes and/or of friends and acquaintances who use drugs or hold attitudes and beliefs supportive of drug use. Some individuals may succumb to peer pressure to use drugs because of intrapersonal factors such as low self-esteem, high anxiety, hopelessness, low personal control, or the need for excitement (i.e., sensation seeking). Moreover, the accumulation of risk factors increases the risk of using and eventually abusing drugs. The greater the number of risk factors, the more likely that an individual will become a drug user and eventually a drug abuser since the presence of multiple risk factors is associated with both initial drug use and the severity of later drug involvement (Newcomb & Felix-Ortiz, 1992; Scheier & Newcomb, 1991).

It therefore seems evident that to be effective, prevention programs must not only take into account the complex array of factors promoting drug use, but also recognize the important role of social factors including influence of friends and family members (Barnes & Welte, 1986; Kandel, 1985; Krosnick & Judd, 1982) and media (Tye, Warner, & Glantz, 1987). Individuals are more likely to use drugs if they view drug use as a normative behavior (Chassin, Presson, Shermon, Corty, & Olshavsky, 1984) or have specific psychological characteristics such as low social confidence, assertiveness, personal control, and self-efficacy (Dielman, Leech, Lorenger, & Horvath, 1984; Jessor & Jessor, 1977; Weir, 1968). It is also important to recognize that drug use is part of a general syndrome or life-style reflecting a particular value orientation and cooccurring with other problem behaviors (Jessor & Jessor, 1982; Newcomb & Bentler, 1986). Prevention approaches that are based on a solid theoretical and empirical foundation, target the broad array of etiologic factors promoting drug use, and take into account the developmental process leading to drug abuse have proved particularly promising.

Life Skills Training

One such approach, called *Life Skills Training* (LST), has been subjected to extensive testing by our group at Cornell University Medical College. This prevention program is an example of a comprehensive, school-based approach to drug abuse prevention that targets an array of etiologic factors. The evidence supporting its effectiveness also indicates how prevention programs can impact drug use at various points along the developmental continuum leading from initial use to more serious levels of drug involvement, including progression from one drug class to another.

The LST program is a drug abuse prevention program that is designed for middle or junior high school students and is intended to be implemented in school classrooms. The program consists of a core curriculum, delivered during the first year of intervention, and a two-year booster curriculum. The program currently consists of 15 class periods in the first year, 10 classes in the second year, and 5 classes in the third year. Except for our initial pilot research, all of the studies evaluating the LST program have been conducted with seventh graders. When booster sessions were included, students received the LST program in the seventh grade and the booster intervention in the eighth and ninth grades. Thus, curriculum materials have now been developed and tested for all three years of junior high school. For school districts with a middle school, the LST program can be implemented with students in grades six, seven, and eight.

The LST prevention program consists of three major components: The first is designed to teach students a set of general self-management skills; the second focuses on teaching general social skills; the third includes information and skills that are specifically related to the problem of drug abuse. The first two components are designed to enhance overall personal competence and decrease both the motivations to use drugs and vulnerability to drug use social influences. The problem-specific component is designed to provide students with material relating directly to drug abuse (drug resistance skills, antidrug attitudes, and antidrug norms).

Personal Self-Management Skills. The personal skills component of the LST program is designed to impact an array of self-management skills. To accomplish this, the personal skills component contains material to (1) foster the development of decision making and problem solving (e.g., identifying problem situations, defining goals, generating alternative solutions, considering consequences); (2) teach skills for identifying, analyzing, interpreting, and resisting media influences; (3) provide students with self-control skills for coping with anxiety (e.g., relaxation training) and anger/frustration (inhibiting impulsive reactions, reframing, using self-statements); and (4) provide students with the basic principles of personal behavior change and self-improvement (e.g., goal setting, self-monitoring, self-reinforcement).

Social Skills. The social skills component is designed to impact several important social skills and enhance general social competence. This social skills component contains material designed to help students overcome shyness and improve general interpersonal skills. This material emphasizes the teaching of (1) communication skills, (2) general social skills (e.g., initiation of social interactions, conversational skills, complimenting), (3) skills related to boy/girl relationships, and (4) both verbal and nonverbal assertive skills.

Drug-Related Information and Skills. The drug-related information and skills component is designed to impact knowledge and attitudes concerning drug use, normative expectations, and skills for resisting drug use influences from the media and peers. The material contained in this component is similar to that contained in many psychosocial drug abuse prevention programs that focus on the teaching of social resistance skills. Included is material concerning the (1) short- and long-term consequences of drug use; (2) knowledge about the actual levels of drug use among both adults and adolescents in order to correct normative expectations about drug use; (3) information about the declining social acceptability of cigarette smoking and other drug use; (4) information and class exercises demonstrating the immediate physiologic effects of cigarette smoking; (5) material concerning media pressures to smoke, drink, or use drugs; (6) information concerning the techniques used by cigarette and alcoholic beverage advertisers to promote the use of these drugs and skills for resisting them; and (7) techniques for resisting direct peer pressure to smoke, drink, or use drugs.

Effectiveness for Preventing Initiation and Escalation of Drug Use

The primary objective of drug abuse prevention research over the past three decades has been to identify approaches capable of preventing the initiation and/or escalation of drug use and provide evidence of their effectiveness. It has become clear that many prevention approaches are able to increase health knowledge and promote antidrug attitudes, but very few are capable of changing behavior and deterring drug use. It was not until the end of the 1970s and beginning of the 1980s that evidence that some prevention approaches could deter drug use began to emerge (Bangert-Drowns, 1988; Botvin, 1999; Botvin & Botvin, 1992; Hansen, 1992). Since then a growing research literature has documented the efficacy of several promising prevention approaches, including the Life Skills Training program.

During the 1980s and 1990s, our team of researchers at Cornell conducted a series of evaluation studies testing the effectiveness of the Life Skills Training (LST) program. These studies were conducted in a logical sequence to determine the effectiveness of this promising approach with different forms of drug use, when implemented by different program providers, and with different populations. The initial LST research focused on cigarette smoking and involved predominantly White middle-class populations. More recent research extended this work to other forms of drug use including the use of alcohol, marijuana, and illicit drugs other than marijuana. In addition, this research examined the effectiveness of the LST approach when used with inner-city minority youth. Finally, this research assessed the long-term durability of the LST prevention model, the impact on hypothesized mediating variables, and the role of implementation fidelity. These studies are briefly described later along with the key findings in order to examine the impact of the LST program on the initiation and developmental progression of drug use.

The primary goal of most studies testing the LST approach was to determine the extent to which it could prevent drug use initiation. In studies in which follow-up data were collected, the impact of the prevention program was also evaluated in terms of measures of more serious drug involvement. Thus, the emphasis of evaluations focusing on the initial impact of the prevention program centered on either lifetime (ever) use or occasional (monthly) use. However, the emphasis usually shifted in studies with intermediate- and/or long-term follow-up to assessment of the impact of the prevention program on regular (weekly or daily) use, "heavy" or problem use, use of multiple drugs, and, in one study, use of illicit drugs other than marijuana.

Preventing Drug Use Initiation

Most drug abuse prevention studies have focused on the capacity of the particular approach to deter drug use initiation. Several studies testing the LST prevention approach indicate that it can significantly reduce the onset of drug use. Studies have shown that the LST approach can reduce the onset of cigarette smoking in the three months between the baseline and the initial posttest when implemented by either project staff or peer leaders. In a study testing the short-term efficacy of the LST program with students ($N = 281$) in the eighth, ninth, or tenth grades, findings showed that the prevention program reduced new (current) cigarette smoking by 75%, comparing the onset rate for students receiving the LST program (4%) to that of the controls (16%) at the initial posttest (Botvin, Eng, & Williams, 1980) and by 67% (6% vs. 18%) at the three-month follow-up (Botvin & Eng, 1980). A second study ($N = 426$) tested the effectiveness of this prevention approach when implemented by older peer leaders (Botvin & Eng, 1982). New (current) cigarette smoking was reduced by 58% when the posttest rates for seventh graders receiving the LST program (8%) were compared to those for controls (19%).

Additional studies have examined the impact of the LST prevention program on alcohol and/or marijuana use. The first study to examine alcohol use was conducted with seventh graders from two comparable New York City public schools ($N = 239$) randomly assigned to experimental and control conditions (Botvin, Baker, Renick, Filazzola, & Botvin, 1984). The intervention was modified to include material concerning the potential consequences of alcohol use, and, where appropriate, skills were taught in relation to situations that might promote alcohol use. At the six-month follow-up, significantly fewer (54%) experimental students reported drinking in the past month compared to controls.

A larger study was conducted to replicate the alcohol results and to test the generalizability of the LST approach to marijuana use. The study included 1,311 seventh-grade students from 10 suburban New York junior high schools (Botvin et al., 1984). Results found significant prevention effects for tobacco, alcohol, and marijuana use at the four-month initial posttest. Adolescents who participated in the LST program drank significantly less alcohol per drinking occasion and were drunk less often. The LST program reduced occasional (monthly) marijuana use by 71% and regular (weekly or daily) marijuana use by 83%.

Research also indicates that drug initiation can be prevented with minority youth. For example, several studies with minority youth show that LST can reduce smoking initiation (Botvin, Dusensbury, Baker, James-Ortiz, & Kerner, 1989; Botvin et al., 1992; Botvin et al., 1989) and occasional use of alcohol (Botvin, Schinke, Epstein, & Diaz, 1994). More recently, a large randomized trial involving a predominantly (97%) minority sample of inner-city girls ($N = 2,209$) from 29 schools found that the LST program significantly reduced lifetime and occasional smoking (Botvin, Griffin, Diaz, Miller, & Ifill-Williams, 1999). Although the effect was significant, the prevention program cut smoking by approximately 30% among inner-city, minority youth rather than the 50% reductions found in studies with White suburban populations.

Preventing Escalation in the Frequency of Use

Evidence also supports the efficacy of school-based prevention programs to prevent escalation in the frequency of use. Research with the LST approach has shown that it is capable of preventing the progression of cigarette smoking from lifetime use to occasional use or from occasional use to regular use. For example, one study indicated that initial prevention effects, assessed in terms of occasional (monthly) smoking during seventh grade, resulted in a 56% reduction in regular (weekly) smoking one year later (Botvin & Eng, 1982). Similarly, a study with 902 seventh graders from suburban schools produced significant reductions in the onset of new smoking at the initial posttest for students who received the LST program. Once again, significant prevention effects were found one year later when these students were eighth graders in terms of more regular (weekly and daily) cigarette smoking and again at the 18-month follow-up (Botvin et al., 1983). Moreover, students receiving booster sessions in the eighth grade included half as many regular (weekly or daily) cigarette smokers as those receiving the LST program in the seventh grade. Finally, a study with minority inner-city girls found that this prevention program was able to prevent escalation from lifetime smoking to occasional smoking over a one-year period (Botvin et al., 1999). Thus, these studies show that either with or without booster sessions this prevention program is able to reduce escalation in the frequency of drug use from either lifetime to occasional smoking or occasional smoking to more regular smoking.

Preventing Heavy or Problem Use

Since most prevention programs focus on preventing early stage drug use, relatively few studies have tested the extent to which a prevention program could prevent "heavy" or problem use. Still, there is at least some evidence from research with the LST program that prevention programs can have an impact on heavy or problem use. One study ($N = 239$) showed substantial reductions in more serious levels of alcohol use: 73% fewer LST students reported heavy drinking (three or more drinks per occasion) and 79% fewer reported getting drunk at least once a month at the six-month follow-up (Botvin, Baker, Botvin, Filazzola, & Millman, 1984). In a study of 1,311 seventh-grade students from 10 suburban New York junior high schools (Botvin et al., 1984), adolescents who participated in the LST program drank significantly less alcohol per drinking occasion and were drunk less often.

Preventing Escalation to Heavy, Multiple, and Illicit Drug Use

Although the studies cited found that the prevention program produced less heavy or problem alcohol use, this finding was not necessarily the result of a disruption in the developmental progression of substance use that began earlier (i.e., that the prevention program first lowered the rate of initiation and/or occasional use of alcohol and that in turn caused lower rates of heavy use further along the developmental sequence). Stronger evidence that the prevention program disrupted a hypothetical developmental progression requires longitudinal research with longer follow-up. Such a study was conducted in the late 1980s (Botvin et al., 1990; Botvin et al., 1995).

Results from this six-year randomized trial show that the LST prevention approach can have an impact over time on more serious levels of drug involvement, including use of multiple Gateway drugs and illicit drug use (Botvin et al., 1995). The study began in 1985 and involved nearly 6,000 seventh graders from 56 public schools in suburban and rural New York State. Schools within each of three geographic regions of the state were randomly assigned to one of two experimental conditions (prevention program with training and support by project staff, or prevention program with no project staff involvement) or the control condition. Students in the two prevention conditions received the LST program during the seventh grade (15 sessions) with booster sessions in the eighth grade (10 sessions) and ninth grade (5 sessions). Although some material targeting tobacco, alcohol, and marijuana use was included in the LST program, most of the prevention program focused on teaching generic personal and social skills.

In the first two years of the intervention, at the end of the 7th and 8th grades, there were significant program effects on cigarette smoking and several etiologic factors in a direction consistent with non-drug use. Follow-up data were published after three years (9th grade), six years (12th grade), and 6.5 years (after high school). Long-term prevention effects were found for cigarette smoking, alcohol and marijuana use, regular (monthly or weekly) use of all three Gateway drugs, and illicit drug use other than marijuana use.

More specifically, data assessing the impact of the prevention program at the end of the 9th grade indicated that the prevention program produced significantly less smoking, marijuana use, and problem drinking in the intervention group than among controls. Long-term follow-up data collected at the end of the 12th grade indicated that there were up to 27% fewer regular smokers, 25% fewer heavy (pack-a-day) smokers, 12% heavy drinkers (three or more drinks of alcohol per occasion), and 44% fewer marijuana users for students who received the LST prevention program during the 7th grade and had booster sessions during the 8th and 9th grades than for controls (Botvin, Baker, Dusenbury, Botvin, & Diaz, 1995).

Impact on the Use of Multiple Gateway Drugs

In order to assess the impact of the prevention program on more serious levels of drug involvement, the Botvin et al. (1995) study also compared prevention and control students in terms of regular (monthly or weekly) use of tobacco, alcohol, *and* marijuana use. At the end of the 12th grade, there were 44% fewer LST students than controls who used all three Gateway drugs one or more times per month and 66% fewer LST students who reported using all three substances one or more times per week. The strongest prevention effects were produced for the students who received the most complete implementation of the prevention program and whose teachers attended annual training workshops and received ongoing support from project staff.

Preventing Illicit Drug Use

Long-term follow-up results from the large-scale prevention trial discussed previously also provided evidence that the LST prevention program can reduce illicit drug use (Botvin, Griffin, Diaz, Scheier, Williams, & Epstein, in 2000). An underlying assumption of primary prevention efforts is that if they prevent or reduce the use of tobacco, alcohol, and/or marijuana they will have a corresponding impact on the use of other substances further along the developmental progression. In other words, preventing Gateway drug use would be expected to reduce the use of illicit drugs such as cocaine or heroin. However, although this rationale is commonly used to justify targeting Gateway drug use, it has never been directly tested.

The impact of the LST program on illicit drug use was addressed by analyzing data collected from an anonymous subsample of students involved in the long-term follow-up study described. Data were collected by mail from 454 individuals (mean age = 18.86) who were contacted after the end of the 12th grade. The length of follow-up was 6.5 years from the initial baseline. The survey assessed the use of 13 illicit drug categories, following those used by the University of Michigan *Monitoring the Future* study (Johnston, O'Malley, & Bachman, 1994). These categories included marijuana, cocaine, amphetamines, methaqvalone [Quaaludes], barbiturates, tranquilizers, heroin, narcotics other than heroin, inhalants, amyl or butyl nitrites, LSD, phenylcyclohexyl piperidine (PCP), and 3, 4–methylenedioxymethamphetamine (MDMA).

Significantly lower levels of drug involvement (relative to those of controls) were found for the LST students on two composite measures of illicit drug use as well as for specific illicit drug categories. There were lower levels of illicit drug use using the composite measure that assessed any illicit drug use and for the measure that assessed use of illicit drugs other than marijuana. More specifically, there were significantly lower levels of heroin use and hallucinogen use for the students who received the LST program in junior high school. Thus, data from this study indicate that preventing Gateway drug use can reduce the use of some illicit drugs. However, the analyses in this study are based on aggregate data involving the comparison of group means and may not adequately capture the pattern of changes occurring on an individual level. Other analytic methods, such as structural equation modeling (SEM), might be more appropriate for studying patterns of individual changes.

Examining Developmental Transitions

Therefore, Scheier, Botvin, & Griffin (2001) conducted a series of SEM analyses to examine further the impact of the LST approach on developmental transitions in drug use. These analyses were conducted with data from a longitudinal sample of students ($N = 2{,}030$) derived from a randomized prevention trial that involved annual assessment from the seventh through the tenth grade. Figure 6.1 presents the analytic framework used to examine the extent to which the intervention disrupted drug use progression and to test the mediational process through which the intervention produced these effects. Figure 6.1 also includes necessary controls for developmental stability and pretest equivalence, two important concerns when using longitudinal data to test program effects.

The SEM models were designed to test one hypothesized mediational mechanism (enhancing assertiveness) through which the LST prevention program may produce any observed effects. The models tested include latent constructs of assertiveness (Assertive Skills) at baseline (7th grade) and one-year follow-up (8th grade) and drug use (Multiple Drug Use) at the end of the 10th grade. Focal measures of assertiveness included assertive behavior (e.g., frequency in returning defective merchandise), assertive efficacy (e.g., perceived assertive mastery), drug refusal skills (frequency of rejecting active offers to use drugs), and drug refusal efficacy (perceived mastery in rejecting drug offers). The assertiveness construct includes important aspects of the prevention program, generic assertiveness, and domain-specific (i.e., drug refusal)

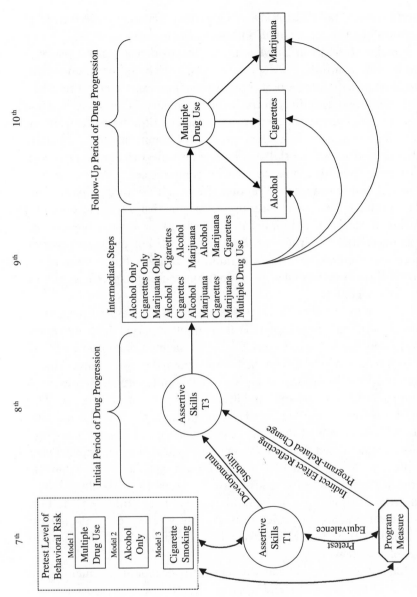

Figure 6.1. General framework for testing intervention effects on developmental progression.

131

assertiveness. The Multiple Drug Use latent construct is derived from measures of cigarette, alcohol, and marijuana use.

A major strength of SEM is the ability to detect general program effects and, controlling for these effects, search for program-related effects on specific prevention components. The exact method to examine general and specific effects involves using post hoc specification searches. Briefly, specification searches include positing paths from the program measure to individual program components (e.g., assertive behavior or drug refusal skills). These paths reflect treatment effects on skills controlling for change in assertive competence.

In addition to testing intervention effects, specification of paths from early (pretest) drug use to later use of specific drugs (e.g., alcohol use) provides a means of examining the plausibility of stage sequences and program-related disruption of those sequences. For instance, program effects can promote reductions in multiple drug use (cigarette, alcohol, and marijuana use) as well as reductions in the use of a specific substance (e.g., alcohol only).

In order to test specific stage sequences on the basis of drug type, inclusion criteria for the analyses based on self-reported drug use varied. The far left-hand side of Figure 6.1 shows the inclusion criteria utilized for each model. Model 1 examined developmental progression and intervention effects by using the entire panel sample (students present at pretest and three follow-ups) and included all patterns of drug use. This model provides a test of the intervention on multiple drug use and tests whether early forms of drug use (e.g., alcohol use) influence later progression to increased drug involvement (e.g., alcohol and marijuana use). To illustrate a stage sequential test, a path was specified from alcohol use in the seventh grade to marijuana use in the ninth grade along with a path from marijuana use in the ninth grade to later Multiple Drug Use. This developmental sequence tests directly whether early alcohol use promotes later and more involved drug use through the intermediate stage of marijuana use.

Model 2 included a test of whether early alcohol involvement influences Multiple Drug Use and whether cigarette use represents a necessary intermediate stage. In contrast to Model 1, Model 2 included a pretest latent construct of alcohol involvement reflected by indicators tapping frequency, intensity, and drunkenness. One important difference between Model 1 and Model 2 is the exclusion of pretest smokers in Model 2, which provides a means to test whether cigarette use represents an essential stage between early alcohol and later multiple drug use.

Model 3 tested whether early smoking behavior (cigarette use) leads to the use of all three Gateway drugs or whether involvement with alcohol represents an essential intermediate step that links smoking behavior with the use of multiple drugs. Specification of this model included a pretest measure of smoking frequency, a latent construct of Alcohol Use in the 9th grade, and a latent construct of Multiple Drug Use in the 10th grade. Model 3 excluded youth reporting pretest alcohol use, thus permitting a test of whether early cigarette use proceeds directly to later multiple drug use or whether alcohol use represents an essential intermediate stage in the drug sequence.

Results from all three models support a stage sequential model of drug use. Specifically, early alcohol use was a determinant of later involvement with multiple drugs. In addition, a small portion of youth initially experimented with alcohol and then progressed directly to marijuana use (manifest indicator). Moreover, findings from Model 2 show that early alcohol involvement led directly to multiple drug use. These findings also show that intense alcohol use (defined by quantity consumed) preceded marijuana use over the course of one year. Results from Model 3 indicate that even with appropriate sample exclusions to eliminate alcohol-using youth, early cigarette use led to alcohol involvement in the 9th grade and multiple drug use in the 10th grade.

In addition to identifying specific facets of developmental progression, the findings also confirm that enhancing assertiveness successfully disrupts the early stages of drug involvement. Regardless of whether these youth drank alcohol or used tobacco as their entry point for drug use, enhancing assertive competence reduced the likelihood of further drug involvement. Reducing risk included limiting alcohol involvement as an intermediate stage as well as further reducing multiple drug use. Across all three models, indirect program effects on assertiveness indicate that for roughly a 10% change in assertiveness, there are corresponding reductions in drug use of 30% to 50%. Thus, a relatively small change in generic assertive skills and drug refusal (assertive) skills over a one-year period (from the seventh to the eighth grade) was responsible for substantial reductions in drug use. Importantly, the impact of the intervention did not vary as a function of drug use reported at baseline. This suggests that targeting assertiveness at this developmental period, regardless of initial drug use status, represents an effective deterrent to later drug involvement.

Taken together, the etiologic and prevention findings of this study underscore the importance of focusing prevention efforts on reducing

Gateway drug use. These findings indicate that the impact of the LST program was mediated by increasing generic assertive skills, assertive efficacy, and drug refusal skills. Among those youth reporting baseline alcohol use, the LST program reduced the risk of later marijuana use as well as multiple drug use. Among youth reporting baseline smoking behaviors but no alcohol use, improvements in assertiveness reduced the likelihood of experimentation with alcohol use and multiple drug involvement. Moreover, the findings of this study provide additional support for the Gateway Hypothesis.

Summary and Conclusions

Advances in drug abuse prevention research have identified several promising approaches. The results of two decades of research with Life Skills Training, a multicomponent prevention approach, provide strong empirical evident that the program can produce substantial reductions in tobacco, alcohol, and marijuana use; booster sessions can both sustain and enhance initial prevention effects; and the program produces prevention effects that are durable and long-lasting. The findings of this research also indicate that Life Skills Training can disrupt the developmental progression of drug use. This prevention approach can reduce initial cigarette smoking, the transition from occasional to regular use, multiple drug use (cigarettes, alcohol, and marijuana), and use of illicit drugs other than marijuana.

Although the prevention research discussed in this chapter was not designed explicitly to examine the Gateway Hypothesis, this body of research does provide general support for it. The findings from 20 years of research with the LST program indicate that preventing the use of substances hypothesized to occur at the very beginning of the developmental progression (tobacco and alcohol use) not only deters the use of those substances, but also deters the use of marijuana and of at least some illicit drugs other than marijuana. Moreover, a study designed to test one hypothesized mediational mechanism for the LST program as well as to examine the impact of the prevention program on deterring the progression of drug use provides further support for the Gateway Hypothesis. Although variations were identified in terms of progression among Gateway substances, the LST program was able to disrupt the progression of drug use regardless of the developmental sequence. Future prevention efforts should focus on preventing the use of all three Gateway drugs both because prevention of Gateway drug use is important to public health and because it is also likely to deter progression to the use of other drugs.

References

Bangert-Downs, R. L. (1988). The effects of school-based substance abuse education: A meta-analysis. *Journal of Drug Education, 18*, 243–265.

Barnes, G. M., & Welte, J. W. (1986). Patterns and predictors of alcohol use among 7–12th grade students in New York State. *Journal of Studies on Alcohol, 47*, 53–62.

Bentler, P. M. (1995). *EQS structural equations program manual*. Encino, CA: Multivariate, Inc.

Botvin, G. J. (1999). Adolescent drug abuse prevention: Current findings and future directions. In C. R. Hartel & M. D. Glantz (Eds.), *Drug Abuse: Origins and Interventions* (pp. 285–308). Washington, DC: APA Books.

Botvin, G. J., Baker, E., Botvin, E. M., Filazzola, A. D., & Millman, R. B. (1984). Prevention of alcohol misuse through the development of personal and social competence: A pilot study. *Journal of Studies on Alcohol, 45*, 550–552.

Botvin, G. J., Baker, E., Dusenbury, L., Botvin, E. M., & Diaz, T. (1995) Long-term follow-up results of a randomized drug abuse prevention trial in a White middle-class population. *Journal of the American Medical Association, 273*, 1106–1112.

Botvin, G. J., Baker, E., Dusenbury, L., Tortu, S., & Botvin, E. M. (1990). Preventing adolescent drug abuse through a multimodal cognitive-behavioral approach: Results of a 3-year study. *Journal of Consulting and Clinical Psychology, 58*, 437–446.

Botvin, G. J., Baker, E., Goldberg, C. J., Dusenbury, L., & Botvin, E. M. (1992). Correlates and predictors of smoking among black adolescents. *Addictive Behaviors, 17*, 97–103.

Botvin, G. J., Baker, E., Renick, N. L., Filazzola, A. D., & Botvin, E. M. (1984). A cognitive-behavioral approach to substance abuse prevention. *Addictive Behaviors, 9*, 137–147.

Botvin, G. J., Batson, H., Witts-Vitale, S., Bess, V., Baker, E., & Dusenbury, L. (1989). A psychosocial approach to smoking prevention for urban black youth. *Public Health Reports, 104*, 573–582.

Botvin, G. J., & Botvin, E. M. (1992). Adolescent tobacco, alcohol, and drug abuse: Prevention strategies, empirical findings, and assessment issues. *Journal of Developmental and Behavioral Pediatrics, 13*, 290–301.

Botvin, G. J., Dusenbury, L., Baker, E., James-Ortiz, S., & Kerner, J. (1989). A skills training approach to smoking prevention among Hispanic youth. *Journal of Behavioral Medicine, 12*, 279–296.

Botvin, G. J., & Eng, A. (1982). The efficacy of a multi-component approach to the prevention of cigarette smoking. *Journal of Preventive Medicine, 11,* 199–211.

Botvin, G. J., Eng, A., & Williams, C. L. (1980). Preventing the onset of cigarette smoking through life skills training. *Preventive Medicine, 9,* 135–143.

Botvin, G. J., Griffin, K. W., Diaz, T., Miller, N., & Ifill-Williams, M. (1999). Smoking initiation and escalation in early adolescent girls: One-year follow-up of a school-based prevention intervention for minority youth. *Journal of the American Medical Women's Association, 54,* 139–143.

Botvin, G. J., Griffin, K. W., Diaz, T., Scheier, L. M., Williams, C., & Epstein, J. A. (2000). Preventing illicit drug use in adolescents: Long-term follow-up data from a randomized control trial of a school population. *Addictive Behavior, 25,* 796–774.

Botvin, G. J., Renick, N., & Baker, E. (1983). The effects of scheduling format and booster sessions on a broad-spectrum psychosocial approach to smoking prevention. *Journal of Behavioral Medicine, 6,* 359–379.

Botvin, G. J., Schinke, S. P., Epstein, J. A., & Diaz, T. (1994). The effectiveness of culturally-focused and generic skills training approaches to alcohol and drug abuse prevention among minority youth. *Psychology of Addictive Behaviors, 8,* 116–127.

Chassin, L., Presson, C. C., Sherman, S. J., Corty, E., & Olshavsky, R. W. (1984). Predicting the onset of cigarette smoking in adolescents: A longitudinal study. *Journal of Applied Social Psychology, 14,* 224–243.

Chou, C. P., & Bentler, P. M. (1990). Model modification in covariance structure modeling: A comparison among likelihood ration, Lagrange multiplier, and Wald tests. *Multivariate Behavioral Research, 26,* 115–136.

Collins, L. M., Graham, J. W., Rousculp, S. S., Fidler, P. L., Pan., J., & Hansen, W. B. (1994). Latent transition analysis and how it can address prevention research questions. In L. M. Collins & L. Seitz (Eds.), *Advances in data analysis for prevention intervention research* (NIDA Research Monograph No. 142). Washington, DC: U.S. Government Printing Office.

Collins, L. M., Graham, J. W., Rousculp, S. S., & Hansen, W. B. (1997). Heavy caffeine use and the beginning of the substance use onset process: An illustration of latent transition analysis. In K. J. Bryant, M. Windle, & S. G. West (Eds.), *The science of prevention: Methodological advances from alcohol and substance abuse research* (pp. 79–99). Washington, DC: American Psychological Association.

Dielman, T. E., Leech, S. L., Lorenger, A. T., & Horvath, W. J. (1984). Health locus of control and self-esteem as related to adolescent health behavior and intentions. *Adolescence, 19,* 935–950.

Goodstadt, M. S. (1986). Drug education: The prevention issues. *Journal of Drug Education, 19,* 197–208.

Graham, J. W., Collins, L. M., Wugalter, S. E., Chung, N. K., & Hansen, W. B. (1991). Modeling transitions in latent stage-sequential processes: A substance use prevention example. *Journal of Consulting and Clinical Psychology, 59,* 48–57.

Hansen, W. B. (1992). School-based substance abuse prevention: A review of the state of the art in curriculum, 1980–1990. *Health Education Research, 7,* 403–430.

Hawkins, J. D., Catalano, R. F., & Miller, J. Y. (1992). Risk and protective factors for alcohol and other drug problems in adolescence and early adulthood: Implications for substance abuse prevention. *Psychological Bulletin, 112,* 64–105.

Jessor, R., & Jessor, S. L. (1977). *Problem behavior and psychosocial development: A longitudinal study of youth.* New York: Academic Press.

Jessor, R., & Jessor, S. L. (1982). Critical issues in research on adolescent health promotion. In T. Coates, A. Peterson, & C. Perry (Eds.), *Promoting adolescent health: A dialogue on research and practice* (pp. 447–465). New York: Academic Press.

Johnston, L. D., O'Malley, P. M., & Bachman, J. G. (1994). National survey results on drug use from the Monitoring the Future Study, 1975–1993. Vol. 1. *Secondary school students.* Rockville, MD: U.S. Department of Health and Human Services.

Kandel, D. B. (1975). Stages in adolescent involvement in drug use. *Science, 190,* 912–914.

Kandel, D. B. (1985). On processes of peer influences in adolescent drug use: A developmental perspective. *Advances in Alcohol and Substance Abuse, 4,* 139–163.

Kandel, D. B., & Faust, R. (1975). Sequence and stages in patterns of adolescent drug use. *Archives of General Psychiatry, 32,* 923–932.

Kandel, D. B., Treiman, D., Faust, R., & Single, E. (1976). Adolescent involvement in legal and illegal drug use: A multiple classification analysis. *Social Forces, 55,* 438–458.

Kandel, D. B., & Yamaguchi, K. (1999). Developmental stages of involvement in substance use. In P. J. Ott, R. E. Tarter, et al. (Eds), *Sourcebook on substance abuse: Etiology, epidemiology, assessment, and treatment* (pp. 50–74). Needham Heights, MA: Allyn & Bacon.

Krosnick, J. A., & Judd, C. M. (1982). Transitions in social influence at adolescence: Who induces cigarette smoking? *Developmental Psychology, 18,* 359–368.

Newcomb, M. D., & Bentler, P. M. (1986). Drug use, educational aspirations, and work force involvement: The transition from adolescence to young adulthood. *American Journal of Community Psychology, 14,* 303–321.

Newcomb, M. D., & Bentler, P. M. (1989). Substance use and abuse among children and teenagers. *American Psychologist, 44,* 242–248.

Newcomb, M. D., & Felix-Ortiz, M. (1992). Multiple protective and risk factors for drug use and abuse: Cross-sectional and prospective findings. *Journal of Consulting and Clinical Psychology, 63,* 280–296.

Scheier, L. M., Botvin, G. J., & Griffin, K. (2001). Preventive intervention effects on developmental progression in drug use: Structural equation modeling analyses using longitudinal data. *Prevention Science, 2,* 89–100.

Scheier, L. M., & Newcomb, M. D. (1991). Psychosocial predictors of drug use initiation and escalation: An expansion of the multiple risk factors hypothesis using longitudinal data. *Contemporary Drug Problems, Spring,* 31–73.

Schinke, S., Botvin, G. J., & Orlandi, M. (1991). *Substance abuse in children and adolescents.* Newbury Park, CA: Sage.

Single, E., Kandel, D. B., & Faust, R. (1974). Patterns of multiple drug use in high school. *Journal of Health and Social Behavior, 15,* 344–357.

Tye, J., Warner, K., & Glantz, S. (1987). Tobacco advertising and consumption: Evidence of a causal relationship. *Journal of Public Health Policy, 8,* 492–507.

Weir, W. R. (1968). A program of alcohol education and counseling for high school students with and without a family alcohol problem. *Dissertation Abstract, 28*(11-A), 4454–4455.

7

The Gateway Theory Applied to Prevention

Mary Ann Pentz and Chaoyang Li

After several years of no change or increase, adolescent drug use in the United States has declined slightly (Johnston, O'Malley, & Bachman, 1999). However, use of tobacco, alcohol, and marijuana, the drugs referred to as *Gateway drugs*, remains at high levels. Gateway or stepping-stone theory posits that early use of Gateway drugs (tobacco, alcohol, marijuana) predisposes adolescents to risk of later use of other, illicit substances, including amphetamines (Marcos & Bahr, 1995; Torabi, Bailey, & Majd-Jabbari, 1993; Yamaguchi & Kandel, 1984). Gateway drug use may account for 39% or more of the variation in adolescent amphetamine use (Marcos & Bahr, 1995).

Theoretical Questions in Applying Gateway Theory to Prevention

Gateway theory has been criticized (DeWit, Offord, & Wong, 1997); however, at least three factors are driving reexamination of its utility for understanding the development and prevention of adolescent drug use. First is the question of whether certain drugs act as a gateway because of their social modeling influence, addictive potential, or psychobiological novelty effect (Bardo, Donohew, & Harrington, 1996; Lindsay & Rainey, 1997; Torabi et al., 1993). The implication is that if other drugs served any of these purposes for young adolescents, they would replace tobacco, alcohol, and marijuana as Gateway drugs. Second is that any assumption of a causal relationship of Gateway drug use to other drug use is

Appreciation is expressed to Dr. James Dwyer for his helpful advice on analyses.

confounded with a temporal effect; that is, the Gateway drugs are used first by adolescents simply because they are currently more socially available and acceptable than other drugs (Clayton, Voss, & LoScuito, 1988). Third is the widely debated question of the efficacy of current universal prevention programs, that is, programs that focus on early population-based prevention for curbing later drug abuse. Little is known about whether conducting such early Gateway drug use prevention on a populationwide basis is more cost effective than waiting to isolate and intervene with smaller numbers of high-risk youth who are further along on a developmental course of drug use.

Criticism notwithstanding, there is substantial epidemiological evidence for a strong predictive relationship between early experimentation with tobacco, alcohol, and/or marijuana and later illicit drug use. Support for the Gateway theory from the field of prevention research, on the other hand, is scanty. Three substance-specific prevention studies have shown generalization of effect *within* the class of Gateway drugs: a smoking prevention study that had an effect on smoking and a smaller effect on alcohol use (Perry, Murray, Kelder, & Klepp, 1992); an alcohol prevention study that showed effects on alcohol and tobacco use (Perry et al., 1996); and an alcohol prevention study that showed effects on both binge drinking and marijuana use (Cheadle et al., 1995). Only one study has reported effects of a Gateway drug use prevention program on delaying progression from no use to trial use to regular use of Gateway drugs (Chou et al., 1998). In these studies, and at least one review of other prevention studies (Tobler & Stratton, 1997), the first and largest effects were obtained on cigarette use; later, smaller effects were obtained on marijuana use; and effects on alcohol use were inconsistent.

A few studies have reported an effect of drug abuse prevention programs *across* Gateway drugs and some illicit drugs such as cocaine (e.g., Botvin, Baker, Dusenbury, Botvin, & Diaz, 1995; Pentz, Dwyer, MacKinnon, et al., 1989; Schinke, Orlandi, & Cole, 1992). As expected, effects on Gateway drug use were always greater than effects of other illicit drug use, reflecting differences in population-based prevalence rates of these substances. Program effects were typically reported on each substance simultaneously at each follow-up, or beginning with the follow-up at which effects began to appear. Presently, then, programs aimed at Gateway drug use prevention are only *assumed* to have later effects on illicit drug use. A true test of the effects of early Gateway drug use prevention on later illicit drug use would model prevention effects on Gateway drug use as a mediational effect on later drug use.

A few studies have evaluated the mediational effects of social variables hypothesized to prevent drug use behavior. For example, drug use refusal skills and perceived social norms for drug use have been shown to act as short-term mediators of drug use behavior change (Donaldson, Graham, & Hansen, 1994; MacKinnon et al., 1991). However, no studies have yet evaluated the mediational effect of preventing Gateway drug use early in adolescence on preventing other illicit drug use later either in short-term or long-term studies. Such an analysis would constitute a test of the Gateway theory applied to prevention. Finding support for the theory from prevention research is important for two reasons. First, such support would counter the argument that prevention efforts would be more cost-effective if they started later in the drug use course, with high-risk youth. Second, supportive evidence from mediational analysis would explain how prevention programs can achieve delayed or sleeper effects on illicit drug use.

In terms of previous research, then, two theoretical questions must apply to testing Gateway theory in a prevention study. One is whether changes in use of any or all of the Gateway drugs achieved from a prevention program can mediate change in other illicit drug use later on. The other is whether any mediational effects that would support the Gateway theory are largely attributable to a change in use of a specific Gateway substance, particularly cigarette and/or marijuana use.

Methodological Questions in Applying Gateway Theory to Prevention

Longitudinal prevention studies pose special problems for estimating mediating effects reliably. One makes several assumptions in the conduct of mediational analyses: The prevention program causes changes in both the mediator and the outcome; the mediator causes the outcome by controlling for effects of the prevention program; and the mediated effect is significant (MacKinnon, 1994). Problems arise in interpretation of mediational effects when one or more of the following situations occur: There are program effects on either the mediator or the outcome, but not both; there are program effects on both, but the mediational effect is not significant; or there are no program effects (MacKinnon, 1994). If the mediator/outcome relationship has already been established, sample sizes are sufficient (e.g., measures of the proportion of mediated intervention effect stabilize at $n => 500$; MacKinnon, 1994), and mediator and outcome measures are reliable, then these problems could be due to suppressor or reciprocal effects among the program, mediator, and outcome. Either of these possibilities is quite likely in prevention studies, where intervention might be expected to decrease a mediator that is considered a risk factor for the outcome variable, but that the normal developmental relationship of risk to outcome is to increase over time.

The most common method of evaluating mediational effects in a longitudinal intervention study is to generate three regression models: the direct intervention effect on the hypothesized mediator, the direct intervention effect on the outcome variable, and the effect of the mediator on the outcome variable. The mediated effect on the outcome variable is then the cross-product of the intervention effect on the mediator and the effect of the mediator on the outcome variable (Dwyer & Feinleib, 1992; MacKinnon et al., 1991; MacKinnon & Dwyer, submitted; Pentz, 1994). Problems arise when one or more of the regression coefficients either has the wrong sign (a relation between two variables opposite to what was expected) or is not significant. Either may produce a situation in which the magnitude of a mediational effect is consistent with a mediational hypothesis, but the direction or the magnitude of the effect relative to the main effect appears illogical. In addition, regression analyses do not control for measurement error in estimating mediational effects. An alternative might be path analysis using structural equation modeling, which can simultaneously model direct and mediational effects and control for measurement error (Pentz & Chou, 1994).

In longitudinal drug abuse prevention research testing the Gateway theory, the problem of estimating mediational effects may be even more complicated. In this case, the prevention program is hypothesized to have a main effect on Gateway drug use early in the adolescent years. This effect is then hypothesized to mediate effects on other illicit drug use later in adolescence and early adulthood, when use prevalence of these substances would be expected to increase. However, analysis of the mediational effect depends on the stability of the relationship between Gateway drug use and later illicit drug use. Epidemiological research has shown repeatedly that this relationship is positive and strong (e.g., Yamaguchi et al., 1984; Clayton, Voss, & LoSciuto, 1988). If a prevention program decreases Gateway drug use early on, it may decrease the strength of the subsequent relationship between Gateway drug use and illicit drug use or even disrupt the normal developmental sequence of the use of these drugs (Pentz & Chou, 1994). A change in this path, between Gateway drug use and later illicit drug use, may suppress a main effect of the program on later illicit drug use, yield the wrong direction of the mediational effect, or both.

Further complications of estimating mediational effects in longitudinal drug abuse prevention research involve assumptions about how to model direct and mediating intervention effects on a youth population accurately as it moves through time (Pentz, 1994). For example, does the mediator, in this case, Gateway drug use, change at the level of the school in which the prevention program is implemented or at the level of the individual? If school is used as the unit of analysis, should mediating effects be weighted by school sample size if samples are selected from within each school? Is a mediational effect best modeled as a baseline-adjusted variable or as a change score? Finally, is regression sufficient for estimating complex mediational relationships?

This chapter explores the mediational relationship of changes in Gateway drug use that were attributed to a prevention program in early adolescence, and to changes in amphetamine use in later adolescence and early adulthood. Two substantive hypotheses are tested. One is that prevention program effects achieved on Gateway drug use early in adolescence serve to mediate effects on amphetamine use later in adolescence and early adulthood. Second is that gateway mediational effects are largely attributable to changes in cigarette use, followed by marijuana use. The methodological questions about mediational analyses are addressed by comparing mediational effects achieved with conditional versus unconditional regression models, school versus individual level units of analysis, and weighting versus no weighting of school sample size.

Method

Data Set

Data for this study were drawn from a large multicommunity-based drug abuse prevention trial (Pentz et al., 1989). All middle schools within each of 26 communities in two large metropolitan areas were assigned to a multi-component, community-based intervention or to a control condition. The intervention consisted of five components introduced into schools and communities at the rate of 6 months to 1 year apart: a school program with a booster, a parent education and organization program, community organization, mass media programming, and local policy change. The primary emphasis was on Gateway drug use (tobacco, alcohol, marijuana use) prevention among adolescents. The data set consisted of 11 years of annual survey data on samples of individuals from two cities ($N = 1,002$ in Kansas City, $N = 8$ schools; $N = 1,206$ in Indianapolis, $N = 57$ schools). Previous studies of this data set showed significant long-term program effects on delaying and reducing use of all three Gateway drugs, with the largest and most immediate effects on cigarette use, followed by marijuana use (e.g., Chou et al., 1998; Johnson et al., 1990; Pentz et al., 1992). Details of the design, intervention, and measurement are provided elsewhere (Pentz et al., 1989). Early results showed that the program prevented and reduced Gateway drug use during the adolescent years (e.g., Pentz et al., 1989; Johnson et al., 1990; Chou et al., 1998). Results of a more recent study showed that the program has had significant lasting effects on both a composite Gateway drug use score and use of each Gateway drug from early adolescence through early adulthood (age 12 through 23), as well as direct program effects on amphetamine use by midadolescence (age 15) (Pentz et al., unpublished manuscript).

Variables

The survey included 133 items on demographic characteristics, drug use, and drug use–related behaviors and attitudes. Demographic characteristics treated as covariates included grade (at baseline, 6 or 7), race (six categories recoded as $0 = $ non-White, $1 = $ White), socioeconomic status (11 categories of father's or proxy's occupation recoded as $0 = $ low, $1 = $ mid/high professional/managerial), and school type ($0 = $ private, $1 = $ public). Gateway drug use variables were selected on the basis of their representing heavy use rather than occasional use. Variables included frequency of cigarette use (recoded as $0 = $ none, $1 = $ any current daily use), drunkenness ($0 = $ none, $1 = $ any in the last month), and heavy marijuana use ($0 = $ none, $1 = $ two or more times in the last week). Amphetamine use represented lifetime use ($0 = $ never, $1 = $ any in lifetime).

Analysis

Different analytical methods were compared to estimate mediational effects, including use of school versus individual level analysis, conditional (baseline-adjusted) versus unconditional (follow-up minus baseline) regression models, and weighted (by school sample size) versus unweighted analyses. Results were then compared to results of multilevel regression and structural equation analyses that were conducted as part of another study (Li, Pentz, Chou, & Dwyer, submitted for publication).

For school level analyses, dichotomous scores for individual demographic and drug use variables were aggregated to create a school level mean proportion (e.g., the proportion of White students in a school). Gateway drug use proportions were standardized and averaged for each school. For individual level analyses, the original dichotomous score for each variable was used; the Gateway drug use composite was created by summing dichotomous scores. The Gateway drug use composites for each year were treated as the mediators for each subsequent year of amphetamine use. Thus, lifetime prevalence rates of amphetamine use in each of the last 3 follow-up years were treated as the outcome variables, and the Gateway drug use composite at each prior year was treated as the mediator. Differentiating cutoff years for Gateway drug and amphetamine use allowed a test of the temporal hypothesis that program effects on late adolescent and early adulthood amphetamine use were mediated by program effects on early adolescent Gateway drug use.

Two dummy variables, city (Kansas City = 1, Indianapolis = −1) and the interaction term between city and group, were created to adjust for effects of city. For one city (Kansas City), amphetamine use in 1986–1987 was treated as a proxy for baseline use, since amphetamine use was not measured in this city until 1986–1987. Also in this city, only one of every four survey forms included socioeconomic status (SES). For this city then, as a result of missing SES information at the individual level, the school level SES was used in the analyses of logistic regression at the individual level. In addition, the numbers of participants in each school differed greatly (range of $n = 5$ to 143). Therefore, school level analyses were conducted with and without weighting for school sample size.

For all analyses, the general mediational model is shown in Figure 7.1.

$$Y = \tau X + \varphi_1 \text{Grade} + \varphi_2 \text{Race} + \varphi_3 \text{SES} + \varphi_4 G_b + \epsilon_1$$

$$M = \alpha X + \alpha_1 \text{Grade} + \alpha_2 \text{Race} + \alpha_3 \text{SES} + \alpha_4 G_b + \epsilon_2$$

$$Y = \tau' X + \beta M + \beta_1 \text{Grade} + \beta_2 \text{Race} + \beta_3 \text{SES} + \beta_4 G_b + \epsilon_3$$

$$\text{Total effect} = \hat{\tau} = \hat{\alpha}\hat{\beta} + \hat{\tau}'$$

$$\text{Mediated effect} = \hat{\alpha}\hat{\beta} = \hat{\tau} - \hat{\tau}'$$

$$SE(\hat{\alpha}\hat{\beta}) = \sqrt{\hat{\alpha}^2 \times SE_{(\hat{\beta})}^2 + \hat{\beta}^2 \times SE_{(\hat{\alpha})}^2}$$

$$t = \frac{\hat{\alpha}\hat{\beta}}{SE_{(\hat{\alpha}\hat{\beta})}}$$

In addition to the general mediational model, several specific models were tested under different assumptions about mediational effect.

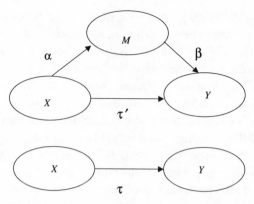

Figure 7.1. General Mediational Model. Where X = intervention (program vs. control). M = Gateway drug use composite score (daily cigarette, monthly drunkenness, and weekly marijuana use); cutoff point: 1991–1992 follow-up (Grades 10–11) for both Kansas City and Indianapolis. Y = amphetamine use at the last three follow-ups (i.e., 1992–1993, 1993–1994, and 1994–1995).

Unconditional Regression Model, School as Unit of Analysis. An unconditional model tests the change in a dependent variable over time (e.g., between follow-up and baseline; Dwyer et al., 1989). The dependent variable is assumed to be continuous. The unit of analysis matches the unit of experimental assignment. In this case, the unit is the school. The unconditional model is useful when experimental assignment is either not random or not entirely random (Dwyer & Feinleib, 1992); the latter being the case in one of the cities (Kansas City) in the data set. Intervention status (program group is coded as 1 and control group is coded as 0) and other demographic variables such as grade, gender, race, and socioeconomic status are included in the regression model as covariates. The program effect can be obtained by calculating the regression coefficients of the intervention group on the change score of the dependent variable (e.g., amphetamine use prevalence rates between 1994 follow-up and the baseline survey). The mediational effects can be tested by using the general procedure and formula described. The following is an example of the unconditional model:
  Where

$$D_{amph} = \alpha_1 X + \alpha_2 \text{ Grade} + \alpha_3 \text{ Race} + \alpha_4 \text{ SES} + \epsilon$$

D_{amph} = difference or change score of amphetamine use prevalence rates between follow-up and baseline

X = intervention group

Grade, Race, and SES = demographic covariates

ϵ = random error

$\epsilon \sim N(0, \sigma^2)$

Conditional Regression Model, School as Unit of Analysis. The analysis of covariance model is the classic conditional model. This model assumes that any baseline variation in Gateway drug use between groups is random and can be adjusted for as an additional covariate. The model also assumes that the direct and mediational effects of the program operate primarily at the school level, on the basis of previous studies that have shown that school-level changes in social norms for drug use are the largest predictors of later drug use in adolescents (e.g., MacKinnon et al., 1991; Donaldson et al., 1994). School as the unit analysis is also considered appropriate for estimating program effects, since it represents the unit of experimental assignment. In longitudinal intervention studies, a conditional model includes Time 1 measures (e.g., amphetamine use at baseline) as a covariate for the dependent variable at Time 2 (e.g., amphetamine use at follow-up). This model assumes that the effects of the intervention and covariates are additive, and it assesses the effect of the intervention at preintervention levels of the dependent variable (Dwyer et al., 1989). Experimental assignment is assumed to be random or mostly random, the latter being the case for the majority of schools in the data set.

The conditional model is as follows:

$$\eta_{1\ amph} = \beta_1\, X + \beta_2\, \text{Grade} + \beta_3\, \text{Race} + \beta_4\, \text{SES} + \beta_5\, \eta_{0\ amph} + \epsilon$$

where

$\eta_{1\ amph}$ = amphetamine prevalence rate at a follow-up

$\eta_{0\ amph}$ = amphetamine prevalence rate at baseline

ϵ = random error

$\epsilon \sim N(0, \sigma^2)$

Logistic Regression Model, Individual as Unit of Analysis. This model assumes that any change in mediators occurs within individuals rather than in schools. When the dependent variable (e.g., amphetamine use) is dichotomous (e.g., use = 1, nonuse = 0), the logistic regression model is appropriate for program effect estimation. In this case, the risk of amphetamine use in the form of log odds is regressed on predictor variables. The maximum likelihood method is used for the parameter estimation. It is assumed that the associations between log odds of amphetamine use risk and the predictors are linear and additive. The following is a conditional logistic regression model

$$\ln \left[\text{odds}(Y = 1) \right] = \gamma_1 X + \gamma_2 \text{ Grade} + \gamma_3 \text{ Race} + \gamma_4 \text{ SES} + \gamma_5 Y_{0 \text{ amph}} + \epsilon$$

where

$\ln$ = natural logarithm

odds $(Y = 1)$ = ratio of probability of amphetamine use over probability of no amphetamine use: prob $(Y = 1)/[1 - \text{prob} (Y = 1)]$

$Y_{0 \text{ amph}}$ = amphetamine use at baseline

ϵ = random error

$\epsilon \sim N(0, \epsilon^2)$

The unconditional logistic model can also be applied at the individual level by using the probit link function to test the total or direct program effects on a dependent variable, for instance, amphetamine use at 1994 follow-up. However, the procedures to conduct mediational analysis using the unconditional model are complicated and impractical because of a lack of available computer programs.

Validation of Regression Analyses. A previous study focused on two specific methodological questions in analyzing mediational effects on amphetamine use (Li et al., under review). The findings from that study, using different analytical techniques, are summarized and compared to results of analyses used for this chapter.

The first methodological question addressed by Li et al., was the question of how multilevel effects should be estimated in a mediational model, and the impact of such estimation on the magnitude of mediational effect obtained. The question is relevant to the data presented in this chapter, which are based on school as the level or unit of randomization in the prevention trial and on individual as the level or unit from which data were collected. If results obtained from multilevel regression analysis in the previous study are similar to those obtained from the separate school and individual level analyses conducted for this chapter, they could be considered a validity check by simultaneously controlling for both levels of variables. It could be hypothesized that the multilevel model yields a magnitude of mediational effect somewhere between the effects obtained from separate school and individual level analyses.

The second methodological question addressed in the Li et al., study was how mediational effects should be estimated in a structural equation model (SEM) and the impact of such estimation on the magnitude of mediational effect obtained. The question is relevant to the use of regression analysis in general to estimate mediational effects. SEM simultaneously estimates the effects of the multiple paths that represent mediation and controls for measurement error. One possible hypothesis is that measurement error produces a bias in the direction of inflating mediational effects. In that case, SEM would be expected to yield a smaller mediational effect than regression analyses.

Results of regression analyses conducted for this chapter then were validated against the two alternative types of analyses conducted in a previous study. First, results of school level and individual level analyses were compared to a multilevel model, which simultaneously examined the effects of group level and individual level variables (Byrk & Raudenbush, 1992). SAS PROC MIXED was used to estimate the multilevel model (SAS Institute, 1996). Second, structural equation modeling, using EQS software, was used to control for measurement error (Bentler, 1989) and simultaneously estimate the multiple paths shown in Figure 7.1. Prevalence rates at the school level were treated as continuous variables (Muthen, 1984). All analyses reported in this chapter were conducted by using PROC REG, PROC LOGISTIC, PROC MIXED, or EQS (Bentler, 1989; SAS, 1996).

Results

Results of all analyses are shown in Tables 7.1–7.3. All tables use the same notations, whereby τ is the relationship between the program and amphetamine use; τ' is the coefficient relating the program to amphetamine use, adjusted for effects of Gateway drug use; β (refers to the Gateway composite score in Tables 7.1 and 7.2 and to each of the specific Gateway drugs in Table 7.3) is the coefficient relating Gateway drug use to amphetamine use adjusted for the program; α (noted at the bottom of each table from a previous study, Pentz et al., unpublished manuscript) is the relationship of the program to changes in Gateway drug use; and the $\alpha \times \beta$ cross-product is the mediational relationship between earlier program effects on Gateway drug use and later amphetamine use.

Mediated Effect of Gateway Drug Use

Table 7.1 summarizes the results of regression analyses at the level of school, the unit of assignment and program implementation. When all potential Gateway drug use relationships are controlled for, the direct or main effect of the program on amphetamine use loses significance, compared to the main effects reported in a previous study (Pentz et al., unpublished manuscript). Two patterns that support Gateway drug use theory are apparent when using the conditional (baseline-adjusted) regression model. One is the consistently positive relationship between early Gateway drug use between 1987 and 1991 and later amphetamine use between 1992 and 1995. The second is the consistently negative relationship of the mediated effect, indicating that the program – by having changed Gateway drug use in early years – reduces amphetamine use later on. Weighting for school size did not change the magnitude of any Gateway relationships. However, Gateway relationships lose all significance with the unconditional model.

Table 7.2 shows results of logistic regression analyses at the level of the individual, the unit of measurement of drug use. The pattern of results is similar to those obtained from the conditional regression model with school as the unit of analysis, with the exception that the Gateway drug use relationships appear slightly stronger, although the larger standard error in the individual level analyses reduces the significance of the mediated effect somewhat.

Results of these analyses were consistent with results of both multilevel regression and structural equation modeling that were conducted as part of the Li et al., study. For multilevel regression, the average $\beta(SE)$ across years of follow-up was .05 (.01) $p < .001$ and $\alpha \times \beta$ (SE) was $-.04$ (.01), $p < .01$. For SEM, the average β (SE) was .13 (.02), $p < .01$, and $\alpha \times \beta$ (SE) was $-.05(.02)$, $p < .01$.

Thus, results of all analyses support Gateway drug use theory in two ways. First, early Gateway drug use is significantly related to later amphetamine use. Second, early program effects on Gateway drug use mediate later effects on amphetamine use.

Table 7.1. *Mediated Prevention Effects on Amphetamine Use (Conditional and Unconditional Regression, School as Unit)*

Method	Parameter	Lifetime Amphetamine Use			
		1992–1993 b (se)	1993–1994 b (se)	1994–1995 b (se)	1992–1995 b (se)
Conditional					
Unweighted					
	τ	−.07 (.05)	−.05 (.06)	−.08 (.06)	−.08 (.06)
	τ'	.01 (.05)	.04 (.05)	.02 (.05)	.03 (.05)
	β	.12 (.02)***	.15 (.02)***	.16 (.02)***	.17 (.02)***
	$\alpha \times \beta$	−.08 (.03)*	−.10 (.04)*	−.11 (.04)*	−.11 (.04)*
Weighted					
	τ	−.05 (.02)*	−.04 (.03)†	−.05 (.02)*	−.04 (.03)*
	τ'	.00 (.02)	.01 (.03)	.01 (.03)	.02 (.03)
	β	.09 (.02)*	.10 (.02)***	.11 (.02)***	.12 (.02)***
	$\alpha \times \beta$	−.05 (.02)*	−.06 (.02)**	−.06 (.02)**	−.07 (.02)**
Unconditional					
Unweighted					
	τ	−.05 (.04)	−.04 (.04)	−.06 (.05)	−.06 (.05)
	τ'	−.04 (.04)	−.01 (.04)	−.04 (.05)	−.00 (.05)
	β	.01 (.01)	.03 (.01)*	.03 (.02)†	.08 (.02)**
	$\alpha \times \beta$	−.01 (.02)	−.03 (.02)	−.03 (.02)	−.07 (.03)*
Weighted					
	τ	−.04 (.02)*	−.04 (.02)*	−.04 (.02)*	−.04 (.02)
	τ'	−.04 (.02)*	−.03 (.02)†	−.04 (.03)†	−.01 (.03)
	β	.01 (.01)	.01 (.01)	.01 (.02)	.06 (.02)**
	$\alpha \times \beta$	−.01 (.01)	−.01 (.00)	−.01 (.02)	−.04 (.02)*

Notes: Covariates = grade, race, SES, school type, city, interaction term between city and program group, and baseline Gateway drug use. Conditional model: α for unweighted analyses = −.67(.26)**; weighted = −.50(.14)*** across all years. Unconditional model: α for unweighted analyses = −.88(37)*; weighted = −.59(.20)**. Note that zero values ranged from .002 to .004, rounded to 0. $N = 65$ schools. One-tailed test: † $p \le 0.1$. * $p \le 0.05$. ** $p \le 0.01$. *** $p \le 0.001$.

Mediated Effects of Gateway Drug Use, by Type of Gateway Drug

Table 7.3 shows the results of mediational analyses for each Gateway drug separately, using regression with school as the unit of analysis. Since results were similar regardless of unit, type (regression or SEM),

Table 7.2. *Mediated Prevention Effects on Amphetamine Use (Conditional Logistic Regression, Individual as Unit)*

Parameter	Lifetime Amphetamine Use			
	1992–1993 b (se)	1993–1994 b (se)	1994–1995 b (se)	1992–1995 b (se)
τ	$-.16\,(.11)^\dagger$	$-.13\,(.11)^\dagger$	$-.09\,(.12)$	$-.11\,(.11)$
τ'	$-.01\,(.13)$	$.01\,(.13)$	$.01\,(.14)$	$-.01\,(.12)$
β	$1.07\,(.08)^{***}$	$1.01\,(.08)^{***}$	$1.038\,(.08)^{***}$	$1.02\,(.07)^{***}$
$\alpha \times \beta$	$-.19\,(.12)^\dagger$	$-.18\,(.11)^*$	$-.19\,(.12)^\dagger$	$-.18\,(.11)^\dagger$

Notes: Covariates in the models are grade, race, SES, school type, city site, and baseline drug use. Collapsed amphetamine was defined as any use of amphetamine in any of the last three follow-ups (1992–1995). $\alpha = -.18\,(.11)^*$. $N = 2,208$ individuals. One-tailed test $^\dagger\,p \le .1$. $^*\,p \le 0.05.\ ^{**}\,p \le 0.01.\ ^{***}\,p \le 0.001.$

Table 7.3. *Mediated Prevention Effects on Amphetamine Use by Each Gateway Drug (Conditional Regression Model, School as Unit)*

Parameter	1992–1993 b (se)	1993–1994 b (se)	1994–1995 b (se)	1992–1995 b (se)
Cigarette use				
τ	$-.02\,(.03)$	$-.00\,(.03)$	$-.02\,(.03)$	$-.02\,(.05)$
τ'	$-.02\,(.02)$	$.00\,(.03)$	$-.01\,(.03)$	$-.01\,(.04)$
β	$.08\,(.02)^{***}$	$.07\,(.02)^{***}$	$.08\,(.02)^{***}$	$.05\,(.02)^{***}$
$\alpha \times \beta$	$-.05\,(.02)^*$	$-.04\,(.02)^*$	$-.05\,(.02)^*$	$-.05\,(.02)^*$
Alcohol use				
τ	$-.02\,(.03)$	$-.00\,(.02)$	$-.02\,(.03)$	$-.02\,(.05)$
τ'	$-.02\,(.03)$	$-.00\,(.03)$	$-.02\,(.03)$	$-.02\,(.04)$
β	$.03\,(.01)^*$	$.50\,(.02)^{**}$	$.07\,(.02)^{**}$	$.05\,(.02)^{**}$
$\alpha \times \beta$	$-.01\,(.01)$	$-.02\,(.01)$	$-.02\,(.01)$	$-.02\,(.01)$
Marijuana use				
τ	$-.02\,(.03)$	$-.00\,(.03)$	$-.03\,(.03)$	$-.02\,(.05)$
τ'	$-.02\,(.02)$	$-.00\,(.02)$	$-.02\,(.02)$	$-.00\,(.04)$
α	$-.49\,(.23)^*$	$-.49\,(.23)^*$	$-.49\,(.23)^*$	$-.49\,(.23)^*$
β	$.06\,(.02)^{***}$	$.08\,(.02)^{***}$	$.08\,(.02)^{***}$	$.06\,(.01)^{***}$
$\alpha \times \beta$	$-.03\,(.02)^\dagger$	$-.04\,(.02)^*$	$-.04\,(.02)^*$	$-.03\,(.02)^\dagger$

Notes: $N = 65$ schools. School was the unit of analysis. Effects were adjusted for grade, race, socioeconomic status, school type, city type, and baseline drug use. The number of subjects in each school was used as a weight in the regression analyses. Collapsed amphetamine was defined as any use of amphetamine in any of the last three follow-ups (1992–1995), α for cigarette use $= -59(.23)^{**}$, alcohol use $= -.49\,(.23)^*$, marjuana use $= -.03\,(.24)$. $^\dagger\,p < .10$. $^*\,p < .05.\ ^{**}\,p < .01.\ ^{***}\,p < .001.$

or weighting, only one table of results is presented here. On the basis of previous studies showing that the earliest and largest program effects were obtained on cigarette use, followed by later effects on marijuana use and/or smaller effects on alcohol use (Botvin et al., 1995; Pentz et al., 1989; Schinke et al., 1992), the strength of mediational effects of use of each type of Gateway drug was hypothesized to vary accordingly. The hypothesis was only partially supported. First, although the relationship between early Gateway drug use and later amphetamine use (β) was slightly stronger for cigarettes and marijuana than for alcohol in some years of follow-up, the differences were not significant. Second, however, a significant mediational effect appeared earliest (1992) and strongest for cigarettes, followed by a later, slightly lesser effect for marijuana. The mediational effect of alcohol use was in the expected direction but was only marginally significant.

Conclusion

Overall, the different models used to estimate the mediational effects of preventing Gateway drug use on later prevention of amphetamine use yielded similar results. Results did not differ substantially by type of regression analysis (conditional or unconditional), unit of analysis (school or individual), or school sample size (weighted or unweighted). On average, the proportion of effect on amphetamine use mediated by earlier program effects on Gateway drug use was 67% (calculated as $\alpha \times \beta/(\alpha \times \beta + \tau')$). The small magnitude of τ' in all of the mediational analysis models is further suggestion that most of the program effect on amphetamine use is mediated by earlier program effects on Gateway drug use.

The difference in mediational effect obtained when the conditional versus unconditional regression model is used is somewhat problematic. There is currently no one accepted method of reporting drug abuse prevention trial results, and studies have varied in their use and reporting of conditional or unconditional analysis models (e.g., Botvin et al., 1995; Johnson et al., 1990; Pentz et al., 1989; Perry et al., 1992). The smaller R's obtained with the unconditional models and the lack of significant group differences at baseline, however, suggest that the conditional model, with adjustment for baseline use, may be the more appropriate model for analysis for this data set and for randomized prevention trials in general that have no or negligible baseline differences between groups.

Three study limitations should be noted. First, the survey was limited to measurement of lifetime prevalence of amphetamine use, since the major focus of the study had been on Gateway drug use rather than use of other illicit drugs. Thus, it is not possible to confirm the mediational effect of Gateway drug use on more frequent or heavier amphetamine use rates. Furthermore, the Gateway drug use variables used in these analyses represented heavy regular use rather than occasional use because of the assumption that regular Gateway drug use would have a more proximal (and therefore more predictive) relationship to the development of use of more illicit substances such as amphetamines. Direct and mediational effects might be different if other measures of Gateway drug use were included in the models. Second, the potential mediational effects of other variables were not considered, for example, changes in perceived social norms and peer pressure resistance skills, both of which were targeted in the original prevention program and thus are considered program mediators. Third, data from the two cities were collapsed to increase power for mediational analyses. Even though city was included as a covariate in analyses, there could be potential differences between the two cities that could have affected mediational relationships in ways not controlled for in the present analyses.

In summary, the results reported in this chapter support the Gateway drug use theory applied to prevention; That is, an early change in Gateway drug use produced by a prevention program can mediate effects on later amphetamine use. However, the difference in significance and magnitude of the mediational effect obtained when a conditional versus unconditional regression model is used to estimate effects suggests that researchers should routinely compare the results from multiple methods of analysis before concluding whether a mediational effect has occurred.

References

Bardo, M. T., Donohew, R. L., & Harrington, N. G. (1996). Psychobiology of novelty seeking and drug seeking behavior. *Behavioural Brain Research*, *77*(1–2), 23–43.

Bentler, P. M. (1989). *EQS structural equations program manual*. Los Angeles: BMDP Statistical Software.

Botvin, G. J., Baker, E., Dusenbury, L., Botvin, E. M., & Diaz, T. (1995). Long-term follow-up results of a randomized drug abuse prevention trial in a white middle-class population. *Journal of the American Medical Association*, *273*, 1106–1112.

Bryk, A. S., & Raudenbush, S. W. (1992). *Hierarchical linear models in social and behavioral research: Applications and data analysis methods.* Newbury Park, CA: Sage.

Cheadle, A., Pearson, D., Wagner, E., Psaty, B. M., Diehr, P., & Koepsell, T. (1995). A community-based approach to preventing alcohol use among adolescents on an American Indian reservation. *Public Health Reports,* 110(4), 439–447.

Chou, C.-P., Montgomery, S. B., Pentz, M. A., Rohrbach, L. A., Johnson, C. A., Flay, B. R., & MacKinnon, D. (1998). Effects of a community-based prevention program on decreasing drug use in high risk adolescents. *American Journal of Public Health, 88*(6), 944–948.

Clayton, R. R., Voss, H. L., & LoSciuto, L. A. (1988). Gateway drugs: What are the stages people go through in becoming drug abusers. *Pharmacy Times, 53,* 28–35.

DeWit, D. J., Offord, D. R., & Wong, M. (1997). Patterns of onset and cessation of drug use over the early part of the life course. *Health Education and Behavior, 24*(6), 746–758.

Donaldson, S. I., Graham, J. W., & Hansen, W. B. (1994). Testing the generalizability of intervening mechanism theories: Understanding the effects of adolescent drug use prevention interventions. *Journal of Behavioral Medicine, 17*(2), 195–216.

Dwyer, J. H., & Feinleib, M. (1992). Introduction to statistical models for longitudinal studies of health. In J. H. Dwyer, M. Feinleib, P. Lippert, & H. Hoffmeister (Eds.), *Statistical models for longitudinal studies of health.* New York: Oxford University Press.

Dwyer, J. H., MacKinnon, D. M., Pentz, M. A., Flay, B. R., Hansen, W. B., Wang, E.Y.I., & Johnson, C. A. (1989). Estimating intervention effects in longitudinal studies. *American Journal of Epidemiology, 130,* 781–795.

Johnson, C. A., Pentz, M. A., Weber, M. D., Dwyer, MacKinnon, D. P., Flay, B. R., Baer, N. A., & Hansen, W. B. (1990). The relative effectiveness of comprehensive community programming for drug abuse prevention with risk and low risk adolescents. *Journal of Consulting and Clinical Psychology, 58,* 447–456.

Johnston, L., O'Malley, P. M., & Bachman, J. G. (1999). National survey results on drug use from the monitoring the future study, 1975–1998. Vol. 1. Secondary school students. *NIH Publication No. 99-4660.* Rockville, MD: National Institute on Drug Abuse.

Kandel, D. B., Yamaguchi, K., & Chen, K. (1992). Stages of progression in drug involvement from adolescence to adulthood: Further evidence for the gateway theory. *Journal of Studies on Alcohol, 53*(5), 447–457.

Li, C., Pentz, M. A., Chou, C.-P., & Dwyer, J. H. A comparison of multilevel and structural equation models for estimating mediational effects of drug abuse prevention programs. Submitted for publication.

Lindsay, G. B., & Rainey, J. (1997). Psychosocial and pharmacologic explanations of nicotine's "gateway drug" function. *Journal of School Health, 67*(4), 123–126.

MacKinnon, D. P. (1994). Analysis of mediating variables in prevention and intervention research. *NIDA Research Monograph, 139*, 127–153.

MacKinnon, D. P., Dwyer, J. H. Mediation effects in prevention studies. *Evaluation Review*, under review.

MacKinnon, D. P., Johnson, C. A., Pentz, M. A., Dwyer, J. H., Hansen, W. B., Flay, B. R., & Wang, E.Y.I. (1991). Mediating mechanism in a school-based drug prevention program: First-year effects of the Midwestern Prevention Project. *Health Psychology, 10*(3), 164–172.

Marcos, A. C., & Bahr, S. J. (1995). Drug progression model: A social control test. *International Journal of the Addictions, 30*, 1383–1405.

Muthen, B. (1984). A general structural equation model with dichotomous, ordered categorical, and continuous latent variable indicators. *Psychometrika, 49*, 115–132.

Pentz, M. A. (1994). Adaptive evaluation strategies for estimating effects of community-based drug abuse prevention programs. *Journal of Community Psychology*, CSAP Special Issue, 26–51.

Pentz, M. A., Chou, C.-P. (1994). Measurement invariance in longitudinal clinical research assuming change from development and intervention. *Journal of Consulting and Clinical Psychology, 62*(3), 450–462.

Pentz, M. A., Dwyer, J. H., MacKinnon, D. P., Flay, B. R., Hansen, W. B., Wang, E.Y.I., & Johnson, C. A. (1989). A multi-community trial for primary prevention of adolescent drug abuse: Effects on drug use prevalence. *JAMA, 261*(22), 3259–3266.

Pentz, M. A., Li, C., Dwyer, J., Chou, C.-P., MacKinnon, D. P., Flay, B. R., Hansen, W. B., & Johnson, C. A. *Long-term effects of a multi-component community-based prevention program on adolescent and young adult amphetamine use.* Unpublished manuscript.

Perry, C. L., Kelder, S. H., Murray, D. M., & Klepp, K. I. (1992). Community-wide smoking prevention: Long-term outcomes of the Minnesota Heart Health Program and the Class of 1989 Study. *American Journal of Public Health, 82*(9), 1210–1216.

Perry, C. L., Williams, C. L., Veblen-Mortenson, S., Toomey, T. L., Komro, K. A., Anstine, P. S., McGovern, P. G., Finnegan, J. R., Forster, J. L., Wagenaar, A. C., et al. (1996). Project Northland: Outcomes of a community wide alcohol use prevention program during early adolescence. *American Journal of Public Health, 86*(7), 956–965.

SAS Institute (2000). SAS/C Online DOC™, Release 8.1. Cary, NC: SAS Institute Inc.

Schinke, S. P., Orlandi, M. A., & Cole, K. C. (1992). Boys and girls clubs in public housing development: Prevention services for youth at risk. *Journal of Community Psychology*, Special Issue; Programs for Change: Office for Substance Abuse Prevention demonstration models, 118–128.

Tobler, N. S., & Stratton, H. H. (1997). Effectiveness of school-based drug prevention programs: A meta-analysis of the research. *Journal of Primary Prevention*, *18*(1), 71–128.

Torabi, M. R., Baily, W. J., & Majd-Jabbari, M. (1993). Cigarette smoking as a predictor of alcohol and other drug use by children and adolescents: Evidence of the "gateway drug effect." *Journal of School Health*, *63*, 302–306.

Yamaguchi, K., & Kandel, D. B. (1984). Patterns of durg use from adolescence to young adulthood. III. Predictors of progression. *American Journal of Public Health*, *74*, 673–681.

8

Intervention Effects on Adolescent Drug Use and Critical Influences on the Development of Problem Behavior

Anthony Biglan and Keith Smolkowski

At least three different paradigmatic frameworks that guide behavioral science research (Biglan, 1995a, 1995b; Biglan & Hayes, 1996; Hayes, Hayes, & Reese, 1988) can be identified. Each is entirely defensible as an intellectual enterprise, yet each may not contribute equally to our ability to prevent or ameliorate problems of human behavior.

The most common framework guiding behavioral science research might be called *mechanism*, since it derives from the intellectual traditions of the physical sciences in which phenomena are conceived of as machinelike (Pepper, 1942). The key feature of this approach is the analysis of the phenomenon of interest into parts and the interrelationships of its parts. The validity of an analysis within this framework is judged by the degree to which a model of the parts and their interrelationships is confirmed by analyses of multiple samples of data. This validity or truth criterion has been labeled *predictive verification*. Because one can always construct a model for a given data set that perfectly fits that data set, there is a premium in this approach on showing that models are generalizable across a wide variety of samples.

A second, and somewhat less common framework has been labeled *contextualism* (Pepper, 1942). This approach derives from the American pragmatist philosophy. According to this approach, an analysis is said to be valid to the extent that it allows the analyst to achieve a stated goal. Because different analysts can have different goals, one can find quite a variety of contextualist approaches (Hayes, Hayes, Sarbin, & Reese, 1993).

Support for this chapter was provided by Grant CA 38273 from the National Cancer Institute and Grant DA09306 from the National Institute on Drug Abuse.

158

One goal that has organized a significant amount of behavioral science research and has contributed to our ability to solve human problems is the *prediction and influence of behavior.* This is the framework that has guided behavior analysis, cultural materialism in anthropology (Harris, 1979), and much of the work in public health and prevention science. The approach has sometimes been called *functional contextualism* because of its focus on identifying the functional relations between behavior and environment (Biglan & Hayes, 1996; Hayes, 1993).

A third paradigm is organicism. This framework has guided most developmental research. Its focus is on the integrated or developed organism, and its emphasis is on examining how phenomena progress through stages toward an integrated whole (Pepper, 1942). The validity of analyses is assessed in terms of their coherence, the degree to which the assembled facts converge to support a given conclusion (Hayes et al., 1988).

It seems to us that much of the research on the Gateway Hypothesis has proceeded within the framework of the mechanistic and organicist approaches to research. The effort has been to identify models of the stages and sequences through which young people move as they become substance users. The identification of structures of sequences of drug initiation is an excellent example of science involving predictive verification.

The work has clarified a great deal about the manner in which young people come to use drugs and has organized much of our thinking in the drug abuse field (Kandel, 1978, 1980, 1982, 1992; Kandel, Kessler, & Margulies, 1978; Kandel, Simcha-Fagan, & Davies, 1986; Kandel & Yamaguchi, 1985, 1993; Kandel, Yamaguchi, & Chen, 1992). However, if this line of work is going to make further advances, some of the ideas from the functional contextualist approach to research may be needed. Specifically, we would argue that Gateway Hypothesis research will move forward to the extent that it focuses on the variables that predict and influence the transitions through drug-using stages.

The strongest test of whether one variable influences another involves the experimental manipulation of the presumed influence and examination of the effect of the manipulation on the dependent variable. As noted in Chapter 1 of this volume, experimental evaluations of the effect of preventing the use of one substance on the use of other substances provide a particularly strong test of the Gateway Hypothesis that the use of one substance influences the subsequent use of other substances. Does, for example, preventing cigarette smoking prevent the use of other, later stage, substances? The present chapter presents data on this issue are from an experimental evaluation of a community intervention that focused on the prevention of cigarette use. Because the intervention focused almost exclusively on preventing young people from smoking cigarettes, it provides a relatively pure test of the question of whether the prevention of smoking could prevent the development of the use of other substances.

Specific Influences on Cigarette Smoking Versus General Influences on Problem Behavior

Examination of whether the prevention of cigarette smoking could prevent the use of other substances requires some discussion of the types of influences on smoking and other problem behaviors. To the extent that the onset of smoking is a function of influences that also affect the use of other substances, it will be impossible to test whether preventing smoking can prevent the use of other substances, since manipulation of these influences will affect both smoking and other substance use. On the other hand, if there are influences that are unique to smoking, they could be manipulated to prevent smoking alone, thus providing a relatively pure test of the Gateway Hypothesis that preventing smoking could prevent the use of other substances.

Figure 8.1 illustrates this issue. The data are from a study of 643 adolescents age 14 to 17 who were assessed at three time points over 18 months (Biglan, Duncan, Ary, & Smolkowski, 1995). Cigarette use at Time 3 could be predicted from two smoking-specific influences as well as two more general influences on youth problem behavior. Both parental smoking and peer smoking at Time 2 predicted the adolescents' smoking at Time 3, and peer smoking had an especially strong relationship. At the same time, variance in Time 3 smoking was also predicted by the adequacy of parental monitoring and by general peer deviance (that is, adolescent-reported peer engagement in deviant behaviors *other than cigarette smoking*).

The analysis suggests that one might prevent cigarette use by modifying cigarette-specific influences such as peer smoking and parental smoking or by modifying general influences on problem behavior. Obviously to test the Gateway Hypothesis, one would want to manipulate only specific influences. Although the Biglan et al. (1995) study identified only two specific influences, we can conceive of a number of others, such as parental communications to their children about not

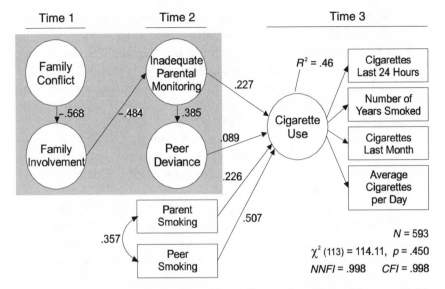

Figure 8.1. General and specific predictors of smoking, adolescents 14–17 years old (Biglan et al., 1995).

smoking, peer communications that oppose smoking, and a reduction in the availability of cigarettes (e.g., Forster et al., 1998).

Does a Tobacco Prevention Intervention Focused on Tobacco-Specific Influences Prevent the Use of Other Substances?

We evaluated the effects of a smoking prevention intervention that targeted influences that were likely to affect only smoking. This provides a relatively clean experimental test of the Gateway Hypothesis. The study is also of general significance for public health prevention efforts, since if preventing tobacco use reduced the initiation of other substances, it would point to an additional reason for preventing tobacco use.

A randomized controlled trial of a community intervention to prevent tobacco use, Project SixTeen, compared the effects of a comprehensive community intervention to prevent tobacco use with those of a school-based program alone. The school-based program involved the provision of a classroom-based prevention curriculum for grades 6 through 12 (Biglan, James, LaChance, Zoref, & Joffe, 1988) that taught about the social influences to use tobacco and other substances and provided young people with skills for resisting these social influences. Eight small Oregon communities were assigned at random to receive the school-based program, and eight matched communities were assigned to receive the school-based program plus the community intervention. The community intervention, which targeted young people in grades 6 through 12, included media advocacy (such as newsletters, newspaper stories, and presentations to community groups) related to the importance of preventing adolescent tobacco use, youth antitobacco activities, a family communications program designed to persuade parents to encourage their children not to smoke (Biglan et al., 1996), and a program to reduce illegal sales of tobacco to young people (Biglan et al., 1995; Biglan et al., 1996). This intervention was conducted over a 2½-year period.

Our primary assessment of the prevalence of tobacco and other substance use was based on annual assessments of seventh- and ninth-grade students in each community. A detailed description of the results of this assessment is presented in Biglan, Ary, Smolkowski, Duncan, and Black (2000). One year after the initiation of the interventions (Time 2) the community intervention communities had a significantly lower prevalence of smoking in the week prior to assessment than the school-based-only communities ($t[14] = 2.57$, $p = .022$). The effect size was $d = 1.18$ standard deviations. Similarly, there was a significant difference in conditions 1 year after the completion of the intervention (Time 5; $t[14] = 2.29$, $p = .038$; $d = 1.03$). The effect approached significance at Time 4 just after the intervention ended ($t[14] = 1.91$, $p = .077$, $d = .81$). In addition, after the first year of intervention, Time 2 smokeless tobacco use among ninth-grade boys was significantly lower in communities that received the community intervention ($t[14]) = 2.50$, $p = .026$, $d = 1.15$).

The intervention was successful to some extent in preventing adolescent smoking and smokeless tobacco use. It therefore provides an opportunity to examine whether preventing tobacco use per se has an impact on the use of other substances. We found two effects that suggested that this was the case. First, for ninth-grade students, there was a significant difference in the slope of the prevalence of alcohol use across the 5 years of assessment ($t(14) = 3.77$, $p = .002$, $d = 1.82$). The result is illustrated in Figure 8.2. In community intervention communities the slope was approximately zero, indicating no change in prevalence over the five years of assessment. However, in school-based-only communities the prevalence of alcohol use increased significantly over this period.

Second, there was an effect on the quadratic parameter for the prevalence of marijuana use in the prior week ($t[14]) = 2.22$, $p = .043$) over the 5 years of assessment. The curve for school-based-only communities was

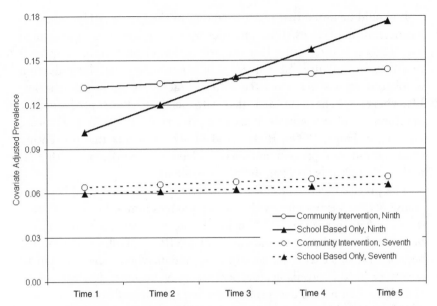

Figure 8.2. Adolescent weekly alcohol prevalence by grade adjusted for covariates (Project SixTeen, seventh and ninth graders from Biglan et al., 2000).

concave up, indicating that use was accelerating over the 5-year period. In community intervention communities the curve was concave down, indicating that the rate of increase slowed over the 5-year period. The prevalence of marijuana use in the last week was lower in community intervention communities than in school-based-only communities; the rates were identical by Time 3; by Time 5 the prevalence in community intervention communities (6.7%) was lower than in school-based-only communites (8.5%). There was no evidence that the intervention affected adolescent-reported antisocial behavior.

These results are consistent with the Gateway Hypothesis in that the prevention of smoking was associated with effects on alcohol and marijuana use; in some way the intervention prevented alcohol and marijuana use. We cannot entirely discount the possibility that our efforts to promote community activities to prevent smoking also had an effect on communications about not using other substances. That undoubtedly happened to some extent. However, it may also be the case that when we prevented young people from smoking that effect made it less likely that they would experiment with alcohol or marijuana.

It should be noted that in other studies of the Gateway Hypothesis it has been difficult to establish an order between tobacco use and alcohol use. Thus it is interesting that the prevention of tobacco use appeared to affect alcohol use. Moreover, it is noteworthy that the reduction in tobacco use was *not* associated with a reduction in antisocial behavior. Elsewhere, we have argued that antisocial behavior precedes the development of any substance use (e.g., Ary et al., 1999a; Ary, Duncan, Duncan, & Hops, 1999b; Biglan et al., 1997). The fact that preventing smoking did not prevent antisocial behavior is consistent with that notion, though it is far from definitive evidence.

The precise mechanism for these effects is unclear. It could be that a young person's experience with cigarettes makes him or her less hesitant to try other substances. This could be because smoking increases a person's susceptibility to the reinforcing effects of other substances, because smokers encounter social environments where other substances are more readily available, or because they become desensitized to violating social norms that prohibit the use of other substances.

It is impossible to say, however, which, if any, of these mechanisms might be involved. One type of experiment might clarify whether it is the prevention of smoking per se or the communication of generalized antisubstance use norms that influences the use of other substances. It would be possible to prevent adolescent tobacco use by focusing only on stopping the illegal sales of tobacco to minors (Forster et al., 1998). Such an intervention would not involve direct communications to young people about not using tobacco. Alternatively, one could prevent adolescent tobacco use through a media campaign (e.g., Flynn et al., 1992). One could then compare these interventions to see whether they differed in the attendant reduction in alcohol or marijuana use.

Predictors of the Initiation of Adolescent Smoking

The Project SixTeen data set also provided an opportunity to examine factors associated with the initiation of smoking. In keeping with the Gateway Hypothesis, we examined the extent to which smoking was more likely when the adolescent was also using alcohol. We also assessed whether engagement in antisocial behavior was associated with smoking, since Jessor and Jessor's work (Jessor & Jessor, 1977a, 1997b) and our own work (described later) suggest that antisocial behavior cooccurs with the use of substances. Our measure of antisocial behavior consisted of the adolescent's self-report on six acts: lying to parents, staying out all night, hitting someone, skipping school, stealing, and vandalism.

In addition, given our contextualist focus on manipulable environmental variables that affect youth problem behavior, we tested whether family and peer variables influenced youth smoking. There is extensive evidence that parents who have frequent conflicts with their children have few positive interactions with them. These interactive patterns are associated with higher rates of aggressive and disruptive behavior (Patterson, 1982; Patterson, Reid, & Dishion, 1992). High conflict discourages parents' attempts to monitor what their children are doing, and inadequate parental monitoring has been shown in numerous studies to influence associations with deviant peers and the development of youth problem behavior (Biglan, 1995a). At the same time, the young person's pattern of aggressive and uncooperative behavior leads him or her to fail academically, be rejected by nondeviant peers, and develop friendships with deviant peers (e.g., Patterson, Debaryshe, & Ramsey, 1989). These deviant peer contacts are believed to increase the likelihood of smoking. This general model is displayed in Figure 8.1, discussed earlier.

For family influences, we looked at three factors: the quality of parent–child interactions, family supportiveness, and parental monitoring. There were nine items involving parent–child interactions; five concerned conflict between parents and children (e.g., "At least once a day we get angry at each other"), and the other four involved positive interactions (e.g., "I enjoy the talks we have"). Five of the items were from the conflict scale of the Family Environment Scale (Moos, 1974), four from the cohesion scale of that instrument. Young people reported on parental monitoring in four items: "Before I go out, I tell my parents when I will be back"; "My parents let me go any place I please without asking"; "I get to do things on weekends without telling my parents exactly where I am"; and "My parents know what I'm doing when I'm away from home." In addition, to assess family supportiveness we used eight items from the Moos (1974) Family Environment Scale (FES), on which lower scores imply greater supportiveness. The peer variable was perceived friends' smoking as reported by the youth; higher scores were associated with more friends' smoking. (These scales ranged from 1 to 5.)

We chose logistic regression as our method of analysis for two reasons. First, we were trying to predict a dichotomous variable, the onset of smoking. Second, in previous work we had used structural equation modeling to investigate these relationships by using continuous measures

Table 8.1. *Significant Predictors of Seventh-Grade Smoking* (N = *1,741*)

		95% Confidence Interval	
Variable[a]	Odds Ratio	Lower	Upper
Perceived friends' smoking	15.78	9.72	25.61
Alcohol in last month	6.52	4.31	9.86
Inadequate monitoring	1.37	1.05	1.77
Parent–child interactions	1.60	1.23	2.10

Note: [a] For inadequate monitoring and parent–child interactions continuous variables range from 1 to 5; odds ratios represent odds per unit change.

of one or more youth behaviors (e.g., Ary et al., 1999a; Ary et al., 1999b; Biglan et al., 1997; Duncan, Duncan, Biglan, & Ary, 1998). Results from one of these studies (Biglan et al., 1995) are presented in Figure 8.1. An analysis using logistic regression allowed us to test the robustness of our findings across statistical methods. Step–down analyses were conducted, and only significant predictors were retained in the models.

We began by examining concurrent factors associated with seventh-grade student's smoking in the prior month. Data were available from 1,741 students. The predictors were antisocial behavior, alcohol use in the past month, parental monitoring, parent–child interactions, supportive family interactions, and friends' smoking. Table 8.1 presents only the variables that significantly predicted smoking in the prior month. Not surprisingly, young people are nearly 16 times more likely to report smoking if their current friends are smoking. Smoking is a social activity at this age (Friedman, Lichtenstein, & Biglan, 1985). Consistent with the problem behavior hypothesis (Jessor & Jessor, 1977a; Donovan, Jessor, & Costa, 1988), seventh graders are more than six times as likely to report smoking if they used alcohol in the last month. Seventh graders were 1.4 times as likely to smoke *per unit change* in inadequate monitoring and 1.6 times as likely to smoke *per unit change* in parent–child interactions.

We next examined whether parenting factors showed an indirect relationship to smoking, through their influence on the variables that predicted smoking. We examined whether parental monitoring, negative parent–child interactions, and family support predicted alcohol use and perceived friends' smoking. As shown in Tables 8.2 and 8.3, inadequate monitoring and the quality of parent–child interaction significantly predicted both alcohol use and associations with peers who smoked.

Table 8.2. *Significant Predictors of Seventh-Grade Alcohol Use* (N = *1,851*)

Variable[a]	Odds Ratio	95% Confidence Interval	
		Lower	Upper
Inadequate monitoring	2.12	1.80	2.49
Parent–child interactions	1.54	1.24	1.91

Note: [a] For each variable continuous variables range from 1 to 5; odds ratios represent odds per unit change.

Table 8.3. *Significant Predictors of Perceived Friends' Smoking in Seventh Grade* (N = *1,866*)

Variable[a]	Odds Ratio	95% Confidence Interval	
		Lower	Upper
Inadequate monitoring	1.86	1.61	2.15
Parent–child interactions	1.84	1.58	2.14

Note: [a] For each variable continuous variables range from 1 to 5; odds ratios represent odds per unit change.

Antisocial behavior was not a significant predictor of smoking, when the parenting practice measures were included in the analysis. It was a significant predictor of smoking (odds ratio [OR] = 2.98, confidence internal [CI] = 1.63 to 5.44) when parenting measures were not included. This suggests that one way inadequate monitoring and negative parent–child interactions influence smoking is by making antisocial behavior more likely. We should therefore expect strong relationships between parenting practices and antisocial behavior, and indeed we find them. As shown in Table 8.4, inadequate monitoring, negative parent–child interactions, and low levels of family support all were associated with a greater likelihood of antisocial behavior.

We next examined the predictors of ninth-grade smoking among seventh grade students who *did not* report smoking in seventh grade. Data were available on 918 students. Although our primary interest was in the longitudinal prediction of smoking onset, we included concurrent variables as predictors in order to assess whether seventh-grade variables predicted ninth-grade smoking after controlling for the ninth-grade value on these variables. The following predictors from ninth grade were included in this analysis: antisocial behavior, alcohol use, perceived friends' smoking,

Table 8.4. *Significant Predictors of Seventh-Grade Antisocial Behavior* (N = *1,945*)

Variable[a]	Odds Ratio	95% Confidence Interval	
		Lower	Upper
Inadequate monitoring	3.80	2.85	5.08
Parent–child interactions	2.08	1.45	3.00
Family support	2.01	1.34	3.01

Note: [a] For each variable continuous variables range from 1 to 5; odds ratios represent odds per unit change.

Table 8.5. *Significant Predictors of Ninth-Grade Smoking for Seventh-Grade Nonsmokers* (N = *918*)

Variable	Odds Ratio	95% Confidence Interval	
		Lower	Upper
Ninth-grade friends' smoking	11.18	6.48	19.29
Alcohol in last month	4.94	3.15	7.76
Current antisocial behavior	3.54	1.77	7.08
Inadequate monitoring in *seventh grade*[a]	1.41	1.04	1.90

Note: [a] Continuous variables range from 1 to 5; odds ratios represent odds per unit change.

parental monitoring, parent–child interactions, and family support. The seventh-grade predictors were perceived friends' smoking, parental monitoring, parent–child interactions, and family support. Table 8.5 presents only the variables that significantly predicted whether or not a ninth grader reported smoking in the month prior to the assessment. Seventh-grade nonsmokers were about 11 times more likely to be smokers in ninth grade if their friends in ninth grade were smokers. They were more than 4 times more likely to smoke if they had used alcohol in the past month. They were 3.5 times more likely to smoke if they were engaging in antisocial behavior. They were 1.4 times as likely to smoke *per unit change* in inadequate monitoring in seventh grade. Note that this result occurred even though ninth-grade monitoring was included in the equation. The influence of parental monitoring in seventh grade can still be seen 2 years later.

Predictors of ninth-grade alcohol use were then analyzed for students who were not smoking in seventh grade (Table 8.6). We included parental monitoring, parent–child interactions, and family support at

Table 8.6. *Significant Predictors of Ninth-Grade Alcohol Use for Seventh- Grade Nonsmokers* (N = 926)

		95% Confidence Interval	
Variable[a]	Odds Ratio	Lower	Upper
Current inadequate monitoring	1.61	1.32	1.97
Current parent–child interactions	1.56	1.17	2.07
Alcohol use in *seventh grade*	8.58	4.58	16.07

Note: [a] For the variables current, inadequate monitoring and current parent–child interactions continuous variables range from 1 to 5; odds ratios represent odds per unit change.

Table 8.7. *Significant Predictors of Having Ninth-Grade Friends Who Smoke for Seventh-Grade Nonsmokers* (N = 965)

		95% Confidence Interval	
Variable[a]	Odds Ratio	Lower	Upper
Current inadequate monitoring	1.26	1.05	1.50
Current parent–child interactions	1.43	1.12	1.82
Current family support	1.43	1.11	1.84
Friends' smoking in *seventh grade*	2.34	1.54	3.55

Note: [a] For the variables current inadequate monitoring, current parent–child interactions, and current family support continuous variables range from 1 to 5; odds ratios represent odds per unit change.

both ninth grade and seventh grade as well as alcohol use in seventh grade. We found that ninth graders were more likely to be using alcohol if they were inadequately monitored, and if they had conflict with their parents in the ninth grade. Their alcohol use in seventh grade made it 8.6 times more likely that they would be using alcohol in ninth grade.

The predictors tested in the analysis of having friends who smoked were parental monitoring, parent–child interactions, and family support at both ninth and seventh grades and friends smoking at seventh grade. Ninth graders who had not smoked in seventh grade were significantly more likely to report having current friends who smoked if they were inadequately monitored, had negative interactions with their parents, or had low levels of family support. When these concurrent parenting variables were included (Table 8.7), seventh-grade parenting did not add anything to the prediction of ninth-grade smoking. However, ninth

Table 8.8. *Significant Predictors of Ninth-Grade Antisocial Behavior for Seventh-Grade Nonsmokers* (N = 997)

Variable[a]	Odds Ratio	95% Confidence Interval	
		Lower	Upper
Current inadequate monitoring	2.51	1.76	3.57
Current parent–child interactions	1.85	1.17	2.91
Current family support	2.22	1.33	3.70
Inadequate monitoring in *seventh grade*	1.68	1.13	2.48

Note: [a] For each variable continuous variables range from 1 to 5; odds ratios represent odds per unit change.

graders were 2.3 times more likely to have friends who smoked in ninth grade if they had had friends who smoked in seventh grade.

There were four significant predictors of self-reported antisocial behavior among these ninth graders (Table 8.8). Inadequate monitoring, the quality of parent–child interactions, and low family support in ninth grade all predicted engagement in antisocial behavior. Even after these ninth-grade variables had been controlled, inadequate monitoring in seventh grade predicted ninth-grade antisocial behavior.

Conclusion

The results of the concurrent and longitudinal analyses are quite consistent. Smoking is more likely among young people who use alcohol and engage in antisocial behavior. However, given that the relationships between smoking and alcohol use and antisocial behavior are only concurrent and that alcohol use and antisocial behavior in seventh grade do not predict smoking in ninth grade, the findings provide only weak support for the Gateway Hypothesis. Considering the 2-year time span between assessments and the fact that smoking often precedes alcohol use, the failure to find longitudinal support for the Gateway Hypothesis is not surprising. The findings are also consistent with problem behavior theory (Jessor & Jessor, 1977a, 1977b) in showing that different types of problem behavior are interrelated. We elaborate on this issue later.

The results also provide information about potentially manipulable social influences on the transition to the use of cigarettes and alcohol. First, they confirm the often replicated finding that adolescent smoking behavior is strongly associated with friends' smoking (U.S. Department of Health and Human Services, 1994). This association has been shown to be a function of both assortative friendship formation and the influence of friends (Kandel, 1978). Assortative friendship formation undoubtedly accounts for some of the concurrent relationship between perceived friends' smoking and the adolescent's smoking. However, seventh-grade friendship with smokers doubles the likelihood that a student will have smoking friends in the ninth grade and ninth-grade friendships with smokers make it 11 times more likely, that the student will begin smoking, suggesting that peers have a substantial influence on young people's initiation of smoking.

Second, the results show the influence of parenting practices on the development of adolescent problem behavior. Inadequate monitoring when young people were in seventh grade predicted concurrent smoking as well as initiation of smoking by ninth grade among seventh-grade nonsmokers. Moreover, inadequate monitoring was a significant predictor of friendships with smokers and of alcohol use and antisocial behavior. Inadequate monitoring in seventh grade predicted greater antisocial behavior in ninth grade, even after ninth-grade monitoring was controlled. When parents and seventh-grade children were having a lot of conflict and few positive interactions the children were more likely to report smoking. Moreover, this pattern of interactions predicted association with smoking peers, alcohol use, and antisocial behavior.

Parents who have high levels of conflict with their children run a greater risk of having children who engage in diverse problem behaviors. Evidence from other studies (e.g., Patterson, Dishion, & Bank, 1984) suggests two reasons why parent–child conflict is related to youth problems. Conflict is probably in part a function of the adolescent's own coercive repertoire. That repertoire also makes it more likely that coercive adolescents will do poorly in school, be rejected by their peers, and drift into deviant peer groups (Patterson et al., 1989). In addition, parent–child conflict probably involves attempts by parents to influence their children, which result in arguments. The arguments imply that the parents are not very successful in their influence attempts and are punished for attempting to set limits on their children's behavior.

Is There a Common Set of Social Influences That Affect the Development of Diverse Problem Behaviors?

The focus of the Gateway Hypothesis is on the influence of the use of one substance on the subsequent use of other substances. The great contribution of this work has been a clear delineation of ordered sequences in the initiation of drugs that points to the importance of preventing the use of cigarettes and alcohol for preventing the development of the abuse of other drugs. As work proceeds on the Gateway Hypothesis we may clarify why it is that the use of cigarettes and alcohol appears to potentiate the use of marijuana and other drugs. As noted both biological and social factors may underlie these relationships.

Although we think that the fine-grained analyses of substance use stages that characterize work on the Gateway Hypothesis are of great importance, there is another line of analysis that, in a sense, runs in the opposite direction yet complements work on the Gateway Hypothesis. In addition to examining the sequencing of the use of different substances, one can analyze young people's general tendency to engage in diverse problems as Jessor and have Jessor (Jessor & Jessor, 1977a, 1977b) and can examine whether there are social influences that make diverse problem behaviors more likely. To the extent that a common set of social influences on the development of diverse problems can be identified, it may be possible to prevent the entire range of youth problems through concentrating on a small number of common factors. We have done a number of studies taking this perspective and summarize them here.

The Interrelationships Among Problem Behaviors. Since 1985, we have been implementing family-, school-, and community-based prevention experiments in which we obtain repeated measures of diverse problem behaviors from adolescents ranging in age from 11 to 18. In the initial studies we simply examined the extent to which a construct of problem behavior could be modeled. For example, in two recently published studies, we replicated the model shown in Figure 8.3, which includes problem behavior as the final outcome. The complete model examines the role of social influences on problem behavior, as discussed in greater detail later. The data were from a study of smoking cessation done with 608 adolescents who were 14 to 17 years old at the outset and were assessed 1 year and 18 months later (Ary et al., 1999a). One in nine persons was not a smoker. Antisocial behavior, high-risk sexual behavior, academic failure, and an index of substance use that included tobacco, alcohol, and marijuana use were sufficiently intercorrelated to justify creating a problem behavior factor. A model with identical paths and very similar beta weights was obtained by Ary et al. (1999b), when they analyzed 3 years of annual data from 204 adolescents, age 11 to 15 at the outset of the study. The problem behavior construct was replicated in modeling studies that did not include measures of high-risk sexual behavior (Biglan et al., 1997), including one in which it was found that the problem behavior construct consisting of antisocial behavior, academic failure, and substance use held across three ethnic groups (Caucasian, Mexican American, and Indian, $n = 500$ in each group) and both genders (Barrera, Biglan, Ary, & Li, in press).

Covariance at one time point leaves many questions unanswered. One involves the degree to which these behaviors develop together. Duncan, Strycker, and Duncan (1999) found significant correlations between the slope for cigarette use and the slopes for alcohol use ($r = .78$), marijuana use ($r = .71$), and risky sexual behavior ($r = .43$). Alcohol and marijuana use slopes were highly correlated (.95) but were not related to the slope for risky sexual behavior. In studies using Latent Growth Modeling, Duncan and Duncan (1996) found that the slopes of the rates of alcohol, cigarette, and marijuana use converged to form a single slope factor; these behaviors had a common trajectory. Duncan et al. (1998) replicated this finding with a different sample of adolescents. In a notable 1999 study, we replicated the factor with a sample of early adolescents (grades 5 through 7 at the outset) who were assessed quarterly over seven quarters (Metzler, Biglan, Li, & Ary, 1999).

Correlational methods assess the degree to which the *rates* of different behaviors (or changes in rate) are correlated, but they do not give a full picture of the extent of overlap in participation in multiple behaviors, for instance, proportion of substance using young people who are also engaging in antisocial behavior. This is important, because from a public health perspective, we need to know what proportion of young people with one problem have another problem. If the proportions are quite high, we might be able to prevent many problems by targeting a small group of young people. In particular, it may be that the majority of drug abusing adolescents were aggressive in childhood. This implies that we might prevent a lot of drug abuse by identifying and ameliorating aggressive behavior problems.

Social Influences on Problem Behavior. Figure 8.3 shows a basic model of peer and parental influences on adolescent problem behavior, described earlier, that we have replicated with slight variations in four studies (Ary et al., 1999a, 1999b; Biglan et al., 1997), including one in which the paths between parenting constructs and problem behavior were found for both genders and three ethnic groups (Barrera et al., in press). The model is based on the work of Patterson, Reid, and Dishion

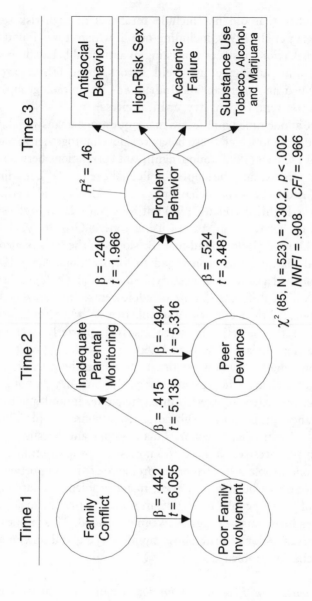

Figure 8.3. Model of social influences on adolescent problem behavior, adolescents 14–17 years old (Ary et al., 1999a).

(e.g., Patterson et al., 1992) at Oregon Social Learning Center (OSLC). As noted, the OSLC group has shown that early aggressive social behavior leads to later delinquency and drug use as a function of a set of parent–child interactions characterized by high levels of coercive behavior. Such patterns of coercive interaction, coupled with low levels of reinforcement for noncoercive means of dealing with conflict, shape up aggressive repertoires that lead to problems in classroom and peer interactions. Coercive response styles in those settings contribute to school failure and peer rejection. In the home, coercive interactions reduce positive family involvement and appear to contribute to parents' doing an inadequate job of monitoring the child and setting limits on out-of-home activities such as associations with deviant peers. By early adolescence highly aggressive children have begun to form deviant peer groups as the result of their rejection by nondeviant peers and their parents' inability to monitor their friendships and guide them away from experimentation with deviant behavior.

A more sophisticated analysis of the social influences on the development of youth substance use and other problem behaviors was provided by Duncan et al. (1998), who examined the predictors of the slope of a construct of substance use. As noted, they established that the slopes for cigarette, marijuana, and alcohol use fit a common factor. They examined how parenting and peer factors were associated with the substance use trajectory factor. Gender was significantly related to slope; males had higher slopes. Perceived peer deviance at Time 1 was *negatively* related to the slope of substance use. The more young people were associating with deviant peers at Time 1, the *lower* the slope of substance use over the subsequent 18 months. This finding is probably due to the fact that young people who had high levels of deviant peers at Time 1 already had high levels of substance use and could not increase their substance use over time. However, increases in parent–child conflict and in association with deviant peers were associated with increasing slopes in substance use over the three time points.

Thus, we consistently find that (a) the use of different substances as well as other problem behaviors are sufficiently intercorrelated to justify the creation of a single construct, (b) these behaviors have a common developmental trajectory, and (c) high levels of parent–child conflict, low levels of family involvement, and inadequate parental monitoring predict increased association with deviant peers and increasing levels of problem behavior. These findings, in conjunction with substantial evidence that interventions that affect parenting practices can reduce aggressive behavior and substance use (Taylor & Biglan 1998; Chamberlain & Moore 1998; Henggeler, Schoenwald, Borduin, Rowland, & Cunningham, 1998), suggest that we have good reason for testing whether the prevalence of diverse problem behaviors can be decreased by an increase in the prevalence of effective parenting practices.

Comparing stage models and problem behavior analyses, Kandel (1989) provided a thoughtful analysis of these two different approaches to the study of the development of youth problem behaviors. She concluded that

> rather than being viewed as two opposed and competing explanations of problem behaviors, the stage and common syndrome perspectives ultimately will need to be reconciled to provide a comprehensive accounting of problem behaviors. (Kandel, 1989: 72)

In Kandel's (1989) view, "... the common syndrome perspective postulates that participation in any one behavior is an opportunistic response to environmental conditions on the part of individuals who share a certain proneness to deviance (p. 70)." Although we think that this is an accurate portrayal of Jessor and Jessor's (1977a) position, we take a somewhat different view. From our contextualist perspective the concept of proneness is problematic because it is not a manipulable variable. This is not to deny that it is possible to characterize individuals in terms of a generalized likelihood of engaging in problem behavior. But even if that is true, it may be more useful to focus on manipulable environmental variables rather than simply to characterize people in terms of their proneness – as though "proneness" were a cause of behavior.

Since our own and others' work on the social environmental influences on problem behavior have consistently identified a set of parenting and peer influences on diverse problem behaviors, the most useful model of the development of problem behavior emphasizes how the social environment makes it more likely that young people will engage in substance use, antisocial behavior, high-risk sexual behavior, and academic failure.

The model is not inconsistent with the notion of stages of drug use or even stages of engagement in diverse problem behaviors (Kandel, 1988). Although most of our studies have not examined stages of substance use, considerable research suggests that oppositional behavior and academic failure precede any substance use as well as more serious delinquent behavior (Patterson et al., 1992) and tobacco use and alcohol use precede marijuana use, which in turn precedes the use of other illicit drugs (e.g., Kandel, 1988). The evidence cited previously indicates that each of these behaviors becomes more likely in the context of high levels of parent–child conflict, low levels of positive family involvement, and, most especially, inadequate parental monitoring. Under these circumstances young people are more likely to be in contact with peers who engage in and reinforce engagement in diverse problem behaviors. To the extent that the development of all youth problem behavior can be characterized by stages (Kandel, 1988), these parenting and peer factors will account for much of the likelihood of transition from one stage to another.

Even if these social influences are common influences on the development of diverse problem behaviors, the question remains why there would be fixed sequences among problem behaviors. One of the most plausible accounts was discussed earlier. Patterson and colleagues (Patterson et al., 1989) argue that a pattern of oppositional and aggressive behavior in early childhood increases the likelihood of both peer rejection and academic failure. Peer rejection and academic failure make association with other rejected and deviant peers more likely, especially when parents have failed to monitor and set limits on their children's peer associations. These unmonitored peer groups form the training ground for substance use experimentation (Dishion, Patterson, & Reid, 1988), increasingly serious forms of delinquency (Patterson et al., 1992), and high-risk sexual behavior (Metzler, Noell, Biglan, Ary, & Smolkowski, 1994). That leaves open the question of why there is a sequencing among the use of different substances. The present volume provides considerable information about the factors that would account for such sequencing.

Do We Know Enough About the Social Influences on Youth Problem Behavior?

Existing evidence provides ample support for at least three conclusions regarding the development of youth problem behavior. First, as evidence presented in this volume shows, the Gateway Hypothesis provides an accurate framework for understanding the sequences in which young people develop substance using behaviors. Second, the evidence presented in this chapter shows clearly that youthful problem behaviors are interrelated. That finding is consistent with a wealth of other evidence, beginning with Jessor and Jessor's original insight (Jessor & Jessor, 1977a; 1977b; Donovan, Jessor, & Costa, 1988; Osgood, Johnston, O'Malley, & Bachman, 1988). Third, it should now be considered well established that coercive family processes and inadequate parental monitoring contribute to adolescents' associations with deviant peers and that associations with deviant peers and inadequate monitoring directly contribute to the development of youth problem behaviors. Further research on these issues will produce diminishing returns, unless we move beyond these basic insights.

The state of our knowledge in the field demands at least two initiatives. First, in keeping with a contextualist orientation (Biglan, 1995a, 1995b) and the developing paradigm in prevention science (Kellam & Rebok, 1992; Coie et al., 1993), the most useful research on the development of youth problem behaviors will involve studies in which purported influences on development are manipulated experimentally. The strongest evidence that a variable does in fact influence development is from experimental manipulations. Such research will be most likely to lead to effective prevention interventions.

Second, research needs to move toward the evaluation of comprehensive interventions to modify the social conditions that produce diverse youth problems. The research reviewed here shows that the same set of social conditions contribute to the development of the *entire range* of youth problem behaviors. Yet most research continues to treat each youth problem separately. Contrary to the reductionist bias of much of the behavioral sciences, research on adolescent problems needs to turn to the question of how we can prevent the development of the entire range of problems. Research on a single problem behavior, or even on the range of substance-using behaviors, ignores considerable evidence that diverse problems stem from the same negative environment. This also means that we need to move beyond the question of what are the influences on problem behavior to the question of how we can modify the family, school, and community conditions that are established influences on problematic development. We need to investigate what have traditionally been the independent variables (e.g., parenting and peer influences) and begin to understand the context that influences them (Biglan, 1995a). We will move toward more effective preventive programs only if we turn to the question of how we can change the social factors that have been shown by overwhelming evidence to be important for youth development.

The wealth of evidence about social influences on youth development has direct implications for public policy. We already know enough to justify calls for the more widespread availability of parenting skills programs (e.g., Taylor & Biglan, 1998), school-based interventions to remediate aggressive and disruptive behavior (Hawkins et al., 1992; Kellam, Rebok, Ialongo, & Mayer, 1994; Walker, 1995), empirically based instructional procedures (Becker, 1986), and school-based prevention programs (Tobler, 1998). We do a disservice to the society that supports us if we do not articulate what we know and work on getting policy-makers and program planners to make use of it.

References

Ary, D. V., Duncan, T. E., Biglan, A., Metzler, C. W., Noell, J. W., & Smolkowski, K. (1999a). Development of adolescent problem behavior. *Journal of Abnormal Child Psychology, 27*, 141–150.

Ary, D. V., Duncan, T. E., Duncan, S. C., & Hops, H. (1999b). Adolescent problem behavior: The influence of parents and peers. *Behaviour Research and Therapy, 37*, 217–230.

Barrera, M., Biglan, A., Ary, D. V., & Li, F. (in press). Modeling family and peer influences on problem behavior of American Indian, Hispanic, and non-Hispanic Caucasian youth.

Becker, W. (1986). *Applied psychology for teachers.* Chicago: Science Research Associates.

Biglan, A. (1995a). *Changing cultural practices: A contextualist framework for intervention research.* Reno, NV: Context Press.

Biglan, A. (1995b). Choosing a paradigm to guide prevention research and practice. *Drugs and Society, 8*, 149–160.

Biglan, A., Ary, D., Koehn, V., Levings, D., Smith, S., Wright, Z., James, L., & Henderson, J. (1996). Mobilizing positive reinforcement in communities to reduce youth access to tobacco. *American Journal of Community Psychology, 24*, 625–638.

Biglan, A., Ary, D. V., Smolkowski, K., Duncan, T. E., & Black, C. (2000). A randomized control trial of a community intervention to prevent adolescent tobacco use. *Tobacco Control, 9*, 24–32.

Biglan, A., Ary, D., Yudelson, H., Duncan, T. E., Hood, D., James, L., Koehn, V., Wright, Z., Black, C., Levings, D., Smith, S., & Gaiser, E. (1996). Experimental evaluation of a modular approach to mobilizing anti-tobacco influences of peers and parents. *American Journal of Community Psychology, 24*, 311–339.

Biglan, A., Duncan, T. E., Ary, D. V., & Smolkowski, K. (1995). Peer and parental influences on adolescent tobacco use. *Journal of Behavioral Medicine, 18*, 315–330.

Biglan, A., Duncan, T. E., Irvine, A. B., Ary, D. V., Smolkowski, K., & James, L. (1997). A drug abuse prevention strategy for rural America. In E. B. Robertson, Z. Sloboda, G. M. Boyd, L. Beatty, & N. Kozel (Eds.), *Rural substance abuse: State of knowledge and issues* (pp. 364–397). Washington, DC: U.S. Department of Health and Human Services.

Biglan, A., & Hayes, S. C. (1996). Should the behavioral sciences become more pragmatic? The case for functional contextualism in research on human behavior. *Applied and Preventive Psychology, 5*, 47–57.

Biglan, A., Henderson, J., Humphreys, D., Yasui, M., Whisman, R., Black, C., & James, L. (1995). Mobilising positive reinforcement to reduce youth access to tobacco. *Tobacco Control, 4*, 42–48.

Biglan, A., James, L. E., LaChance, P., Zoref, L., & Joffe, J. (1988). Videotaped materials in a school-based smoking prevention program. *Preventive Medicine, 17*, 559–584.

Chamberlain, P., & Moore, K. (1998). A clinical model for parenting juvenile offenders: A comparison of group care versus family care. *Clinical Child Psychology and Psychiatry, 3*, 375–386.

Coie, J. D., Watt, N. F., West, S. G., Hawkins, J. D., Asarnow, J. R., Markman, H. J., Ramey, S. L., Shure, M. B., Long, B., Watt, N. F., West, S. G., & Hawkins, J. D. (1993). The science of prevention: A conceptual framework and some directions for a national research program. *American Psychologist, 48*, 1013–1022.

Dishion, T. J., Patterson, G. R., & Reid, J. B. (1988). Parent and peer factors associated with early adolescent drug use: Implications for treatment. In E. Rahdert & J. Grabowski (Eds.), Adolescent drug abuse: Analyses of treatment research Washington, DC: U.S. Department of Health and Human Services.

Donovan, J. E., Jessor, R., & Costa, F. M. (1988). Syndrome of problem behavior in adolescence: A replication. *Journal of Consulting and Clinical Psychology, 56*, 762–765.

Duncan, S. C., & Duncan, T. E. (1996). A multivariate latent growth curve analysis of adolescent substance use. *Structural Equation Modeling, 3*, 323–347.

Duncan, S. C., Duncan, T. E., Biglan, A., & Ary, D. (1998). Contributions of the social context to the development of adolescent substance use: A multivariate latent growth modeling approach. *Drug and Alcohol Dependence, 50*, 57–71.

Duncan, S. C., Strycker, L. A., & Duncan, T. E. (1999). Exploring associations in developmental trends of adolescent substance use and risky sexual behavior in a high-risk population. *Journal of Behavioral Medicine, 22*, 21–34.

Flynn, B. S., Worden, J. K., Secker-Walker, R. H., Badger, G. J., Geller, B. M., & Costanza, M. C. (1992). Prevention of cigarette smoking through mass media intervention and school programs. *American Journal of Public Health, 82*, 827–834.

Forster, J. L., Murray, D. M., Wolfson, M., Blaine, T. M., Wagenaar, A. C., & Hennrikus, D. J. (1998). The effects of community policies to reduce youth access to tobacco. *American Journal of Public Health, 88*, 1193–1198.

Friedman, L. S., Lichtenstein, E., & Biglan, A. (1985). Smoking onset among teens: An empirical analysis of initial situations. *Addictive Behaviors, 10*, 1–13.

Harris, M. (1979). *Cultural materialism: The struggle for a science of culture.* New York: Simon & Schuster.

Hawkins, J. D., Catalano, R. F., Morrison, D. M., O'Donnell, J., Abbott, R. D., & Day, L. E. (1992). The Seattle Social Development Project: Effects of the first four years on protective factors and problem behaviors. *Preventing antisocial behavior: Interventions from birth through adolescence* (pp. 139–161). New York: Guilford Press.

Hayes, S. C. (1993). Goals and the varieties of scientific contextualism. In S. C. Hayes, L. J. Hayes, T. R. Sarbin, & H. W. Reese (Eds.), *The varieties of scientific contextualism* (pp. 11–27). Reno, NV: Context Press.

Hayes, S. C., Hayes, L. J., & Reese, H. W. (1988). Finding the philosophical core: A review of Stephen C. Pepper's *World hypotheses. Journal of the Experimental Analysis of Behavior, 50,* 97–111.

Hayes, S. C., Hayes, L. J., Sarbin, T. R., & Reese, H. M. (1993). *The varieties of scientific contextualism.* Reno, NV: Context Press.

Henggeler, S. W., Schoenwald, S. K., Borduin, C. M., Rowland, M. D., & Cunningham, P. B. (1998). *Multisystemic treatment of antisocial behavior in children and adolescents.* New York: The Guildford Press.

Jessor, R., & Jessor, S. L. (1977a). The conceptual structure of problem-behavior theory. In R. Jessor & S. Jessor (Eds.), *Problem behavior and psychosocial development: A longitudinal study of youth* (pp. 19–67). New York: Academic Press.

Jessor, R., & Jessor, S. L. (1977b). *Problem behavior and psychosocial development: A longitudinal study of youth.* New York: Academic Press.

Kandel, D. B. (1978). Convergences in prospective longitudinal surveys of drug use in normal populations. In D. B. Kandel (Ed.), *Longitudinal research on drug use: Empirical findings and methodological issues* (pp. 3–38). Washington, DC: Hemisphere.

Kandel, D. B. (1980). Drug and drinking behavior among youth. *Annual Review of Sociology, 6:* 235–285.

Kandel, D. B. (1982). Epidemiological and psychosocial perspectives on adolescent drug use. *Journal of the American Academy of Child Psychiatry, 21* (4), 328–347.

Kandel, D. B. (1989). Issues of sequencing of adolescent drug use and other problem behaviors. *Drugs and Society, 3,* 55–76.

Kandel, D. B. (1992). Epidemiological trends and implications for understanding the nature of addiction. In C. P. O'Brien & J. H. Jaffe (Eds.), *Addictive states: Association for research in nervous and mental disease,* Vol. 70, (pp. 23–40). New York: Raven Press.

Kandel, D. B., Kessler, R. C., & Margulies, R. Z. (1978). Antecedents of adolescent initiation into stages of drug use: A developmental analysis. *Journal of Youth and Adolescence, 7,* 13–40.

Kandel, D., Simcha-Fagan, O., & Davies, M. (1986). Risk factors for delinquency and illicit drug use from adolescence to young adulthood. *Journal of Drug Issues, 16*, 67–90.

Kandel, D. B., & Yamaguchi, K. (1985). Developmental patterns of the use of legal, illegal, and medically prescribed psychotropic drugs from adolescence to young adulthood. In *Etiology of drug abuse: Implications for prevention* (pp. 193–235). Washington, DC: USDHHS.

Kandel, D., & Yamaguchi, K. (1993). From beer to crack: Developmental patterns of drug involvement. *American Journal of Public Health, 83*, 851–855.

Kandel, D. B., Yamaguchi, K., & Chen, K. (1992). Stages of progression in drug involvement from adolescence to adulthood: Further evidence for the gateway theory. *Journal of Studies on Alcohol, 53*, 447–457.

Kellam, S. G., & Rebok, G. W. (1992). Building developmental and etiological theory through epidemiologically based preventive intervention trials. In J. McCord & R. E. Tremblay (Eds.), *Preventing antisocial behavior: Interventions from birth through adolescence* (pp. 162–195). New York: Guilford Press.

Kellam, S. G., Rebok, G. W., Ialongo, N., & Mayer, L. S. (1994). The course and malleability of aggressive behavior from early first grade into middle school: Results of a developmental epidemiologically-based preventive trial. *Journal of Child Psychology, 35*, 259–281.

Metzler, C. W., Biglan, A., Li, F., & Ary, D. V. (1999). The relative influence of parents and peers on the developmental trajectory of problem behaviors in early adolescence. Unpublished manuscript.

Metzler, C. W., Noell, J., Biglan, A., Ary, D., & Smolkowski, K. (1994). The social context for risky sexual behavior among adolescents. *Journal of Behavioral Medicine, 17*, 419–438.

Moos, R. H. (1974). Determinants of physiological responses to symbolic stimuli: The role of the social environment. *International Journal of Psychiatry in Medicine, 5*, 389–399.

Osgood, D. W., Johnston, L. D., O'Malley, P. M., & Bachman, J. G. (1988). The generality of deviance in late adolescence and early adulthood. *American Sociological Review, 53*, 81–93.

Patterson, G. R. (1982). *Coercive family process*. Eugene, OR: Castalia.

Patterson, G. R., DeBaryshe, B. D., & Ramsey, E. (1989). A developmental perspective on antisocial behavior. *American Psychologist, 44*, 329–335.

Patterson, G. R., Dishion, T. J., & Bank, L. (1984). Family interaction: A process model of deviancy training. *Aggressive Behavior, 10*, 253–267.

Patterson, G. R., Reid, J. B., & Dishion, T. J. (1992). *Antisocial boys: A social interactional approach* (Vol. 4). Eugene, OR: Castalia.

Pepper, S. C. (1942). *World hypotheses: A study in evidence*. Berkeley: University of California Press.

Taylor, T. K., & Biglan, A. (1998). Behavioral family interventions for improving childrearing: A review of the literature for clinicians and policy makers. *Clinical Child and Family Psychology Review, 1*, 41–60.

Tobler, N. S. (1998). Updated meta-analysis of school-based drug abuse prevention programs: Preliminary results. Presentation at the 6th Annual Meeting of the Society for Prevention Research, June 4–7, Park City, UT.

U.S. Department of Health and Human Services. (1994). *Preventing tobacco use among young people: A report of the Surgeon General.* Atlanta: U.S. Department of Health and Human Services, Public Health Service, Centers for Disease Control and Prevention, National Center for Chronic Disease Prevention and Health Promotion, Office on Smoking and Health.

Walker, H. M. (1995). *The acting-out child: Coping with classroom disruption* (2nd ed.) Longmont, CO: Sopris West.

Part IV

Methodological Issues and Approaches

Advantages and Limitations of Alternate Methods

9

Log Linear Sequence Analyses

Gender and Racial/Ethnic Differences in Drug Use Progression

Kazuo Yamaguchi and Denise B. Kandel

This chapter, a companion to Chapter 4, clarifies the logic underlying the notion of stages of drug use progression and its relation to two related models for the analysis of progressions. These log linear models were introduced in our previous research (Yamaguchi & Kandel, 1984a; Kandel, Yamaguchi, & Chen, 1992; Kandel & Yamaguchi, 1993; Yamaguchi & Kandel, 1996) and are further refined here. The models are applied to gender/ethnic differences in progression patterns among five drugs: alcohol, cigarettes, marijuana, cocaine, and heroin. The models that under- lie the substantive results presented in Chapter 4 are discussed in detail in this chapter to illustrate the use of the methods.

In order for a stage of progression in drug use to be substantiated, two conditions must be met (Yamaguchi & Kandel, 1984a; 1984b). The first condition is that of a *sequential* order between two states. The sequential order of initiations between a lower-stage drug A and a higher-stage drug B is such that *all systematic pathways* of drug use progression, except random progressions, *must not* include the reverse sequence B-A (Yamaguchi & Kandel, 1984a). As a result, all pathways of progres- sion other than the random type fall into one of the following three groups: (1) reaches neither stage A nor B; (2) reaches only stage A; and (3) reaches both stages A and B, stage A first. Under these conditions,

Work on this chapter was partially supported by Grant DA09110 and the Senior Scientist Award (K05DA00081), Denise Kandel, Principal Investigator, from the National Institute on Drug Abuse. Partial support for computer costs was provided by Mental Health and Clinical Research Center Grant MH30906 from the National Institute on Mental Health (NIMH) to the New York State Psychiatric Institute. The research assistance of Christine Schaffran is gratefully acknowledged.

the pathways of drug use progression satisfy the condition that stage A must precede stage B.

The second condition is that of *association* between two states. Being in stage A implies a higher risk of initiating (or progressing to) stage B than being in any stage lower than stage A. Ultimately, to establish causality, this higher risk must not be a spurious effect of common antecedents of using drugs in stages A and B (Yamaguchi & Kandel, 1984b). This implies the nonspurious association of the initiation of the use of drugs at two different stages or, more specifically, the nonspurious effect of the initiation of a lower-stage drug on the rate (or the odds) of initiating a higher-stage drug. Aside from spuriousness, this association can be analyzed by a hazard rate model. However, we employ a parametric log linear model to analyze simultaneously sequencing and association in the initiations of the use of multiple drugs.

The distinction between sequencing and association is most easily illustrated for the case involving two drugs. Figure 9.1 shows that there are five distinct patterns of drug use progression: (1) no lifetime use of either drug (F_0); (2) lifetime use of drug A without lifetime use of drug B (F_A); (3) lifetime use of drug B without lifetime use of drug A (F_B); (4) lifetime use of both drugs with drug A initiated first (F_{A-B}); and (5) lifetime use of both drugs, with drug B initiated first (F_{B-A}). F_0, F_A, F_B, F_{A-B}, and F_{B-A} indicate the frequency expected from a given model. The lifetime use of each drug depends on current age, and this factor is taken into account in the analysis. However, for simplicity we omit reference to this control in the following description of sequencing and association.

The association of lifetime use between two drugs does not depend on the distinction between patterns 4 (F_{A-B}) and 5 (F_{B-A}), and only involves their sum, because it is measured by the log odds-ratio $\log[F_0(F_{A-B} + F_{B-A})/(F_A F_B)]$. Sequencing between two drugs does not depend on the frequency of pattern 1 (F_0), the case in which use of neither drug is initiated. The sequential tendency of A–B versus B–A is measured by the log odds of the A–B versus B–A sequences. We can define either an unconditional sequencing tendency, which takes into account four patterns in which at least one drug is initiated, or a conditional sequencing tendency, restricted to the two patterns in which both drugs are initiated, that is, patterns 4 and 5. Yamaguchi and Kandel (1996) showed, however, that if sequencing is measured as the conditional tendency by $\log (F_{A-B}/F_{B-A})$ by fixing the marginal distributions of the frequencies in the four-fold table, the parameter estimate does not differ from the estimate based on the unconditional tendency.

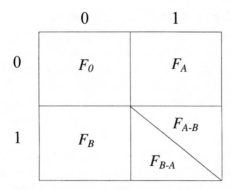

Figure 9.1. Distinction of five progression patterns with two drugs.
Note: Association: $F_0 (F_{A-B}+F_{B-A})/(F_A F_B)$; conditional sequencing: F_{A-B}/F_{B-A}.

Furthermore, the likelihood function becomes the independent product of parameters for (a) the sequencing of initiations between two drugs and (b) the initiation of each drug and the association of initiations between the two drugs. Hence, we measure sequencing by the conditional tendency to attain the independence of the two groups of parameters, without a loss of generality.

To elaborate further the stage notion and its two underlying components, sequencing and association, for cases involving three or more stages it is useful to relax the condition of a strict sequential order among the drugs. Ideally, we would like to observe a true hierarchical Guttman scale–like pattern, such that those who initiate a higher-level drug must initiate all prior lower-stage drugs in sequence. However, empirically observed sequences never satisfy a Guttman scale in this strict sense.

One standard solution is to allow some "random errors" or "noises" in the sequential requirement. Such noise, however, should reflect non-systematic patterns with no sequential tendency or association in the initiation of multiple drugs. We employ a log linear model that assumes two latent classes of persons: (1) those who represent this random progression pattern and (2) those who take various pathways of drug use progression nonrandomly. By a *pathway*, we mean an entire trajectory of progression, not a component path from one stage to another.

A second type of relaxation is often needed, however, because the Guttman scale–like condition is not usually met even when random errors are allowed. With three or more drugs, stages of drug use progression can be defined even when a set of sequences among drugs satisfies only a partial order and when substitutability exists between two drugs as alternative prerequisites to progression to a higher-stage drug. The Guttman scale notion of drug use progression, even when some random errors are allowed, assumes the presence of a complete order. A partial order will exist when both directions of sequences between two drugs are allowed for some stages but not all, and only the transitivity of a sequential order is required to hold among ordered stages, such that if A must precede B and B must precede C, then A must precede C. As shown later, the best fitting model of drug use progression does not require a sequential order between alcohol and cigarettes and between cocaine and heroin and, therefore, satisfies only a partial order among the five drugs (these four drugs plus marijuana). However, the absence of order between drugs A and B does not imply that both directional sequences are equally likely. Although sequence A-B may be more likely than sequence B-A, these two sequences are both allowed as pathways of progression.

A partial order may arise in part when substitutability exists between two drugs as alternative prerequisites to progression to a third drug. For example, the requirement that either alcohol drinking or cigarette smoking, but not necessarily both, must precede marijuana use reflects such substitutability. We define below a weak condition and two strong conditions of substitutability, using these three drugs as an example. The weak condition is met if all pathways of progression satisfy the condition that alcohol drinking or cigarette smoking, but not necessarily both, must precede marijuana use. There are two strong conditions of substitutability between two drugs, one for sequence and the other for association. Both involve negative interactions between the initiation of two drugs, such as alcohol and cigarettes, with the initiation of a third drug, such as marijuana. The sequencing requirement for substitutability is defined as a negative interaction between the prior initiation of one licit drug and the *subsequent sequencing* of initiation between the use of the other licit drug and marijuana. Once one licit drug is initiated, the sequencing tendency between the initiation of the other licit drug and marijuana use is significantly weakened. For example, when alcohol is already initiated, there are increased odds of the marijuana–cigarette versus the cigarette–marijuana sequence because use of only one licit drug is required to precede marijuana initiation.

The association requirement for substitutability is defined as a negative interaction of the initiation of two drugs on *the rate (or the odds)* of initiating the use of a third drug. Once one licit drug is initiated, the impact of initiation of the other licit drug in increasing the risk of initiating marijuana use becomes smaller than if the effects of the two licit drugs were additive. In the log linear model we employ, the association requirement for substitutability is tested by examining whether there is a significant negative three-factor interaction *among the initiations* of alcohol drinking, cigarette smoking, and marijuana use.

Models and Methods

We apply two groups of log linear models developed in our previous research. One is the quasi-independence model (Goodman, 1975) for the analysis of event sequence data (Yamaguchi & Kandel, 1984a; Kandel et al., 1992; Kandel & Yamaguchi, 1993). The model hypothesizes a latent group of persons in the population who follow one of a set of specified pathways of drug use progression and a latent group of persons for whom sequencing among drug use initiations depends only on random probabilities of the initiation of various drugs. This model identifies the types of nonrandom patterns of drug use progression and the proportions of nonrandom and random progression types. This analysis identifies a set of pathways of progression that satisfies only a partial order. The model can test only the weak condition of substitutability between two drugs as alternative prerequisites for progression to a third drug.

The second model is the log linear model for parametric event sequence analysis, which identifies group differences in the extent of sequencing and association among events (Yamaguchi & Kandel, 1996). Unlike the quasi-independence model, this model cannot test any hypothesis about the entire trajectory of drug use progression. However, it can assess the extent both of a sequencing tendency and of the association of initiations between two drugs by simultaneously taking into account sequencing and association, and more than two drugs. The simultaneous analysis of three or more drugs is required to test the strong conditions of substitutability between alcohol drinking and cigarette smoking regarding the sequencing and association requirements for substitutability discussed previously

Log Linear Quasi-Independence Model for the Analysis of Sequence Data

The log linear quasi-independence model assumes that data are given in the form of a cross-classification of (a) the presence/absence of initiation of each drug and (b) the sequential order among initiated drugs. For five classes of drugs, 326 progression patterns are possible: 1 progression pattern for no use of any drug; 5 (= $_5P_1$), possible progression patterns for the initiation of one class of drugs (where $_mP_n$ indicates the number of permutations of n numbers chosen from m numbers); 20 (= $_5P_2$) possible progression patterns for the initiations of two classes of drugs; 60 (= $_5P_3$) possible progression patterns for the initiations of three classes of drugs; 120 (= $_5P_4$) possible progression patterns for the initiations of four classes of drugs; and 120 (= $_5P_5$) possible progression patterns for the initiations of five classes of drugs. The quasi-independence model hypothesizes that some patterns result only from chance occurrences that are due to the presence of a latent class of persons who have nonsystematic or random progression patterns, and other patterns result from both chance occurrences and nonchance occurrences, the latter due to the presence of a latent class of persons who progress in their drug use by following specific pathways.

Let A, C, M, K, and H be the labels of five classes of drugs (i.e., alcohol, cigarette, marijuana, cocaine, and heroin). Let U, V, W, X, and Y be variables that can take any value of A, C, M, K, and H. Let F^U be the expected frequency for the lifetime use of drug U without lifetime use of the other four classes of drugs; F^{UV} be the expected frequency for the initiations of drugs U and V in this order without the lifetime use of the other three classes of drugs; F^{UVW} be the expected frequency of initiations of drugs U, V, and W in this order without the lifetime use of the other two classes of drugs. Expected frequencies of initiations for four or five classes of drugs, that is, F^{UVWX} and F^{UVWXY}, are defined in a similar manner. Thus, F^{AMC} is the expected frequency of initiations of alcohol, marijuana, and cigarette in this order, without the lifetime use of cocaine and heroin.

In cases in which a single class of drugs, denoted by U, is initiated, the model hypothesizes

$$\log(F^U) = \lambda + \lambda^A_i + \lambda^C_j + \lambda^M_k + \lambda^K_l + \lambda^H_m + \delta(U)\alpha^U \qquad (1)$$

The lambda parameters represent the chance occurrence of initiating each drug among persons in the latent random-type group, who yield all nonscale-type outcomes, and the chance occurrences of scale-type outcomes for the distinction between scale types and nonscale types made by a given model. The subscripts of the lambda parameters, i, j, k, l, and m, take a value of either 1 (initiation occurs) or 2 (initiation does not occur), and the two values of each lambda parameter are standardized to sum to zero, that is, $\lambda^A_1 + \lambda^A_2 = 0$, $\lambda^C_1 + \lambda^C_2 = 0$, $\lambda^M_1 + \lambda^M_2 = 0$, $\lambda^K_1 + \lambda^K_2 = 0$, and $\lambda^H_1 + \lambda^H_2 = 0$.

In formula (1), one of i, j, k, l, and m takes a value of 1 depending on what drug U is, and others take a value of 2. For example, if $U = C$, $j = 1$, and $i = k = l = m = 2$. A dummy variable $\delta(U)$ distinguishes scale types (for which $\delta = 1$) from nonscale types (for which $\delta = 0$). The distinction between scale types and nonscale types varies with models. If a model hypothesizes that the first drug to be initiated must be either alcohol or cigarettes, then $\delta(A) = \delta(C) = 1$ and $\delta(M) = \delta(K) = \delta(H) = 0$. Since parameter α_U is specific to each scale type, the observed and expected frequencies are equal for the scale types. The expected frequency for nonscale types is determined only by the estimated lambda parameters.

Similarly, for cases in which two classes of drugs are initiated, the model hypothesizes.

$$\log(F^{UV} \times 2!) = \lambda + \lambda^A_i + \lambda^C_j + \lambda^M_k + \lambda^K_l + \lambda^H_m + \delta(U, V)\alpha^{UV} \quad (2)$$

where two of i, j, k, l, and m take a value of 1 depending on what U and V are, and three others take a value of 2. $\delta(U, V)$ is the dummy variable that takes a value of 1, if and only if the initiations of drugs U and V in this order is one of the scale types, and takes a value of zero otherwise. For example, if the model hypothesizes that scale types include only (A, C), (C, A), (A, M), and (C, M) for the initiation of the first two drugs, $\delta(U, V)$ takes a value of 1 for each of these four cases and a value of zero for each of other 16 $(= {}_5P_2 - 4)$ cases of the first two drugs. The multiplicative constant 2! exists in the left-hand side of equation (2) because among random-type progressions each permutation among initiated drugs is assumed to have an equal probability of occurrence.

Similarly, for the cases when three, four, or five drugs are initiated, the model hypothesizes, respectively,

$$\log(F^{UVW} \times 3!) = \lambda + \lambda^A_i + \lambda^C_j + \lambda^M_k + \lambda^K_l + \lambda^H_m \\ + \delta(U, V, W)\alpha^{UVW} \quad (3)$$

$$\log(F^{UVWX} \times 4!) = \lambda + \lambda^A_i + \lambda^C_j + \lambda^M_k + \lambda^K_l + \lambda^H_m \\ + \delta(U, V, W, X)\alpha^{UVWX} \quad (4)$$

$$\log(F^{UVWXY} \times 5!) = \lambda + \lambda^A_i + \lambda^C_j + \lambda^M_k + \lambda^K_l \\ + \lambda^H_m + \delta(U, V, W, X, Y)\alpha^{UVWXY} \quad (5)$$

A given model applies equations (1) through (5) simultaneously to the data.

Parametric Event Sequence Analysis

Although we can apply sequence models to data for a larger number of events, we illustrate later how we parameterize sequencing effects by using the three-event case because we apply the model separately to alcohol, cigarette, and marijuana, and marijuana, cocaine, and heroin. Increases in the number of events increase the complexity of the analysis. See Yamaguchi and Kandel (1996) for cases with four or more events.

We first present models without covariates to describe a basic model that uses parameters representing the conditional odds of a particular sequence versus the reverse sequence for pairs of events, by extending the log linear model for the occurrence and association of events. We include additional parameters for sequencing effects characterizing interactions between the sequence of two events and the occurrence of a third event. Models with covariates are described later.

In the case of three events A, B, and C, data without covariates are structured into 16 cells, which divide the $2 \times 2 \times 2$ cross-classification of the occurrence versus nonoccurrence of the events into distinct sequential patterns for cells that represent the occurrence of two or more events. At most eight parameters each are possible for the occurrence and association of events and for sequencing effects. We first describe the model with three parameters, γ^A, γ^B, and γ^C, for the odds of occurrence of each event; three parameters, γ^{AB}, γ^{BC}, and γ^{AC}, for pairwise association; and three parameters, π^{AB}, π^{BC}, and π^{AC}, for pairwise sequencing established when at least one of the two events occurs. For example, the sequencing effect parameter π^{AB} contrasts sequence A–B versus B–A. For this model, Model 1, the expected frequency $F_{ijk,s}$, where the subscripts i, j, k indicate the occurrence ($= 1$) or nonoccurrence ($= 0$) of events A, B, and C, respectively, and the subscript s indicates a sequence among events, is given as follows:

$$F_{ijk,s} = [\gamma\gamma^A{}_i\gamma^B{}_j\gamma^C{}_k\gamma^{AB}{}_{ij}\gamma^{BC}{}_{jk}\gamma^{AC}{}_{ik}][\pi^{AB}{}_s\pi^{BC}{}_s\pi^{AC}{}_s /$$
$$\Sigma_{t|ijk}\pi^{AB}{}_t\pi^{BC}{}_t\pi^{AC}{}_t] \equiv g_{ijk}(\gamma)h_s(\pi) \qquad (6)$$

where

$$\gamma^A{}_1 = (\gamma^A{}_0)^{-1},\ \gamma^B{}_1 = (\gamma^B{}_0)^{-1},\ \gamma^C{}_1 = (\gamma^C{}_0)^{-1},$$
$$\gamma^{AB}{}_{00} = \gamma^{AB}{}_{11} = (\gamma^{AB}{}_{01})^{-1} = (\gamma^{AB}{}_{10})^{-1}$$
$$\gamma^{BC}{}_{00} = \gamma^{BC}{}_{11} = (\gamma^{BC}{}_{01})^{-1} = (\gamma^{BC}{}_{10})^{-1},$$
$$\gamma^{AC}{}_{00} = \gamma^{AC}{}_{11} = (\gamma^{AC}{}_{01})^{-1} = (\gamma^{AC}{}_{10})^{-1}$$

and $\pi^{LM}_s = \pi^{LM}$ for events L and M if the sequence s of events that occurred establishes the order L-M, $\pi^{LM}_s = (\pi^{LM})^{-1}$ if s establishes the reverse order M-L, and $\pi^{LM}_s = 1$ when neither event L nor event M occurs. For example, $\pi^{AB}_s = \pi^{AB}_{A\text{-}B\text{-}C} = \pi^{AB}_{A\text{-}C\text{-}B} = \pi^{AB}_{C\text{-}A\text{-}B} = \pi^{AB}_{A\text{-}B} = \pi^{AB}_{A\text{-}C} = \pi^{AB}_{C\text{-}A} = (\pi^{AB}_{B\text{-}A\text{-}C})^{-1} = (\pi^{AB}_{B\text{-}C\text{-}A})^{-1} = (\pi^{AB}_{C\text{-}B\text{-}A})^{-1} = (\pi^{AB}_{B\text{-}A})^{-1} = (\pi^{AB}_{B\text{-}C})^{-1} = (\pi^{AB}_{C\text{-}B})^{-1}$, and $\pi^{AB}_s = 1$ otherwise, and π^{BC} and π^{AC} are defined in a similar manner. The summation $\Sigma_{t|ijk}\pi^{AB}_t\pi^{BC}_t\pi^{AC}_t$ means that $\pi^{AB}_t\pi^{BC}_t\pi^{AC}_t$ are to be summed over all sequences t for each distinct combination ijk of event occurrences/nonoccurrences. When a sequence s indicates the occurrence of only one event, we can set parameters $\pi^{LM}_s = 1$ for any pair of events L and M without loss of generality because $h_s(\pi) = 1$ always holds for such cases.

Model 1 has the following characteristics: (1) The ratio between two expected frequencies having the same combination of event occurrences and differing only in the sequence of two events L and M, such as $F_{111,A\text{-}B\text{-}C}/F_{111,B\text{-}A\text{-}C}$ and $F_{110,A\text{-}B}/F_{110,B\text{-}A}$ when L = A and M = B, is $(\pi^{LM})^2$; and (2) the expected marginal frequencies, summed across different sequences within each combination of event occurrences/nonoccurrences, are $F_{ijk} = g_{ijk}(\gamma)$, that is, a function of the γ parameters only. Thus, Model 1 employs each π parameter for the conditional odds of a particular sequence versus the reverse sequence for a pair of events and γ parameters for the marginal odds and the odds ratios of frequencies summed across sequence patterns for each combination of event occurrences/nonoccurrences. The γ parameters are those for a hierarchical log linear model for frequencies obtained without distinguishing sequences.

For the three sequencing effect parameters π^{AB}, π^{BC}, and π^{AC}, the following equations are derived from equation (6):

$$(\pi^{AB})^2 = F_{111,C\text{-}A\text{-}B}/F_{111,C\text{-}B\text{-}A} \tag{7a}$$

$$= F_{111,A\text{-}B\text{-}C}/F_{111,B\text{-}A\text{-}C} \tag{7b}$$

$$= F_{110,A\text{-}B}/F_{110,B\text{-}A} \tag{7c}$$

$$(\pi^{BC})^2 = F_{111,A\text{-}B\text{-}C}/F_{111,A\text{-}C\text{-}B} \tag{8a}$$

$$= F_{111,B\text{-}C\text{-}A}/F_{111,C\text{-}B\text{-}A} \tag{8b}$$

$$= F_{011,B\text{-}C}/F_{011,C\text{-}B} \tag{8c}$$

$$(\pi^{AC})^2 = F_{111,B\text{-}A\text{-}C}/F_{111,B\text{-}C\text{-}A} \tag{9a}$$

$$= F_{111,A\text{-}C\text{-}B}/F_{111,C\text{-}A\text{-}B} \tag{9b}$$

$$= F_{101,A\text{-}C}/F_{101,C\text{-}A} \tag{9c}$$

For this model, $(\pi^{AB})^2$ represents simultaneously three conceptually different kinds of odds: (1) the odds of having sequence A-B versus sequence B-A, given that the three events A, B, and C occur and that C occurs first (equation [7a]); (2) the odds of having sequence A-B versus sequence B-A, given that the three events A, B, and C occur and that C occurs last (equation [7b]), and (3) the odds of having sequence A-B versus sequence B-A, given that only events A and B occur (equation [7c]). Similarly, $(\pi^{BC})^2$ and $(\pi^{AC})^2$ each represent three conceptually different kinds of odds, indicated by equations (8a), (8b), and (8c) and equations (9a), (9b), and (9c), respectively.

These three kinds of odds need not be identical. If the prior occurrence of a third event affects the sequencing of two events, the first quantity is different from the last two quantities: $(7a) \neq (7b) = (7c)$, $(8a) \neq (8b) = (8c)$, and $(9a) \neq (9b) = (9c)$. Parameters for these effects measured by odds ratios are expressed as $\pi^{AB|C}$, $\pi^{BC|A}$, and $\pi^{AC|B}$, where $\pi^{AB|C}$ represents the dependence of the odds of sequence A-B versus B-A on the prior occurrence of event C, and so on. If we hypothesize that the prior establishment of a particular sequence between two events, rather than the reverse sequence, affects the occurrence of the third event, the second quantity is different from the third quantity: $(7b) \neq (7c)$, $(8b) \neq (8c)$, and $(9b) \neq (9c)$. Parameters for these effects measured by odds ratios are expressed as $\pi^{C|AB}$, $\pi^{A|BC}$, and $\pi^{B|AC}$, where $\pi^{C|AB}$, for example, represents the dependence of the odds of occurrence of event C on the prior establishment of the sequence A-B versus B-A.

These two sets of parameters characterize the interaction effects between the sequencing of two events and the occurrence of a third event. In our particular example, parameters that represent the dependence of the sequence between two events on the prior occurrence of a third event provide a test of the strong sequencing condition involving substitutability between alcohol drinking (A) and cigarette smoking (C) as alternative prerequisites for progression to marijuana use (M). We will be concerned with whether either $\pi^{AM|C}$ or $\pi^{CM|A}$ or both are significantly negative such that the prior initiation of use of one licit drug reduces the odds of sequencing from the initiation of use of the other licit drug to the initiation of marijuana use.

An important characteristic of the six interaction parameters, $\pi^{AB|C}$, $\pi^{BC|A}$, $\pi^{AC|B}$, $\pi^{C|AB}$, $\pi^{A|BC}$, and $\pi^{B|AC}$, is that only five of the six are independent because the constraint $[(7a)/(7b)][(8a)/(8b)][(9b)/(9a)] = 1$ always exists. Because the use of five interaction parameters leads to saturated sequencing effects, all combinations of five parameters become equivalent and the interpretation of findings becomes ambiguous. Fewer than five of these effects should be used; thereby the ambiguity is reduced. However, nonindependence of the six interaction effect parameters means that each parameter may modify some quantities that the other parameters represent, as described in Appendix A for an empirical application that is analyzed later. The interpretation of interaction effect parameters requires caveats.

Parameters for sequencing effects and for the occurrence and association of events can be estimated independently because the likelihood function can be decomposed into two components, a marginal likelihood that includes only λ parameters and a conditional likelihood that includes only π parameters (see Yamaguchi & Kandel, 1996). Since the marginal likelihood component, which includes γ parameters, is identical to the full likelihood function of the hierarchical log linear model, log linear analysis can be applied to the data. For the conditional likelihood component, the estimates of the π parameters can be obtained independently of the γ parameters. Therefore, in estimating the π parameters we can assume, without loss of generality, that the model for the marginal likelihood component is saturated. In that case, however, the entire model can be reparameterized as a log linear model without replacing the π parameters. In the three-event case with parameters π^{AB}, π^{AC}, and π^{BC}, for example, the model with a saturated marginal likelihood component can be written as

$$F_{ijk,s} = \gamma^{ABC}_{ijk}[\pi^{AB}_s \pi^{BC}_s \pi^{AC}_s / \Sigma_{t|ijk} \pi^{AB}_t \pi^{BC}_t \pi^{AC}_t] \tag{10a}$$

$$= \tau^{ABC}_{ijk} \pi^{AB}_s \pi^{BC}_s \pi^{AC}_s \tag{10b}$$

where γ^{ABC}_{ijk} is a set of γ parameters for each combination of event occurrences/nonoccurrences that saturates the marginal likelihood component, that is, satisfies $F_{ijk} = f_{ijk}$, where f_{ijk} are observed frequencies, and $\tau^{ABC}_{ijk} \equiv \gamma^{ABC}_{ijk}/(\Sigma_{t|ijk} \pi^{AB}_t \pi^{BC}_t \pi^{AC}_t)$ is a set of rescaled parameters that retains equations $F_{ijk} = f_{ijk}$ without changing the estimates of the π parameters. Because equation (10b) is a log linear model, we can estimate the π parameters by using a program for log linear analysis.

For a given set of γ and π parameters, we can extend the model to a regression model, so that the logarithm of these parameters are linear functions of covariates. If $\lambda = \log(\gamma)$ and $\varphi \equiv \log(\pi)$, for a given set of λ and φ parameters included in the model

$$\lambda' = B_1 x_1' \tag{11}$$
$$\varphi' = B_2 x_2' \tag{12}$$

where λ' is a $n_\lambda \times 1$ column vector of λ parameters, B_1 is a $n_\lambda \times k_1$ matrix of regression coefficients, x_1' is a $k_1 \times 1$ column vector of covariates, φ' is a $n_\varphi \times 1$ vector of φ parameters, B_2 is a $n_\varphi \times k_2$ matrix of regression coefficients, and x_2' is a $k_2 \times 1$ column vector of covariates.

Methods of Parameter Estimation and Model Selection

For the quasi-independence model, a previously used FORTRAN program based on the maximum likelihood method (Yamaguchi & Kandel, 1984a) was used to obtain chi-square test statistics. In contrast to contingency table data, the quasi-independence model cannot be applied to the analysis of sequence data using available programs for log linear analysis. For parametric event sequence analysis, the SPSS LOGLINEAR procedure, which employs the maximum likelihood method based on the Newton–Raphson algorithm, is used to estimate parameters for the λ regression in the multinomial logit model. The model saturated with respect to the λ regression component is used to estimate the parameters of the φ regression as if they were those of a multinomial logit model.

Model selection is based on the Bayesian information criterion (BIC) (Raftery, 1986), defined as $G^2 - (df)\log(N)$, where G^2 is the likelihood ratio chi-square statistic for comparison of the tested model against the saturated model and N is the sample size. A model with a smaller BIC value indicates a better fit. A model with a negative BIC value is better than the saturated model, where the number of parameters is equal to the number of observed frequencies and, therefore, has zero degree of freedom and fits the data perfectly. The choice of BIC as a criterion for the selection of a model for a stage analysis is in part based on the fact that, with a large sample size, the likelihood ratio test may detect many minor progression patterns as being significant, whereas the identification of the best fitting model by BIC depends less on sample size, which may differ greatly among subgroups. Since the log linear quasi-independence model is applied separately for each gender or racial/ethnic group, it is important to use a criterion for selecting the best fitting model that depends less on group differences in sample size. However, BIC tends to capture only major patterns and ignores minor ones, which can be detected by the likelihood ratio test. When we are concerned with the significance of specific parameters of substantive interest, we employ the likelihood ratio test instead of BIC.

Data

The data are from the National Household Survey on Drug Abuse conducted by The Substance Abuse and Mental Health Services Administration (SAMHSA, 1996, 1997) for men and women 18–40 years of age from the aggregated 1994–1995 survey (see Chapter 4). The analysis by racial/ethnic groups and the analysis using a covariate for racial/ethnic groups are restricted to non-Hispanic Whites (Whites), non-Hispanic African Americans (Blacks), and Hispanics, excluding non-Hispanics other than Whites and Blacks.

Analysis

Analysis of the Overall Patterns of Drug Use Progression: Main Results and Gender Differences

The identification of the best model of pathways of drug use progression for each gender group is based on a series of tests that examine whether each particular sequence is a necessary step in the progression, except for individuals who progress randomly with no systematic order. After a test of the random progression model, we first test the basic ordered model that hypothesizes sequences supported in our previous research: (1) use of at least one licit drug, alcohol drinking or cigarette smoking, precedes marijuana use, and (2) marijuana use precedes the use of other illicit drugs (Yamaguchi & Kandel, 1984a; Kandel et al., 1992; Kandel & Yamaguchi, 1993). In the present application, cocaine and heroin are the two specific illicit drugs of interest. We test further various hypotheses that modify the sequences (1) between the use of marijuana and of cocaine and heroin, (2) between cocaine and heroin use, and (3) between the use of each of two licit drugs and each of three illicit drugs in order to see whether these modifications improve the fit of the basic model. Fifteen separate models were tested.

Table 9.1 presents the results of these tests. Model 0 is the independence model, which hypothesizes no sequencing tendency among drugs (i.e., equally probable sequences conditional upon occurrences). The sequences observed among drugs are solely due to the different probabilities and independent occurrences of the onset of the five drugs. This model, which hypothesizes that everyone in the population belongs to a latent group of random progression types, does not fit the data (as indicated by large positive BIC values). Model 1 is the basic model, which hypothesizes that (1) either alcohol drinking or cigarette smoking must precede marijuana use, (2) marijuana use must precede cocaine use, and (3) marijuana use must precede heroin use. Model 1 hypothesizes that there are two latent groups, one with nonrandom progression that satisfies the three hypothesized requirements of drug use progression, and one with random progression. The negative BIC value indicates that this model is more parsimonious than the saturated model for both women and men and, therefore, fits the data well.

As the next step, we test two hypotheses, each of which modifies the basic model regarding the sequence between the use of marijuana and use of one of the two other illicit drugs. Marijuana use need not precede either cocaine use or heroin use, but either alcohol drinking or cigarette smoking must precede the use of all three illicit drugs.

In Model 2 marijuana use must precede heroin use but need not precede cocaine use. Either alcohol drinking or cigarette smoking must precede both marijuana use and cocaine use.

In Model 3 marijuana use must precede cocaine use but need not precede heroin use. Either alcohol drinking or cigarette smoking must precede both marijuana use and heroin use.

Both Models 2 and 3 provide a worse fit than Model 1 for men and women because these models have larger BIC values (negative and smaller absolute values) (Table 9.1). Both hypotheses that (1) marijuana use need not precede cocaine use and (2) marijuana use need not precede heroin use are rejected. A sequential order between marijuana use and the use of the two other illicit drugs must be satisfied as necessary requirements of drug use progression for both men and women, except for individuals in the latent class characterized by random drug use progression.

The next model tests whether cocaine use must precede heroin use and hypothesizes the following: In Model 4, in addition to the requirements of Model 1, cocaine use must precede heroin use.

For both men and women, Model 4 is worse in fit than Model 1. Cocaine use need not precede heroin use.

The following two sets of hypotheses are concerned with possible modifications of Model 1 regarding whether (1) alcohol drinking must precede the use of some illicit drugs and (2) cigarette smoking must precede the use of some illicit drugs. These models hypothesize that marijuana use must precede cocaine and heroin use. Four alternative models regarding the sequential order between alcohol drinking and the use of illicit drugs were tested:

Table 9.1. *Results from Models for Men and Women, NHSDA 1994B–1995, Ages 18–40*

Models[a]	Women (N = 11,856)			Men (N = 8,779)		
	G^2	df	BIC	G^2	df	BIC
1. Model 0: Independence model	17,283.00	320	14,281.21	13,650.67	320	10,535.03
2. Baseline model (Model 1) and two modifications about sequencing between marijuana use and the use of other illicit drugs						
Model 1	556.62	273	–2,004.38	697.75	273	–1,781.77
Model 2	451.50	249	–1,884.26	575.18	249	–1,685.77
Model 3	548.42	249	–1,787.34	660.89	249	–1,600.06
3. Modifications of Model 1 for the sequence between cocaine and heroin use						
Model 4	786.18	291	–1,943.57	970.53	291	–1,671.78
4. Modifications of Model 1 for the sequence between the use of each licit drugs and the use of illicit drugs						
Model 5A	2,889.34	289	188.35	2,058.21	289	–565.95
Model 5B	615.59	283	–2,039.11	705.84	283	–1,863.83
Model 5C	596.33	280	–2,030.24	703.32	280	–1,839.11
Model 5D	589.17	280	–2,037.39	700.44	280	–1,841.99
Model 6A	1,261.54	289	–1,449.45	1,882.60	289	–741.55
Model 6B	683.93	283	–1,970.78	1,072.69	283	–1,496.98
Model 6C	682.97	280	–1,943.59	1,070.10	280	–1,432.33
Model 6D	558.40	280	–2,068.16	721.78	280	–1,820.65
Model 5B–6D (Model 7)	617.16	290	–2,103.21	729.68	290	–1,903.55
Model 5D–6D	596.75	287	–2,101.48	724.50	287	–1,881.44

Notes: [a] Model 1 hypothesizes that (1) either alcohol or cigarette use must precede marijuana use; (2) marijuana use must precede cocaine use; or (3) marijuana use must precede heroin use. See text for the definition of other models.

In Model 5A, in addition to the requirements of Model 1, alcohol drinking must precede marijuana use (and logically both cocaine and heroin use).

In Model 5B, in addition to the requirements of Model 1, alcohol drinking must precede both cocaine use and heroin use but need not precede marijuana use.

In Model 5C, in addition to the requirements of Model 1, alcohol drinking must precede cocaine use but need not precede marijuana use and heroin use.

In Model 5D, in addition to the requirements of Model 1, alcohol drinking must precede heroin use but need not precede marijuana use and cocaine use.

Similarly four alternative Models 6A–6D, parallel to Models 5A–5D, related to the sequential order between cigarette smoking and the use of illicit drugs were tested.

Models 5B, 5C, and 5D improve the fit of Model 1, whereas Model 5A does not, for both men and women. Model 5B is the best model for men and women, although the difference between Models 5B and 5D is small for women. Alcohol drinking must precede cocaine use and heroin use for men and women, whereas alcohol drinking does not have to precede marijuana use. As regards the sequential order between cigarette smoking and the use of illicit drugs, only Model 6D improves the fit of Model 1 for women and men. Cigarette smoking must precede heroin use for men and women, whereas cigarette smoking does not have to precede marijuana or cocaine use.

The last two models confirm that Model 5B-6D, which adds the conditions of Models 5B and 6D, that is, simultaneous consideration of the sequential order between alcohol drinking and cigarette smoking with the use of illicit drugs, is the best model for women and men.

1. Either alcohol drinking or cigarette smoking must precede marijuana use.
2. Alcohol drinking and marijuana use must precede cocaine use.
3. Alcohol drinking, cigarette smoking, and marijuana use must precede heroin use.

The proportion of individuals in the scale type, who take one of the pathways of progression hypothesized by Model 5B-6D, is decomposed into two components: the estimated proportion that results from chance occurrence among those whose progression pattern is random and the estimated proportion of scale type persons not explained by chance occurrences. Model 5B-6D characterizes 95.6% of women in the sample, including 90.5% not by chance and 5.1% by chance. Only 4.4% of women do not satisfy this progression pattern. Thus, 90.5% of women in the population are estimated to be in the latent group of non-random progression type, and the remaining 9.5% in the latent group of random progression type. Similarly, Model 5B-6D characterizes 94.8% of men in the sample as the scale type, including 89.5% not by chance and 5.3% by chance. Only 5.2% of men do not satisfy this progression pattern.

Figure 9.2 presents the decomposition of scale-type responses into progression patterns in the sample by gender. These numbers sum to the sample proportion of persons in the scale type, that is, 95.6% for women

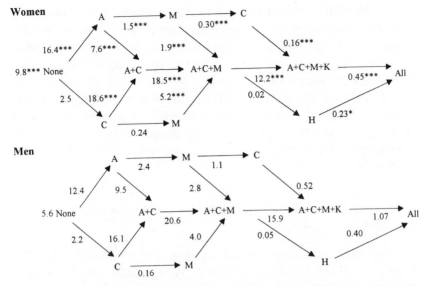

Figure 9.2. Proportions of scale-type individuals who followed specific pathway among women and men. Note: A = alcohol; C = cigarettes; M = marijuana; K = cocaine; H = heroin. Statistically significant gender differences are indicated for women: $^*p < .05.$ $^{***}p < .001.$

and 94.8% for men. For example, 16.4% of women used alcohol but did not make any further progression in drug use. Similarly, the arrow from "A + C + M" to "A + C + M + K" indicates that 12.2% of women first used alcohol, cigarettes, and marijuana and progressed to the use of cocaine without progressing to the use of heroin. Some characteristics of these decomposed proportions are similar for men and women. Even though only one licit drug is required to progress to marijuana use, the large majority of individuals initiate marijuana use after the initiation of both alcohol and cigarette use. Similarly, although cigarette smoking is not a prior requirement for cocaine use, the large majority still progress to cocaine use after cigarette use as well as the use of alcohol and marijuana, which are required predecessors. The majority of heroin users use cocaine first. Heroin users who use heroin before cocaine almost always progress to cocaine use, whereas only a minority of cocaine users who use cocaine first go on to use heroin.

Asterisks attached to the numbers in the women's diagram indicate significant gender differences. Although the scale-type progression patterns are identical for men and women, the proportions who fall into each distinct scale-type progression pattern differ significantly by gender. Most differences indicate that greater proportions of men than women progress to the use of higher-stage drugs, partly because smaller proportions of men than women did not use any drugs and used alcohol only. However, two progression patterns show significantly greater proportions for women than men: (1) cigarette first, alcohol second, no further drug use; and (2) cigarette first, marijuana second, alcohol third, no further drug use. The initial use of cigarettes is a better indicator of further progression in drug use for women than for men. We confirm this hypothesis by the parametric event sequence analysis presented later in the chapter.

Analysis of the Overall Patterns of Drug Use Progression: Race/Ethnic Differences

A similar analysis was implemented to identify potential racial/ethnic differences in patterns of progression among Whites, Blacks, and Hispanics. We apply the model identified as the best fitting model for men and women, Model 5B-6D, labeled Model 7, to each racial/ethnic group and test whether selected modifications improve the fit for a particular racial/ethnic group. Model 7 hypothesizes that (1) either alcohol drinking or cigarette smoking must precede marijuana use; (2) alcohol drinking and marijuana use must precede cocaine use; and (3) alcohol drinking, cigarette smoking, and marijuana use must precede heroin use. The following hypotheses, which either weaken or strengthen Model 7, are each tested by a model that modifies a particular sequencing requirement of Model 7 while retaining all other requirements. Each model is referred to as Model 7 + H1, Model 7 + H2, and so on, in Table 9.2.

H1. Alcohol drinking must precede marijuana use. (This strengthens requirement [1].)

H2. Cigarette smoking must precede marijuana use. (This strengthens requirement [1].)

H3. Alcohol drinking need not precede cocaine use. (This weakens requirement [2].) But use of one licit drug must precede cocaine use because marijuana use must precede cocaine use.

H4. Marijuana use need not precede cocaine use. (This weakens requirement [2].)

H5. Cigarette smoking must precede cocaine use. (This strengthens requirement [2].)

H6. Cigarette smoking need not precede heroin use. (This weakens requirement [3].)

Table 9.2. *Results From Models for Whites, Blacks, and Hispanics, NHSDA 1994B–1995, Ages 18–40*

Models	df	Whites (N = 9,866)		Blacks (N = 4,714)		Hispanics (N = 5,513)	
		G^2	BIC	G^2	BIC	G^2	BIC
Model 7	290	667.06	−2,000.03	428.87	−2,024.03	360.97	−2,137.34
Model 7 + H1	296	2,755.28	−33.02	870.18	−1,633.47	714.21	−1,835.79
Model 7 + H2	299	1,773.21	−976.55	799.44	−1,779.59	615.19	−1,960.65
Model 7 + H3	287	656.50	−1,983.00	428.27	−1,999.26	355.47	−2,116.99
Model 7 + H4	277	577.78	−1,969.75	377.26	−1,965.69	274.90	−2,111.42
Model 7 + H5	293	973.06	−1,721.62	473.19	−2,005.09	419.80	−2,104.35
Model 7 + H6	283	654.29	−1,948.42	423.79	−1,969.90	341.31	−2,096.69
Model 7 + H7	284	655.54	−1,956.35	426.50	−1,975.65	350.85	−2,095.77
Model 7 + H8	298	886.26	−1,854.40	589.43	−1,931.14	457.80	−2,109.43

H7. Marijuana use need not precede heroin use. (This weakens requirement [3].)

H8. Cocaine use must precede heroin use. (This strengthens requirement [3].)

None of the modifications specified by hypotheses H1 through H8 improves the fit of Model 7 for any racial/ethnic group (see Table 9.2). Model 7 is the best fitting common model not only for men and women, but also for all three racial/ethnic groups. Model 7 characterizes 95.5% of Whites in the sample as the scale type, including 90.7% not by chance and 4.7% by chance. Respective percentages are 92.8%, 84.0%, and 8.9% for Blacks, and 95.2%, 89.6%, and 5.6% for Hispanics. Although the same model characterizes the pattern of drug use progression for all three racial/ethnic groups, the proportions of persons who fall into the scale-type progression patterns differ significantly among racial/ethic groups, especially users of an illicit drug.

Table 9.3 summarizes the proportions of individuals with scale-type progression patterns among all members of each racial/ethnic group, and among marijuana users, cocaine users, and heroin users in each group. Asterisks next to the Black and Hispanic proportions indicate significant differences from the corresponding White proportions.

The proportions of persons who fall into scale types are smaller for Blacks and Hispanics than for Whites, especially among users of illicit drugs. Because no systematic progression patterns specific only to

Table 9.3. *Proportions of Individuals With a Scale-Type Progression Pattern by Race/Ethnicity, NHSDA 1994B–1995, Ages 18–40*

	Proportion of Individuals with a Scale Type Progression Pattern		
	Whites	Blacks	Hispanics
In the total sample	0.955	0.928***	0.952
Among marijuana users	0.924	0.823***	0.862***
Among cocaine users	0.886	0.753***	0.766***
Among heroin users	0.848	0.695*	0.714*

* $p < .05$. *** $p < .001$.

Blacks and/or Hispanics were found by testing hypotheses H1 through H8, these results indicate that minorities have more nonsystematic and unordered drug use progression patterns, especially among users of illicit drugs, than Whites.

The detailed decomposition of scale-type responses into progression patterns for each racial/ethnic group is displayed in Figure 9.3.

Parametric Event Sequence Analysis: Progression From the Use of Licit Drugs to Marijuana Use

It is of interest to analyze in greater detail sequencing and association in the initiations of the five drug classes. This is done in two steps because the joint analysis of all five drugs complicates the analysis unnecessarily with little gain in additional insight. Separate analyses are conducted on sequencing and association in the initiations of alcohol drinking, cigarette smoking, and marijuana use (presented in this section), and on initiations of marijuana, cocaine, and heroin use (presented in the next section). We separate these two steps because marijuana use is a prerequisite for initiation of use of the other illicit drugs. The procedure for the selection of the final models presented in Tables 9.4 and 9.5 is described in Appendix B.

Table 9.4 presents estimates for selected substantively important parameters of the best fitting model for the initiation of alcohol drinking, cigarette smoking, and marijuana use for (1) the sequencing tendency between initiations of two drugs for each pair of drugs and (2) the association of initiation between two drugs for each pair of drugs. The effects of gender, race/ethnicity, and birth cohort (measured by age) are also presented. The sequencing tendency is measured by one half the log odds of having a particular sequence versus the reverse sequence of initiation of two drugs. The multiplier 1/2 is determined by coding one

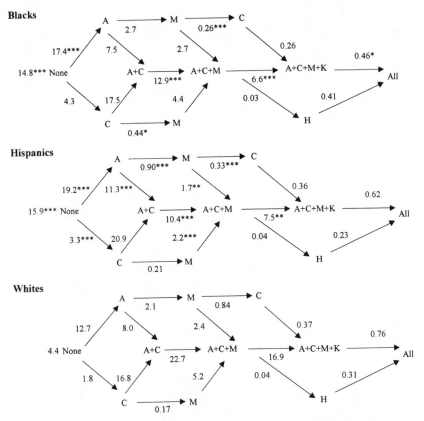

Figure 9.3. Proportions of scale-type individuals who followed specific pathways among Blacks, Hispanics and Whites. Note: A = alcohol; C = cigarettes; M = marijuana; K = cocaine; H = heroin. Statistically significant differences between each minority group and Whites are indicated for Blacks and Hispanics. $^*p < .05.$ $^{**}p < .01.$ $^{***}p < .001.$

sequence versus the reverse sequence as 1 versus −1. Association is measured by one fourth the log odds ratio between the dichotomous distinction of having ever versus never initiated use of each of two drugs. The multiplier 1/4 is determined by coding the presence versus the absence of initiation as 1 versus −1. Table 9.4 does not present the estimates of the other parameters included in the model, such as the effects of covariates on the log odds of the presence or absence of initiation of each drug, because they are not of central interest in the analysis. The effects of the three covariates are based on the use of standard dummy variable expressions (i.e., values 0 for the baseline category and 1 for each contrast category).

Table 9.4. *Parameter Estimates From the Parametric Sequence Analysis of the Initiations of Alcohol Drinking, Cigarette Smoking, and Marijuana Use, NHSDA 1994B–1995, Ages 18–40*[a]

	Main Effects	Interaction Effects with					
		AGE: 24–29 (vs. 18–23)	AGE: 30–35 (vs. 18–23)	AGE: 36–40 (vs. 18–23)	Women (vs. Men)	Black (vs. White)	Hispanic (vs. White)
1. Covariate effects on the sequencing from X to Y (versus Y to X) (φ^{XY})[b]							
φ^{AC}	−0.169	−0.048	−0.148	−0.193	−0.151	−0.020	0.021
	(6.61)	(1.67)	(5.24)	(6.50)	(7.49)	(0.78)	(0.87)
φ^{CM}	0.632	−0.129	−0.101	−0.058	0.134	−0.312	−0.175
	(13.97)	(2.67)	(2.16)	(1.14)	(4.07)	(8.10)	(4.26)
φ^{AM}	0.779	−0.137	0.136	0.045	−0.089	−0.189	−0.062
	(18.17)	(3.08)	(3.19)	(0.97)	(2.86)	(5.80)	(1.74)
$\varphi^{CM|A}$	−0.124	−0.054	−0.158	−0.126	(—)	(—)	(—)
	(5.61)	(1.22)	(3.86)	(2.64)			
G^2				242.37			
df				167			
BIC				−1,412.93			
2. Covariate effects on the association of X and Y (λ^{XY})[b]							
λ^{AC}	0.296	0.012	0.000	0.026	0.008	0.065	0.055
	(5.77)	(0.34)	(0.01)	(0.69)	(0.13)	(1.25)	(1.03)
λ^{CM}	0.596	−0.025	−0.092	−0.076	0.147	−0.145	0.007
	(13.60)	(0.72)	(2.76)	(2.10)	(6.10)	(5.17)	(0.22)

	Main Effects	Interaction Effects with					
		AGE: 24–29 (vs. 18–23)	AGE: 30–35 (vs. 18–23)	AGE: 36–40 (vs. 18–23)	Women (vs. Men)	Black (vs. White)	Hispanic (vs. White)
λ^{AM}	0.794	0.114	0.176	-0.057	0.008	-0.339	-0.260
	(10.02)	(1.50)	(2.34)	(0.79)	(0.13)	(4.71)	(3.11)
λ^{ACM}	-0.088	—	—	—	—	—	—
	(2.64)						
G^2				268.80			
df				113			
BIC				-863.27			

Notes: [a] The numbers in parentheses are the absolute values of the ratios of parameter estimates to their standard errors, that is, $|b|/s.e.(b)$. Other parameter estimates included in the model are omitted from the table.

[b] A = alcohol; C = cigarette; M = marijuana.

Three-factor interactions among the three drugs are present for both sequencing and association, although there are no significant covariate effects on these interactions. The estimate of the sequence parameter $\varphi_{CM|A}$ is significant and negative and indicates that, when alcohol drinking is already initiated, the sequencing tendency from cigarette smoking to marijuana use is weaker than when alcohol drinking is not yet initiated. In the baseline group (i.e., White men aged 18–23), the odds of the cigarette–marijuana sequence (versus the reverse sequence) are 2.76 (= exp[2(.632 – .124)]) when alcohol is already initiated, whereas the same odds are 4.54 (= exp[2(.632 + .124)]) when alcohol is not yet initiated, yielding the odds ratio of 0.608 (= exp[4(–.124)]). This odds ratio is higher for the two oldest cohorts, indicating a higher substitutability of alcohol drinking for cigarette smoking in the progression to marijuana use among them, yielding, for example, the odds ratio of 0.324 (= exp[4 (–.124 – .158)]) for those aged 30–35. This same parameter ($\varphi_{CM|A}$) also affects the alcohol–marijuana sequence versus the reverse sequence (see Appendix A for an explanation), such that the odds of the alcohol–marijuana sequence versus the reverse sequence for the baseline group becomes 0.780 (= exp[2(–.124)]). This value is the same when cigarette use is already initiated as when it is not. However, the significance of the $\varphi_{CM|A}$ parameter combined with the nonsignificance of $\varphi_{AM|C}$ indicates that the role of alcohol drinking as a substitute for cigarette smoking is stronger than the reverse as a prerequisite for the progression to marijuana use. In conclusion, the *strong sequencing condition* that alcohol drinking and cigarette smoking be substitutes as a prerequisite for the progression to marijuana use is empirically satisfied.

Table 9.4 also shows that there is a significant negative three-factor interaction among the initiations of alcohol drinking, cigarette smoking, and marijuana use (λ^{ACM}). In the baseline group, the odds ratio of the presence (versus absence) of initiating alcohol drinking and that of marijuana use is 16.8 (= exp[4(.794 – .088)]) for individuals with prior experience of cigarette smoking, and the odds ratio is 34.1 (= exp [4(.794 + .088)]) without prior experience of cigarette smoking. Similarly, the odds ratio of the initiation (versus non initiation) of cigarette smoking and of marijuana use is 7.6 (= exp[4(.596 – .088)]) for individuals with prior alcohol drinking experience, whereas the odds ratio is 15.4 (= exp[4(.596 + .088)]) for individuals without the experience of prior alcohol drinking. In conclusion, the *strong association condition* that alcohol drinking and cigarette smoking be substitutes as a prerequisite for the progression to marijuana use is also empirically satisfied.

There are significant gender effects on the sequencing from cigarette smoking and from alcohol drinking to marijuana use (Table 9.4). The odds of sequencing from cigarette smoking to marijuana use (versus the reverse sequence) are 1.31 (= exp[2 × .134]) times as high for women as for men, and the odds of sequencing from alcohol drinking to marijuana use (versus the reverse sequence) are 0.84 (= exp[2 × −.089]) time as high for women as for men. There is also a strong gender effect on the association of the initiations between cigarette smoking and marijuana use; the odds ratio is 1.80 (= exp[4 × .147]) times as high for women as for men. In conclusion, cigarette smoking is a better precursor of marijuana use initiation for women than for men not only because the sequence from the initiation of cigarette smoking to that of marijuana use is better established for women than for men, but because cigarette smoking predicts a greater increase in the odds of marijuana use initiation for women than for men. On the other hand, although the tendency for alcohol drinking to precede marijuana use is better established for men than for women, there is no gender difference in the effect of alcohol drinking on the odds of marijuana use initiation. There is also a strong gender effect on the sequencing between alcohol drinking and cigarette smoking such that, compared with men, women have greater odds of the cigarette–alcohol than the alcohol–cigarette sequence.

Regarding racial/ethnic differences, both the sequencing tendency and the association between the initiation of use of each of the two licit drugs and marijuana are weaker for Blacks than Whites. Alcohol drinking and cigarette smoking are better precursors of marijuana use for Whites than for Blacks. Not only is the sequence between the initiation of use of each licit drug and marijuana use initiation better established for Whites than for Blacks, but the initiation of use of a licit drug is a better predictor of increased risk of marijuana use initiation for Whites than for Blacks.

The use of licit drugs as the stage preceding marijuana use is also weaker for Hispanics than for Whites. Sequencing between cigarette smoking and marijuana use is less well established for Hispanics than for Whites, and the association of the initiations between alcohol drinking and marijuana use is weaker for Hispanics than for Whites.

Parametric Event Sequence Analysis: Progression from Marijuana Use to Cocaine/Heroin Use

Table 9.5 presents parameter estimates for (1) the sequencing tendency between the initiations of marijuana and cocaine use and between those

Table 9.5. *Parameter Estimates From the Parametric Sequence Analysis of the Initiations of Marijuana Use, Cocaine Use, and Heroin Use, NHSDA 1994B–1995, Ages 18–40*[a]

	Main Effects	Interaction Effects with					
		AGE: 24–29 (vs. 18–23)	AGE: 30–35 (vs. 18–23)	AGE: 36–40 (vs. 18–23)	Women (vs. Men)	Black (vs. White)	Hispanic (vs. White)
1. The covariate effects on the sequencing from X to Y (versus Y to X) (φ^{XY})[b]							
φ^{MK}	2.124	−0.034	0.179	−0.005	0.050	−0.579	−0.528
	(10.10)	(0.16)	(0.83)	(0.02)	(0.37)	(3.61)	(3.40)
φ^{KH}	0.943	−0.016	−0.145	−0.801	−0.341	−0.082	−0.051
	(3.03)	(0.05)	(0.45)	(2.51)	(2.32)	(0.46)	(0.28)
φ^{MH}	1.372	—	—	—	—	—	—
	(6.49)	(—)	(—)	(—)	(—)	(—)	(—)
G^2				108.06			
df				177			
BIC				−1,647.60			
2. Covariate effects on the association of X and Y (I^{XY})[b]							
λ^{MK}	1.151	−0.084	−0.052	0.018	−0.000	−0.159	−0.155
	(12.91)	(0.96)	(0.61)	(0.18)	(0.01)	(2.11)	(2.51)
λ^{KH}	0.753	0.242	0.470	0.239	−0.052	0.130	−0.054
	(4.18)	(1.09)	(1.98)	(1.25)	(0.35)	(0.70)	(0.31)
λ^{MH}	1.264	−0.617	−0.890	−0.800	−0.095	−0.318	−0.168
	(1.96)	(0.97)	(1.46)	(1.32)	(0.49)	(1.03)	(0.54)
G^2				204.42			
df				118			
BIC				−966.02			

Notes: [a] The numbers in parentheses are the absolute values of the ratios of parameter estimates to their standard errors, that is, $|b|/s.e.(b)$. Other parameter estimates included in the model are omitted from the table.

[b] M = marijuana; K = cocaine; H = heroin.

of cocaine and heroin use; the effects of gender, race/ethnicity, birth cohort on sequencing tendencies; and the main effect of sequencing between the initiations of marijuana use and heroin use; and (2) the association of the initiations of use between two drugs for each pair of drugs and the effects of gender, race/ethnicity, and birth cohort on the associations. Covariate effects on sequencing between the initiations of marijuana use and heroin use are omitted from the model because of their nonsignificance and instability. Table 9.5 presents estimates for selected substantively important parameters of the best fitting model (see Appendix B for model selection).

There is a significant negative gender effect on the sequencing from cocaine to heroin use, such that for the baseline group (Whites aged 18–23) the odds of the sequence from cocaine to heroin use (versus the reverse sequence) are 3.33 (= exp[2 × (.943 − .341)]) for women but 6.59 (= exp[−2 × .943]) for men. However, there is no significant gender effect on the association of initiation between cocaine and heroin use. Although the sequencing from cocaine to heroin use is better established for men than for women, the significant effect of cocaine use in increasing the odds of heroin use does not differ significantly by gender.

There are strong significant effects of race/ethnicity on the sequence of initiations between marijuana and cocaine use, but not between cocaine and heroin use. The sequential order from marijuana to cocaine is significantly less well established, and the association of initiation between marijuana and cocaine use is significantly weaker for Blacks and Hispanics than for Whites. Although we established in the first part of the analysis that marijuana use is a prerequisite for the initiation of cocaine and heroin use, marijuana use as the prior stage of the use of other illicit drugs is weaker for Blacks and Hispanics than for Whites. This occurs mainly because there is a greater proportion of individuals with random-type progression patterns, especially among users of illicit drugs, among Blacks and Hispanics than among Whites, as noted. There are neither the effect of the prior use of one drug on the subsequent sequencing between the other two drugs nor the three-factor interaction on the association among the initiations of marijuana, cocaine, and heroin use. There is no substitution effect between marijuana and cocaine use in the progression to heroin use.

Conclusion

This chapter has presented a conceptual distinction between sequencing and association underlying drug use progressions and illustrated in detail the application of log linear approaches to the analysis of these progressions. The chapter demonstrated the usefulness of these approaches, which permit the specification of parameters that match theoretical concepts of interest. Two log linear analyses of drug use progression were presented. Log linear quasi-independence models for sequence data permit the identification of overall sequencing patterns of drug use progression by allowing (a) the presence of noises, or random patterns of progression; (b) a partial rather than a complete order among stages of drug use progression; and (c) substitutability between two drugs, by the weak criterion, as alternative prerequisites to progression to the use of a higher-stage drug. Log linear parametric event sequence analysis permits the assessment and significance testing of the extent of sequencing and association between two drugs, while sequencing and association between other drugs are simultaneously taken into account. This analysis also permits a test of substitutability in sequencing and association by strong criteria of substitutability. These two log linear methods/models complement each other for identifying patterns of drug use progression.

The illustrative empirical application to gender and racial/ethnic differences in patterns of drug use progression in a national sample confirmed several major findings reported in our previous research and provided new findings. There is a significant commonality between men and women and among three racial/ethnic groups (Whites, Blacks, and Hispanics) in pathways of drug use progression. These satisfy the following three conditions, except for a small proportion of persons with random patterns of drug use progression: (1) either alcohol drinking or cigarette smoking must precede marijuana use; (2) alcohol drinking and marijuana use must precede cocaine initiation; and (3) alcohol drinking, cigarette smoking, and marijuana use must precede heroin initiation.

This chapter has also demonstrated that alcohol drinking and cigarette smoking are substitutes as a prerequisite for marijuana use not only because all pathways of progression satisfy the condition that either alcohol drinking or cigarette smoking, but not necessarily both, must precede marijuana use (the weak substitutability condition), but also because the following two characteristics of sequencing and association exist (the strong substitutability conditions). First, when alcohol drinking is already initiated, the sequencing tendency between cigarette smoking and marijuana use is weakened. Similarly, when cigarette smoking is already initiated, the sequencing tendency between alcohol drinking and marijuana use is weakened, although the extent of this weakening is smaller than in the first case. The extent to which alcohol drinking is a substitute for cigarette smoking as a prerequisite for marijuana use is stronger than the extent to which cigarette smoking is a substitute for alcohol drinking. Second, there is also a negative three-factor interaction among the initiations of alcohol drinking, cigarette smoking, and marijuana use; once use of one licit drug is initiated, the effect of the other licit drug in increasing the odds of marijuana use initiation becomes smaller.

Despite the commonality of pathways of drug use progression among different groups, there are gender and racial/ethnic differences. The main gender difference is the greater importance of cigarette smoking as a precursor to marijuana initiation among women than among men. Not only is the cigarette–marijuana sequence better established for women than for men, but cigarette smoking is a more effective predictor of marijuana use initiation for women than for men because of the stronger association of initiations between the two drugs. This finding replicates similar findings in our earlier studies (Yamaguchi & Kandel, 1984a; Kandel & Yamaguchi, 1993; Yamaguchi & Kandel, 1996). New gender effects include the fact that both the alcohol–marijuana and the marijuana–cocaine sequences are less well established for women than for men. The first finding was not observed in a previous study based on a different data set (Yamaguchi & Kandel, 1996), and the second finding was not tested in any previous research. In both cases, however, there are no gender effects on the association of the initiations between the two drugs involved. Although the reverse sequence is more likely for women than for men, the effectiveness of alcohol drinking in predicting the risk of marijuana use initiation and that of cocaine use in predicting the risk of heroin use initiation do not differ significantly between men and women, once the first of the two drugs is initiated.

Racial/ethnic differences are not due to the fact that Blacks and Hispanics have certain pathways of drug use progression that differ from those of Whites, but to the fact that a greater proportion of minority groups, especially among users of illicit drugs, are classified into the random type, whose progression patterns do not show any systematic sequencing patterns. Although the use of at least one licit drug is a prerequisite for the progression to marijuana initiation, and marijuana use is the prerequisite for the progression to the use of cocaine or heroin, the sequential order between the initiations of these drugs is less well established for Blacks and Hispanics than for Whites. This characteristic holds for all aspects of the progression for Blacks but only for certain aspects for Hispanics. In addition, the association of initiations between use of licit drugs and use of marijuana and between use of marijuana and use of cocaine are also weaker for Blacks and Hispanics than for Whites. The use of a lower-stage drug is a much less effective precursor of further drug use progression for Blacks and Hispanics than for Whites.

Appendix A: Parameterization of Final Sequence Model

Table 9.A1 presents the main elements of the design matrix of the final model (Model 7 in Table 9.B of Appendix B) of sequencing among alcohol drinking, cigarette smoking, and marijuana use, excluding the components related to covariate effects on the sequencing parameters. Table 9.A1 shows two alternate covariates, x_4 and x_4^*, for parameter $\varphi^{CM|A}$, where x_4 takes the value 1 for the sequences C-M with prior alcohol initiation or M-C without prior alcohol initiation, and the value-1 for the sequences C-M without prior alcohol initiation or M-C with prior alcohol initiation. In the original model, with $\varphi^{CM|A}$ as the coefficient for variable x_4, $\varphi^{CM|A}$ affects the sequences A-C and A-M when the third drug is not initiated first; in the alternate equivalent

Table 9.A1. *Design Matrix for the Final Sequence Model for the Estimation of the φ Parameters for the Sequence Analysis*[a]

Occurrence				Sequencing Parameters[b]				
				φ^{AC}	φ^{CM}	φ^{AM}	$\varphi^{CM|A}$	$[\varphi^{CM|A}]$
A	C	M	Sequence	x_1	x_2	x_3	x_4	$[x_4^* = x_4 - x_1 + x_3]$[c]
1	1	1	A-C-M	1	1	1	1	[1]
1	1	1	A-M-C	1	−1	1	−1	[−1]
1	1	1	C-A-M	−1	1	1	−1	[1]
1	1	1	C-M-A	−1	1	−1	−1	[−1]
1	1	1	M-A-C	1	−1	−1	1	[−1]
1	1	1	M-C-A	−1	−1	−1	1	[1]
1	1	0	A-C	1	1	1	1	[1]
1	1	0	C-A	−1	1	1	−1	[1]
0	1	1	C-M	−1	1	−1	−1	[−1]
0	1	1	M-C	−1	−1	−1	1	[1]
1	0	1	A-M	1	−1	1	−1	[−1]
1	0	1	M-A	1	−1	−1	1	[−1]

Notes: [a] A = alcohol; C = cigarette; M = marijuana. [b] Parameters for covariate effects on φ^{AC}, φ^{CM}, and φ^{AM} are included in the model but not shown here. [c] x_4^* is a rescaled value of x_4 (see text).

Table 9.A2. *Log Odds and Log Odds Ratios for the Original and Alternative Parameterizations of Models That Include* $\varphi^{CM|A}$

Log Odds and Log Odds Ratios	Original With x^4	Alternative With x^{4*a}
$\log[(2a)] \equiv \log(F_{111,M\text{-}A\text{-}C}/F_{111,M\text{-}C\text{-}A})$	$2\varphi^{AC}$	$2\varphi^{AC} - 2\varphi^{CM|A}$
$\log[(2b)] \equiv \log(F_{111,A\text{-}C\text{-}M}/F_{111,C\text{-}A\text{-}M})$	$2\varphi^{AC} + 2\varphi^{CM|A}$	$2\varphi^{AC}$
$\log[(2c)] \equiv \log(F_{110,A\text{-}C}/F_{110,C\text{-}A})$	$2\varphi^{AC} + 2\varphi^{CM|A}$	$2\varphi^{AC}$
$\log[(3a)] \equiv \log(F_{111,A\text{-}C\text{-}M}/F_{111,A\text{-}M\text{-}C})$	$2\varphi^{CM} + 2\varphi^{CM|A}$	$2\varphi^{CM} + 2\varphi^{CM|A}$
$\log[(3b)] \equiv \log(F_{111,C\text{-}M\text{-}A}/F_{111,M\text{-}C\text{-}A})$	$2\varphi^{CM} - 2\varphi^{CM|A}$	$2\varphi^{CM} - 2\varphi^{CM|A}$
$\log[(3c)] \equiv \log(F_{011,C\text{-}M}/F_{011,M\text{-}C})$	$2\varphi^{CM} - 2\varphi^{CM|A}$	$2\varphi^{CM} - 2\varphi^{CM|A}$
$\log[(4a)] \equiv \log(F_{111,C\text{-}A\text{-}M}/F_{111,C\text{-}M\text{-}A})$	$2\varphi^{AM}$	$2\varphi^{AM} + 2\varphi^{CM|A}$
$\log[(4b)] \equiv \log(F_{111,A\text{-}M\text{-}C}/F_{111,M\text{-}A\text{-}C})$	$2\varphi^{AM} - 2\varphi^{CM|A}$	$2\varphi^{AM}$
$\log[(4c)] \equiv \log(F_{101,A\text{-}M}/F_{101,M\text{-}A})$	$2\varphi^{AM} - 2\varphi^{CM|A}$	$2\varphi^{AM}$
$\log[(2a)/(2b)] = \log[(2a)/(2c)]$	$-2\varphi^{CM|A}$	$-2\varphi^{CM|A}$
$\log[(2b)/(2c)]$	0	0
$\log[(3a)/(3b)] = \log[(3a)/(3c)]$	$4\varphi^{CM|A}$	$4\varphi^{CM|A}$
$\log[(3b)/(3c)]$	0	0
$\log[(4a)/(4b)] = \log[(4a)/(4c)]$	$2\varphi^{CM|A}$	$2\varphi^{CM|A}$
$\log[(4b)/(4c)]$	0	0

Note: [a] x_4^* is a rescaled value of x_4 (see text).

model, which uses the variable $x_4^* \equiv x_1 - x_1 + x_3$ instead of x_4, $\varphi^{CM|A}$ affects the sequences A-C and A-M when the third drug is initiated first. We employed x_4^* in our analysis.

Table 9.A2 show how the selected log odds and log odds ratios can be characterized by the original and alternative parameterizations in the final model that includes parameters φ^{AC}, φ^{CM}, φ^{AM}, and $\varphi^{CM|A}$.

Appendix B: Model Selection for the Parametric Sequence Analysis

Because the likelihood function becomes the product of the marginal likelihood component, which includes the association parameters, and the conditional likelihood component, which includes the sequencing parameters, model selection can be done independently for the sequencing and association components (Yamaguchi & Kandel, 1996).

Since we are interested in the effects of gender and race/ethnicity on sequencing and association, the main effects of these covariates and those of age, as a control on sequencing and association, are included regardless of their significance, except for effects on sequencing between marijuana use and heroin use. These effects are omitted because they are unstable and become nonsignificant as per chi-square tests, once the covariate effects on the sequences between marijuana use and cocaine use and between cocaine use and heroin use are taken into account.

We also considered three-factor interactions for association or sequencing among three drugs and the main effects of each covariate on the significant three-factor interactions. For these tests, we employed the standard likelihood ratio test so as not to miss any significant effect because these effects are related to the substitution hypotheses we discussed and are of primary theoretical interest in our analysis.

After the significant effects were included in the model, we considered the interaction effects of two covariates at a time among gender, race/ethnicity, and age on the initiation of each drug and the sequencing between two drugs. If tests on drug use initiation showed that there was an interaction effect of two covariates on the same set of two drugs, we also considered the interaction effect of these two covariates on the association of initiations between the two drugs. For those additional tests we employed BIC to identify the model with only strong major effects. We employed this liberal criterion, which may omit minor effects that can be numerous in a large sample, because we were not interested in these interaction effects in our analysis.

Table 9.B presents the results on model selection for four factors: (1) sequencing among alcohol drinking, cigarette smoking, and marijuana use; (2) association among these three drugs; (3) sequencing among marijuana use, cocaine use; and heroin use; and (4) association among these three drugs. The baseline model that includes only the main effects of covariates fits the data very well for factor (3) ($L^2 = 108.06$, $df = 170$). Therefore, the models are elaborated only for factors (1), (2), and (4), whose results are summarized in Table 9.B.

Part I shows that for sequencing among alcohol drinking, cigarette smoking, and marijuana use, Model 2, which adds $\varphi^{CM|A}$, reflecting the dependence of the cigarette–marijuana sequence on the prior initiation of alcohol drinking, improves the fit of the baseline model (Model 1). Among the covariate effects on $\varphi^{CM|A}$, only age effects are present identifying Model 7 as the better model. The remainder of Part I shows that no interaction effects of two covariates improve the fit of Model 7 according to BIC. Hence, we took Model 7 as the final model. Note that this is a different Model 7 than that discussed earlier in Table 9.2.

Part II shows that there is a three-factor interaction of initiations among alcohol drinking, cigarette smoking, and marijuana use, as shown

Table 9.B. *Results for Model Selection in the Parametric Sequence Analysis*

Model Selection	G^2	df	BIC
I. Sequencing among initiations of alcohol, cigarettes, and marijuana use			
Model 1: (φ^{AC}, φ^{CM}, φ^{AM}, $\varphi^{AC*}S$, $\varphi^{AC*}R$, $\varphi^{AC*}Y$, $\varphi^{CM*}S$, $\varphi^{CM*}R$, $\varphi^{CM*}Y$, $\varphi^{AM*}S$, $\varphi^{AM*}R$, $\varphi^{AM*}Y$)	365.14	171	−1,329.81
I-1. Test of the dependence of sequencing between a licit drug and marijuana on prior use of another licit drug			
Model 2: Model 1 + $\varphi^{CM \mid A}$	259.72	170	−1,425.32
Model 3: Model 1 + $\varphi^{AM \mid C}$	350.16	170	−1,334.88
Model 4: Model 1 + $\varphi^{CM \mid A}$ + $\varphi^{AM \mid C}$	257.78	169	−1,423.35
Models 2 vs. 1	105.42	1	$p < .001$
Models 3 vs. 1	14.98	1	$p < .001$
Models 4 vs. 2	1.94	1	$p > .05$
Models 4 vs. 3	92.38	1	$p < .001$
I-2. Main effects of covariates on $\varphi^{CM \mid A}$			
Model 5: Model 2 + $\varphi^{CM \mid A*}S$	255.76	169	−1,419.37
Model 6: Model 2 + $\varphi^{CM \mid A*}R$	259.10	168	−1,406.12
Model 7: Model 2 + $\varphi^{CM \mid A*}Y$	242.37	167	−1,412.93
Model 8: Model 2 + $\varphi^{CM \mid A*}S$ + $\varphi^{CM \mid A*}Y$	240.32	166	−1,405.07
Models 5 vs. 2	3.96	1	$p < .05$
Models 6 vs. 2	0.62	2	$p > .05$
Models 7 vs. 2	17.35	3	$p < .001$
Models 8 vs. 5	15.44	3	$p < .01$
Models 8 vs. 7	2.05	1	$p < .05$
I-3. Effects of covariates on sequencing			
Model 9: Model 7 + $\varphi^{AC*}S^*R$	239.33	165	−1,396.15
Model 10: Model 7 + $\varphi^{CM*}S^*R$	241.06	165	−1,394.42
Model 11: Model 7 + $\varphi^{AM*}S^*R$	241.09	165	−1,394.39
Model 12: Model 7 + $\varphi^{AC*}S^*Y$	227.16	164	−1,398.41
Model 13: Model 7 + $\varphi^{CM*}S^*Y$	236.87	164	−1,388.70
Model 14: Model 7 + $\varphi^{AM*}S^*Y$	239.27	164	−1,386.98
Model 15: Model 7 + $\varphi^{AC*}R^*Y$	221.12	161	−1,374.71
Model 16: Model 7 + $\varphi^{CM*}R^*Y$	236.03	161	−1,359.08
Model 17: Model 7 + $\varphi^{AM*}R^*Y$	225.02	161	−1,369.12
II. Associations among initiations of alcohol, cigarette, and marijuana use			
Model 1: (S^*R^*Y, A^*C, A^*M, C^*M, A^*S, A^*R, A^*Y, C^*S, C^*R, C^*Y, M^*S, M^*R, M^*Y)	535.39	126	−713.52

(continued)

Table 9.B *(continued)*

Model Selection	G^2	df	BIC
II-1. Test of the three-factor interaction of drug use initiations			
Model 2: Model 1 + A^*C^*M	529.11	125	−709.52
Models 2. vs. 1	6.28	1	$p < .01$
II-2. Test of the main effects of each covariate on A^*C^*M			
Model 3: Model 2 + $A^*C^*M^*S$	525.35	124	−703.75
Model 4: Model 2 + $A^*C^*M^*R$	523.62	123	−695.56
Model 5: Model 2 + $A^*C^*M^*Y$	525.95	122	−683.14
Models 3 vs. 2	3.76	1	$p > .05$
Models 4 vs. 2	5.49	2	$p > .05$
Models 5 vs. 2	3.16	3	$p > .05$
II-3. Nine tests of interaction effects of two covariates on the initiation of each drug			
Model 6: Model 2 + A^*S^*R	363.49	123	−855.69
Model 7: Model 2 + A^*S^*Y	510.62	122	−698.64
Model 8: Model 2 + A^*R^*Y	502.71	119	−676.72
Model 9: Model 2 + C^*S^*R	444.82	123	−773.36
Model 10: Model 2 + C^*S^*Y	526.30	122	−682.96
Model 11: Model 2 + C^*R^*Y	465.01	119	−714.52
Model 12: Model 2 + M^*S^*R	516.55	123	−702.63
Model 13: Model 2 + M^*S^*Y	517.24	122	−692.02
Model 14: Model 2 + M^*R^*Y	474.65	119	−704.88
II-4. Test of three models that combine two factors included in Models 3–11 and improve the fit of Model 1			
Model 15: Model 1 + A^*S^*R + C^*S^*R	338.01	121	−861.34
Model 16: Model 1 + A^*S^*R + C^*R^*Y	302.16	117	−857.54
Model 17: Model 1 + C^*S^*R + C^*R^*Y	381.97	117	−773.73
II-5. Test of two models that combine three factors included in Models 6–14 and improve the fit of Model 2			
Model 18: M2 + A^*S^*R + C^*S^*R + C^*R^*Y	276.61	115	−863.27
Model 19: Model 15 + $A^*C^*S^*R$	268.80	113	−851.26
III. Sequencing among initiations of marijuana, cocaine, and heroin use			
Model 1: $(\varphi^{MK}, \varphi^{KH}, \varphi^{MH}, \varphi^{MK*}S, \varphi^{MK*}R,$ $\varphi^{MK*}Y, \varphi^{KH*}S, \varphi^{KH*}R, \varphi^{KH*}Y)$	108.06	177	−1,647.60
IV. Associations among initiations of marijuana, cocaine, and heroin use			
Model 1: $(S^*R^*Y, M^*K, M^*H, K^*H, M^*S, M^*R,$ $M^*Y, K^*S, K^*R, K^*Y, H^*S, H^*R, H^*Y)$	325.76	126	−924.03

Model Selection	G^2	df	BIC
IV-1. Test of the three-factor interaction of drugs			
Model 2: Model 1 + M^*K^*H	322.36	125	−917.42
Models 2. vs. 1	3.40	1	
IV-2. Nine tests of interaction effects of two covariates on the initiation of each drug			
Model 3: Model 1 + M^*S^*R	295.02	124	−934.94
Model 4: Model 1 + M^*S^*Y	322.93	123	−897.11
Model 5: Model 1 + M^*R^*Y	277.97	120	−912.31
Model 6: Model 1 + K^*S^*R	296.89	124	−933.07
Model 7: Model 1 + K^*S^*Y	314.43	123	−905.61
Model 8: Model 1 + K^*R^*Y	235.32	120	−954.96
Model 9: Model 1 + H^*S^*R	324.53	124	−905.43
Model 10: Model 1 + H^*S^*Y	323.40	123	−896.64
Model 11: Model 1 + H^*R^*Y	284.48	120	−905.80
IV-3. Test of three models that combine two factors included in models IV-3–IV-11 and improve the fit of Model IV-1			
Model 12: Model 1 + M^*S^*R + K^*S^*R	284.06	122	−926.06
Model 13: Model 1 + M^*S^*R + K^*R^*Y	204.42	118	−966.02
Model 14: Model 1 + K^*S^*R + K^*R^*Y	206.22	118	−964.22
IV-4. Test of a model that combines three factors included in Models 3–11 and improves the fit of Model 1			
Model 15: M1 + M^*S^*R + K^*S^*R + K^*R^*A	193.34	16	−957.27

Notes: A = alcohol drinking; C = cigarette smoking; M = marijuana use; K = cocaine use; H = heroin use; S = gender; R = race/ethnicity; Y = age.

in the improvement in fit of Model 2 over the baseline model (Model 1), but there are no significant covariate effects on the three-factor interactions. Three kinds of interaction effects of two covariates on drug use initiations, the interaction effects of gender and race/ethnicity on alcohol and cigarette use initiations and the interaction effect of race/ethnicity and age on cigarette use initiation, are significant according to BIC. Model 18, which adds these three factors to Model 2, is the best model among those considered.

We further tested in Model 19 the interaction effect of gender and race/ethnicity on the association of alcohol and cigarette use initiations; it was found to be nonsignificant. Model 18 was retained as the final model.

Part III on sequencing among marijuana, cocaine, and heroin use initiations presents only the results for the baseline model, which fits the data very well.

The results of Part IV show that the three-factor interaction of initiations among marijuana, cocaine, and heroin use is not significant (Model 1 is more parsimonious than Model 2). Two kinds of interaction effects of two covariates on drug initiations, the interaction effects of gender and race/ethnicity on marijuana use initiation and of race/ethnicity and age on cocaine use initiation, were found to be significant according to BIC. Model 13, which adds these two factors to Model 1, was identified as the best fitting model.

References

Goodman, L. A. (1975). A new model for scaling response patterns: An application of quasi-independence concept, *Journal of the American Statistical Association, 70,* 755–768.

Kandel, D. B., & Yamaguchi, K. (1993). From beer to crack: Developmental patterns of involvement in drugs. *American Journal of Public Health, 83,* 851–855.

Kandel, D. B., Yamaguchi, K., & Chen, K. (1992). Stages of progression in drug involvement from adolescence to adulthood: Further evidence for the gateway theory. *Journal of Studies on Alcohol, 53,* 447–457.

Raftery, A. (1986). A note on Bayes Factor for log-linear contingency models with vague prior information. *Journal of Royal Statistical Society, Series B, 48,* 249–250.

Substance Abuse and Mental Health Services Administration (1996). *National Household Survey on Drug Abuse: Main Findings 1994.* U.S. Department of Health and Human Services. Rockville, M.D.

Substance Abuse and Mental Health Services Administration (1997). *National Household Survey on Drug Abuse: Main Findings 1995.* U.S. Department of Health and Human Services. Rockville, M.D.

Yamaguchi, K., & Kandel, D. B. (1984a). Patterns of drug use from adolescence to young adulthood II. Sequences of progression. *American Journal of Public Health, 74,* 668–672.

Yamaguchi, K., & Kandel, D. B. (1984b). Patterns of drug use from adolescence to young adulthood III. Predictors of progression. *American Journal of Public Health, 74,* 673–681.

Yamaguchi, K., & Kandel, D. B. (1996). Parametric event sequence analysis: An application to an analysis of gender and racial/ethnic differences in patterns of drug-use progression. *Journal of the American Statistical Association, 91,* 1388–1399.

10

Cigarette Use and Drug Use Progression

Growth Trajectory and Lagged Effect Hypotheses

Peter M. Bentler, Michael D. Newcomb, and Marc A. Zimmerman

We propose a new way of thinking conceptually and methodologically about drug use sequences. In terms of biopsychosocial views on drug use, such as Noble's (1996) theory on genetic variations that imply a genetically based differential rewarding effect of alcohol and drug use on the dopamine system, the effect of initial drug use on later drug use can be conceptualized as a sensitizing effect that influences the subsequent growth in use of other substances. Extensive use of a Gateway drug may serve to determine a higher initial level of use of a consequent drug or a faster trend of growth in use of the consequent drug across time. Additionally, a greater rate of growth across time in extent of use of the Gateway drug may itself serve to determine a faster trend of growth in extent of use of the consequent drug. This growth trajectory hypothesis for progression of drug use can be tested with a variant of structural equation modeling known as *growth curve modeling*. The more traditional cross-lag autoregressive model can be used to study lagged effects of one substance use on another. We compare these two ways of looking at drug use involvement in a sample of 679 African American and White high school youths assessed at three time points. In addition, we cross-validate our results on a previously published data set.

The research reported here was funded by the National Institute on Drug Abuse (NIDA) Grants DA01070 and DA00017. The first study was further supported by NIDA Grant DA07484. The research reported here does not represent the views or policies of NIDA.

Drug Use Sequences

The sequential model of drug use acquisition and escalation was formally proposed and tested over two decades ago (Kandel, 1975; Kandel & Faust, 1975). Since then, many attempts have been made to validate and expand the notion that use of one drug precedes use of another in a fixed sequence. A 1995 review (Werch & Anzalone, 1995) concluded that there is substantial research evidence that confirms a general sequence beginning with nonuse, progressing to legal or licit drug use, and then proceeding to illegal or illicit drug involvement.

Yet, this sequence is not without ambiguity and contrary evidence. Newcomb and Bentler (1986a) found that heavy use of cannabis as a teenager predicted increases in both cocaine use and alcohol use one year later. Newcomb and Bentler (1986b) found that higher frequency of cannabis use during earlier adolescence predicted increases in both hard drug use and cigarette use four years later. Early alcohol use did not predict later cannabis use, and there were no cross-lagged associations between cigarette use and alcohol use. The most glaring contradictions occur within the group of legal or licit drugs (e.g., cigarettes, smokeless tobacco, beer, wine, and hard liquor). Werch and Anzalone (1995) concluded that "the exact sequence of alcohol and tobacco products in the progression of other drug use is equivocal" (p. 92).

The Role of Cigarettes

The placement of cigarettes in the sequence has been particularly troublesome. The use of tobacco often precedes the use of other drugs in regard to the age of initial use (e.g., Fleming, Leventhal, Glynn, & Ershler, 1989; Mills & Noyes, 1984). Kandel, Yamaguchi, and Chen (1992) found that for women either cigarette use or alcohol use was the Gateway to marijuana use. Fleming and associates (1989) concluded that cigarette was the entry-level drug for their sample. Clearly, early tobacco use is a critical stage in the progression to use of other drugs. However, at higher levels of involvement with other licit and illicit drugs, these other drugs may deepen the involvement and addiction to tobacco (e.g., Newcomb & Bentler, 1986a, 1986b).

Accounting for Discrepancies

Many factors may explain discrepancies among studies, including study design, definition of a stage, and differing analytic procedures.

Conceptual Variations. Stage and sequential models are distinct but share several common features (Werch & Anzalone, 1995). Stage models describe the phases of acquiring a particular behavior, such as cigarette use, and represent intradomain, in general for health behaviors, or intradrug, in particular, patterns of behavioral involvement (Weinstein, Rothman, & Sutton, 1998). Interdomain behavior sequences involve the transition from one behavior to another in a progression, in this case the progression of the use of one drug to use of another in a specific order. This is often called the gateway hypothesis.

One critical characteristic of both these models is the definition of state or stage of drug use sequences. These have included (1) use versus nonuse of a drug, (2) level or degree of drug involvement, and (3) problem or inappropriate drug use. Conclusions about the nature and ordering of the drug use sequence can depend on the chosen definition. In the following we use the second operationalization.

The use versus nonuse distinction seems simplistic. Early experimentation with drugs may be ephemeral and transient, dependent on circumstances and availability. Using this criterion, the typical sequence of drug initiation begins with nonuse, progresses to use of alcohol and/or cigarettes, and then to marijuana use (e.g., Ellickson, Hays, & Bell, 1992). Kandel, Yamaguchi, and Chen (1992) tightened the definition of use to more than 10 times and found that alcohol preceded marijuana, which preceded other illicit drugs. However, as before (e.g., Kandel & Faust, 1975), the placement of cigarettes in relationship to alcohol was not clearly delineated.

When stages are constructed on type of drug use, rather than use per se, more complicated patterns emerge. Ellickson et al. (1992) found that regular use of alcohol occurred subsequent to use of marijuana and legal drugs, and regular use of cigarettes emerged after use of all legal drugs, pills, and regular alcohol use. Donovan and Jessor (1983) found that problem drinking was subsequent to the use of marijuana and legal drugs. Further, considering changes of settings, Newcomb (1988) found that use of drugs at work began after use of legal drugs, marijuana, and cocaine.

Using a more realistic appraisal of drug use, as recommend by Kandel and Faust (1975), whereby greater involvement with one drug increases the likelihood or probability of using a different drug higher in the sequence (Newcomb & Bentler, 1989), complex and contradictory results also have emerged. For example, heavy use of cannabis increased both alcohol use and cocaine use over a 1-year period (Newcomb & Bentler, 1986a). Over a 4-year period greater involvement with cigarettes led to increased marijuana use and heavy marijuana involvement led to increased cigarette use (Newcomb & Bentler, 1986b). This reciprocal sequence may reflect factors, such as common genetic influences, a similar route of administration (i.e., volatilization), or pharmacological similarities, that are rarely considered in drug sequence theories.

Methodological Variations. These studies use different study designs and populations. The basic design variation is that of cross-sectional versus prospective data, and the primary sample variations are on age or developmental period and nature of the sample. Ideally, a temporal ordering must be demonstrated within individuals. Although cross-sectional data test whether correlations on use of various substances correspond to the simplex pattern that is consistent with stage theory, such studies (e.g., Huba & Bentler, 1983; Huba, Wingard, & Bentler, 1981) do not describe individual subjects' trends. A true test of a causal sequence requires longitudinal data.

Age or developmental stage has also varied across studies. Most investigations have examined adolescence, but some have examined young and later adulthood. Different conclusions may thus be reached as a result of the different processes and forces occurring at distinct periods of life. And, with some exceptions (e.g., Brook, Whiteman, & Gordon, 1983; Okwumabua & Duryea, 1987), most studies have examined European American teenagers in school. Only rarely have high-risk samples or ethnic minority groups been studied. In the following we examine a high-risk African American sample of teenagers.

Analytic Variations. Various procedures have been used to analyze data related to the sequence of drug use involvement. Dichotomous variables of drug use are often analyzed with Guttman scalogram methods using cross-sectional (e.g., Donovan & Jessor, 1983) and prospective data (e.g., Ellickson et al., 1992). Life event history analysis (e.g., Kandel et al., 1992) is concerned with the impact of factors on the timing and sequence of transitions, especially the rate of change in a discrete dependent variable such as smoking (or not). Continuous and near-continuous frequency data have been recoded to categorical variables and analyzed with Guttman scales and conditional probabilities (e.g., Kandel & Faust, 1975). In the following we accept the variables as continuous and use path or structural equation models that have latent constructs (e.g., Huba et al., 1981; Newcomb & Bentler, 1986b; Hays, Widaman, DiMatteo, & Stacy, 1987) or measured variables (e.g., Newcomb & Bentler, 1986a).

Better appreciation of individual change in drug use over time is given by the longitudinal Guttman simplex (e.g., Collins & Cliff, 1990), in which for each person there is a joint items–occasions ordering. Ellickson et al. (1992) used such a method to show that increased involvement with legal drugs is a step in the transition to hard drug use for most adolescents. Similarly, latent transition analysis (Collins & Wugalter, 1992) is concerned with sequences of qualitative changes (see Chapter 11). A model of quantitative change is the multilevel model for longitudinal data (e.g., Duncan et al., 1997; Chou, Bentler, & Penz, 1998). A basic two-level hierarchy is obtained when measurement occasions are nested within subjects. Especially interesting are methodologies that permit evaluating whether and how an individual's pattern and progression of one type of drug use influence the progression and involvement with a different drug. A new method to accomplish this with qualitative sequences was developed by Flaherty and Collins (1999). Their extension of latent transition analysis estimates two sequences simultaneously and allows stages in one sequence to affect the other. However, when applied to inherently quantitative data, recoding to a few categories can destroy valuable information. Growth curve modeling for quantitative data (discussed later) is a promising technique for testing evolving extensiveness of drug use involvement and how extent of use of one type of drug influences extent of use of another drug. However, it is unclear whether this approach will yield insights beyond those available from the cross-lag approach (Curran, Stice, & Chassin, 1997).

Context and Predictors of Progression

Many risk and protective factors have been identified and tested as predictors of drug use and abuse (e.g., Hawkins, Catalano, & Miller, 1992; Newcomb & Felix-Ortiz, 1992). Some of these have been tested as direct predictors of greater involvement in the purported drug use sequence (e.g., Brook Whiteman, & Gordon, 1983; Kandel, Kessler, & Margulies, 1978; Yamaguchi & Kandel, 1984). In general, these influences are personal (i.e., demographic, personality) and social (i.e., family, peers) in nature (e.g., Kandel, 1978; Newcomb, 1995). The context within which drug use occurs (i.e., availability), as well as sociocultural norms and beliefs about drugs, no doubt also affect the nature and character of a drug use sequence. For example, centuries ago in China, tobacco was considered more harmful and undesirable than opium (Westermeyer, 1988), and hence it is unlikely that tobacco would have been the initial drug of choice at the time.

Structural Equation Models for Research on Gateway Drugs

Cross-Lagged Autoregressive Models

The simplex model is a natural model for a continuous variable such as alcohol use (A) measured at several time points. The relative amount of use at one time point affects only the relative amount of use at the immediately subsequent time point, as in the sequence $A_1 \rightarrow A_2 \rightarrow A_3 \rightarrow A_4$, where the time lag between measurements is appropriate. Here each arrow represents a regression coefficient, and the residuals are not shown. The coefficients should be positive and large. Thus $A_1 \rightarrow A_2$ implies that people with higher alcohol use at Time 1 also will have higher alcohol use at Time 2. There may be additional such sequences, for example, for illicit drug use (I), the sequence $I_1 \rightarrow I_2 \rightarrow I_3 \rightarrow I_4$.

If use of a Gateway drug such as smoking tobacco (S) is a precursor to such a sequence, then $S_0 \rightarrow A_1 \rightarrow A_2 \rightarrow A_3 \rightarrow A_4$, although S might also affect A at a later time in the sequence. An effect that skips a time point, such as $A_1 \rightarrow A_3$, is no longer a simplex, but it is not necessarily inconsistent with the spirit of this kind of model. An invariant cross-drug use sequence might be $S_0 \rightarrow A_1 \rightarrow I_2$, or $S_1 \rightarrow A_2 \rightarrow I_3$. Reverse sequences such as $I_1 \rightarrow A_2 \rightarrow S_3$ are inconsistent with tobacco as a Gateway drug for alcohol and illicit drug use. These sequences imply restricted covariance structures (e.g., Huba et al., 1981; Newcomb & Bentler, 1986a; 1986b), and hence are testable. As in regression, the means are not of interest. However, there is nothing in the theory to prevent adding a mean structure. Then mean drug use at each time point, and increments in means, also would be modeled (e.g., Bentler, 1995, Ch. 8). This has not been done in Gateway research.

Because observed variables contain errors of measurement, sequences are ideally modeled with latent variables with appropriate indicators of use (e.g., Huba et al., 1981; Newcomb & Bentler, 1986b; Hays et al., 1987). Because drug use variables often have skewed and kurtotic distributions, normality-assuming tests can be seriously distorted (Bentler & Dudgeon, 1996). The Satorra–Bentler (1994) chi-square and robust standard errors in EQS remain today's best performing statistics (Hu, Bentler, & Kano, 1992).

Latent Growth Curve Models

Linear models allow several ways to evaluate growth, for example, hierarchical regression with linear or quadratic trends. A more flexible approach is given by growth curve modeling (see e.g., McArdle & Epstein, 1987; Meredith & Tisak, 1990; Stoolmiller, 1994; Curran, Stice, & Chassin, 1997; and especially Duncan & Duncan, 1996; Duncan et al., 1997; and Duncan et al., 1999).

Basic Ideas. One hypothesizes that two or more special factors underlie repeatedly measured variables, such as alcohol use measured at three time points (see Figure 10.1). The Intercept and Linear Growth factors explain the means, variances, and correlations among the variables. The factor loadings are fixed at 1.0 on the Intercept factor, and at 0.0, 1.0, and 2.0 across time. This is a very restricted covariance structure model. Further, the Constant is a hypothetical variable scored 1.0 for all subjects (called *V999* in EQS), and its inclusion makes this a mean structure model. "The coefficient for regression on a constant is an intercept" (Bentler, 1995, p. 166), and an intercept is a mean for a variable that is otherwise an independent variable. Thus a, a free parameter, is the Intercept factor mean, and b is the Linear Growth factor mean. Individual differences in Intercept generate the variance D1, and individual differences in Linear Growth generate the variance D2. Thus the Intercept factor has mean a and variance D1, and the Linear Growth factor has mean b and variance D2. Not shown in the Figure, D1 and D2 can be correlated.

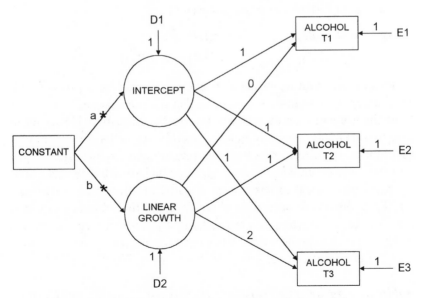

Figure 10.1. Generic growth curve model example for alcohol.

The factors generate the observed variables according to path tracing rules. The mean of a dependent variable such as Alcohol-T1 (or just T1 for short) is given by the total effect (sum of direct plus indirect effects) of the Constant on the variable. Calculations show the mean of T1 is a, and the mean for T2 is $(a + b)$. Thus b represents the increment in mean from T1 to T2. The mean for T3 is $(a + 2b)$. Hence $2b$ is the mean increment of T3 over T1, and b is the mean increment over T2. Clearly, b is the mean increment from time to time. Equal increments yield linear growth. With more frequent measurement, quadratic or other higher-order trends in mean shifts could be evaluated.

Using the usual path tracing rules, the variances are the following:

var(T1):	var(D1) + var(E1)
var(T2):	var(D1) + var(D2) + var(E2)
var(T3):	var(D1) + 4var(D2) + var(E3)

Clearly, aside from error, the variance of T1 reflects variance in the Intercept factor alone. Thus individual differences in Intercept reflect systematic individual differences in T1, that is, at the starting point of the sequence. Individual differences at a later time point also reflect individual differences in D2, that is, Linear Growth. The covariances are the following:

cov(T1, T2):	var(D1)
cov(T1, T3):	var(D1)
cov(T2, T3):	var(D1) + 2var(D2)

This model, with its strong restrictions, may not be consistent with any data set. One solution is to assume that the slope factor, here Linear Growth, has some paths that are free to be estimated. Hence mean growth is no longer precisely equal across time segments – but then, why should it be so? If time gaps between measurement are not equal, equal growth would be unlikely, and perhaps unequal growth may occur even for equal intervals at different ages. Finally, ideally the measurements T1, T2, ... would be spaced on physical ages of the subjects, but this is often not practical when data are gathered by grade, not age. If growth by age rather than grade is critical to a theory, some parameter inaccuracy may result from the use of grade (Mehta & West, 2000).

Application to Growth Trajectory Hypothesis. Now we can illustrate our growth trajectory hypothesis with a prototype model. In Figure 10.2,

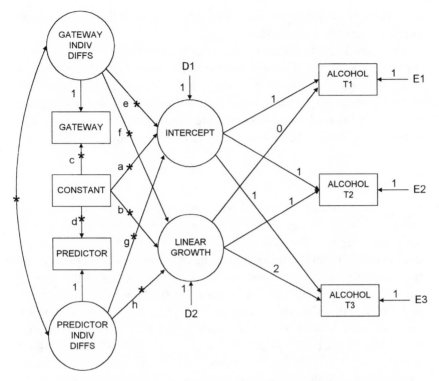

Figure 10.2. Generic growth curve model with Gateway effects for alcohol.

we add a Gateway variable and a predictor variable. These are illustrative of more complex setups.

Gateway and predictor variables are both influenced by the Constant, and paths c and d represent their means. The circled Gateway Individual Differences and Predictor Individual Differences are residuals: That is, they are the Gateway and predictor deviation scores. Thus any subject's score on a variable equals a mean plus a deviation from mean. Gateway and predictor circled variables are correlated, as shown by the two-way arrow connecting them, and both influence the Intercept and Linear Growth factors. Suppose that the Gateway variable is smoking. Then e represents the effect of smoking on subsequent alcohol Intercept; that is, higher levels of smoking would be predicted to lead to higher levels of beginning alcohol use. Path f would represent the effect of smoking on subsequent Linear Growth in alcohol use. Similar interpretations would hold for the effects g and h of the predictor variable on Intercept and Linear Growth. In any particular application, not all paths might be expected; for example, a Gateway drug might influence only the Intercept, or only Linear Growth.

In Figure 10.2, the means of the Gateway and predictor variables have no influence on the alcohol Intercept and Linear Growth factors and hence have no effect on the means of T1–T3. This could be allowed by moving paths e and f (and/or g and h) from the circled to their rectangular variables. This setup would be meaningful primarily when the left-side variables are in a similar metric as the right-side variables.

Current Study

In this study, we test whether cigarette involvement is a driving force for other licit drug involvement, specifically, alcohol use, as well as for illicit drug use. We also evaluate whether alcohol use affects illicit drug use. We do this by using the two model types described previously, the cross-lagged autoregressive model for covariances and the growth curve model for means and covariances. On the basis of prior literature and our growth trajectory hypothesis, we expect that extent of cigarette use will contribute to increased involvement with alcohol and illicit drugs, that alcohol use will affect illicit drug use, and perhaps that illicit drug use will affect alcohol use. In the specific context of growth curve analysis, we predict that heavier involvement with tobacco at an early time point will both (1) be related to higher Intercepts for alcohol and illicit drug use and (2) increase the Linear Growth rate for alcohol consumption, which in turn we expect will accelerate the Linear Growth rate of illicit drug use involvement. We also expect these patterns to be influenced by various risk and protective factors representing demographic and psychosocial influences. We analyze three waves of data in a primarily African American sample of teenagers.

Method

Participants. The sample is from the four main public high schools in the second largest school district in Michigan (Ramirez-Valles, Zimmerman, & Newcomb, 1998). At the start of fall 1994, ninth-grade students with grade-point averages of 3.0 and below were selected to participate. Students who were diagnosed as either emotionally impaired or developmentally disabled were not included. The sample includes 679 African American youths (80%), 145 White youths (17%), and 26 mixed African American and White youths (3%) and is about equally divided

Table 10.1. *Sample Characteristics by Race and Gender for Each Year of the Study*

| | Number (Percentage) | | |
	Year 1	Year 2	Year 3
African American	679 (80%)	647 (80%)	626 (80%)
Male	340 (50%)	313 (48%)	298 (48%)
Female	339 (50%)	334 (52%)	328 (52%)
White	145 (17%)	140 (17%)	132 (17%)
Male	80 (55%)	77 (55%)	71 (54%)
Female	65 (45%)	63 (45%)	61 (46%)
African American and White	26 (3%)	25 (3%)	25 (3%)
Male	12 (46%)	11 (44%)	11 (44%)
Female	14 (54%)	14 (56%)	14 (56%)
Total sample	850	812	783

Note: Year 1 = fall 1994; Year 2 = fall 1995; Year 3 = fall 1996.

by sex (see Table 10.1). Ranging in age from 14 to 17 (mean = 14.6, $SD = .66$), their prevalence of lifetime smoking and marijuana use was 46.1% and 47.7%, respectively. These teenagers were followed for 3 years. The response rate from Year 1 to Year 2 was 96%, from Year 2 to Year 3 was 96%, and from Year 1 to Year 3 was 92%.

Procedure. Face-to-face interviews were conducted by trained African American and European American male and female interviewers. Students were called from their regular classrooms and taken to select areas within the school to be interviewed. Interviews lasted for 50–60 minutes. Youths who no longer attended school were interviewed in a community setting (e.g., home, Urban League office).

Measures. Data were gathered at three waves separated by 1-year periods. Identical measures of past year alcohol and illicit drug use were assessed at each year. Cigarette use and psychosocial predictors were taken from the first wave of data.

Drug Use. Two items were used to reflect a latent construct of Cigarette Use at Time 1: (1) lifetime use of cigarettes (*cigever*, ranging from never [0] to regularly now [5]); and (2) rate of cigarette smoking in the past 30 days (*cig30day*, ranging from not at all [0] to two packs or more per day [7]). Alcohol use was a measured variable assessing the frequency of consuming alcoholic beverages in the past 12 months, at each of three time points (*alct1, alct2, alct3*, each ranging from 0 time [0] to

Table 10.2. *Summary Statistics for Variables in Figures 10.3 and 10.4*

Variable	Mean	Standard Deviation	Skewness	Kurtosis
sex	1.51	.50	−.04	−2.00
parntsup	3.94	1.03	−1.03	.18
frnusedr	1.32	.39	1.74	3.19
depressn	1.66	.71	1.62	2.82
anxiety	1.59	.64	1.76	3.61
gpa	4.78	1.91	−.08	−.61
planhsg	4.60	.78	−1.95	3.38
cigever	1.83	1.19	1.44	1.29
cig30day	.81	1.16	1.84	4.18
alct1	1.52	1.79	1.24	.95
alct2	1.66	1.87	1.01	.13
alct3	1.62	1.99	1.16	.34
illic1	1.56	2.38	2.32	8.28
illic2	2.02	2.58	1.29	1.86
illic3	10.63	4.54	−.77	1.09

40+ times [7]). Illicit drug use (*illic1, illic2, illic3*) was the sum of 11 types of drugs (i.e., marijuana lysergic acid dethylamide [LSD], phenylcyclohexyl piperidine [PCP], cocaine, uppers, downers), rated for their frequency of use during the past 12 months on the same scale as for alcohol.

Psychosocial Variables. Sex was coded male (1) and female (2). Single scales were used to capture parent support (*parntsup*) and friends' use of drugs (*frnusedr*) as measured variables. A latent construct of Academic Orientation was reflected by two items: (1) self-reported grade-point average (*gpa*, coded [1] to [9]) and (2) likelihood of graduation from high school (*planhsg*, rated on a scale from not at all likely [1] to very likely [5]). Finally, a latent construct of Psychological Distress was reflected in two multiitem scales (1) depression (*depressn*) and (2) anxiety.

Analysis. All models were estimated with normal theory maximum likelihood using the EQS for Windows program. Two subjects made extreme contributions to Mardia's normalized multivariate kurtosis, and to the robust parameter variances, and hence were eliminated from further analyses. The basic statistics on the final sample are shown in Table 10.2. There is evident nonnormality. As a result, the autoregressive model was evaluated statistically by using the Satorra–Bentler (1994) corrected test statistic and the robust standard errors, but these corrections were not possible in the growth curve model, because these methods are not yet implemented in mean structure models. Thus, the root mean square error of approximation (RMSEA), the comparative fit index (CFI), and the standardized root mean square residual (SRMR) were used to evaluate models (Hu & Bentler, 1998). The former two indexes are reliable under a wide variety of modeling conditions, and the latter is the most sensitive to model misspecification.

First, an a priori model was set up. Model modification was done by using the Lagrange multiplier test on theoretically meaningful parameters. Finally, models were pruned by eliminating nonsignificant parameters having small absolute standardized size. In view of our plan to cross-validate, we were not unduly worried about capitalization on chance.

Cross-Lagged Autoregressive Model

The final model is presented in Figure 10.3, which shows the predictor variables in the left part of the figure, the Gateway drug tobacco in the bottom right, and two sets – alcohol use and illicit drug use – of cross-lagged consequent drug use variables across 3 years in the right-hand side. The figure gives the Wright standardized solution, so that coefficients are standardized partial beta (β) weights. Overall, this is an acceptable model (Satorra–Bentler $\chi^2 = 68.7$, $df = 65$, $p = .35$, robust $CFI = .999$, $RMSEA = .021$, $SRMR = .025$).

Drug Use Effects. In the right-hand side, standardized coefficients from .29 to .42 show that alcohol use and illicit drug use are not very stable across 3 years. Alcohol has a longer memory than anticipated by a simplex, with a small time 1–3 effect. Nonetheless, controlling for their predictors, relative amount of alcohol use at times 1 and 2 (T1 and T2) significantly predicts relative amount of illicit drug use 1 year later. There is one feedback effect of illicit use at T2 on alcohol use at T3. There are significant residual associations (.43–.55 in a correlation metric) within time. The variables in the model account for .17–.40% of the variance (i.e., $1 - residual \beta^2$) in drug use.

Gateway Effects. Cigarette Use, based on two very highly loading indicators of cigarette smoking, is the primary Gateway drug use of interest. Given the personal controls, amount of smoking significantly positively

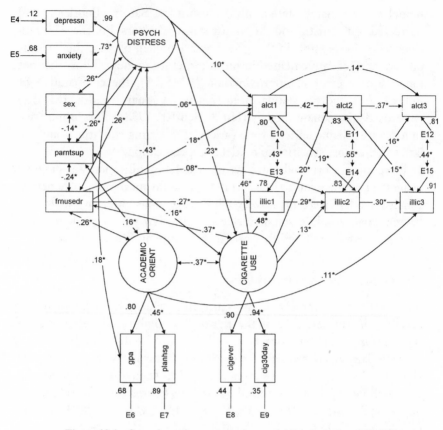

Figure 10.3. Cross-lagged autoregressive model for alcohol and illicit drugs.

impacts alcohol use at T1 and T2 (.46, .20), as well as illicit use at T1 and T2 (.48, .13). Note that the larger coefficients at T1, but not those at T2, are inflated by contemporaneous measurement. Importantly, Cigarette Use has a further impact on subsequent substance use via its significant indirect effects (all $p < .01$) on both alcohol use and illicit drug use at T2 and T3.

Predictor Effects. Four of the seven predictor variables depend on two latent factors, Psychological Distress and Academic Orientation. Each factor has highly loading indicators. There was an unanticipated small (.18) loading of grade-point average (GPA) on Psychological Distress. This effect was significant by ML, but not by the correct robust standard error, so we consider it an uninteresting suppressor effect. The predictors are typically correlated, always in the logical direction. Correlations omitted among predictors were nonsignificant, and hence set to zero.

The higher subjects' levels of Psychological Distress, and being female as compared to male, the more alcohol is used at T1. Parent support has no impact, whereas as expected during adolescence, friends' use has a significant impact on both alcohol use and illicit drug use at T1. Friends' use has a trivially small but significant, unanticipated additional impact at T2. Finally, Academic Orientation has a significant and unanticipated small (.11) impact on illicit drug use at T3. We interpret this as an uninteresting suppressor effect, because no comparable effect shows up in the growth curve model later.

Summary. The cross-lag autoregressive model clearly indicates that, controlling for personal predictors, greater use of the cigarette Gateway drug impacts subsequent greater use of alcohol and illicit drugs. There is also a tendency for alcohol to be a gateway for increased use of illicit drugs, with some indication of feedback.

Latent Growth Curve Model

Figure 10.4 shows the final model. The figure differs from the previous one in that Sex, Parent Support, and Friends' Use of Drugs are deviation scores shown in circles. The covariances of these variables are carried by these deviation scores. In order to minimize clutter, a number of key model features are omitted from the figure. Some parts that are not shown are virtually the same as in Figure 10.3 or represent uninteresting parameters. Covariances among the predictors are virtually the same as earlier (differing by .02 maximum). Also not shown are the Constant and its emanating paths, which are 0.0 in the standardized solution. The coefficients of the respective indicators on the two Alcohol and Illicits factors are fixed nonzero (1, 1, 1 or 0, 1, 2) values as in Figures 10.1–10.2, but they show in Figure 10.4 as standardized coefficients instead. Also, the correlations between the error terms of alct1 and illic1 (.13) and alct2 and illic2 (.47) are not shown.

For each of the seven predictor variables and the two smoking variables, there is a path from the Constant to that variable, carrying information about the mean of that variable. But these means were already given in Table 10.2. Because they do not propagate the means of the growth factors or variables, there is no important new information in

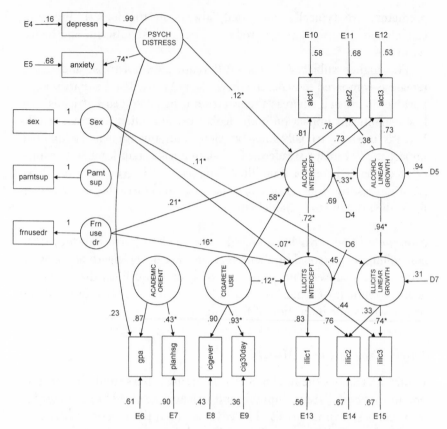

Figure 10.4. Growth curve model of cigarettes, alcohol, and illicit drugs.

them. The Constant does have a significant unstandardized effect on Alcohol Intercept (1.54), Alcohol Linear Growth (.30), and Illicit Linear Growth (.37). An intercept (7.46) for the specific T3 illicit drug use variable was unanticipated but needed.

Statistics on this model are based on maximum likelihood. All indexes imply a well-fitting model (χ^2 = 89.7, df = 71, p = .07, CFI = .995, $RMSEA$ = .020, $SRMR$ = .023).

Drug Use Factors. Both alcohol use and illicit drug use have Intercept and Linear Growth factors. However, the loading of illicit drug use at T3 on the Illicit Linear Growth factor could not be maintained at the fixed value of 2 and was estimated at 3.8 (.74 standardized), significantly larger (p < .01) than 2. Thus growth from T2 to T3 in illicit drug use was greater than expected from the linear model.

Gateway Effects. Cigarette Use has a large .58 standardized effect on the Alcohol Intercept factor. Individual differences in alcohol use at T1 are substantially dependent on prior smoking. However, this interpretation is unclear because Alcohol Intercept is largely an indicator of T1 use, which is contemporaneous with cigarette use. Smoking also marginally (.12) predicts the Illicit Intercept factor. The higher the initial use of alcohol, the lower subsequent growth in alcohol use, as shown by the $-.33$ regression coefficient of Alcohol Linear Growth on Alcohol Intercept. The largest influences are from alcohol to illicit drug use factors. Alcohol Intercept strongly (.72) predicts Illicits Intercept. Even more strongly (.94), Alcohol Linear Growth predicts Illicits Linear Growth. Cross-paths between intercept and linear growth factors were investigated but were not significant. Similarly, paths from illicit intercept and growth factors were allowed to affect alcohol intercept and growth factors, but the paths were not significant. The absence of a path from the use of illicits to alcohol use is a difference from the cross-lag model reported previously.

Predictor Effects. Higher levels of Psychological Distress predicted increased levels on Alcohol Intercept (.12). Girls were less likely to have high starting levels of illicit drug use ($-.07$) but then increased more rapidly in their use as compared to boys (.11). Friends' Use of Drugs significantly predicted Alcohol Intercept (.21) as well as Illicits Intercept (.16) factors. A suppressor effect of Psychological Distress on GPA (.23) is visible here as in Figure 10.3 and again is unlikely to be meaningful.

Mean Effects. The means of alcohol and illicit drug use variables except illic3 were not presumed to be directly affected by the Constant. Thus the means of alct1, alct2, alct3, illic1, and illic2 are indirect effects given by path tracing from the Constant to the variable through the alcohol and illicit factors, and the mean of illic3 is a total effect (sum of direct plus indirect effect). The large significant 1.54 coefficient for Constant →Alcohol Intercept indicates that mean alcohol use at T1 also accounts for mean alcohol use at T2 and T3, but also by path tracing, to the mean illicit drug use through Illicits Intercept and hence to the 3 illicit indicators at T1–T3. The small but significant .30 coefficient for Constant →Alcohol Linear Growth implies a small positive mean increase in alcohol use across time but also offsets the negative mean forward propagation of Alcohol Intercept on Alcohol Linear Growth. There are no direct effect of the Constant on Illicits Intercept and a small .37 effect of

Constant →Illicits Linear Growth. Thus the mean increment due to the Illicits Linear Growth factor is quite small. And, as already noted, the separate path Constant → illic3 with the value of 7.46 indicates that $7.46/10.63 = 70\%$ of the increment in mean illicit drug use at T3 is not mediated by any of the other drug factors.

Summary. Although the Gateway Hypothesis could imply strong effects of Cigarette Use on both intercepts and linear growth factors, contrary to expectation there were essentially no direct effects of Cigarette use on Alcohol and Illicits Linear Growth. The impacts were primarily on the intercept factors and, as noted, could be a result of a contemporaneous measurement. This is an unfortunate aspect of this study's design.

There are some significant indirect effects. The effect of Cigarette Use on Alcohol Linear Growth is a significant negative indirect effect ($p < .01$) through Alcohol Intercept, implying that although Cigarette Use impels strong initial use of alcohol, it does not impel further growth in alcohol use. The indirect effect of Cigarette Use on Illicits Intercept is also significant ($p < .01$), but as expected positive. Again, simultaneous measurement at T1 of cigarette use and illic1 make this a somewhat ambiguous finding.

Cross-Validation Study

We sought to strengthen our substantive conclusions by cross-validating findings using data from Duncan and Duncan (1996). Although their report provides a beautiful discussion, analysis, and account of alternative growth curve models, they did not report on Gateway theories and results.

The data are based on 321 adolescents who had complete data on four annual assessments of social context for drug use (parent–child conflict; *ParChCon*; parent drug use; peer encouragement of use; *Peer Encr*; gender; family status; age) and four repeated assessments of alcohol use, cigarette use, and marijuana use. Drug variables were scored on 5-point scales to represent current status and frequency of use. We make use of all of the drug use measures as well as the three predictor variables (ParChCon, Peer Encr, gender) that are parallel to our own study. Although the variables are not identical to those in our study, there is great conceptual overlap. The sample, however, is quite different in race and educational background from our own. Subjects ranged in age from

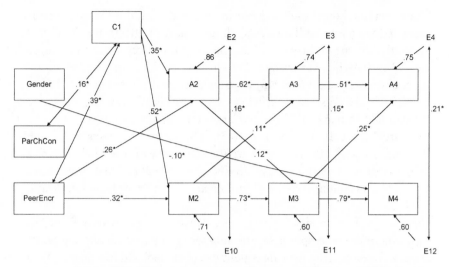

Figure 10.5. Cross-lag model on Duncan and Duncan (1996) data for cigarettes, alcohol, and marijuana.

11 to 15 (mean = 13.11, *SD* = 1.49), were mainly girls (57%), were from single-parent homes (44.5%), and were largely White (>90%) and from professional homes (>80%).

Cross-Lagged Autoregressive Model

Cigarette use at T1 (C1) is the primary Gateway drug use in a model in which alcohol use (A2, A3, A4) and marijuana use (M2, M3, M4) are measured at three consecutive occasions. Thus, there is no simultaneous measurement confounding for the Gateway Hypothesis. The final standardized solution is shown in Figure 10.5. Because raw scores were not accessible, maximum likelihood was used. The model fits the data well (χ^2 = 32.6, *df* = 28, *p* = .25, *CFI* = .997, *RMSEA* = .023, *SRMR* = .039). The SRMR means that the correlations among the variables were reproduced to within .039 on average.

The three predictor variables (Gender, ParChCon, Peer Encr) are contemporaneous with cigarette use at T1 (C1). Gender is scored so that male subjects have higher scores. Only two correlations are significantly nonzero, indicating that parent–child conflict and peer encouragement of use are associated with the subjects' cigarette use. Cigarette use is a significant gateway precursor to subsequent alcohol (C1→A2) and marijuana (C1→M2) use, with coefficients of .35 and .52 moderate to substantial.

The effect of C1 on alcohol and marijuana use at T3 and T4 is significantly mediated via its direct T2 effects; all four indirect effects are significant ($p < .01$). In the right side of the figure are the repeatedly measured alcohol and marijuana variables. Stabilities (e.g., A2 → A3) and all cross-lag coefficients (e.g., A2 → M3) were included in the initial model. All but the A3 → M4 cross-lag coefficient were significant. The stabilities are substantial (from .51 to .79), much larger than in our own data (.29 to .42; compare Figure 10.5 to Figure 10.3). The cross-lag effects are small. Reverse cross-lag effects, which are inconsistent with use of alcohol as a Gateway drug to marijuana use, are also seen. Small residual correlations (.16, .15, .21) among errors within time are not interpretively important.

Summary. This model is remarkably consistent with results from our own data in several respects: Controlling for personal predictors, cigarettes act as a Gateway drug for subsequent use of alcohol and marijuana. That is, heavier smoking of cigarettes yields increased subsequent use of alcohol and marijuana. Cigarette use at T1 not only directly affects subsequent alcohol and marijuana use at T2 but also significantly indirectly affects these variables at T3 and T4 (all four $p < .01$). Alcohol is a weaker Gateway drug for marijuana as compared to our data on illicit drugs, and marijuana use also more strongly affects alcohol use when compared to the previous results.

Latent Growth Curve Model

As in the cross-lag model, the Gateway variable (cigarette use) is measured at T1, and the growth curve factors are based on drug use data obtained subsequently. Figure 10.6 gives the standardized solution from the final model. The fit is extremely good ($\chi^2 = 20.1$, $df = 23$, $p = .63$, $CFI = 1.000$, $RMSEA = .000$, $SRMR = .035$). The left-most variables are gender (reverse scored in this model as Sex, to have the same directionality as the Michigan data), parent–child conflict, and peer encouragement to use drugs. These variables are similar in meaning to their counterparts in Figure 10.4. Cigarette use is measured at T1. The circled variable is just the deviation observed variable, not a factor with two indicators as in Figure 10.4. In the right part of the figure are two sets of growth curve factors, one for alcohol (top) and one for marijuana (below). The path structure of these factors was taken as in Figure 10.4, though other possibilities were explored and found not to be an improvement. The alcohol growth factors influence the marijuana growth factors,

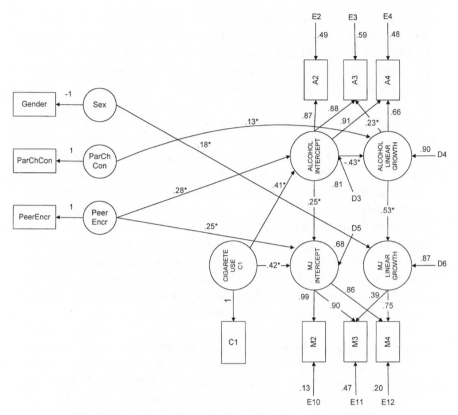

Figure 10.6. Growth curve model on Duncan and Duncan (1996) data for cigarettes, alcohol, and marijuana.

but only within factor type (intercept, or slope). Not shown are residual covariances between the growth factors, covariances among the residual error terms for the drug variables measured at the same time, and mean and intercept effects.

Drug Use Factors. The intercept and linear growth loadings for both alcohol and marijuana were initially the usual (1, 1, 1) and (0, 1, 2) fixed values in the unstandardized solution. However, the path from Alcohol Linear Growth to A3 could not be maintained at the fixed 1 value, and hence it was freed and estimated at .74 (.23 standardized). Thus on average, growth at T3 was a bit slower than expected from the model, and hence this factor no longer represents equal growth across intervals. This effect mirrors the data, because the means of A2, A3, and A4

(2.56, 2.69, 2.96) show a smaller A2–A3 difference, as compared to A3–A4. In general, the standardized factor loadings are higher than in Figure 10.4, indicating that alcohol use and marijuana use were more strongly correlated across time than in the Michigan data (as can also be seen by comparing Figures 10.3 and 10.5).

Gateway Effects. Cigarette Use is a significant Gateway drug use for both Alcohol (.41) and Marijuana (.42) Intercept factors in these data. However, it is not a Gateway drug for the corresponding Alcohol and MJ Linear Growth factors. Cigarette Use also significantly indirectly affects all six subsequent alcohol and marijuana variables ($p < .01$). Alcohol Intercept and Linear Growth factors affect their corresponding MJ Intercept and Linear Growth factors significantly, and there are no cross-effects of different factor types. The only intercept to linear growth effect is for alcohol (−.43), indicating the higher one starts, the slower the subsequent growth. Although the loading sizes are not identical, these results are similar to those of Figure 10.4, representing a substantial cross-validation of gateway effects.

Predictor Effects. Female subjects showed somewhat greater Marijuana Linear Growth as compared to boys (.18). Peer encouragement for substance use predicted increased Alcohol Intercept (.28) and Marijuana Intercept (.25) levels. Each of the preceding effects mirrors a comparable effect in our own data, as shown in Figure 10.4. An effect in these data, but not ours, is that parent–child conflict predicted increased Alcohol Linear Growth (.13). An effect in our data, but not Duncan and Duncan, is a sex difference effect on MJ Intercept. As expected, the predictor variables correlate, precisely at the values given by Duncan and Duncan in their Table 10.1. Additionally, residual errors for substance use measured at the same time are correlated (E2 and E10: − .78; E3, E11: .18; E4, E12: − .42), as are residuals in growth factors (D3, D6: .22, D5, D6: − .30). To minimize clutter, these correlations are not shown.

Mean Effects. The Constant, part of the model but not shown in Figure 10.6, significantly affects Gender, ParChCon, PeerEncr, and C1. These unstandardized effects simply reproduce the sample means of these variables and hence are not interpretively interesting. Again, remarkably mirroring the results in our own data, the Constant affects Alcohol Intercept (2.559), Alcohol Linear Growth (.595), and Marijuana Intercept (.942), whereas there is no direct effect on Marijuana Linear

Growth. The meaning and interpretation of these effects are identical to those in the Michigan model.

Summary. Key results from our study cross-validate remarkably well in the Duncan and Duncan data, though there are some differences in the relative size of coefficients. For example, the positive cross-growth factor effects of Alcohol Intercept on Marijuana Intercept and of Alcohol Linear Growth on Marijuana Linear Growth parallel our own results, though the effect sizes (.25, .53) are smaller than obtained in our own data (.72, .94). More important than these details, however, is that the pattern of Gateway effects is remarkably similar: namely, cigarette use has a relationship as a Gateway drug to both Alcohol and Illicits or Marijuana Intercept factors, but not to either of the growth factors in both data sets. In neither data set is there a feedback effect of Illicits or Marijuana use growth factors on Alcohol growth factors. Even some of the gender and peer effects are similar in both data sets.

Discussion

We compared cross-lag autoregressive structural models with latent growth curve models to examine the role of cigarettes as Gateway drugs in the hypothesized increasing involvement sequence of alcohol to illicit (marijuana) drug use. We also evaluated other drug use sequences in extent of drug use and included some risk and protective variables that might influence drug use progression. Our analyses were conducted on two data sets of similar variables, but quite different samples of teenagers. One sample is a high-risk sample of primarily African American teenagers, and the other a more privileged sample of primarily White adolescents. Certain of the results are surprisingly consistent across methods and data sets, whereas others are distinct and imply different conclusions depending on the methodology used and the nature of the groups.

Tobacco as a Gateway Drug

One of the most consistent results of these analyses is that smoking is an important Gateway drug in both samples of subjects and as evaluated by the two different types of models. In each of the four main analyses (Figures 10.3–10.6), cigarette use was a significant and substantial precursor to subsequent use of other substances, namely, alcohol, marijuana, and other illicit drugs. Although there was some confounding of within

T1 effects (but not to T2) in our high-risk sample, there was no such confounding in the Duncan and Duncan data, making the results quite strong indeed. Of course, these results are not entirely unexpected, because prior research has shown that teenagers who are heavy users of cigarettes subsequently also tend to drink more alcohol and use more illicit drugs (e.g., Newcomb & Bentler, 1986a, 1986b). Similarly, Flaherty and Collins (1999) found that advancement in tobacco use predicts advancement in alcohol use.

On the other hand, smoking's role is not precisely that envisioned by a classic stage theory. Cigarette use played a prominent role in driving increases in both alcohol use and illicit drug use over time. Although the cigarettes to alcohol effect can be predicted by the drug progression hypothesis, the cigarettes to illicit (and marijuana) drug use effect is not part of this hypothesis. In fact, the cigarettes to illicit drug use path violates the stage notion and provides disconfirming evidence for the simplistic version of the drug use progression hypothesis. A similar effect has been found in previous research (e.g., Newcomb & Bentler, 1986b) and further emphasizes the need to reevaluate the hypothesized stage model of drug use acquisition. Although we did not specifically differentiate onset of use from escalation of use, the consequences of cigarette use are clear. Our results emphasize the central role of tobacco in drug use progression and clearly identify cigarette use as a major Gateway to both other licit use and illicit drug use.

We had proposed that higher levels of use of a Gateway drug may influence individual differences in progression in use of a substance. Although as hypothesized smoking strongly influenced subsequent levels of both alcohol and illicit drug use – the effect on Intercept factors shown in Figures 10.4 and 10.6 – contrary to our proposal, it did not influence the linear growth in use of the subsequent drugs. That is, there was no impact of smoking on any of the Linear Growth factors. To our knowledge, this is the first study evaluating such a growth-effect hypothesis. If the finding holds up in other research, it would seem that the Gateway effect is limited to an initial level effect and its indirect consequences. This implies that a Gateway drug's sensitization effect on use of other drugs can be seen relatively quickly.

Alcohol as a Gateway Drug

Results concerning alcohol as a Gateway drug are also positive, though more complex in nature, and depend somewhat on the methodology used. In all four models, evidence could be found for alcohol as a

Gateway drug to illicit (including marijuana) drugs. In the two cross-lag models, levels of alcohol use at one time point significantly predicted increased illicit drug use 1 year later. This effect was significant in three out of four possible cross-lag effects (Figures 10.3 and 10.5). In these models, initial levels of illicit use are controlled, so even though the effect sizes are not very large, their consistency is remarkable. Similarly, in both growth curve models (Figures 10.4 and 10.6), there is a strong effect of Alcohol Intercept on Illicits and MJ Intercepts, meaning that higher levels of alcohol use predict higher levels of illicit drug use. Furthermore, there is also a strong effect of Alcohol Linear Growth on Illicits (MJ) Linear Growth, indicating that an increasing trajectory of alcohol use across time predicts an increasing trajectory of illicit drug use over time. These consistent findings provide very strong support for the hypothesized drug use acquisition sequence that leads from alcohol use to illicit drug use (Kandel, 1975; Kandel & Faust, 1975; Kandel & Yamaguchi, 1999).

The complexity in interpretation involves the existence of feedback effects of illicit drug use on alcohol use. Although such effects were explicitly evaluated, they were not observed in the growth curve models of Figures 10.4 and 10.6. In contrast, the autoregressive models show that three of four possible effects of the "higher" drug in the sequence (illicits, marijuana) significantly affect subsequent levels of use of the "lower" drug in the sequence, alcohol. In other words, higher levels of earlier illicit drug use increased the levels of later alcohol use. In conjunction with the effect of alcohol on illicit drug use, this shows a reciprocal or feedback effect between alcohol use and illicit drug use over time. The absence of a clear feedback effect in the growth curve models may reflect that there is no explicit parameter for a lag effect in these models. Although we cannot fully explain the inconsistent results between the two methodologies, the result we obtained from two data sets has been observed in other research (e.g., Newcomb, 1988; Newcomb & Bentler, 1986a). Indeed, it can be argued that these cross-lag results are more rich and detailed regarding drug use sequences than the results obtained from the growth curve models.

Reverse effects are in direct contradiction to a theory implying a specific drug use acquisition and influence sequence. There are several possible explanations for this apparent reverse sequence in which a drug higher in the hierarchy exerts a strong effect on a drug lower in the sequence. For instance, the present analyses are based on intensity of drug use and not simply on whether or not a drug is used. Sequences of initiation or onset of use alone, ignoring magnitude of use, may not show reciprocal effects (e.g., Flaherty & Collins, 1999). But magnitude or level of use is a critical aspect of drug use, because it is frequent and high quantity use that will yield negative personal and social consequences. In fact, high levels of alcohol consumption may reflect problem alcohol use, which may occur higher in the drug progression sequence than simple alcohol consumption (e.g., Newcomb, 1988). Nevertheless, in spite of the methodological inconsistency, we suspect that a simple one-directional drug acquisition model may be too simplistic to capture the complex interplay that seems to occur in use of various kinds of drugs. We need to broaden our theories to incorporate the more interactive nature of drug use acquisition and escalation.

Personal Vulnerabilities

Only a few personal vulnerability variables were included in these models as control or predictor variables, but some results are remarkably consistent across methodologies and data sets. In all models, peers had a strong effect on contemporaneous and subsequent substance use. This is seen in the effects of friends' drug use on alct1 and illic1 as well as illic2 in Figure 10.3, and its effect on Alcohol and Illicits Intercepts in Figure 10.4. Similar results were obtained with the peer encouragement of substance use variable in Figures 10.3 and 10.5. The growth curve models showed that these influences were limited to initial levels of subsequent use (Intercept factors) and do not involve subsequent individual differences in growth (Linear Growth factors). Female subjects showed higher Marijuana or Illicits Linear Growth trends in two data sets (Figures 10.4, 10.6). In the cross-lag model, this shows up as a small increment among females on marijuana use at T4. These results are consistent with research showing that although women may start drug use later, they may progress faster to problem use, as compared to men (e.g., Lex, 1991). Finally, in our high-risk sample, Psychological Distress is a small but significant predictor of alcohol use. Because the Distress factor involves depression and anxiety, this is not a surprising result. Further research on, and discussion of, predictors of alcohol use can be found in Barnes, Murray, Patton, Bentler, & Anderson (2000).

Alternate Explanations

We investigated some risk factors for drug use and investigated drug use sequences starting with tobacco use. Some of the influences that we studied in relation to the Gateway Hypothesis, and its very sequence, may not be primary causes in the most fundamental sense. Instead of being exogenous predictors, the academic and psychological variables used as predictors of the sequence may in reality represent mediational influences. They may be a consequence of more basic precursors, such as genetic attributes of individuals. This is not idle speculation because research has shown that personality variables related to drug use progression may themselves be substantially determined by genetic variation (e.g., Rose, 1995). Also, smoking may be substantially under genetic control (e.g., Spitz et al., 1998), as may the hypothesized intermediate variable of alcohol use (e.g., Li, 2000). In fact, evidence is accumulating for at least some common genetic origins for use of various drugs (e.g., Koopmans, van Doornen, & Boomsma, 1997), and for common precursors to the association between personality and drug use (e.g., Tambs, Harris, & Magnus, 1997).

On the other hand, it is hard to argue that friends' use or peers' encouragement of substance use are genetically controlled. In this research, peer variables provided a moderately strong influence on subsequent substance use. This is not a new result (e.g., Kandel, 1973; 1978). Thus social influences clearly play a role. Of course, a theorist could argue that genetically based personal attributes may lead to a selection of certain types of friends who might be drug users. To evaluate such a hypothesis requires a study design not envisioned in our research.

Clearly, key predictors in our work and the work of others might lose their explanatory power in the presence of such omitted prior variables. Drug sequence and progression studies so far have not included measures of genetic or physiological liabilities. Their incorporation may lead to new interpretations of Gateway drugs and drug progression sequences, and to a more fundamental understanding of their very nature.

References

Barnes, G. E., Murray, R. P., Patton, D., Bentler, P. M., & Anderson, R. E. (2000). *The addiction prone personality.* New York: Kluwer Academic/Plenum.

Bentler, P. M. (1995). *EQS structural equations program manual.* Encino, CA: Multivariate Software (www.mvsoft.com).

Bentler, P. M., & Dudgeon, P. (1996). Covariance structure analysis: Statistical practice, theory, directions. *Annual Review of Psychology, 47,* 563–592.

Brook, J. S., Whiteman, M., & Gordon, A. S. (1983). Stages of drug use in adolescence: Personality, peer, and family correlates. *Developmental Psychology, 19,* 269–277.

Chou, C.-P., Bentler, P. M., & Pentz, M. A. (1998). Comparisons of two statistical approaches to study growth curves: The multilevel model and latent curve analysis. *Structural Equation Modeling, 5*, 247–266.

Collins, L. M., & Cliff, N. (1990). Using the longitudinal Guttman simplex as a basis for measuring growth. *Psychological Bulletin, 108*, 128–134.

Collins, L. M., & Wugalter, S. E. (1992). Latent class models for stage-sequential dynamic latent variables. *Multivariate Behavioral Research, 27*, 131–157.

Curran, P. J., Stice, E., & Chassin, L. (1997). The relation between adolescent alcohol use and peer alcohol use: A longitudinal random coefficients model. *Journal of Consulting and Clinical Psychology, 55*, 130–140.

Donovan, J., & Jessor, R. (1983). Problem drinking and the dimension of involvement with drugs: A Guttman scalogram analysis of adolescent drug use. *American Journal of Public Health, 73*, 543–552.

Duncan, S. C., & Duncan, T. E. (1996). A multivariate latent growth curve analysis of adolescent substance use. *Structural Equation Modeling, 3*, 323–347.

Duncan, T. E., Duncan, S. C., Alpert, A., Hops, H., Stoolmiller, M., & Muthén, B. (1997). Latent variable modeling of longitudinal and multilevel substance use data. *Multivariate Behavioral Research, 32*, 275–318.

Duncan, T. E., Duncan, S. C., Strycker, L. A., Li, F., & Alpert, A. (1999). *An introduction to latent variable growth curve modeling: Concepts, issues, and applications.* Mahwah, NJ: Erlbaum.

Ellickson, P. L., Hays, R. D., & Bell, R. M. (1992). Stepping through the drug use sequence: Longitudinal scalogram analysis of initiation and regular use. *Journal of Abnormal Psychology, 101*, 441–451.

Flaherty, B. P., & Collins, L. M. (1999). *Modeling transitions in two stage-sequences simultaneously.* Technical Report 99-33, Methodology Center, Pennsylvania State University.

Fleming, R., Leventhal, H., Glynn, K., & Ershler, J. (1989). The role of cigarettes in the initiation and progression of early substance use. *Addictive Behaviors, 14*, 261–272.

Hawkins, J. D., Catalano, R. F., & Miller, J. Y. (1992). Risk and protective factors for alcohol and other drug problems in adolescence and early adulthood: Implications for substance abuse prevention. *Psychological Bulletin, 112*, 64–105.

Hays, R. D., Widaman, K. F., DiMatteo, M. R., & Stacy, A. W. (1987). Structural equation models of drug use: Are appropriate models so simple(x)? *Journal of Personality and Social Psychology, 52*, 134–144.

Hu, L., & Bentler, P. M. (1998). Fit indices in covariance structural equation modeling: Sensitivity to underparameterized model misspecification. *Psychological Methods, 3*, 424–453.

Hu, L., Bentler, P. M., & Kano, Y. (1992). Can test statistics in covariance structure analysis be trusted? *Psychological Bulletin, 112*, 351–362.

Huba, G. J., & Bentler, P. M. (1983). Test of a drug use causal model using asymptotically distribution free methods. *Journal of Drug Education, 13*, 3–14.

Huba, G. J., Wingard, J. A., & Bentler, P. M. (1981). A comparison of two latent variable causal models for adolescent drug use. *Journal of Personality and Social Psychology, 40*, 180–193.

Kandel, D. B. (1973). Adolescent marihuana use: Role of parents and peers. *Science, 181*, 1067–1070.

Kandel, D. B. (1975). Stages in adolescent involvement in drug use. *Science, 190*, 912–914.

Kandel, D. B. (1978). Convergences in prospective longitudinal surveys of drug use in normal populations. In D. B. Kandel (Ed.), *Longitudinal research on drug use* (pp. 3–38). New York: Wiley.

Kandel, D. B. & Faust, R. (1975). Sequence and stages in patterns of adolescent drug use. *Archives of General Psychology, 32*, 923–932.

Kandel, D. B., Kessler, R. C., & Margulies, R. Z. (1978). Antecedents of adolescent initiation into stages of drug use: A developmental analysis. *Journal of Youth and Adolescence, 7*, 13–40.

Kandel, D., & Yamaguchi, K. (1999). Developmental stages of involvement in substance use: In P. J. Ott, R. E. Tarter, & R. Ammerman (Eds.), *Sourcebook on substance abuse: Etiology, epidemiology, assessment, and treatment* (pp. 50–74). Boston: Allyn & Bacon.

Kandel, D., Yamaguchi, K., & Chen, K. (1992). Stages of progression in drug involvement from adolescence to adulthood: Further evidence for the gateway theory. *Journal of Studies on Alcohol, 53*, 447–457.

Koopmans, J. R., van Doornen, L. J. P., & Boomsma, D. I. (1997). Association between alcohol use and smoking in adolescent and young adult twins: A bivariate genetic analysis. *Alcoholism: Clinical and Experimental Research, 21*, 537–546.

Lex, B. W. (1991). Some gender differences in alcohol and polysubstance users. *Health Psychology, 10*, 121–132.

Li, T.-K. (2000). Pharmacogenetics of responses to alcohol and genes that influence alcohol drinking. *Journal of Studies on Alcohol, 60*, 5–12.

McArdle, J. J., & Epstein, D. (1987). Latent growth curves within developmental structural equation models. *Child Development, 58*, 110–133.

Mehta, P. D., & West, S. G. (2000). Putting the individual back in individual growth curves. *Psychological Methods, 5*, 23–43.

Meredith, W., & Tisak, J. (1990). Latent curve analysis. *Psychometrika, 55*, 107–122.

Mills, C. J., & Noyes, H. L. (1984). Patterns and correlates of initial and subsequent drug use among adolescents. *Journal of Consulting and Clinical Psychology, 52*, 231–243.

Newcomb, M. D. (1988). *Drug use in the workplace: Risk factors for disruptive substance use among young adults.* Dover, MA: Auburn House.

Newcomb, M. D. (1995). Identifying high-risk youth: Prevalence and patterns of adolescent drug abuse. In E. Rahdert, D. Czechowicz, & I. Amsel (Eds.), *Adolescent drug abuse: Clinical assessment and therapeutic intervention* (pp. 7–38). Rockville, MD: National Institute on Drug Abuse.

Newcomb, M. D., & Bentler, P. M. (1986a). Cocaine use among adolescents: Longitudinal associations with social context, psychopathology, and use of other substances. *Addictive Behaviors, 11*, 263–273.

Newcomb, M. D., & Bentler, P. M. (1986b). Frequency and sequence of drug use: A longitudinal study from early adolescence to young adulthood. *Journal of Drug Education, 16*, 101–120.

Newcomb, M. D., & Bentler, P. M. (1989). Substance use and abuse among children and teenagers. *American Psychologist, 44*, 242–248.

Newcomb, M. D., & Felix-Ortiz, M. (1992). Multiple protective and risk factors for drug use and abuse: Cross-sectional and prospective findings. *Journal of Personality and Social Psychology, 63*, 280–296.

Noble, E. P. (1996). The gene that rewards alcoholism. *Scientific American Science & Medicine, 3*, 52–56.

Okwumabua, J. O., & Duryea, E. J. (1987). Age of onset, periods of risk, and patterns of progression in drug use among American Indian high school students. *The International Journal of the Addictions, 22*, 1269–1276.

Ramirez-Valles, J., Zimmerman, M. A., & Newcomb, M. D. (1998). Sexual risk behavior among youth: Modeling the influence of prosocial activities and socioeconomic factors. *Journal of Health and Social Behavior, 39*, 237–253.

Rose, R. J. (1995). Genes and human behavior. *Annual Review of Psychology, 46*, 625–654.

Satorra, A., & Bentler, P. M. (1994). Corrections to test statistics and standard errors in covariance structure analysis. In A. von Eye & C. C. Clogg (Eds.), *Latent variables analysis: Applications for developmental research* (pp. 399–419). Thousand Oaks, CA: Sage.

Spitz, M. R., Shi, H., Yang, F., Hudmon, K. S., Jiang, H., Chamberlain, R. M., Amos, C. I., Wan, Y., Cinciripini, P., Hong, W. K., & Wu, X. (1998). Case-control study of the D2 dopamine receptor gene and smoking status in lung cancer patients. *Journal of the National Cancer Institute, 90*, 358–363.

Stoolmiller, M. (1994). Antisocial behavior, delinquent peer association, and unsupervised wandering for boys: Growth and change from childhood to early adolescence. *Multivariate Behavioral Research, 29*, 263–288.

Tambs, K., Harris, J. R., & Magnus, P. (1997). Genetic and environmental contributions to the correlation between alcohol consumption and symptoms of anxiety and depression: Results from a bivariate analysis of Norwegian twin data. *Behavior Genetics, 27*, 241–250.

Weinstein, N. D., Rothman, A. J., & Sutton, S. R. (1998). Stage theories of health behavior: Conceptual and methodological issues. *Health Psychology, 17*, 290–299.

Werch, C. E., & Anzalone, D. (1995). Stage theory and research on tobacco, alcohol, and other drug use. *Journal of Drug Education, 25,* 81–98.

Westermeyer, J. (1988). The pursuit of intoxication: Our 100 century-old romance with psychoactive substances. *American Journal of Drug and Alcohol Abuse, 14,* 175–187.

Yamaguchi, K., & Kandel, D. (1984). Patterns of drug use from adolescence to young adulthood: III Predictors of progression. *American Journal of Public Health, 74,* 673–681.

11

Using Latent Transition Analysis to Examine the Gateway Hypothesis

Linda M. Collins

According to the Gateway Hypothesis, in some cases one substance serves as a gateway for another, more advanced substance. In other words, it is necessary to go through this gateway in order to reach the more advanced substance. In a series of studies (Kandel & Faust, 1975; Yamaguchi & Kandel, 1984a, 1984b; Kandel, 1988; Kandel & Yamaguchi, 1993), Kandel and colleagues have examined the Gateway Hypothesis in detail. In general, these researchers have found that the legal drugs alcohol and tobacco appear to act as gateways for more advanced substances; alcohol plays a somewhat more important role for men and cigarettes play a somewhat more important role for women. Marijuana comes next, followed by cocaine and crack. Collins and colleagues (Graham, Collins, Wugalter, Chung, & Hansen, 1991; Collins, Graham, Long, & Hansen, 1994; Collins, Graham, Rousculp, & Hansen, 1997; Collins, Hyatt, & Graham, 2000; Hyatt & Collins, 2000) have examined the very early part of the onset process, looking at a sample of junior high and high school students. They have found that the onset process usually starts with alcohol; individuals go on either to try tobacco and then have a first experience with drunkenness or to have a first experience with drunkenness followed by trying tobacco. However, a small subset of individuals start their substance use experience with tobacco, go on to try alcohol, and then have a first experience with drunkenness. These researchers found that marijuana came next,

The author is grateful to Stephanie L. Hyatt for providing assistance with the data analysis, and to John W. Graham and William B. Hansen for allowing the Adolescent Alcohol Prevention Trials (AAPT) data to be analyzed for this chapter. This research was supported by Grant P50 DA10075 from the National Institute on Drug Abuse.

254

followed by cocaine. They did not have data on any more advanced substances. However, they did find that a high level of caffeine use was a prospective risk factor for trying alcohol (Collins et al., 1997).

The Gateway Hypothesis has two testable implications. The first implication is that there is an order in which people try substances, such that the gateway substance precedes other substances. However, there is more to the hypothesis than an order of substances. Its second implication is that a substance does not act as a gateway just because it precedes another. Instead, a gateway substance must be associated with increased risk of more advanced substance use. For example, although nearly every American tries broccoli before he or she tries alcohol, no one would argue that broccoli is a gateway for alcohol, because those who have tried broccoli are not at increased risk for trying alcohol compared with those who have not tried it. In the case of a highly normative "substance" such as broccoli, which virtually everyone has tried, there may be no basis for establishing this increased risk. Risk can be established only when a group who has used the putative gateway substance can be compared with a group who has not used the substance. Thus, in order for a substance to be considered a gateway for another substance, there must be *both* ordering such that the gateway substance is precedent *and* increased risk associated with having tried the gateway substance.

In the work of Kandel and colleagues, primarily event history and related log linear methods have been used to test the Gateway Hypothesis. The event history data were collected retrospectively, by asking individuals to recall their substance use experience over a period of years between surveys in a longitudinal panel study. The data analyzed by Collins and colleagues were gathered by using a longitudinal panel study with annual waves of data collection. Individuals were asked whether they had ever tried a substance and were asked some other questions about use in the very recent past (previous week or month) but were not asked when they had first tried a substance. This data collection approach has the disadvantage of not providing event history information. If a participant reports never having tried a substance at one observation then reports having tried it at the next observation, it is known that the substance was tried at some point during the interval, but the exact date when it occurred is not known. However, retrospective event history designs often involve asking participants to recall substance use over a long period, even their entire life. Panel designs, particularly those with closely spaced (i.e., 1 year or less) waves of data, have the advantage of asking study participants to recall their use over a much shorter period, a method that may produce more accurate reports.

This chapter discusses a statistical method for estimating and testing gateway type models, as well as other stage sequential models, in longitudinal panel data with closely spaced data collection points. Latent transition analysis (LTA; Collins & Wugalter, 1992) is, as the name implies, a latent variable model. LTA fits under the general rubric of latent class models (Goodman, 1974; Clogg & Goodman, 1984). Latent class models are an approach to multiway contingency table modeling that involves an underlying categorical latent variable. There are several parallels between latent class models and factor analysis models. Both postulate an underlying error-free latent variable measured by fallible manifest variables, or indicators. In the factor analysis model, this latent variable and its indicators are continuous (although this term is often loosely defined for the indicators); by contrast, in latent class models, the latent variable and its indicators are categorical. As do all statistical models, both attempt to reproduce data. In the case of factor analysis, the model attempts to reproduce the covariance matrix among the set of indicators. Latent class models attempt to reproduce the cell frequencies of the multiway contingency table formed by cross-tabulating the set of categorical indicators. In factor analysis models, factor loadings, which are regression coefficients, express the relationship between variables and factors. In latent class models, the analogous parameters express the probability of a particular observed response conditional on latent class membership.

LTA is an extension of latent class models to longitudinal data. LTA models transitions among discrete stages over time. Using this procedure, it is possible to estimate and test models of substance use onset, including gateway models, in longitudinal panel data. This chapter illustrates the use of LTA to model the substance use onset process, using data from a longitudinal prevention study. It will also show how LTA can be used to examine one particular Gateway Hypothesis: the hypothesis that marijuana is a gateway substance for cocaine.

Methods

Subjects

The sample used in the present chapter is a subsample of participants in the Adolescent Alcohol Prevention Trials (AAPT; Graham, Rohrbach, Hansen, Flay, & Johnson, 1989; Hansen & Graham, 1991).

This subsample consists of all 8,316 individuals present for 9th-grade measurement who were asked whether they had tried marijuana and whether they had tried cocaine. (Although the AAPT study collected data from 5th grade on, these questions were not asked before 9th grade.) The sample, from Southern California, is approximately 45% White, 30% Latino, 16% Asian, and 9% members of other ethnic groups, primarily African American. Participants were in 9th grade at the first observation used here (approximately 14 years old) and in 10th grade at the second observation (approximately 15 years old). This was a cohort-sequential design; depending on the cohort, participants started 9th grade in the fall of 1990 or 1991. Missing data procedures allowed us to use the entire sample of 8,316 in the analyses reported here.

Measures

The substance use variables used are listed in Table 11.1. Some of these variables were originally multicategory and were dichotomized for these analyses. In general the variables asked about whether the individual had ever tried a substance, rather than whether he or she practiced ongoing use of substances. They asked whether the individual had ever tried alcohol, ever tried tobacco, ever tried marijuana, ever tried cocaine, and ever been drunk. In addition, because drunkenness is a subjective state, a variable asking the largest number of drinks the individual had consumed in one day was included. This was dichotomized so that two drinks or fewer was coded as one, and three drinks or more was coded as 2.

Table 11.1. *Drug Use Items Used in the Analysis*

Multicategory items from the AAPT questionnaire were recoded so that they were effectively the following, (No = 1, Yes = 2)

Lifetime Alcohol Use: Have you ever had even a sip of alcohol (excluding for religious service)?

Lifetime Tobacco Use: Have you ever had even a puff of tobacco?

Lifetime Marijuana Use: Have you ever tried marijuana?

Lifetime Cocaine Use: Have you ever tried cocaine?

Lifetime Drunkenness: Have you ever been drunk?

In addition, participants were asked to indicate the following: Number of Alcoholic Drinks on Day When Had Most Alcohol: 2 or fewer = 1; 3 or more = 2

The Model

Consider a model expressing the onset process as a sequence of stages, in which each stage is a different substance tried. The existence of a gateway relationship between two substances has some implications for which stages will be observed in data. If marijuana is a gateway substance for cocaine, there will be stages involving trying marijuana without having tried cocaine, but no stages involving having tried cocaine without having tried marijuana. On the other hand, if cocaine is a gateway for marijuana, there will be stages involving trying cocaine without having tried marijuana but no stages involving trying marijuana without having tried cocaine. If there is no ordering between the substances, so that either one may be tried first, both stages will be observed with approximately equal frequency.

In the example presented in this chapter, we are skipping an important step: selection of a model of the substance use onset process. An in–depth treatment of this topic is outside the scope of the current chapter; for more discussion of the model selection process see Collins et al. (1994) and Collins, Schafer, Hyatt, and Flaherty (in preparation). Here we will rely on past research with the AAPT data set (Collins, Hyatt, & Graham, 2000; Hyatt & Collins, 2000), which strongly suggests that the model depicted in Figure 11.1 is a reasonable representation of the data. In Figure 11.1, the circles represent stages in the model and the arrows represent possible stage transitions. According to this model, which we will call *Model 1*, the early part of the onset process involves several alternative paths: either alcohol

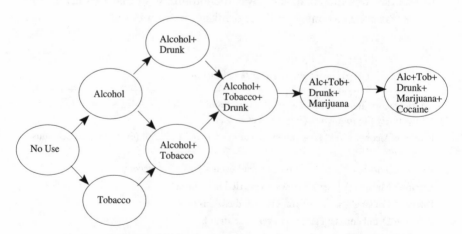

Figure 11.1. Model 1: Stage sequential model of substance use onset (Collins et al., 2000; Hyatt & Collins, 2000).

first, then drunkenness, then tobacco; or alcohol first, then tobacco, then drunkenness; or tobacco first, then alcohol, then drunkenness. From this point, the next substance tried is marijuana, followed by cocaine.

Model 1 omits a stage that would be necessary if marijuana is *not* a gateway substance for cocaine: the stage involving having tried every substance, including cocaine, *except* marijuana. In order to address the question of whether marijuana is a gateway substance for cocaine, we can compare Model 1 to a different model, Model 2, which is exactly the same as Model 1 with the addition of this stage.

The LTA Model

Suppose there are two times of measurement, Time t and Time $t + 1$. (The model can incorporate more than two times.) In our example the times are 9th grade and 10th grade. Further suppose a stage-sequential process involving S stages. For technical reasons, in the LTA framework stages are referred to as *latent statuses*. Suppose $p, q = 1, \ldots, S$ with p denoting a latent status at Time t and q denoting a latent status at Time $t + 1$. In our example this is the substance use onset latent variable, with $S = 8$ latent statuses, as described in reference to Model 1.

Suppose there are six manifest indicators (items or variables) of the dynamic latent variable at each occasion:

Item 1, with $i, i' = 1, \ldots, I$ response categories
Item 2, with $j, j' = 1, \ldots, J$ response categories
Item 3, with $k, k' = 1, \ldots, K$ response categories
Item 4, with $l, l' = 1, \ldots, L$ response categories
Item 5, with $m, m' = 1, \ldots, M$ response categories
Item 6, with $o, o' = 1, \ldots, O$ response categories

where $i, j, k, l, m,$ and o refer to responses obtained at Time t, and $i', j', k', l', m',$ and o' refer to responses obtained at Time $t + 1$. These correspond to the six substance use items listed in Table 11.1.

Let $Y = \{i, j, k, l, m, o, i', j', k', l', m', o'\}$ represent a response pattern, that is, a cell of the multiway contingency table. Then

$$P(Y) = \sum_{a=1}^{s} \sum_{b=1}^{s} \delta_a \rho_{i|a}\, \rho_{j|a}\, \rho_{k|a}\, \rho_{l|a}\, \rho_{m|a}\, \rho_{o|a}\, \tau_{b|a}\, \rho_{i'|b}\, \rho_{j'|b}\, \rho_{k'|b}\, \rho_{l'|b}\, \rho_{m'|b}\, \rho_{o'|b}$$

where

δ_a = probability of membership in latent status a at Time t, for example, the probability of membership in the Tried Alcohol Only latent status at Time 1

$\tau_{b|a}$ = probability of membership in Latent Status b at Time $t + 1$, conditional on membership in Latent Status a at Time t, for example, the probability of membership in the Tried Alcohol Only latent status at Time 2, conditional on membership in the No Use latent status at Time 1

$\rho_{i|a}$ = probability of response i to Item 1 at Time t, conditional on membership in Latent Status a, for example, the probability of responding yes to the question "Have you ever had even a sip of alcohol?" conditional on membership in the Alcohol Only latent status

It is possible to incorporate an exogenous categorical manifest or latent variable in LTA models. This allows the comparison of probabilities of stage membership and transition probabilities across groups. Groups can be experimental condition, gender, attitude, and others. For more about the technical details of this see Collins and Wugalter (1992); for empirical examples, see Graham et al. (1991), Collins et al. (2000) or Hyatt and Collins (2000).

LTA performs maximum likelihood estimation by means of the Expectation–Maximization (EM) algorithm (Dempster, Laird, & Rubin, 1977). Missing data are averaged over by using a standard maximum-likelihood procedure. Software to perform LTA analyses is available free of charge by downloading from the website http://METHODOLOGY. PSU.EDU.

Results

First the results from estimating and testing Model 1 are reviewed; a comparison of Model 1 and Model 2 follows.

*Examining the Basic Model of the Substance Use
Onset Process: Model 1*

Model 1 appears to fit the data reasonably well. The G^2 associated with Model 1 is 3,453 with 4,051 *df.* Table 11.2 shows the ρ parameters estimated for Model 1. In much the same way that factor loadings are the

Table 11.2. ρ Parameter Estimates for the Dynamic Latent Variable, Representing the Probability of a Yes Response to Each Item Conditional on Latent Status Membership

Latent Status	Ever Tried Alcohol	Ever Tried Tobacco	Ever Been Drunk	Ever Had 3 + Drinks	Ever Tried Marijuana	Ever Tried Cocaine
No use	.153	.057	.033	.049	.014	.003
Alcohol	.988	.057	.033	.049	.014	.003
Tobacco	.153	.960	.033	.049	.014	.003
Alcohol + tobacco	.988	.960	.033	.049	.014	.003
Alcohol + drunk	.988	.057	.850	.848	.014	.003
Alcohol + tobacco + drunk	.988	.960	.850	.848	.014	.003
Alcohol + tobacco + drunk + marijuana	.988	.960	.850	.848	.891	.003
Alcohol + tobacco + drunk + marijuana + cocaine	.988	.960	.850	.848	.891	.572

Note: These parameters were constrained to be equal across times and across genders. They were also constrained so that only two parameters per item were estimated.

basis for interpreting the meaning of factors, so the ρ parameters are the basis for interpreting the latent statuses. For example, the first latent status shows ρ parameters that are small across the board, indicating that the probability of having tried any of the substances is low. Thus it seems reasonable to label this latent status No Use. The next latent status shows a similar pattern of ρ parameters, with the exception that the probability of responding Yes to Tried Alcohol is high, suggesting that this latent status is characterized by having tried Alcohol Only. The remaining latent statuses can be interpreted in a similar manner. Constraints were imposed on the ρ parameters to limit the amount of estimation and to arrive at a more parsimonious model. The constraints specified that only two ρ parameters would be estimated per variable.

Because the ρ parameters are probabilities, they are interpreted somewhat differently than factor loadings, which are regression coefficients. A ρ parameter close to 0 or 1 represents a strong relationship with the latent status. For example, the probability of responding yes to the cocaine question is only .003 for those in the No Use latent status. This means that the response to the cocaine question is almost completely determined by latent status membership. Most of the ρ parameters in this study reflect a strong relationship between the manifest variables and the latent statuses. In general, a strong pattern of rho parameters is one in which most of the rho parameters are smaller than .3 or greater than .7. (Contrast this with factor loadings, in which a loading close to zero means there is no relationship between the variable and the factor.) In these data there is one weaker ρ parameter, a ρ of .572 associated with the cocaine variable and the last latent status. These two ρ parameters associated with the cocaine item suggest that the probability that a respondent will indicate having tried cocaine when he or she has not tried cocaine is only .003, but the probability of indicating not having tried cocaine when the individual has tried it is $1 - .572 = .428$.

Table 11.3 shows the δ parameters for grade 9 and grade 10. Only the δ parameters for the first time of measurement are actually estimated in LTA; δ's for any subsequent times can be computed from other parameters in the model. The δ parameters show that 24.5% of 9th graders have engaged in no substance use, and that this declines to 18.5% by grade 10. As expected, over time more children are engaging in experimentation with substances. Table 11.3 reflects this pattern. For example, in grade 9 about 4.8% of students had tried cocaine, whereas in grade 10

Table 11.3. *δ Parameter Estimates, Representing the Probability of Latent Status Membership at Each Grade*

Latent Status	Grade 9	Grade 10
No use	.245	.185
Alcohol	.219	.189
Tobacco	.031	.017
Alcohol + tobacco	.164	.147
Alcohol + drunk	.052	.061
Alcohol + tobacco + drunk	.152	.183
Alcohol + tobacco + drunk + marijuana	.090	.138
Alcohol + tobacco + drunk + marijuana + cocaine	.048	.080

Table 11.4. *Estimated Prevalence Rates for Having Tried Each Substance at Each Grade, Plus Estimated Prevalence of Drunkenness*

	Percentage	
	Grade 9	Grade 10
Alcohol	72	80
Tobacco	48	51
Marijuana	14	21
Cocaine	5	8
Drunkenness	34	46

this number had increased to 8%. Table 11.4 shows estimated marginal prevalence rates, based on the δ parameter estimates. These estimates indicate that by grade 10, the majority of children had tried alcohol and tobacco, nearly half had been drunk, and over 20% had tried marijuana.

Table 11.5 shows the τ parameters. These parameters express the probability of transitioning from one latent status to another between grade 9 and grade 10. According to Model 1, many of these transitions will involve passing through other latent statuses. For example, according to the model an individual in Alcohol Only at grade 9 passes through the Alcohol and Tobacco latent status before arriving at the Alcohol, Tobacco, and Drunkenness latent status at grade 10. Some τ parameters were fixed at a value of zero. These are indicated in Table 11.5 by a single dash. These correspond to transitions that are not consistent with Model 1.

Table 11.5. *τ Parameter Estimates, Representing the Probability of Transitioning to the Column Latent Status by Grade 10, Conditional on Membership in the Row Latent Status at Grade 9*

Latent Status at Grade 9	Latent Status at Grade 10							
	(1)	(2)	(3)	(4)	(5)	(6)	(7)	(8)
(1) No Use	.755	.112	.014	.038	.030	.030	.002	.018
(2) Alcohol	—	.735	—	.073	.090	.068	.015	.020
(3) Tobacco	—	—	.436	.357	—	.156	.000	.050
(4) Alcohol + Tobacco	—	—	—	.676	—	.220	.068	.036
(5) Alcohol + Drunk	—	—	—	—	.653	.187	.130	.030
(6) Alcohol + Tobacco + Drunk	—	—	—	—	—	.729	.214	.057
(7) Alcohol + Tobacco + Drunk + Marijuana	—	—	—	—	—	—	.931	.069
(8) Alcohol + Tobacco + Drunk + Marijuana + Cocaine	—	—	—	—	—	——		1.00

Examining Whether Marijuana Is a Gateway for Cocaine: Model 1 Versus Model 2

In order to establish whether marijuana is a gateway substance for cocaine, the first step was to determine whether Model 1 or Model 2 (which includes an additional latent status reflecting the possibility of trying cocaine without having tried marijuana) is a more appropriate fit to the data. The principle of parsimony states that if Model 1, which is simpler, does not fit worse than Model 2, it is assumed that the additional complexity is not necessary. Unfortunately, Model 1 and Model 2 are not nested, so they can be compared only informally. The G^2 associated with Model 2 is 3,452 with 4,043 *df*. The G^2 statistics are almost identical, suggesting that the more parsimonious Model 1 is not a worse fit than Model 2. An even better indication that Model 2's additional latent status is not necessary is that this latent status is estimated to be nearly empty. At both Grade 9 and Grade 10 the delta parameters indicate that only about .001 of the sample are in this latent status. These results suggest that there is no need for an additional latent status representing having tried cocaine without having tried marijuana. Additionally, the transition probability matrix indicates that there is virtually no movement into this latent status between grade 9 and grade 10 from any of the other latent statuses. This suggests that prospectively few individuals are moving into this latent status.

The preceding results establish that there is an ordering such that trying marijuana precedes trying cocaine. The second requirement for establishing that marijuana is a gateway substance for cocaine is that those who have not tried marijuana are at less risk for trying cocaine than are those who have tried marijuana. In these data, it appears that there is no evidence that anyone tries cocaine without having tried marijuana. Thus, those who have not tried marijuana appear to be at extremely small risk of trying cocaine. Table 11.5 shows that those who have tried marijuana by 9th grade appear to have approximately a 6.9% chance of trying cocaine by 10th grade. Implicit in Table 11.5 is the idea that the risk of trying cocaine is effectively zero for those who have not tried marijuana.

Discussion

Marijuana as a Gateway for Cocaine

The results of these analyses indicate that marijuana is a gateway substance for cocaine. It appears that in this sample few individuals tried cocaine without having first tried marijuana. What does this mean? Clearly there is a relationship between trying marijuana and trying cocaine. However, it would be inappropriate to call this relationship causal. Over time an increasing tendency to experiment with drugs is developing within these individuals. The cause of this development is a complex network of intrapsychic factors, such as self-esteem and perceived stress; biological factors, including the individual's reaction to a drug; social factors, such as peer pressure and parental modeling; and societal factors, such as availability of drugs in the individual's environment. In fact, it is possible that the gateway sequence observed in the present study represents nothing more than increasing desire for involvement in drugs, so that whichever untried substance is most readily available is tried next (L. Cooper, personal communication, June 1998). This would mean that the gateway order is completely culturally determined – nothing more than a reflection of the availability of substances in that place at that time. It is possible that trying marijuana may play a truly causal role if it somehow alters one's brain or body chemical characteristics in such a way as to make one more likely to desire cocaine, or if it introduces one to people who are likely to encourage the use of cocaine or make it easily available. But solely on the basis of the results presented in this chapter, trying marijuana can more appropriately be called a *marker*. It flags a high-risk situation without saying very much about how it came about, or about what is likely to distinguish those who will eventually go on to try cocaine from those who will not.

Nevertheless, establishing a gateway sequence can be highly valuable. It is important to understand the progression of substance use onset so that risk factors can be studied treating the progression itself as a dependent variable. It is likely that different risk factors are relevant at different points along the onset process. For example, parental modeling and availability of substances in the home may be more important risk factors for trying alcohol and tobacco, whereas peer pressure may be more important for a first experience with drunkenness and trying marijuana. Establishing a gateway sequence may also be important for prevention programming. A teenager who has tried marijuana may require a very different kind of intervention from that required by one who has not progressed this far in the gateway sequence.

Evidence for Other Gateways

In this chapter formal evidence has been presented that marijuana is a gateway for cocaine. Similar formal tests can be done to investigate other interesting Gateway Hypotheses, for example, to test whether legal substances are a gateway for marijuana. But even without formal tests, it is easy to see from the results presented here that the evidence is strong that alcohol and tobacco, and a first experience with drunkenness, appear to be gateways for marijuana in this data set. As mentioned earlier, considerable preliminary work with the AAPT data has established that this model of substance use onset fits the data well. On the basis of this previous work, there is no indication that there is a need for a latent status involving having tried marijuana without having tried alcohol and tobacco, and having been drunk. Such a latent status is necessary in a model allowing marijuana to be tried without first having tried alcohol and tobacco. However, recent latent transition analyses (Collins, Hyatt, & Flaherty, 1999) on the Add Health data set (Resnik et al., 1997) suggest that although tobacco is a gateway for marijuana, alcohol may not be. There are several possible reasons for these emerging differences in results. One is that Add Health is a nationally representative sample, whereas the AAPT sample is not nationally representative. Another is that the Add Health data were collected more recently than the AAPT data; perhaps the role of alcohol in the onset process has changed. A third possibility is that differences in questionnaire wording or other procedures between the two studies account for the difference. We are currently investigating this finding further.

Limitations and Strengths of LTA

Potential users of LTA should be aware of some significant limitations. Because it is a contingency table model, it is limited in the size and complexity of models it can address. Every variable and time added increases the size of the contingency table. For example, the contingency table used for the analyses discussed here, involving six variables measured at two times, had 4,096 cells. Although LTA can handle considerably larger contingency tables, problems the size of typical large Structural equation models would be unwieldy. A related problem is sample size. A rough rule of thumb is that the ratio of sample size to number of cells should not fall much below about .2. This suggests that for a problem like the one analyzed in this chapter, the sample size should not be less than about 800. However, sample size requirements are dramatically affected by the strength of the ρ parameters. If the ρ parameters are strong, that is, close to 1 or 0 then smaller sample sizes will be sufficient. If the ρ parameters are weaker, larger sample sizes are needed. In any case, LTA in its current form is not a small sample procedure. Another problem associated with LTA is model selection. With large degrees of freedom and sparse data, as are typical of LTA analyses, the G^2 is not reliably distributed as a χ^2. Unfortunately, the true distribution is not known, although it is known that its expectation is considerably less than the degrees of freedom (Collins, Fidler, Wugalter, & Long, 1993). The distribution may be much closer to a χ^2 for comparisons of nested models associated with small degrees of freedom.

Nevertheless, as an approach to examining the Gateway Hypothesis or to testing other stage-sequential models, LTA has some advantages. One advantage is that it allows the user to compare models that express different gateway sequences and investigate which appear most appropriate for the data. In our analyses, it was clear that the more complex Model 2, which allowed the possibility that some individuals tried cocaine before marijuana, was no better than the simpler Model 1, and therefore the additional stage allowing trying cocaine without having tried marijuana was unnecessary. Another advantage to LTA is that because it is a latent variable approach, it adjusts for measurement error. This adjustment is particularly important in the τ parameters. In categorical data, the effect of measurement error is to misclassify individuals. In any square matrix with more than four elements, there are more off-diagonal elements than diagonal elements. Because of this, random measurement error is more likely to place an element that should be on the diagonal somewhere off the diagonal than it is to move an off-diagonal element onto the diagonal. The net effect of measurement error is thus to increase the size of the off-diagonal elements at the expense of the diagonal elements. Because the diagonal elements in the transition probability matrix contain individuals who are in the same latent status at Time 2 as they were in at Time 1, underestimating the diagonal elements makes it appear that there has been more change over time than has really occurred. Adjusting for this, as is done in LTA, can give a more realistic assessment of the amount of change.

References

Clogg, C. C., & Goodman, L. A. (1984). Latent structure analysis of a set of multidimensional contingency tables. *Journal of the American Statistical Association, 79,* 762–771.

Collins, L. M., Fidler, P. L., Wugalter, S. E., & Long, J. L. (1993). Goodness-of-fit testing for latent class models. *Multivariate Behavioral Research, 28,* 375–389.

Collins, L. M., Graham, J. W., Long, J., & Hansen, W. B. (1994). Crossvalidation of latent class models of early substance use onset. *Multivariate Behavioral Research, 29,* 165–183.

Collins, L. M., Graham, J. W., Rousculp, S. S., & Hansen, W. B. (1997). Heavy caffeine and the beginning of the substance use onset process: An illustration of latent transition analysis. In K. Bryant, M. Windle, & S. West (Eds.), *The science of prevention: Methodological advances from alcohol and substance abuse research* (pp. 79–99). Washington, DC: American Psychological Association.

Collins, L. M., Hyatt, S. L., & Flaherty, B. P. (October, 1999). Latent transition analysis: A method for estimating and testing stage-sequential models in longitudinal contingency tables. Presented at Measuring Change in Complex Social Systems: Best Practices and State-of-the-Art Developments for Measuring Change in Organizations, College Park, MD.

Collins, L. M., Hyatt, S. L., & Graham, J. W. (2000). LTA as a way of testing models of stage-sequential change in longitudinal data. In T. D. Little, K. U. Schnabel, & J. Baumert (Eds.), *Modeling longitudinal and multiple-group data: Practical issues, applied approaches, and specific examples* (pp. 147–161). Hillsdale, NJ: Erlbaum.

Collins, L. M., & Wugalter, S. E. (1992). Latent class models for stage-sequential dynamic latent variables. *Multivariate Behavioral Research, 27,* 131–157.

Dempster, A. P., Laird, N. M., & Rubin, D. B. (1977). Maximum likelihood from incomplete data via the EM algorithm. *Journal of the Royal Statistical Society (B), 39*, 1–38.

Goodman, L. A. (1974). Exploratory latent structure analysis using both identifiable and unidentifiable models. *Biometrika, 61*, 215–231.

Graham, J. W., Collins, L. M., Wugalter, S. E., Chung, N. K., & Hansen, W. B. (1991). Modeling transitions in latent stage-sequential processes: A substance use prevention example. *Journal of Consulting and Clinical Psychology, 59*, 48–57.

Graham, J. W., Rohrbach, L., Hansen, W. B., Flay, B. R., & Johnson, C. A. (1989). Convergent and discriminant validity for assessment of skill in resisting a role play alcohol offer. *Behavioral Assessment, 11*, 353–379.

Hansen, W. B., & Graham, J. W. (1991). Preventing alcohol, marijuana, and cigarette use among adolescents: Peer pressure resistance training versus establishing conservative norms. *Preventive Medicine, 20*, 414–430.

Hyatt, S. L., & Collins, L. M. (2000) Using latent transition analysis to examine the relationship between parental permissiveness and the onset of substance use. In J. Rose, L. Chassin, C. Presson & S. Sherman (Eds.), *Multivariate applications in substance use research* (pp. 259–288). Hillsdale, NJ: Erlbaum.

Kandel, D. B. (1988). Issues of sequencing of adolescent drug use and other problem behaviors. In *Drugs and Society* (Vol. 3). New York: Hawthorne Press.

Kandel, D., & Faust, R. (1975). Sequence and stages in patterns of adolescent drug use. *Archives of General Psychiatry, 32*, 923–932.

Kandel, D., & Yamaguchi, K. (1993). From beer to crack: Developmental patterns of drug involvement. *American Journal of Public Health, 83*, 851–855.

Resnick, M. D., Bearman, P. S., Blum, R. W., Bauman, K. E., Harris, K. M., Jones, J., Tabor, J., Beuhring, T., Sieving, R. E., Shew, M., Ireland, M., Bearinger, L. H., & Udry, J. R. (1997). Protecting adolescents from harm: Findings from the National Longitudinal Study of Adolescent Health. *Journal of the American Medical Association, 278*, 823–832.

Yamaguchi, K., & Kandel, D. B. (1984a). Patterns of drug use from adolescence to young adulthood. II. Sequences of progression. *American Journal of Public Health, 74*, 668–672.

Yamaguchi, K., & Kandel, D. B. (1984b). Patterns of drug use from adolescence to young adulthood. III. Predictors of progression. *American Journal of Public Health, 74*, 673–681.

12

Stages of Drug Use Progression

A Comparison of Methods, Concepts, and Operationalizations

Kazuo Yamaguchi

The notion of stages of drug use progression implies two conditions: (1) sequencing, that is, regularities in the sequential patterns of progression that are reflected in partially ordered discrete states, namely stages, and (2) association, that is, stages that are significant indicators of greater risk of progression into higher stages than the risk from any lower stage. As was noted earlier, association implies causation, when nonspuriousness has been definitely established. However, control for all spurious factors cannot be easily implemented. Although the presence of such stages would make it easier to identify individuals who are at greater risk than others for a particular kind of drug use, and thereby to design more effective intervention programs, researchers do not always agree about which conceptualization of stages is the most meaningful and what the stages are. In order to clarify the important relationship between the conceptualization of stages and their operationalization through various methods and models, this chapter discusses three methodological approaches to the study of drug use progression, and the testing of the Gateway Hypothesis in particular, that are analyzed in the present volume: structural equation models with latent variables and linear growth curve models, discussed by Bentler, Newcomb, and Zimmerman in Chapter 10 (Huba, Wingard, & Bentler, 1981; Newcomb and Bentler, 1986a, 1986b); latent transition analysis, (LTA) discussed by Collins in Chapter 11 (Graham, Collins, Wugalter, Chuny, & Hansen, 1991; Collins, 1991; Collins et al., 1994a, 1994b; Collins & Wugalter, 1992); and log linear quasi–independence models, models for parametric event sequence analysis, and hazard rate models for the analysis of drug use initiation, discussed by Yamaguchi and Kandel in Chapters 4 and 9 (Kandel & Yamaguchi, 1993; Yamaguchi & Kandel, 1984a, 1984b, 1997).

Commonalities and Differences in the Conceptualization of Stages and Their Measurement

The Notion of Stages of Drug Use Progression

The notion of stages of drug use progression differs greatly in the approaches of Bentler et al. and those of the other two groups of investigators. Yamaguchi and Kandel and Collins share a concern with developing and applying a *dynamic* extension of Guttman scale–like analysis to identify stages of drug use progression. Guttman scale analysis is well suited to the study of stages of drug use progression because of cumulativeness and unidimensionality among ordered states. Earlier studies that employed Guttman scale analysis to identify stages in drug use include Single, Kandel, and Faust (1974) and Donovan and Jessor (1983).

However, the early studies that identified Guttman scale–like characteristics among drug use states were based on cross-sectional data and identified states from interindividual differences in drug use behavior, whereas the notion of drug use progression concerns intraindividual changes in drug use behavior. Hence, Yamaguchi and Kandel (1984a) developed a dynamic version of Goodman's (1975) quasi-independence model for Guttman scale analysis of longitudinal data on drug use progression. Collins, Cliff, and Dent (1988) also proposed the "longitudinal Guttman-simplex model" to assess Guttman scalability in patterns of intraindividual change, although the original application was not to drug use progression. The idea of identifying cumulative patterns of intraindividual change is also reflected in the Collins et al., applications of latent transition analysis (LTA) to drug use progression (e.g., Collins, 1991; Collins et al., 1994b; also see Chapter 11).

These two groups of studies are also concerned with identifying stages when unidimensionality of the Guttman scale, characterized by complete order, does not hold among stages. When there is only a partial order, there may exist stages among which no order can be established, such as between alcohol use and tobacco use, although transitivity must hold among ordered stages.

On the other hand, studies by Bentler et al. are concerned with identifying patterns of drug use progression within the framework of causal analysis of drug use states using linear structural equation models with latent variables (e.g., Huba et al., 1981; Newcomb & Bentler, 1986a; also see Chapter 10). Because of the continuous characterization of drug use states, the Bentler et al. approach is less consonant with the discrete notion of stages of drug use progression than the other two approaches. In particular, Bentler et al. identify the Gateway Hypothesis, in which marijuana use is assumed to precede progression to use of other illicit drugs, with the "simplex model," and the rejection of the Gateway Hypothesis with the alternative "common factor model" (Huba et al., 1981). I define these models later and discuss how Bentler and colleagues' conceptualization of the Gateway Hypothesis differs greatly from that of the other two approaches.

Typical Drug Use Variables Chosen for Analyzing Progression

The difference between the Bentler et al. approach and the other two in the conceptualization of drug use progression leads to differences in the typical variables employed in identifying drug use states. Generally, four kinds of variables can be employed to measure the usage state of each class of drugs: (1) presence/absence of lifetime use and (2) presence/ absence of current use (or use at each time of a panel survey), both measured by dichotomous variables, and (3) frequency/quantity of lifetime use and (4) frequency/quantity of current use (or use at each time of a panel survey), both measured by continuous variables. The presence/ absence of lifetime use of a drug can be defined at each time (or age) by the presence/absence of initiation of any use, or by the presence/ absence of initiation of a certain level of use, such as problem use, daily use, or use that produces symptoms of dependence. Both Yamaguchi and Kandel and Collins et al. rely mainly on a discrete characterization of drug use states by the first group of variables because it is especially useful in revealing Guttman scale–like characteristics among drug use stages. A stage of drug use is typically defined as the attainment of lifetime use of a certain class of drugs, such as having ever used alcohol, cigarettes, and marijuana, but no other illicit drugs in the Yamaguchi–Kandel analysis, or having ever tried alcohol and tobacco and ever having been drunk, but not having reached "advanced use," in the Collins et al. analysis.

Bentler, Newcomb, and their associates rely mainly on a continuous characterization of drug use states by the fourth group of variables, which measure the frequency/quantity of current use, because they are especially suitable for causal analysis. The Bentler et al. approach differs from the other two not only in the scale of variables employed (continuous rather than discrete) but also in the measurement of drug use by current rather than lifetime use. This difference in choice of variables has several consequences. The studies of Yamaguchi and Kandel and of Collins et al. are primarily concerned with progression across different classes of drugs rather than progression within the same class of drugs in quantity and frequency of use. The studies of Bentler et al. focus on both cross-class and within class progressions in drug use, but they are less concerned than the other two approaches with identifying a sequential order in the attainment of various drug use states.

Latent Versus Manifest States for Stages

In another respect, the Bentler et al. and Collins et al. approaches are similar, and the Yamaguchi–Kandel approach is distinct. Although the scale of their variables differs, both Bentler et al. and Collins et al. assume that true stages (or true drug use states) are latent and that only indicators with *measurement error* are observable. The stage notion of drug use carries as a necessary condition that each stage be strongly associated with the use (or a certain level of use) of a set of drugs and with the nonuse (or a lower level of use) of other drugs. Bentler et al. and Collins et al. differ in the way they relate latent variable states and drug use stages. In the Bentler et al. approach each continuous latent variable is formulated in such a way that it is significantly associated with the use (or heavier use) of a set of drugs and is not associated with the use of other drugs. Hence, a stage may be defined as a particular state of a set of relations with those latent variables. For example, the stage of marijuana use is positively associated with the first two latent variables, which represent use of licit drugs and use of marijuana, and is negatively associated with the third latent variable, which represents use of other illicit drugs. The extent of such positive and negative associations varies and stages are not directly identified.

In the Collins et al. approach, each latent state of the discrete latent class variable represents a drug use stage, which has a close to 1 probability of ever having used one set of drugs and a close to 0 probability of ever having used other drugs. However, the association between each latent state and the used/nonused set of drugs is not complete because the model assumes measurement error.

In both approaches, however, the assumption of measurement error allows *observed* patterns of drug use to deviate from patterns represented by stages. Each observed pattern of drug use cannot be identified with a particular stage, because of the incomplete association between latent drug use states and their indicators.

Unlike the other two approaches, the Yamaguchi–Kandel approach identifies stages by manifest (i.e., observed) patterns of drug use rather than by latent patterns. In analyses based on the quasi-independence model, which they use to identify the best fitting set of "scale type" trajectories, or sequences of stages, of drug use, they can identify stages for the great majority (about 95%) of observed drug use patterns in the sample (e.g., Yamaguchi and Kandel, 1984a; also see Chapter 9). Their model does not assume measurement error. Instead, it assumes a latent class of persons whose drug use progression patterns do not conform to any of the hypothesized scale type patterns, although they may become scale types by chance. This is an alternative explanation of deviant progression patterns. Later I discuss these alternative choices for handling deviant cases further, assuming measurement error and unobserved population heterogeneity, in the historical context of methodological developments.

Association of Stages and Tests of the Gateway Hypothesis

Despite different conceptualizations of stages in drug use progression by Bentler et al. and the other two groups, and different characterizations of drug use states by Yamaguchi and Kandel (manifest) and the other two groups (latent), all three groups agree that the notion of stages requires that among drug use stages A-B-C, ordered from lower to higher levels of use, being in a higher-stage B rather than a lower-stage A implies a significantly higher risk of progressing to a still higher-stage C. I call this the assumption of significant *association* between adjacent stages.

In the Collins et al. LTA, this association is measured by significant differences in transition probabilities among stages of origin. If the stage sequence A-B-C exists, the probability of reaching stage C is moderate or high from stage B, depending on the proportion of people who progress to stage C for a given time interval, but low from stage A.

Yamaguchi and Kandel's quasi-independence model is designed only to analyze sequencing among drug use initiations and not association among them. Hence, they present complementary analyses of association using either the hazard rate model, in their early studies

(Yamaguchi & Kandel, 1984a, 1984b), or parametric event sequence analysis in their more recent studies. (Yamaguchi & Kandel, 1997; also see Chapter 9).

In the Bentler et al. approach, association is measured by partial correlation between two latent variables, each of which is highly correlated with a distinct set of drug use indicator variables. However, their approach is unique in that the pattern of associations itself is also used to characterize the order among stages, and to test the Gateway Hypothesis in particular. An early study based on cross-sectional data (Huba et al., 1981) employed the relative goodness of fit between the simplex model and the common factor model to test the Gateway Hypothesis. According to the authors, the simplex model holds if, among three latent drug use variables, namely, variable 1 (use of licit drugs), variable 2 (marijuana use), and variable 3 (use of other illicit drugs), there is an association between variables 1 and 2 and between variables 2 and 3 but not between variables 1 and 3. On the other hand, the common factor model holds when all three pairwise associations are significant. Although Bentler et al. identified the Gateway Hypothesis with the simplex model and favored rejecting the hypothesis, this identification does not coincide with the way the other two approaches conceptualize the Gateway Hypothesis. Yamaguchi and Kandel consider that although the Gateway Hypothesis requires a well-established temporal order or sequence among the initiations of different drugs, it only requires significant associations between adjacent stages. Significant associations across more than one stage do not violate the requirement of the hypothesis. In other words, as long as licit drugs, marijuana, and other illicit drugs are initiated in this sequential order and the use of each lower-stage drug increases the risk of initiation of the next stage drug, the Gateway Hypothesis holds. It holds regardless of whether the use of licit drugs is uniquely associated with the use of other illicit drugs, as when the use of licit drugs further increases the risk of initiating the use of other illicit drugs among marijuana users.

Whether unique association between licit and illicit drugs other than marijuana contradicts the Gateway Hypothesis is related to two factors. One factor is the definition regarding what sense the notion of stages requires that among ordered stages A-B-C, the "effect" of A on progression to C must be *indirect* and through B. As described, Bentler et al. require this condition for association among drug use states, whereas Yamaguchi and Kandel require it only for the sequential order of initiations but not for association among drug use classes. The second factor is the conceptualization of stages in drug use regression. A positive partial correlation $(\rho_{13|2})$ between the use of licit and the use of other illicit drugs may not always indicate that the use of licit drugs increases the risk of progression to the use of other illicit drugs, controlling for marijuana use. A positive $\rho_{13|2}$ value may indicate instead that the use of licit drugs reduces the risk of regression from the use of other illicit drugs, controlling for marijuana use. If we consider that the former violates the Gateway Hypothesis but the latter does not, we must employ some method to distinguish between the two.

Therefore, the distinction between stages of progression and those of regression in drug use is important, although most analyses of drug use stages have been concerned with progression patterns only. In principle, progression and regression can be distinguished when we treat stages as discrete states and are concerned with transition probabilities (or transition rates) as in the Collins et al. LTA analysis and Yamaguchi and Kandel's hazard rate analysis that distinguishes initiation, cessation, and resumption of drug use. In conventional structural equation models based on correlational data, this distinction cannot be made even with panel or longitudinal data. The linear growth curve model that Bentler et al. have advocated recently, however, can make such a distinction because it can identify the effects of covariates (such as use of lower-stage drugs) on both level of use (for which the covariate effect must be positive for progression and negative for regression) and rate of change in use (which shows whether covariates increase or decrease the extent of within group progression or regression in drug use).

Although recent studies by Bentler et al. are based on the analysis of panel data that include information on time ordering, their logic in testing the Gateway Hypothesis seems to be the same as before: that is, they are concerned only with the pattern of association. For example, in Chapter 10, they cite the following two examples as contradicting the Gateway Hypothesis: "Heavy use of cannabis as a teenager predicted increases in both cocaine use and alcohol use one year later [Newcomb & Bentler, 1986a]," and "higher frequency of cannabis use during earlier adolescence predicted increases in both hard drug use and cigarette use four years later [Newcomb & Bentler, 1986b]." Although Bentler et al. take temporal order into account, in testing the Gateway Hypothesis they consider order in terms of the direction of causal influence, which is a characteristic of association, rather than the sequential order of drug initiations. They regard the fact that a higher-stage drug use (cannabis use) increases the risk of using a lower-stage drug (alcohol or cigarette) as contradicting the Gateway Hypothesis. However, these findings do not contradict the hypothesis according to the Yamaguchi–Kandel and Collins et al. conceptualizations, as stated before.

In addition, a difference between the variables used by Yamaguchi and Kandel and those by Bentler et al. may affect this conclusion. Yamaguchi and Kandel employ a dichotomous distinction between presence or absence of lifetime drug use, whereas Bentler et al. employ continuous measures of quantity currently used at each survey. This difference can affect the associations observed among stages. Given a well-established temporal order from the initiation of licit drugs to the initiation of marijuana, reverse causation such that marijuana initiation affects the initiation of a licit drug is very unlikely if not impossible. Only when we are concerned with current rather than lifetime use and with quantity used rather than presence versus absence of use does reverse causation become likely. The contradiction between Yamaguchi and Kandel and Bentler et al. regarding whether empirical data support the Gateway Hypothesis is only apparent. It is the result of different conceptualizations of the hypothesis and consequently different operationalizations of its empirical test.

The Formal Relation Between the Yamaguchi–Kandel QI Model and the Collins LTA Model

Not only are the Yamaguchi and Kandel and Collins et al. conceptualizations of stages similar, the Yamaguchi–Kandel quasi-independence (QI) model and the Collins et al. LTA model are, in a sense, distant kin. This observation is worth explaining because the models reflect alternative approaches to handling "nonscalable" cases that do not fit any of the hypothesized Guttman scale–like stages of drug use progression. The difference between the two models also means that for simplicity of modeling the data, each ignores an aspect that the other takes into account. In order to identify their distant kinship and to clarify their differences, I show how Yamaguchi and Kandel's QI model and the Collins et al. LTA model are special cases of a larger group of models. Figure 12.1 outlines the hierarchical relations among related models.

The mixed Markov latent class (MMLC) model is a general model for the analysis of panel and discrete time data (van de Pol & Langeheine, 1990). This model assumes both discrete states and discrete time. Furthermore, the model assumes (1) *latent states* among which transitions occur

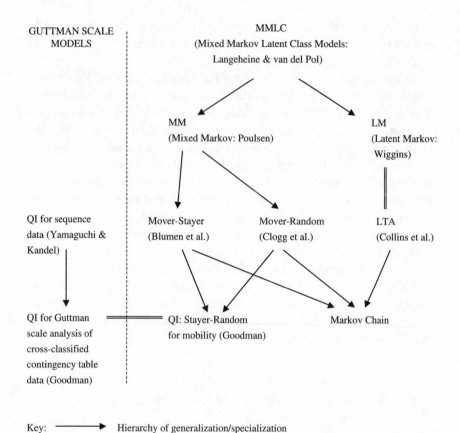

Figure 12.1. Hierarchical relations among log linear models including the Yamaguchi–Kandel quasi-independence model and Collins et al. latent transition analysis.

over time, while the states are reflected by some observable indicators, and (2) *latent classes* of persons, each class having, a distinct transition probability matrix. The first latency reflects *measurement error* for discrete states with transitions among them; it assumes that true states are not directly observable and are reflected only by their indicators. The second latency reflects *unobserved population heterogeneity* in the transition probability matrix; it assumes that there are latent groups of persons with different patterns of transitions among the stages. Generally, parameters of an MMLC model cannot be estimated without setting some strong constraints. As a result, two special cases of the general model, which omit one aspect of latency, are more often considered. One is the mixed Markov (MM) model, described by Poulsen (1982) and Langeheine and van de Pol (1990). This model assumes that discrete states, among which transitions occur, are observed and not latent although there are latent classes of persons each of which has a distinct transition probability matrix. It ignores measurement error but assumes unobserved heterogeneity in the transition probability matrix. The other is the latent Markov (LM) model introduced by Wiggins (1955) and van de Pol and de Leeuw (1989). This model assumes latent states with observed indicators and a single transition probability matrix among those latent states. It ignores unobserved heterogeneity in the transition probability matrix but assumes measurement error for states among which transitions occur. The Collins et al. LTA is basically an application of the LM model assuming latent states for drug use stages. However, Collins et al. elaborate the method in several ways. In particular, they developed a method that imposes a certain set of equality constraints on parameters so that the LM model can be used to identify the stages of drug use progression that satisfy a partial order and to test hypotheses about the presence or absence of particular stages.

The MM model still cannot be applied without constraints on its parameters because various alternative mixtures of transition matrices can predict the same observed transition data. Hence, more restricted models are advocated and used in applications. One such restricted model is the mover–stayer model (Blumen et al., 1955), which assumes $I + 1$ latent classes for I states. There are I latent classes, one for each state, of stayers who stay in the same state over time, and an additional latent class of movers (though they may stay in the same state by chance), whose pattern of transition is Markovian; their probabilities of being in each state at $t + 1$ depend on their states at t. Another model is what we may call the *mover-random* mixture model introduced by Clogg et al. (1995), which assumes two latent classes, one that follows a Markovian process, and another that satisfies the condition that states at $t + 1$ are independent of states at t. The model requires some constraints on the form of the Markovian transition.

Earlier, Goodman (1969) introduced the quasi-independence model for the analysis of social mobility. The QI model can be regarded as a stayer-random model with I latent groups of stayers for I states and a latent group of random movers whose states at $t + 1$ are independent of states at time t. This model is a special case of both the mover–stayer model and the mover-random mixture model described. Although this QI model is not very useful for mobility research because it rarely fits the data, the QI model later introduced by Goodman (1975) for Guttman scale analysis for a set of response items likely fits many data sets and is therefore very useful. The assumptions of this model are basically the same as for the QI model for mobility data: The model assumes for I response items $I + 1$ latent groups of people, each of which satisfies a particular set of nonrandom Guttman scale responses, such as $X_1 = X_2 = \cdots = X_m = 1$, and $X_{m+1} = \cdots = X_I = 0$ for a set of X_i, $i = 1, \ldots, I$, and a latent group of random respondents for whom responses to $X_1, \ldots, X_I$ are mutually independent. The model assumes that observed patterns of responses that do not conform to any of the Guttman scale response patterns are the result of a single random type latent class.

Yamaguchi and Kandel's QI model (1984a) extends Goodman's QI model for Guttman scale analysis. The major extension is for analyzing data on sequencing of events, such as initiation among different groups of drugs, for a Guttman scale analysis of *intraindividual* change. By contrast, the original Goodman model, whose application would be based on the pattern of presence or absence of responses (drug use) at a given time, is for a Guttman scale analysis of *interindividual* differences. The Yamaguchi–Kandel QI model assumes various latent groups, each following one of a set of specified "scale type" trajectories of drug use progression and a single latent group with random non–scale type response patterns. The model also relaxes the strict Guttman scale condition of a complete order, requiring only a partial order in the initiations of drugs to be satisfied among the scale types. As in Goodman's original QI model, however, latent classes are used to introduce unobserved population heterogeneity in progression patterns and not measurement error. The assumption of unobserved population heterogeneity made here is a strong one because only one random type is assumed to characterize all the types that deviate from the scale type progression patterns.

As Figure 12.1 shows, the Collins et al. LTA model and Yamaguchi and Kandel's QI model are distant kin. Each uses latent classes to allow nonscale types to appear in the observed data, but each regards the source of such error type observations differently, measurement error for one and the presence of a latent class with random progression patterns for the other. A model that assumes both measurement error and unobserved heterogeneity in progression patterns is theoretically possible, but the parameters of such a model would be very difficult to identify with stability.

Advantages and Limitations of the Three Alternative Approaches

The Bentler and Associates Approach

The most significant advantage of the Bentler et al. approach is that it is naturally suited for analyzing drug use progressions that take into account quantity and frequency of use, because of the reliance on continuous variables. Although it is possible to categorize level of use with the Collins et al. LTA model or Yamaguchi and Kandel QI model, some information is lost by categorization besides the fact that it is difficult to measure reliably the exact timing of the initiation of a certain level of use, such as daily use. When researchers wish to define drug use states by taking into account frequency or quantity of use and conceptualizing progression within the same group of drugs as well as across different classes of drugs, the Bentler et al. approach, especially the linear growth curve model, is more advantageous than the other two approaches.

A major limitation of the Bentler et al. approach is that it cannot easily analyze sequential order in the attainment of various drug use stages; for that the other two approaches are more suitable. As a result, the stage notion is more abstract and the measurement of stages more indirect in the Bentler et al. approach than in the other two.

An additional limitation of conventional confirmatory factor analytic models based on correlation data is that they cannot analyze changes in level of use or distinguish regression from progression in drug use. This limitation does not apply to the linear growth curve model, which can assess covariate effects on level of use (intercept) and linear growth separately. However, time-lagged reciprocal effects can be assessed by conventional confirmatory factor analytic models but not by the linear growth curve model. An assumption of unidirectional influence is usually made: whereas the level and linear growth of alcohol use can affect the level and linear growth of marijuana use, the reverse effects of level and growth of marijuana use on alcohol use are assumed to be absent. Hence, the linear growth curve model has its own limitations, despite its important advantages when compared with conventional structural equation models.

The Collins and Associates Approach

The major advantage of the LTA approach is that although it retains the notion of stages of drug use progression based on Guttman scale–like sequencing of drug use initiations, it can assess simultaneously transition probabilities among the stages and measurement error. In particular, Collins has elaborated LTA in several ways, including the cross-validation method (1994a), so that it is useful in identifying stages of drug use progression. The major elaboration is the strategic use of equality constraints on the conditional probabilities of having ever used each class of drugs so that persons in each state of the latent class variable, which represents a distinct stage, have either a very small (i.e., near 0) or a very large (i.e., near 1) probability of having ever used each class of drugs; the stage can then be characterized by the lifetime use of a set of drug classes and lifetime nonuse of another set of drug classes. These constraints can also be used to test a particular hypothesis about whether another stage exists between stages A and B, because such an intermediate stage must be characterized by large probabilities of lifetime use of all stage A drugs and some, but not all, stage B drugs and small probabilities of lifetime use of all drugs associated only with stages higher than B. The model tests the presence of a latent drug use state that satisfies the characterisatics of conditional probabilities that the intermediate stage must satisfy.

The limitations of LTA are largely technical and can in principle be remedied in the future. First, no procedure for comparing relative good-ness of fit among latent class models with different numbers of latent classes has yet been established. Since the test of such a comparison involves boundary conditions for some parameters, conventional tests, such as likelihood ratio tests or Bayesian information criteria (BIC), cannot be employed for that purpose. Thus, if two models that differ in the number of latent classes both fit the data, there is ambiguity as to which model is better and how many stages (latent classes) exist. Second, LTA cannot currently introduce covariates parametrically, and, there-fore, comparisons can be made among groups only for a single group variable. Third, applications to data with three or more time points have a practical limitation. Because the first-order Markovian assumption is unlikely to hold, the model must incorporate higher-order Markovian dependence for transitions among multiple latent states. This makes the model unwieldy because it involves a large number of transition probability parameters.

The Yamaguchi–Kandel Approach

I discuss the advantages and limitations of the QI model and of para-metric event sequence analysis (PESA) separately. The major advantage of the QI model for the analysis of event sequences is that it can assess alternative hypotheses about the whole trajectory of drug use progression and identify what proportions of the sample fall into each stage in the scale-type progression pattern of drug use. No other approach permits such an analysis. However, there are several major limitations to the approach. First, since this analysis identifies only patterns in the temporal order of initiations, and not associations, it has to be supplemented by additional analysis of association. Second, the assumption of a single latent class with a random progression pattern to explain all non–scale type progression patterns is a strong one. To the extent that the assumption does not capture the underlying causes of deviant patterns, the results of the model will be artifactual even if the model fits the data at the aggregate frequency level. Third, the model cannot employ covariates; therefore, comparisons can be made only among groups for a single group variable.

These three limitations of the QI model do not apply to PESA, however. PESA can treat both sequencing and association simultaneously, can introduce covariates, and does not make a strong assumption about the underlying causes of deviant progression patterns. It can also test the substitution hypotheses between two drugs (such as between alcohol and cigarette use on the progression to marijuana use) for both sequencing and association in drug use progression (see Chapter 9). However, unlike the QI model, PESA cannot analyze the whole trajectory of progression and can assess only the unique sequencing tendency between two drug use states for multiple pairs, controlling for age effects on the probability of initiating each drug and sequencing tendencies among other drugs.

Current Limitations in Establishing Causality. In testing the Gateway Hypothesis with respect to initiation into the use of different drugs, Yamaguchi, Kandel and Collins analyze both sequencing and association whereas Bentler et al. analyze association among stages of drug use. However, association is a necessary but not a sufficient condition for establishing causality because of potential spuriousness. In the analysis of nonexperimental data, one needs to control for the selection bias of individuals into the use of a lower-stage drug when predicting progression to the next stage. Statistical models that can introduce many control variables, such as hazard rate models or other regression-type models, are more advantageous than others in this respect, although such controls do not completely eliminate the possibility of spuriousness. In the future, all approaches need to improve the handling of selection bias into the preceding stage in establishing association and eventually causation between adjacent stages of drug use in order to provide a more rigorous test of the Gateway Hypothesis.

Conclusion

The three approaches are all useful, but they each have distinct advantages and limitations. Differences in the conceptualizations of stages of drug use progression, which are closely related to differences in the analytical methods employed by Bentler et al. and by the other two approaches are especially important to recognize. In particular, Yamaguchi and Kandel's and the Bentler et al. differing conclusions about whether the Gateway Hypothesis holds empirically are due to differences in their conceptualizations, and resulting operationalizations of the hypotheses and do not reflect a real contradiction. Which particular conceptualization is most useful is in part a matter of theoretical choice. I believe that as long as researchers qualify the implications they draw from results of their analyses, apparent inconsistencies between the implications of different approaches will be resolvable in most cases. The different approaches will for the most part be mutually complementary in enriching theory and research on drug use progression.

References

Blumen, L., Kogan, M., & McCarthy, P. J. (1955). *The Industrial Mobility of Labor as a Probability Process.* Ithaca, NY: Cornell Studies in Industrial and Labor Relations, Cornell University.

Clogg, C. C., Rudas, T., & Xi, L. (1995). A new index of structure for the analysis of models for mobility tables and other cross-classifications. *Sociological Methodology, 25,* 197–222.

Collins, L. M. (1991). Measurement in longitudinal research. In L. M. Collins and J. H. Horn (Eds.), *Best methods for the analysis of change: Recent advances, unanswered questions, future directions* (pp. 137–148). Washington, DC: APA.

Collins, L. M., Cliff, N., & Dent, V. W. (1988). The longitudinal guttman simplex: A new methodology for measurement of dynamic constructs in longitudinal panel studies. *Applied Psychological Measurement, 21,* 217–230.

Collins, L. M., Graham, J. W., Long, J. D., & Hansen, W. B. (1994a). Cross-validation of latent class models of early substance use onset. *Multivariate Behavioral Research, 29,* 165–183.

Collins, L. M., Graham, J. W., Rousculp, S. S., Filder, P. L., Pan, J., & Hansen, W. B. (1994b). Latent transition analysis and how it can address prevention research. In L. M. Collins and L. Seltz (Eds.), *Advances in data analysis for prevention research* (pp. 81–111). National Institute on Drug Abuse Research Monograph 142. National Institute on Drug Abuse, US Department of Health and Human Services. Rockville, MD.

Collins, L. M., & Wugalter, S. E. (1992). Latent class models for stage-sequential dynamics latent variables. *Multivariate Behavioral Research, 27,* 131–157.

Donovan, J. E., & Jessor, R. (1983). Problem drinking and the dimension of involvement in drugs: A Guttman scalogram analysis of adolescent drug use. *American Journal of Public Health, 73,* 542–552.

Goodman, L. A. (1969). On the measurement of social mobility: An index of status persistence. *American Sociological Review, 34,* 831–850.

Goodman, L. A. (1975). A new model for scaling response patterns: An application of the quasi-independence concept. *Journal of the American Statistical Association, 70,* 755–768.

Graham, J. W., Collins, L. M., Wugalter, S. E., Chung, N. K., & Hansen, W. B. (1991). Modeling transitions in latent stage-sequential processes: A substance use prevention example. *Journal of Consulting and Clinical Psychology, 59,* 48–57.

Huba, G. J., Wingard, A., & Bentler., P. M. (1981). A comparison of two latent variable causal models for adolescent drug use. *Journal of Personality and Social Psychology, 40,* 180–193.

Kandel, D. B., & Yamaguchi, K. (1993). From beer to crack: Developmental patterns of drug involvement. *American Journal of Public Health, 83,* 851–855.

Kandel, D. B., & Yamaguchi, K. (2000). Stages of drug involvement in the U.S. population. Chapter 4 in this book.

Langeheine, R., & van de Pol, F. (1990). A unifying framework for Markov modeling in discrete space and discrete time. *Sociological Methods and Research, 18,* 416–441.

Newcomb, M. D., & Bentler, P. M. (1986a). Cocaine use among adolescents: Longitudinal association with social context, psychology, and the use of other substances. *Addictive Behavior, 11,* 263–273.

Newcomb, M. D., & Bentler, P. M. (1986b). Frequency and sequence of drug use: A longitudinal study from early adolescence to young adulthood. *Journal of Drug Education, 16,* 101–120.

Poulsen, C. S. (1982). *Latent structure analysis with choice modeling applications.* Ph.D. dissertation, Wharton School, The University of Pennsylvania.

Single, E., Kandel, D. B., & Faust, R. (1974). Pattern of multiple drug use in high school. *Journal of Health and Social Behavior, 15,* 344–357.

Van de Pol, F., & de Leeuw, J. (1989). A latent Markov model for correcting measurement errors. *Sociological Methods and Research, 15,* 118–141.

Van de Pol, F., & Langeheine, R. (1990). Mixed Markov latent class models. *Sociological Methodology, 20,* 213–247.

Wiggins, L. M. (1955). *Panel analysis, latent probability models for attitude and behavior processes*. Amsterdam: Elsevier.

Yamaguchi, K., & Kandel, D. B. (1984a). Patterns of drug use from adolescence to young adulthood. II. Sequences of progression. *American Journal of Public Health, 74*, 668–672.

Yamaguchi, K., & Kandel, D. B. (1984b). Patterns of drug use from adolescence to young adulthood. III. Predictors of progression. *American Journal of Public Health, 74*, 673–681.

Yamaguchi, K., & Kandel, D. B. (1996). Parametric event sequence analysis: Racial/ethnic differences in patterns of drug-use progression. *Journal of American Statistical Association, 91*, 1388–1399.

Part V

Animal Models and Biological Processes

Implications for Drug Progression

13

The Value of Animal Models to Examine the Gateway Hypothesis

Neil E. Grunberg and Martha M. Faraday

Despite extensive correlational data and discussion of the Gateway Hypothesis, there is little direct empirical evidence that addresses its potential causal mechanisms. The possible causes for initial drug use and subsequent transition from use of one drug to use and abuse of other drugs include psychological, sociological, economic, behavioral, and biological variables. It is difficult, if not impossible, directly to examine and manipulate any of these possible explanations in children. The existing literature on reasons for drug use initiation and maintenance in children is restricted to self-reports. In contrast, the literature on adult drug initiation and maintenance includes self-reports as well as experimental examination of behavioral and biological effects of drugs. Importantly, continued drug use in adults, as self-reported and as indicated in experiments, largely results from the behavioral and biological effects of the self-administered substance. Self-report studies in children also suggest that young people use drugs because of their behavioral and biological effects. It is possible that these drug effects in young people are part of the causal mechanism of the Gateway Hypothesis.

Animal models have contributed substantially to the study of drugs of abuse and allow testing of causal hypotheses regarding drug effects. Although most of these studies have examined drug effects in adult animals, the paradigms and methods are readily applicable to younger animals. Animal models to evaluate human drug use are only valuable if they parallel and predict the human condition. This chapter presents rodent experiments that have (1) directly addressed the Gateway Hypothesis; (2) addressed relevant behavioral and biological effects of the

Gateway drugs, nicotine and alcohol; (3) examined variables (e.g., stress) that interact with drug effects and drug use; and (4) examined genotypic differences (i.e., sex and strain of rodents) that result in different drug effects. In addition, this chapter discusses how animal studies could be conducted to examine more fully behavioral and biological drug effects that may be relevant to the Gateway Hypothesis.

The Gateway Hypothesis Has Not Been Causally Examined

The Gateway Hypothesis – the idea that drugs such as nicotine and alcohol constitute a gateway in the path to illicit drug use – is a vivid description of the fact that some children and adolescents who initiate and maintain use of licit drugs go on to illicit drug use. This conceptualization is easy for scientists and the public to grasp and is consistent with correlational self-report data from epidemiological studies that use of nicotine and alcohol precedes use of illicit drugs (Kandel, 1975; Kandel & Yamaguchi, 1985; Kandel, Yamaguchi, & Chen, 1992). Despite the tendency to assume that correlations reflect causality, they may or may not. In fact, the reasons for initial drug use and transition to use and abuse of other drugs are not clear. The causal relationships underlying the Gateway Hypothesis are complex, multifactorial, and likely to include psychological, sociological, economic, behavioral, and biological variables. Until mechanisms in the relationship between licit drug use and subsequent illicit drug use are determined, it is difficult to predict who may be at risk, craft effective interventions, and engage meaningfully in prevention efforts. Until the Gateway Hypothesis is evaluated, it cannot and should not guide policy.

The complexity of investigating this multicausal process is exemplified by examining reasons children and youth report using one Gateway drug: nicotine self-administered via cigarettes. Young people report that they smoke cigarettes to try something new, to appear cool, to fit in with smoking friends and family; because cigarettes are cheap and accessible; for the euphoric effects; because they are addicted; to focus attention and cope with stress; and to control body weight and appetite (e.g., Sarason, Mankowski, Peterson, & Dinh, 1992; Nye, Haye, McKenzie-Pollock, Caughley, & Housham, 1980; French & Perry, 1996; Beaglehole, Eyles, & Harding, 1978; Ary & Biglan, 1988; Wang, Fitzhugh, Westerfield, & Eddy, 1995; CDC, 1994; Stanton, Mahalski, McGee, & Silva, 1993; Tuakli, Smith, & Heaton, 1990; Klesges, Elliot, & Robinson, 1997;

Milberger, Biederman, Faraone, Chen, & Jones, 1997). Adolescents' reasons for experimenting with alcohol are similarly complex and include psychosocial as well as biobehavioral reasons (e.g., to be cool, to get high, to fit in with friends, to release restraints) (Cronin, 1997; Hughes, Power, & Francis, 1992; Knibbe, Oostveen, & van de Goor, 1991; Pedersen, 1990; Bettes, Dusenbury, Kerner, James-Ortiz, & Botvin, 1990; Windle & Barnes, 1988; Snow & Wells-Parker, 1986; Earleywine & Finn, 1991). Given the complexity of reasons for using licit drugs, why do certain young smokers or drinkers progress to illicit drug use? Also, why do other young smokers or drinkers *not* progress to illicit drug use?

One can speculate about the intricacy of psychological, social, and biological reasons for licit drug use. A young smoker or drinker might progress to illicit drug use because he or she wants to assert independence, because friends or family members also are using other drugs, because small quantities of illicit drugs are relatively affordable, because illicit drugs exert desired effects similar to or more intense than those of licit drugs, because he or she wants to get high, because exposure to licit drugs during adolescence biologically primes the brain's reward mechanisms in a way that provokes future drug-seeking behavior, and so on. Examination of this network of potential causal variables is challenging, given that the population of interest consists of children and adolescents. For ethical reasons, it is impossible to manipulate and examine these explanations in children because these efforts would involve the administration of addictive substances. This restriction contrasts with methods that have been used to examine causal reasons for drug use in adults. In adults the effects of the licit Gateway drugs nicotine and alcohol have been examined extensively in experimental situations in which drug dose as well as drug cost have been manipulated and behavioral drug effects have been measured. Using nicotine as an example, experiments in adult humans have indicated that nicotine alters hedonic feelings, affect, attention, interactions with stress, aggressive social behaviors, relaxation, physiological variables, and subjective reward experiences (USDHHS, 1988; Heishman, Taylor, & Henningfield, 1994; Grunberg, 1982; Cherek, Bennett, & Grabowski, 1991; Pomerleau, Turk, & Fertig, 1984; Kassel & Shiffman, 1997). These reports have been central to establishing that adults smoke because they are addicted to nicotine, and because nicotine exerts multiple desired behavioral effects. In addition, this work established that nicotine caused these effects and led to the design and implementation of cessation therapies using nicotine replacement.

Although such experiments cannot be conducted with children, experimental findings from adults are informative in the context of the Gateway Hypothesis. The existing self-report literature on reasons for drug use initiation and maintenance in children indicates that, although initiation of nicotine and alcohol use may be the result of psychosocial factors such as peer influences (e.g., van Roosmalen & McDaniel, 1989, 1992; Sarason et al., 1992; French & Perry, 1996; Flay et al., 1994; Beaglehole et al., 1978; Aloise-Young, Graham, & Hansen, 1994), children continue smoking and drinking for much the same reasons as do adults. The younger smoker is addicted and smokes for feelings of reward, affect regulation, stress relief, body weight control, and attentional effects (Mitic, McGuire, & Neumann, 1985; CDC, 1994; USDHHS, 1994; Sarason et al., 1992; Tuakli et al., 1990; Stanton et al., 1993; Klesges et al., 1997; Milberger et al., 1997). The fact that the adolescent appears to smoke in order to obtain nicotine's behavioral and biological effects may be partially a result of biologically mediated factors in this age group relevant to maintenance of licit drug use as well as progression to illicit drug use. Although it is not possible to test these hypotheses experimentally in children, it is possible to employ a powerful methodology that has been used extensively to examine drug effects and mechanisms of action relevant to adult humans: the use of animal models.

Animal Models Are Valuable

Studies of Behavior, Health, and Drug Use

Animal research has a long history of providing valuable information relevant to disease states, potential treatments, and behaviors that affect health. Animal studies have provided critical information regarding the development and treatment of infectious diseases (Grunberg & Schnitzer, 1951, 1952), cardiovascular diseases (Manuck, Kaplan, & Matthews, 1986; Kaplan et al., 1982), cancers (Herberman & Holden, 1978), and so on. Animals also have been used as subjects in important studies of behavior over the past 100 years (e.g., Pavlov, 1927; Skinner, 1938; Miller, 1948; Brady, 1962; Thompson, 1962).

Moreover, animals have been used to study complex phenomena, such as the behavioral and biological aspects of drug use and abuse. Self-administration of a substance is considered an essential element to establish that the substance is addictive. Animals self-administer the same drugs self-administered by humans: cocaine, alcohol, nicotine, amphetamines, heroin, and other opiates (e.g., Corrigall & Coen, 1989; Goldberg, Spealman, & Goldberg, 1981; Goldberg, Morse, & Goldberg, 1976; Pallares, Nadal, Hernandez-Torres, & Ferre, 1997; van Erp & Miczek, 1997; Heyser, Schulteis, & Koob, 1997; Hyytia, Schulteis, & Koob, 1996; Horger, Giles, & Schenk, 1992; Schenk, Robinson, & Amit, 1988). In addition, behavioral and biological effects of drugs interact with drug history, environment, and psychological variables, and these complex interactions have been demonstrated in animals (e.g., Siegel, 1975; Schenk, Lacelle, Gorman, & Amit, 1987; Barrett, 1992; Shaham, Alvares, Nespor, & Grunberg, 1992; Shaham, Klein, Alvares, & Grunberg, 1993; Klein, Popke, & Grunberg, 1997). Further, the actions of putative treatments for addictions can be tested in animal models for efficacy as well as for toxicity. Despite the scientific and medical importance of these studies and the information revealed, animal models have *not* been widely used to study why drug use develops and whether use of one drug leads to the use of other drugs, that is, a testing of the Gateway Hypothesis.

Why Animal Models Have Not Been Used in Prevention Research

The relative omission of animal studies in the drug prevention literature does not indicate that animal models cannot be used in this context. Although the paradigms have been extensively employed in adult animals, they are readily applicable to younger subjects. The lack of application of animal models to study development and prevention of drug use reflects underlying assumptions operating in the various disciplines involved in drug research.

First, most prevention researchers do not use animal models and most animal researchers do not focus on prevention. Therefore, prevention researchers lack experience with and knowledge of the utility of animal models, and investigators who use animals to study drug effects lack knowledge about prevention issues.

Second, it has been tacitly or explicitly assumed in the prevention field that the variables that contribute most to the development and continuation of drug use in humans are variables that can only be studied in humans (e.g., economic, psychological, social, environmental, developmental). Many of these variables, however, are amenable to study in animal models. Both the adult and adolescent drug use literature indicate that the behavioral and biological effects of drugs (in addition to drug addiction per se) are potent motivators of continued drug self-administration. Prevention and intervention efforts in young people, however, have rarely focused on these drug effects. Animal models are well suited to examine and quantify drug effects in young subjects but have not been employed systematically to address these questions.

Third, most scientists who use animals to study drug effects have focused on classical effects that maintain drug addiction (e.g., dopamine release, physical dependence, tolerance, withdrawal) rather than on the behavioral and biological effects of addictive drugs that contribute to initiation and maintenance – for example, effects on appetitive behaviors and body weight, attention, stress, and affect regulation. It is noteworthy that these additional drug effects are among those indicated by adolescent self-reports as potent motivators for continued licit drug use.

Animal Models Could Be Used to Examine the Gateway Hypothesis

Although animal models have not been used to date to address underlying causal mechanisms for the Gateway Hypothesis for the reasons articulated, they provide a valuable tool. Animal studies can complement and parallel human studies by examining, in detail, causal hypotheses drawn from the human literature. In a study of a multicausal phenomenon in which psychological, sociological, economic, behavioral, and biological variables all are potentially relevant, animal models allow the explicit separation of variables so that individual causal contributions can be evaluated. Animal models can be conceptualized as a way to peel away psychological, sociological, and economic factors in order to focus on behavioral and biological effects of drugs that may be relevant to the Gateway Hypothesis. Animal models also can be used to determine the influence of nonbiological variables and their interactions with behavioral and biological variables, including psychological and economic factors. Economic factors contributing to drug initiation and maintenance can be operationalized by using operant conditioning paradigms in which access to drugs depends on the amount of work (measured in bar presses) the animal is willing to perform (e.g., Bickel, De Grandpre, & Higgins 1995; Pickens, 1979). Psychological variables, such as the influence of stress and its predictability or controllability, can be manipulated and examined in animal studies to determine possible causal contributions (e.g., Klein et al., 1997). Use of animals allows assessment of possible underlying biological mechanisms for observed behaviors, such as assay of peripheral and central biochemicals and neurotransmitters. Animal studies can be used to develop and test possible pharmacological or psychopharmacological interventions and can lead to new hypotheses that can be tested in humans. Further, the contributions that individual differences, such as sex and genotype, make to a given process can be assessed by measuring responses of animals of both sexes and multiple genotypes, for instance, different inbred and outbred rat strains.

The Three Major Ways That Animal Models Can Be Conceptualized

The small body of animal work performed to date that is relevant to determining causal mechanisms of the Gateway Hypothesis is reviewed later. Experiments that can and should be done also are discussed. To design and understand animal research relevant to complex human behavior, it is important to recognize that there are three major ways in which animal models can be conceptualized: (1) to provide *face valid models* to parallel human conditions or phenomena directly (e.g., studies of drug intravenous self-administration); (2) *to study underlying behavioral, psychological, and biological mechanisms* (e.g., study of the release of dopamine in the nucleus accumbens in response to administration of a putative addictive); and (3) *to examine similarities and differences in responses to reveal similarities and differences in effects* but with measures that do not have face validity to the human condition (e.g., studies of changes in locomotion to compare drug effects).

Face Valid Animal Models Can Be Used to Study the Gateway Hypothesis

Klein (1997) developed a face valid animal model to study Kandel's (1975) Gateway Hypothesis. Klein (1997) used male and female Wistar rats to examine effects of nicotine administration during adolescence on subsequent opioid consumption during adulthood. The subjects (41–day-old rats) received saline solution or nicotine (6 or 12 mg/kg/day) for 19 days subcutaneously via osmotic minipump. After a 7-day cessation from nicotine, animals had access to fentanyl (a potent opiate) solution for 4 weeks. In addition, half of the subjects were exposed to a mild physical stressor (immobilization for 20 minutes a day) during the period of fentanyl availability in order to determine the extent to which this variable would interact with opiate self-administration.

This experiment's results partially confirmed the Gateway Hypothesis. In nonstressed male rats, exposure to 6 mg/kg/day nicotine during adolescence was associated with increased fentanyl self-administration. Adolescent exposure to 12 mg nicotine kg/day did not have this effect. Exposure to nicotine did not enhance opiate self-administration in male rats that were stressed during opiate availability. In fact, stress exposure attenuated the effect of 6 mg/kg/day nicotine. In addition, female subjects did not significantly alter opiate self-administration after exposure to nicotine with or without stress. Klein (1997) suggested that the sex differences might indicate that simple pharmacological exposure to nicotine results in increased opiate consumption in males, whereas other biological mechanisms and social or cultural variables may be necessary to explain Gateway phenomena in females. Klein (1997) also suggested that future studies need to evaluate more fully the dose response curves relevant to progression from nicotine to opiate use and that the sex differences might disappear with lower dosages of nicotine.

This experiment is valuable because of the new data that it reports as well as the fact that it establishes a relatively face valid model to study the Gateway Hypothesis. It is "relatively" face valid because the nicotine was administered subcutaneously by continuous infusion, rather than by self-administration. Now that several investigators have reported that rats can self-administer nicotine intravenously (e.g., Goldberg et al., 1981; Corrigall & Coen, 1989), it would be useful to blend Klein's (1997) paradigm with nicotine self-administration. Further, it is relevant to consider that Klein (1997) used sequential, nonoverlapping exposure to nicotine and fentanyl. She followed this protocol to isolate the separate drug effects, but typical opiate users also continue to self-administer nicotine via cigarettes. It is possible that the simultaneous use of these different drugs (a central nervous system [CNS] stimulant and a CNS depressant) causes them to act jointly. Therefore, Klein's paradigm should be expanded to include simultaneous administration of both drugs. The fact that stress counteracted effects of nicotine in males to increase opiate self-administration also suggests that, in addition to gender, stress may be an important variable in whether or not nicotine exposure leads to opiate self-administration. The possible role of individual differences in these patterns also has not been explored. Other investigators using rats (see the section, Stress) have found that individual differences in stress sensitivity predict subsequent self-administration of stimulants (e.g., Piazza et al., 1989, 1990, 1991; Deminiere et al., 1989, 1992). Whether important differences in how individuals respond to stress also are relevant to the likelihood of opiate self-administration, concurrent with or subsequent to nicotine self-administration, is not known. Careful evaluation of the role of stress in the Gateway process, however, may illuminate who is at highest risk. The effects of different types of stressors (e.g., social, psychological, environmental) also should be examined. In addition, this animal study suggests that stress should be assessed in human self-report studies. Schenk (Chapter 14) discusses studies with adult male rats that examine effects of acute administration of nicotine, amphetamines, or caffeine on subsequent cocaine intracerebral self-administration. These studies provide examples of additional ways that animal research could be used to develop face valid models to examine the Gateway Hypothesis.

Animal Models Can Be Used to Study Behavioral, Biological, and Psychological Mechanisms Relevant to the Gateway Hypothesis

Humans self-administer drugs for many reasons. These reasons include positive reinforcement, or direct rewarding effects of the administered substance, and negative reinforcement, or administration of the substance to offset unpleasant withdrawal symptoms. These classic drug reward and withdrawal effects have been studied extensively with animal subjects and are discussed in the chapters by Koob and by Schenk (Chapters 15 and 14).

Addictive drugs also have other important behavioral and biological effects that maintain their use. These effects are relevant in the context of the Gateway Hypothesis because the Gateway drugs nicotine and alcohol exert many effects desired by users other than traditional reward or withdrawal prevention effects. These additional effects may contribute to initiation, maintenance, and progression of drug use.

Appetitive Behaviors and Body Weight. One of the most commonly cited reasons for smoking cigarettes, especially among young women, is to control appetite and body weight (Klesges et al., 1989; Grunberg, Winders, & Wewers, 1991). These reasons for smoking also are cited by adolescents, especially White girls (Klesges et al., 1997; Page & Gold, 1983). Importantly, the inverse relationship between tobacco use and body weight is well documented (e.g., Grunberg, Bowen, & Winders, 1986; Grunberg & Bowen, 1985; Grunberg, Winders, & Popp, 1987; Grunberg, 1992), and the role of nicotine per se in these effects was established empirically in studies with rats (Grunberg, 1982). It has been suggested that the appetitive effects of nicotine, particularly to alter specific food consumption and insulin levels in plasma and brain, are likely to be underlying biological and psychobiological mechanisms of reward in addition to dopaminergic effects (Grunberg & Raygada, 1991). Alcohol consumption also affects feeding behaviors. Ingestion of moderate amounts of alcohol may result in increased feeding (Orozco & de Castro, 1991), although this topic has not been studied extensively. Opiate effects on feeding are complex, with stimulation at low levels and suppression at higher levels (e.g., Yim & Lowy, 1984). The extent to which these effects motivate individuals to self-administer these drugs, however, has not been studied in detail because of the focus on these drugs as addictive, abused, or analgesic substances.

Drug effects that alter appetite, feeding, and body weight may be relevant in the context of the Gateway Hypothesis in several ways. It is possible that the effects of nicotine to control body weight and specific appetites may habituate over time (e.g., several years) and that people who desire these effects progress to use of opiates to reinstate these actions. The long-term effects of nicotine on body weight have not been systematically examined in animal models, but these experiments could easily be performed. It also is possible that appetitive effects of nicotine may come to serve as interoceptive and exteroceptive cues for drug reward, and, therefore, any introduction of drugs with similar effects may share these reinforcing actions and make drug progression more likely. This idea can be tested in animals by using drug discrimination paradigms in which subjects' preferences for opiates with and without concurrent nicotine administration can be assessed. In addition, it is possible that individuals use nicotine to counteract undesired appetitive effects of other reinforcing drugs such as alcohol, including increased feeding. Use of nicotine concurrent with alcohol may prevent this disinhibition. Further, if effects of nicotine to control body weight and appetite wane over time but the individual continues to self-administer alcohol, then progression to other appetite-controlling drugs also might occur. This idea can be tested in animals by examining the long-term appetitive effects of concurrently administered nicotine and alcohol, and the effects on body weight and appetite when opiates are introduced.

The appetitive effects of addictive drugs also may be part of the centrally mediated rewarding effects (Grunberg & Baum, 1985). It has been suggested that drugs that affect central appetitive mechanisms come to exert actions on the body that mimic those of essential food-stuffs. As a result, craving for addictive drugs and withdrawal symptoms may involve the same mechanisms that underlie hunger and food crav-ings. If this postulate is correct, then cross-dependence and cross-tolerance to other addictive drugs may result from a generalization of hungers across drugs qua foods. This possibility could be involved in Gateway type drug progression and could be examined in animals.

Attentional Effects. Because humans self-administer drugs to obtain behavioral, biological, and cognitive effects, it is possible that attention altering properties of Gateway and illicit drugs are relevant to initiation, maintenance, and progression. It is well established that nicotine, alcohol, and illicit drugs alter attentional processes in humans and in animals. With regard to nicotine, some smokers, generally men, report smoking specifically to focus attention (Zuckerman, Ball, & Black, 1990). Among adolescents, certain subgroups such as individuals diagnosed with attention deficit hyperactivity disorder (ADHD) report dispropor-tionately high smoking rates (Milberger et al., 1997). In experiments with adults, tobacco or nicotine enhances performance on simple repeti-tive tasks and some vigilance-based cognitive tasks (Heishman et al., 1994). Parallel animal studies indicate that nicotine enhances sensory gating, a possible index of attention, in certain strains of rats and impairs it in others (Acri, Morse, Popke, & Grunberg, 1994; Acri, 1994; Faraday, Rahman, Scheufele, & Grunberg, 1998; Faraday, O'Donoghue, & Grunberg, 1999). Taken together, the human and animal data suggest that some individuals use nicotine to improve attention and others may use nicotine to blunt attention or in spite of the attention impairing effects. The effects of alcohol and opiates can impair attentional processes (e.g., Arnsten, Segal et al., 1983; Post, Lott, Maddock, & Beede, 1996; Koelega, 1995; Lamb & Robertson, 1987).

In the context of the Gateway Hypothesis, it is likely that the attention enhancing properties of nicotine maintain cigarette use in individuals for whom this is a desired effect. It is possible that long-term exposure to nicotine containing products creates a hypervigilant or hyperattentive state that is unpleasant for some people. Despite these now-undesired effects, it may be difficult for individuals to quit smoking because of other addictive properties of nicotine. If this is so, then alcohol, opiates, or other CNS depressants may be particularly reinforcing as they offset these effects on attention. This idea can be tested in animal subjects by measuring effects of long-term nicotine administration on attention and other behaviors indicative of vigilance and then either administering or allowing animals to self-administer alcohol and measuring effects on the same behaviors.

It also is possible that individuals who are hypervigilant may begin using alcohol to attenuate this unpleasant attentional state. Having learned that this CNS depressant can alleviate this condition, individuals might be motivated to try other vigilance and anxiety reducing drugs such as the opiates. This hypothesis also can be assessed in animals by examining preferences for alcohol and opiates in different rat strains bred for high or low fearfulness (e.g., Roman Low Avoidance, Roman High Avoidance, Fischer-344, Lewis) and in the same animals when exposed to stressful or fear-inducing situations, with concurrent measurement of attentional indices.

Another, quite different, possibility is that individuals for whom nicotine impairs attentional processes consider this effect desirable. It may be, for example, that these individuals are hyperattentive at baseline and nicotine is experienced as calming. Progression to opiates, therefore, might occur in pursuit of similar calming effects. This idea can be tested by using two strains of rodents in which the effects of nicotine on attention are opposite in direction. Specifically, nicotine enhances indices of attention in Sprague-Dawley rats (Acri, 1994; Acri et al., 1994; Faraday et al., 1999) but impairs the same indices in Long-Evans rats (Faraday et al., 1998, 1999). Each strain could be exposed to nicotine and then opiate self-administration behavior measured to determine the extent to which nicotine's attentional effects are predictive of opiate self-administration. Because both strains will self-administer nicotine, this experiment could be done with concurrent nicotine and opiate availability to address the same question.

The interaction of early concurrent use of alcohol and cigarettes may be relevant to the Gateway Hypothesis. In addition to being Gateway drugs, cigarettes and alcohol are positively correlated in epidemiological studies (Kozlowski et al., 1993). Further, alcohol use is a risk factor for relapse to habitual smoking (Borland, 1990). Popke (1997) examined behavioral and biological effects of nicotine and alcohol in adult Sprague-Dawley rats and reported that nicotine offset the effects of alcohol to increase attentional processes. Ethanol also attenuated effects of nicotine on central biochemical mechanisms related to dopamine and its turnover, suggesting that the use of the two drugs together may be more classically reinforcing than separate use. Popke (1997) suggested that in addition to affecting indices of reward, the two drugs when used concurrently might counteract each other's aversive behavioral or biological effects.

In the context of the Gateway Hypothesis, nicotine and alcohol as well as the illicit drugs might similarly be used to counteract each other's aversive effects while causing rewarding effects. For example, if the ability of nicotine to attenuate unwanted effects of alcohol diminished over time, then other sympathomimetics, such as cocaine, might be tried, to reinstate the desired effect. This idea could be tested by using long-term nicotine and alcohol administration in animals, measuring behaviors that index attention and giving subjects access to cocaine and measuring the same behaviors.

Stress. In addition to interaction with other drugs, attentional effects of nicotine may interact with attentional effects of stress in ways that might explain why people smoke more under stress (Acri, 1994; Faraday et al., 1999). Male Sprague-Dawley and male Long-Evans rats administered nicotine and subjected to a mild physical stressor had attentional processes indistinguishable from those of control subjects that did not receive nicotine and did not experience stress (Acri, 1994; Faraday et al., 1999). The effects of nicotine to counteract stress induced changes in attention also occurred in female Long-Evans rats, but not in female Sprague-Dawley rats, in which the attentional effects of nicotine were additive with effects of stress (Faraday et al., 1999).

To the extent that behavioral and biological effects of drugs are altered by stress, a stress by drug interaction may be relevant to the Gateway Hypothesis. Individuals under stress may use drugs for different effects than individuals who are not under stress. Further, a person who uses nicotine to maintain attentional processes despite stress may be more likely to continue smoking than an individual who is not experiencing stress. The effects that drugs may have on the behavioral and biological manifestations of stress as well as those that stress may have on the behavioral and biological effects of Gateway and illicit drugs can be tested in animal models.

It is well known that stress is positively correlated with substance use. Stress is a frequently reported reason for use of tobacco and alcohol among adults (USDHHS, 1988; Pohorecky, 1991) as well as among adolescents (Tuakli et al., 1990; Byrne, Byrne, & Reinhart, 1995; Friedman et al., 1985; Botvin & McAlister, 1981). Animal studies have been used to test the causality of this relationship and have indicated that a number of variables affect the stress–drug use relationship. Shaham and colleagues (1992) gave male Sprague-Dawley and male Wistar rats, half of which underwent daily mild physical stress (immobilization), access to opiate solutions (morphine and fentanyl). Over the course of the 55-day experiment, stressed subjects increased their preference for the morphine solution to double the level of control, nonstressed subjects, indicating that stress caused increased opiate self-administration (Shaham et al., 1992). In a follow-up experiment using footshock and making fentanyl subsequently available in an operant self-administration paradigm, stressed male Wistar rats self-administered more fentanyl than did nonstressed controls (Shaham et al., 1993). A similar paradigm in female Wistars, however, revealed sex differences in the stress–drug self-administration relationship. Half of the stressed female subjects self-administered more fentanyl on stress days than on nonstress days, but half of the subjects did not (Klein et al., 1993). All subjects, however, exhibited physical dependence to fentanyl when challenged with the opioid antagonist naloxone. These findings in an animal model are consistent with clinical reports that men and women differ in patterns of drug use and abuse (Grunberg et al., 1991; Lex, 1991).

The extent to which psychological variables, such as the predictability of a stressor, may be relevant in the stress–drug use relationship has been examined by using an animal model. Klein and colleagues (1997) gave male and female Wistar rats access to fentanyl solution after predictable stress (footshock reliably preceded by a tone) or unpredictable stress (footshock with random tones not related temporally to the shock). The predictable stressor resulted in greater fentanyl self-administration than did the unpredictable stressor, and female rats self-administered more fentanyl than did male rats but displayed fewer physical dependence symptoms than did males when challenged with naloxone (Klein et al., 1997). These findings suggest that sex and environmental cues may play powerful roles in the stress–drug use relationship.

With regard to the Gateway Hypothesis, it may be that stress (including biological, emotional, social, psychological, environmental stressors) experienced during adolescence contributes to drug use and progression from use of one drug to another in several ways. First, adolescents may self-administer various drugs to reduce psychological, cognitive, behavioral, or biological effects of stress that are unpleasant. For example, stress can result in negative mood states, impaired cognitive functioning, and physiological states such as increased heart rate that may be perceived as unpleasant. Gateway drugs as well as illicit drugs can lift mood, offset effects of stress on cognition, and alter arousal. If an individual uses Gateway drugs to alleviate symptoms of stress, and the effects of these drugs wane over time, then that person may be likely to turn to illicit drugs to obtain similar or more intense stress relief. The animal work reviewed here suggests that once opiate use is initiated, males may become more physically dependent than females. In addition, the kind of stress the individual experiences, whether predictable or unpredictable, may affect the extent to which the illicit drugs are self-administered. With regard to the Gateway Hypothesis, these findings in animals suggest that stress, including the specific type of stressor (e.g., predictable or unpredictable), should be systematically measured in human studies.

In addition, links between stress sensitivity and drug self-administration have been demonstrated, indicating that biologically based individual differences may be relevant to illicit drug progression. Individual rats that exhibited the greatest behavioral and biological responses to mild stressors also were the animals most likely to self-administer addictive drugs (e.g., Piazza, Deminiere, Le Moal, & Simon, 1989; Piazza et al., 1990, 1991). Sprague-Dawley males that exhibited the greatest locomotor responses to stress and to a single injection of amphetamine were the most likely to develop subsequent amphetamine self-administration (Deminiere, Piazza, Moal, & Simon, 1989; Deminiere et al., 1992). In addition, male rats (strain not reported) that exhibited the largest catecholamine responses to stress also demonstrated the largest decreases in catecholamine levels when given ethanol (Livezey, Balabkins, & Vogel, 1987). Mechanisms for these differences appear to be differential corticosterone reactivity and the properties of corticosterone to modify activity of the mesocorticolimbic dopaminergic system (De Kloet, 1991; Faunt & Crocker, 1988; Rothchild et al., 1984). Exploratory responses to novelty also are positively correlated with peripheral corticosterone levels, propensity to self-administer various drugs, responsivity to food reinforcement, and activity of dopaminergic systems (Dellu, Mayo, Le Moal, & Simon, 1993; Piazza et al., 1989, 1990, 1991; Dellu, Piazza, Mayo, Le Moal, & Simon, 1996). Importantly, these studies have focused for the most part on the responses of male Sprague-Dawley rats. Whether similar patterns exist in responses of female rats and rats of other strains is not known but may be relevant to understanding of differential drug progression patterns.

Individuals also may mistake the symptoms of stress for symptoms of drug withdrawal and self-administer drugs to a greater extent when stressed than when not stressed (Grunberg & Baum, 1985). If a young person experiencing stress misinterprets stress symptoms as signs of withdrawal, then he or she may be more likely to increase self-administration of Gateway drugs. If use of Gateway drugs is not sufficient to alleviate symptoms, then the individual may seek relief of presumed withdrawal from illicit drugs. This hypothesis can be tested in an animal model by creating dependence in animal subjects on Gateway drugs, inducing physiological symptoms similar to those of withdrawal, and providing access to harder drugs.

Social Interaction. Social interactions are central to the human experience and are particularly salient during adolescence (Erikson, 1959). Drugs alter social interaction and, therefore, may be used to alter social interactions in desired ways. In addition, social interactions can be a source of stress and, thereby, contribute to drug use. These effects can be studied in animals to evaluate these influences carefully without the confound of expectations and social history. Scheufele et al. (2000) examined effects of nicotine on social interaction in Long-Evans male and female rats. These investigators found that nicotine reduced aggressive behaviors, consistently with reports in the human literature (Cherek et al., 1991). Social situations in the form of housing conditions also can alter drug self-administration in animals and may interact with subjects' sex. Crowded housing conditions increased fentanyl self-administration by female Wistars when compared to the individual housing condition, but differential housing did not alter fentanyl self-administration by males (Brown, Klein, Rahman, & Grunberg, 1995). Housing conditions during development also have been reported to alter subsequent drug self-administration behavior. For example, rats raised in isolation consume more opioids and are less sensitive to the effects of opioids compared with animals raised in groups (Schenk, Britt, Atalay, & Charleson, 1982; Alexander, Coambs, & Hadaway, 1978; Schenk, Ellison, Hunt, & Amit, 1985). Also, rats raised in groups do not reliably self-administer cocaine, whereas rats raised in isolation do (Schenk et al., 1987).

With regard to the Gateway Hypothesis, it is possible that young people use Gateway drugs and progress to use of harder drugs in order to modify social behaviors or to ameliorate the stress of social situations. As the studies reviewed here indicate, these ideas can be tested in animal models. Animals could be exposed to repeated social interactions with novel conspecifics, with and without licit drug administration, and biological and behavioral stress responses measured. Animals also could be given access to Gateway and harder drugs while in the social interaction paradigm in order to determine whether stressful social encounters result in progressive drug-taking behaviors. Further, the influence of housing conditions on initial and subsequent drug self-administration behavior also can be assessed by these paradigms.

Animal Models Can Be Used to Examine Similarities and Differences in Drug Effects

Animal models can be used to determine whether different drugs or drug combinations result in similar behavioral effects or similar interoceptive effects. This type of animal study is useful in two ways. First, it provides a way of indexing the extent to which drugs in the same class (e.g., sympathomimetics, depressants) exert similar behavioral effects qualitatively and quantitatively. From these behavioral effects, it may be possible to extrapolate to reasons for human drug use. Second, models of drug discrimination provide a window into each animal's subjective experience, that is, the extent to which the animal experiences drug effects as the same or different.

Locomotion. Spontaneous locomotion is a widely used behavioral index of animal health, drug effects, stress effects, and sex and genotypic differences. The effects of nicotine, alcohol, and the opiates are well documented. Nicotine when administered acutely to male Sprague-Dawley rats depresses locomotion but in a nicotine tolerant animal increases locomotion (Hildebrand, Nomikos, Bondjers, Nisell, & Svensson, 1997; Stolerman, Garcha, & Mirza, 1995; Welzl, Allessandri, Oettinger, & Battig, 1988; Clarke & Kumar, 1983). Alcohol and the opiates have complex effects on locomotion that depend on dosage, measurement time course, and genotype of subject (e.g., Vaccarino, Amalric, Swerdlow, & Koob, 1986; Judson & Goldstein, 1978; Phillips & Shen, 1996; Smoothy & Berry, 1985, 1984). The effects of nicotine on locomotion also can be modified by variables such as the sex and strain of subject as well as the subject's housing condition. For example, Faraday et al. (1999) reported that in Long-Evans rats chronic nicotine administration interacted with housing such that nicotine decreased locomotion of males and females that were singly housed and increased locomotion of subjects that were group-housed. These animal findings highlight the importance of environment and individual differences in drug effects.

In the context of the Gateway Hypothesis, these data suggest that an individual's social environment (e.g., isolated vs. grouped vs. crowded) may alter the effects of drugs experienced. If humans self-administer licit and illicit drugs to obtain specific behavioral actions, then modifying the environment may be one means of preventing drug use and progression. That is, if the environment in which the drug is available results in an aversive drug effect, then the individual will be less likely to continue use. Conversely, if an individual's environment maximizes rewarding drug effects, then that person may be more likely to progress to harder drug use. These important issues are poorly understood but merit research attention. As the Faraday et al. (1999) experiment indicates, the influence of environment on behavioral drug actions can be readily studied in animals.

Drug Discrimination. Drug discrimination paradigms in animals provide a means of assessing how a particular drug or drug combination compares in terms of its interoceptive effects to other drugs or drug combinations (e.g., Signs & Schechter, 1986; Gordon, Meehan, & Schechter, 1993; de la Garza & Johanson, 1985; Shoaib & Stolerman, 1996). With regard to the Gateway Hypothesis, this approach could be used to indicate the extent to which drugs provide similar interoceptive cues that may signal reward. This information may indicate whether cues for reward are important in drug progression. With regard to nicotine by alcohol interactions as a gateway to illicit drug use, it is possible that the combined interoceptive effects of an arousing drug and a sedating drug on attention, affect, stress relief, and appetitive behaviors come to serve as cues for drug reward. If so, then other combinations of arousing and sedating drugs also may provide similar cues and make the individual more likely to initiate and maintain use. Animal subjects could be used to test this possibility by administering concurrent nicotine and alcohol and testing drug discrimination responses to other stimulant–depressant combinations.

Genotype Is Important and Can Be Studied in Animal Experiments of Drug Effects

Although we have not explicitly addressed the role of animal genotype in the studies reviewed, in our discussion of animal work we have specified the strain and sex of rat. A complete discussion of the research possibilities involving systematic variation of genotype broadly construed to include sex is beyond the space allotted for this chapter. However, it is relevant to note that sex and strain (i.e., two major manifestations of different genotype) matter when studying effects of addictive drugs. Nicotine, for example, generally has greater behavioral effects on females than on males, but females may be less responsive to interoceptive cues associated with nicotine administration (Grunberg et al., 1991; Perkins, 1996; Faraday et al., 1999). With regard to strains of rodents, nicotine has opposite effects on some behaviors (i.e., attentional indices) but similar effects on others (body weight, locomotion); alcohol is preferred or not preferred; some addictive drugs are readily self-administered but others are not; susceptibility to stress is high or low; emotionality is high or low; and so on. Further, genetically altered knock-out mice and transgenic mice can be used to study effects of addictive drugs and to infer from them the role of specific genes or proteins in drug sensitivity and behavioral effects (e.g., Picciotto et al., 1995; Pomerleau, 1995). All of these variables are potentially relevant to the Gateway Hypothesis and provide a means of investigating the role of biologically based individual differences in addiction and addiction progression liability. As molecular biological techniques continue to progress, the possibilities of studying genetic variables involved in drug use and abuse continue to expand.

So Now What?

The Gateway Hypothesis needs to be examined empirically and animal models can be used to do that. Thoughtful use of animal models would allow direct evaluation of biological, behavioral, and psychological variables that may help to explain why some individuals progress from the use and abuse of licit to use and abuse of illicit drugs and why other individuals do not. Animal experiments allow causal examination of variables that may contribute to the progression from the use of one drug to the use of another. Moreover, results of such animal studies may suggest where uniquely human responses (e.g., desires to be rebellious, concerns about the opinions of others) are likely to operate. That is, when a drug progression occurs in a human sample but hypothetical biological or behavioral mechanisms are disconfirmed in animal studies, then uniquely human responses are likely to be operating. Therefore, animal studies that are designed to test the Gateway Hypothesis and specific underlying mechanisms would provide valuable information regardless of whether the questions under study confirm or disconfirm the Gateway Hypothesis per se. Although to date little work has been done on this theme, several laboratories are now pursuing these questions.

It is important for prevention researchers and epidemiologists to communicate with animal researchers to determine the key questions to examine, to share research findings, and to use these findings to guide each other's work. For this communication to be effective, scientists from the many related disciplines must be trained to understand and to be able to critique each other's work. Over the past 20 years scientists have drawn from each others' findings, techniques, and methods. Multidisciplinary and interdisciplinary collaborations and training have moved scientific knowledge forward. It is now time to try to understand and to incorporate each other's ways of thinking about problems and each other's ways of solving problems such as why certain people progress from one drug to another and others do not. This transdisciplinary (Rosenfield, 1992) approach certainly is challenging, but it is a logical next step to make the best use of the intellectual and human-made tools that now are available.

References

Acri, J. B. (1994). Nicotine modulates effects of stress on acoustic startle reflexes in rats: Dependence on dose, stressor and initial reactivity. *Psychopharmacology, 116*, 255–265.

Acri, J. B., Morse, D. E., Popke, E. J., & Grunberg, N. E. (1994). Nicotine increases sensory gating measured as inhibition of the acoustic startle reflex in rats. *Psychopharmacology, 114*, 369–374.

Alexander, B. K., Coambs, R. B., & Hadaway, P. F. (1978). The effect of housing and gender on morphine self-administration in rats. *Psychopharmacology, 58*, 175–179.

Aloise-Young, P. A., Graham, J. W., & Hansen, W. B. (1994). Peer influence on smoking initiation during early adolescence: A comparison of group members and group outsiders. *Journal of Applied Psychology, 79*, 281–287.

Arnsten, A. F., Segal, D. S., Neville, H. J., Hillyard, S. A., Janowsky, D. S., Judd, L. L., & Bloom, F. E. (1983). Naloxone augments electrophysiological signs of selective attention in man. *Nature, 304*, 725–727.

Ary, D. V., & Biglan, A. (1988). Longitudinal changes in adolescent cigarette smoking behavior: Onset and cessation. *Journal of Behavioral Medicine, 11*, 361–382.

Barrett, J. E. (1992). Historical influences affecting the behavioral actions of abused drugs. *NIDA Research Monograph 124*, 161–172.

Beaglehole, R., Eyles, E., & Harding, W. (1978). Cigarette smoking habits, attitudes and associated social factors in adolescents. *New Zealand Medical Journal, 87,* 239–242.

Bettes, B. A., Dusenbury, L., Kerner, J., James-Ortiz, S., & Botvin, G. J. (1990). Ethnicity and psychosocial factors in alcohol and tobacco use in adolescence. *Child Development, 61,* 557–565.

Bickel, W. K., De Grandpre, R. J., & Higgins, S. T. (1995). The behavioral economics of concurrent drug reinforcers: A review and reanalysis of drug self-administration research. *Psychopharmacology, 188,* 250–259.

Borland, R. (1990). Slip-ups and relapse in attempts to quit smoking. *Addictive Behaviors, 15,* 235–245.

Botvin, G., & McAlister, A. (1981). Cigarette-smoking among children and adolescents: Causes and prevention. In C. B. Arnold, L. H. Kuller, & M. R. Greenlick (eds.), *Advances in Disease Prevention* (Vol. 1). New York: Springer.

Brady, J. V. (1962). Psychophysiology of emotional behavior. In A. J. Bachrach (Ed.), *Experimental foundations of clinical psychology* (pp. 343–385). New York: Basic Books.

Brown, K. J., Klein, L. C., Rahman, M. A., & Grunberg, N. E. (1995). Acoustic startle responses as predictors of fontanyl self-administration in rats. Presented at American Psychological Association, New York.

Byrne, D. G., Byrne, A. E., & Reinhart, M. I. (1995). Personality, stress and the decision to commence cigarette smoking in adolescence. *Journal of Psychosomatic Research, 39,* 53–62.

CDC (1994, October 21). Reasons for tobacco use and symptoms of nicotine withdrawal among adolescent and young adult tobacco users – United States, 1993. *Morbidity and Mortality Weekly Report, 43,* 745–750.

Cherek, D. R., Bennett, R. H., & Grabowski, J. (1991). Human aggressive responding during acute tobacco abstinence: Effects of nicotine and placebo gum. *Psychopharmacology, 104,* 317–322.

Clarke, P.B.S., & Kumar, R. (1983). The effects of nicotine on locomotor activity in non-tolerant and tolerant rats. *British Journal of Pharmacology, 80,* 587–594.

Corrigall, W. A., & Coen, K. M. (1989). Nicotine maintains robust self-administration in rats on a limited-access schedule. *Psychopharmacology, 99,* 473–478.

Cronin, C. (1997). Reasons for drinking versus outcome expectancies in the prediction of college student drinking. *Substance Use and Misuse, 32,* 1287–311.

De Kloet, E. R. (1991). Brain corticosteroid receptor balance and homeostatic control. *Frontiers in Neuroendocrinology, 12,* 95–164.

De la Garza, R., & Johanson, C. E. (1985). Discriminative stimulus properties of cocaine in pigeons. *Psychopharmacology, 85,* 23–30.

Dellu, E., Mayo, W., Le Moal, M., & Simon, H. (1993). Individual differences in behavioral responses to novelty in rats: Possible relationship with the sensation-seeking trait in man. *Personality and Individual Differences, 14,* 411–418.

Dellu, E., Piazza, P., Mayo, W., Le Moal, M., & Simon, H. (1996). Novelty-seeking in rats—biobehavioral characteristics and possible relationship with the sensation-seeking trait in man. *Neuropsychobiology, 34,* 136–145.

Deminiere, J. M., Piazza, P. V., Guegan, G., Abrous, N., Maccari, S., Le Moal, M., & Simon, H. (1992). Increased locomotor response to novelty and propensity to intravenous amphetamine self-administration in adult offspring of stressed mothers. *Brain Research, 586,* 135–139.

Deminiere, J. M., Piazza, P. V., Le Moal, M., & Simon, H. (1989). Experimental approach to individual vulnerability to psychostimulant addiction. *Neuroscience and Biobehavioral Reviews, 13,* 141–147.

Earleywine, M., & Finn, P. R. (1991). Sensation seeking explains the relation between behavioral disinhibition and alcohol consumption. *Addictive Behaviors, 16,* 123–128.

Erikson, E. (1959). *Identity and the life cycle.* New York: Norton.

Faraday, M. M., O'Donoghue, V. A., & Grunberg, N. E. (1999). Effects of nicotine and stress on startle amplitude and sensory-gating depend on rat strain and sex. *Pharmacology Biochemistry and Behavior, 62,* 273–284.

Faraday, M. M., Rahman, M. A., Scheufele, P. M., & Grunberg, N. E. (1998). Nicotine impairs startle and sensory-gating in Long-Evans rats. *Pharmacology Biochemistry and Behavior, 61,* 281–289.

Faraday, M. M., Scheufele, P. M., Rahman, M. A., & Grunberg, N. E. (1999). Effects of chronic nicotine administration on locomotion depend on rat sex and housing condition. *Nicotine and Tobacco Research, 1,* 143–151.

Faunt, J. E., & Crocker, A. D. (1988). Adrenocortical hormone status affects responses to dopamine receptor agonists. *European Journal of Pharmacology, 152,* 255–261.

Flay, B. R., Hu, F. B., Siddiqui, O., Day, L. E., Hedeker, D., Petraitis, J., Richardson, J., & Sussman, S. (1994). Differential influence of parental smoking and friends' smoking on adolescent initiation and escalation of smoking. *Journal of Health and Social Behavior, 35,* 248–265.

French, S. A., & Perry, C. L. (1996). Smoking among adolescent girls: Prevalence and etiology. *Journal of the American Medical Women's Association, 51,* 25–28.

Friedman, L. S., Lichtenstein, E., & Biglan, A. (1985). Smoking onset among teens: An empirical analysis of initial situations. *Addictive Behaviors, 10,* 1–13.

Gordon, T. L., Meehan, S. M., & Schechter, M. D. (1993). P and NP rats respond differently to the discriminative stimulus effects of nicotine. *Pharmacology Biochemistry & Behavior, 45,* 305–308.

Goldberg, S. R., Morse, W. H., & Goldberg, D. M. (1976). Behavior maintained under second-order schedule by intramuscular injection of morphine or cocaine in rhesus monkeys. *The Journal of Pharmacology and Experimental Therapeutics, 199*, 278–286.

Goldberg, S. R., Spealman, R. D., & Goldberg, D. M. (1981). Persistent behavior at high rates maintained by intravenous self-administration of nicotine. *Science, 214*, 573–575.

Grunberg, E., & Schnitzer, R. J. (1951). Chemotherapy of murine leprosy. *Annals of the New York Academy of Sciences, 54*, Art. 1, 107–114.

Grunberg, E., & Schnitzer, R. J. (1952, January). Studies on the activity of hydrazine derivatives of isonicotinic acid in the experimental tuberculosis of mice. *Quarterly Bulletin, Sea View Hospital*, 3–11.

Grunberg, N. E. (1982). The effects of nicotine and cigarette smoking on food consumption and taste preferences. *Addictive Behaviors, 7*, 317–331.

Grunberg, N. E. (1992). Cigarette smoking and body weight: A personal journey through a complex field. *Health Psychology, 11*(suppl.), 26–31.

Grunberg, N. E., & Baum, A. (1985). Biological commonalities of stress and substance abuse. In S. Shiffman & T. A. Wills (Eds.), *Coping and substance use* (pp. 25–62). New York: Academic Press.

Grunberg, N. E., & Bowen, D. J. (1985). The role of physical activity in nicotine's effects on body weight. *Pharmacology Biochemistry & Behavior, 23*, 851–854.

Grunberg, N. E., Bowen, D. J., & Winders, S. E. (1986). Effects of nicotine on body weight and food consumption in female rats. *Psychopharmacology, 90*, 101–105.

Grunberg, N. E., & Raygada, M. (1991). Effects of nicotine on insulin: Actions and implications. In *Advances in pharmacological sciences: Effects of nicotine on biological systems* (pp. 131–142). Basel: Birkhauser Verlag.

Grunberg, N. E., Winders, S. E., & Popp, K. A. (1987). Sex differences in nicotine's effects on consummatory behavior and body weight in rats. *Psychopharmacology, 91*, 221–225.

Grunberg, N. E., Winders, S. E., & Wewers, M. E. (1991). Gender differences in tobacco use. *Health Psychology, 10*, 143–153.

Heishman, S. J., Taylor, R. C., & Henningfield, J. E. (1994). Nicotine and smoking: A review of effects on human performance. *Experimental and Clinical Psychopharmacology, 2*, 345–395.

Herberman, R. B., & Holden, H. T. (1978). Natural cell-mediated immunity. *Advances in Cancer Research, 27*, 305–377.

Heyser, C. J., Schulteis, G., & Koob, G. F. (1997). Increased ethanol self-administration after a period of imposed ethanol deprivation in rats trained in a limited access paradigm. *Alcoholism: Clinical & Experimental Research, 21*, 784–791.

Hildebrand, B. E., Nomikos, G. G., Bondjers, C., Nisell, M., & Svensson, T. H. (1997). Behavioral manifestations of the nicotine abstinence syndrome in the rat: Peripheral versus central mechanisms. *Psychopharmacology, 129*, 348–356.

Horger, B. A., Giles, M. K., & Schenk, S. (1992). Preexposure to amphetamine and nicotine predisposes rats to self-administer a low dose of cocaine. *Psychopharmacology, 107*, 271–276.

Hughes, S. O., Power, T. G., & Francis, D. J. (1992). Defining patterns of drinking in adolescence: A cluster analytic approach. *Journal of Studies on Alcohol, 53*, 40–47.

Hyttia, P., Schulteis, G., & Koob, G. F. (1996). Intravenous heroin and ethanol self-administration by alcohol-preferring AA and alcohol-avoiding ANA rats. *Psychopharmacology, 125*, 248–254.

Judson, B. A., & Goldstein, A. (1978). Genetic control of opiate-induced locomotor activity in mice. *Journal of Pharmacology and Experimental Therapeutics, 206*, 56–60.

Kandel, D. B. (1975). Stages of adolescent involvement in drug use. *Science, 190*, 912–914.

Kandel, D. B., & Yamaguchi, K. (1985). Developmental patterns of the use of legal, illegal, and medically prescribed psychotropic drugs from adolescence to young adulthood. In C. L. Jones & R. J. Battjes (Eds.), *Etiology of drug abuse: Implications for prevention, NIDA Research Monograph 56* (pp. 193–235). U.S. Department of Health and Human Services, Public Health Services, Alcohol, Drug Abuse, and Mental Health Administration, National Institute on Drug Abuse. DHHS Pub. No. (ADM) 85–1335. Washington, DC: U.S. Government Printing Office.

Kandel, D. B., Yamaguchi, K., & Chen, K. (1992). Stages of progression in drug involvement from adolescence to adulthood: Further evidence for the gateway theory. *Journal of Studies on Alcohol, 53*, 447–457.

Kaplan, J. R., Manuck, S. B., Clarkson, T. B., Lusso, F. M., & Taub, D. M. (1982). Social status, environment, and atherosclerosis in cynomolgous monkeys. *Atherosclerosis, 53*, 283–295.

Kassel, J. D., & Shiffman, S. (1997). Attentional mediation of cigarette smoking's effect on anxiety. *Health Psychology, 16*, 359–368.

Klein, L. C. (1997). *Sex differences and the effects of stress on subsequent opioid consumption in adult rats following adolescent nicotine exposure: A psychopharmacologic examination of the Gateway Hypothesis.* Unpublished doctoral dissertation, Bethesda, MD: Uniformed Services University of the Health Sciences.

Klein, L. C., Popke, E. J., & Grunberg, N. E. (1997). Sex differences in effects of predictable and unpredictable footshock on fentanyl self-administration in rats. *Experimental and Clinical Psychopharmacology, 5*, 99–106.

Klein, L. C., Shaham, Y., Alvares, K., & Grunberg, N. E. (1993). Effect of stress on oral fentanyl consumption in rats in an operant self-administration paradigm. *Pharmacology Biochemistry & Behavior, 46*, 315–322.

Klesges, R. C., Elliot, V. E., & Robinson, L. A. (1997). Chronic dieting and the belief that smoking controls body weight in a biracial, population-based adolescent sample. *Tobacco Control, 6,* 89–94.

Klesges, R. C., Meyers, A. W., Klesges, L. M., & La Vasque, M. E. (1989). Smoking, body weight, and their effects on smoking behavior: A comprehensive review of the literature. *Psychological Bulletin, 106,* 1–27.

Knibbe, R. A., Oostveen, T., & van de Goor, I. (1991). Young people's alcohol consumption in public drinking places: Reasoned behaviour or related to the situation? *British Journal of Addiction, 86,* 1425–1433.

Koelega, H. S. (1995). Alcohol and vigilance performance: A review. *Psychopharmacology, 118,* 233–249.

Kozlowski, L. T., Henningfield, J. E., Keenan, R. M., Lei, H., Leigh, G., Jelinek, L. C., & Haertzen, C. A. (1993). Patterns of alcohol, cigarette, and caffeine use in two drug-abusing populations. *Journal of Substance Abuse Treatment, 10,* 171–179.

Lamb, M. R., & Robertson, L. C. (1987). Effect of acute alcohol on attention and the processing of hierarchical patterns. *Alcoholism: Clinical & Experimental Research, 11,* 243–248.

Lex, B. W. (1991). Some gender differences in alcohol and polysubstance users. *Health Psychology, 10,* 121–132.

Livezey, G. T., Balabkins, N., & Vogel, W. H. (1987). The effect of ethanol (alcohol) and stress on plasma catecholamine levels in individual female and male rats. *Neuropsychobiology, 17,* 193–198.

Manuck, S. B., Kaplan, J. R., & Matthews, K. A. (1986). Behavioral antecedents of coronary heart disease and atherosclerosis in cynomolgous monkeys. *Psychosomatic Medicine, 6,* 1–14.

Milberger, S., Biederman, J., Faraone, S., Chen, L., & Jones, J. (1997). ADHD is associated with early initiation of cigarette smoking in children and adolescents. *Journal of the American Academy of Child and Adolescent Psychiatry, 36,* 37–44.

Miller, N. E. (1948). Studies of fear as an acquirable drive. I. Fear as motivation and fear-reduction as reinforcement in the learning of new responses. *Journal of Experimental Psychology, 38,* 89–101.

Mitic, W. R., McGuire, D. P., & Neumann, B. (1985). Perceived stress and adolescents' cigarette use. *Psychological Reports, 57*(3 Pt. 2), 1043–1048.

Nye, P. A., Haye, K. L., McKenzie-Pollock, D. J., Caughley, B. L., & Housham, R. W. (1980). What encourages and discourages children to smoke? Knowledge about health hazards and recommendations for health education. *New Zealand Medical Journal, 91,* 432–435.

Orozco, S., & de Castro, J. M. (1991). Effects of alcohol abstinence on spontaneous feeding patterns in moderate alcohol consuming humans. *Pharmacology Biochemistry & Behavior, 40,* 867–873.

Page, R. M., & Gold, R. (1983). Assessing gender differences in college cigarette smoking intenders and non-intenders. *Journal of School Health, 53*, 531–535.

Pallares, M. A., Nadal, R. A., Hernandez-Torres, M., & Ferre, N. A. (1997). EtOH self-administration on shuttle box avoidance learning and extinction in rats. *Alcohol, 14*, 503–509.

Pavlov, I. (1927). *Conditioned reflexes*. New York: Oxford University Press.

Pedersen, W. (1990). Drinking games adolescents play. *British Journal of Addiction, 85*, 1483–1490.

Perkins, K. A. (1996). Sex differences in nicotine versus nonnicotine reinforcement as determinants of tobacco smoking. *Experimental and Clinical Psychopharmacology, 4*, 166–177.

Phillips, T. J., & Shen, E. H. (1996). Neurochemical bases of locomotion and ethanol stimulant effects. *International Review of Neurobiology, 39*, 243–282.

Piazza, P., Deminiere, J., Le Moal, M., & Simon, H. (1989). Factors that predict individual vulnerability to amphetamine self-administration. *Science, 245*, 1511–1513.

Piazza, P., Deminiere, J., Maccari, S., Mormede, P., Le Moal, M., & Simon, H. (1990). Individual reactivity to novelty predicts probability of amphetamine self-administration. *Behavioral Pharmacology, 1*, 339–345.

Piazza, P., Maccari, S., Deminiere, J., Le Moal, M., Mormede, P., & Simon, H. (1991). Corticosterone levels determine individual vulnerability to amphetamine self-administration. *Proceedings of the National Academy of Sciences, 88*, 2088–2092.

Picciotto, M., Zoli, M., Léna, C., Bessis, A., Lallemand, Y., LeNovère, N., Vincent, P., Pich, E.M., Brûlet, P., & Changeux, J. P. (1995). Abnormal avoidance learning in mice lacking functional high-affinity nicotine receptor in the brain. *Nature, 374*, 65–67.

Pickens, R. (1979). A behavioral program for treatment of drug dependence. *NIDA Research Monograph 25*, 44–54.

Pohorecky, L. A. (1991). Stress and alcohol interaction: An update of human research. *Alcoholism: Clinical & Experimental Research, 15*, 438–459.

Pomerleau, O. F. (1995). Individual differences in sensitivity to nicotine: Implications for genetic research on nicotine dependence. *Behavioral Genetics, 25*, 161–177.

Pomerleau, O. F., Turk, D., & Fertig, J. (1984). The effects of cigarette smoking on pain and anxiety. *Addictive Behaviors, 9*, 256–271.

Popke, E. J. (1997). *Effects of nicotine and ethanol on indices of reward and sensory-motor function in rats: Implications for the positive epidemiologic relationship between the use of cigarettes and the use of alcohol.* Unpublished doctoral dissertation, Bethesda, MD: Uniformed Services University of the Health Sciences.

Post, R. B., Lott, L. A., Maddock, R. J., & Beede, J. I. (1996). An effect of alcohol on the distribution of spatial attention. *Journal of Studies on Alcohol, 57*, 260–266.

Rosenfield, P. L. (1992). The potential of transdisciplinary research for sustaining and extending linkages between the health and social sciences. *Social Sciences in Medicine, 35*, 1343–1357.

Rothchild, A. J., Langlais, P. J., Schatzberg, A. F., Walsh, F., Cole, J., & Bird, E. (1984). Dexamethasone increases plasma free dopamine in man. *Journal of Psychological Research, 18*, 217–223.

Sarason, I. G., Mankowski, E. S., Peterson, A. V., & Dinh, K. T. (1992). Adolescents' reasons for smoking. *Journal of School Health, 62*, 185–190.

Schenk, S., Britt, M. D., Atalay, J., & Charleson, S. (1982). Isolation rearing decreases opiate receptor binding in rat brain. *Pharmacology Biochemistry & Behavior, 16*, 841–842.

Schenk, S., Ellison, F., Hunt, T., & Amit, Z. (1985). An examination of heroin conditioning in preferred and nonpreferred environments and in differentially housed mature and immature rats. *Pharmacology Biochemistry & Behavior, 22*, 215–220.

Schenk, S., Lacelle, Gorman, K., & Amit, Z. (1987). Cocaine self-administration in rats influenced by environmental conditions: Implications for the etiology of drug abuse. *Neuroscience Letters, 81*, 227–231.

Schenk, S., Robinson, B., & Amit, Z. (1988). Housing conditions fail to affect the intravenous self-administration of amphetamine. *Pharmacology Biochemistry & Behavior, 31*, 59–62.

Scheufele, P. M. (1997). *Effects of nicotine administration, cessation, and differential housing conditions on aggressive behaviors of male and female rats.* Unpublished master's thesis, Bethesda, MD: Uniformed Services University of the Health Sciences.

Scheufele, P. M., Faraday, M. M., & Grunberg, N. E. (2000). Differential effects of nicotine on social and non-social behaviors in male and female Long-Evans rats. *Nicotine & Tobacco Research, 2*, 169–178.

Shaham, Y., Alvares, K., Nespor, S. M., & Grunberg, N. E. (1992). Effect of stress on oral morphine and fentanyl self-administration in rats. *Pharmacology Biochemistry & Behavior, 41*, 615–619.

Shaham, Y., Klein, L. C., Alvares, K., & Grunberg, N. E. (1993). Effect of stress on oral fentanyl consumption in rats in an operant self-administration paradigm. *Pharmacology Biochemistry & Behavior, 46*, 315–322.

Shoaib, M., & Stolerman, I. P. (1996). Brain sites mediating the discriminative stimulus effects of nicotine in rats. *Behavioral Brain Research, 78*, 183–188.

Siegel, S. (1975). Evidence from rats that morphine tolerance is a learned response. *Journal of Comparative Physiology, 89*, 498–506.

Signs, S. A., & Schechter, M. D. (1986). Nicotine-induced potentiation of ethanol discrimination. *Pharmacology Biochemistry & Behavior, 24*, 769–771.

Skinner, B. F. (1938). The behavior of organisms: An experimental analysis. New York: Appleton-Century-Crofts.

Smoothy, R., & Berry, M. S. (1984). Alcohol increases both locomotion and immobility in mice: An ethological analysis of spontaneous motor activity. *Psychopharmacology, 83,* 272–276.

Smoothy, R., & Berry, M. S. (1985). Time course of the locomotor stimulant and depressant effects of a single low dose of ethanol in mice. *Psychopharmacology, 85,* 57–61.

Snow, R. W., & Wells-Parker, E. (1986). Drinking reasons, alcohol consumption levels, and drinking locations among drunken drivers. *International Journal of Addiction, 21,* 671–689.

Stanton, W. R., Mahalski, P. A., McGee, R., & Silva, P. A. (1993). Reasons for smoking or not smoking in early adolescence. *Addictive Behaviors, 18,* 321–329.

Stolerman, I. P., Garcha, H. S., & Mirza, N. R. (1995). Dissociations between the locomotor stimulant and depressant effects of nicotinic agonists in rats. *Psychopharmacology, 117,* 430–437.

Thompson, R. F. (1962). Role of the cerebral cortex in stimulus generalization. *Journal of Comparative Physiology and Psychology, 55,* 279-287.

Tuakli, N., Smith, M. A., & Heaton, C. (1990). Smoking in adolescence: Methods for health education and smoking cessation. *Journal of Family Practice, 31,* 369–374.

U.S. Department of Health and Human Services (1988). *The health consequences of smoking: Nicotine addiction. A report of the Surgeon General.* DHHS Pub. No. (CDC)88–8406. Washington, DC: U.S. Government Printing Office.

U.S. Department of Health and Human Services (1994). *Preventing tobacco use among young people: A report of the Surgeon General.* Atlanta, Georgia: U.S. Department of health and Human Services, Public Health Service, Centers for Disease Control and Prevention, National Center for Chronic Disease Prevention and Health Promotion, Office on Smoking and Health. Washington, DC: U.S. Government Printing Office.

Vaccarino, F. J., Amalric, M., Swerdlow, N. R., & Koob, G. F. (1986). Blockade of amphetamine but not opiate-induced locomotion following antagonism of dopamine function in the rat. *Pharmacology Biochemistry & Behavior, 24,* 61–65.

Van Erp, A., & Miczek, K. A. (1997). Increased aggression after ethanol self-administration in male resident rats. *Psychopharmacology, 131,* 287–295.

Van Roosmalen, E. H., & McDaniel, S. A. (1989). Peer group influence as a factor in smoking behavior of adolescents. *Adolescence, 24,* 801–816.

Van Roosmalen, E. H., & McDaniel, S. A. (1992). Adolescent smoking intentions: Gender differences in peer context. *Adolescence, 27,* 87–105.

Wang, M. Q., Fitzhugh, E. C., Westerfield, R. C., & Eddy, J. M. (1995). Family and peer influences on smoking behavior among American adolescents: An age trend. *Journal of Adolescent Health, 16,* 200–203.

Welzl, H., Allessandri, B., Oettinger, R., & Battig, K. (1988). The effects of long-term nicotine treatment on locomotion, exploration and memory in young and old rats. *Psychopharmacology, 96,* 317–323.

Windle, M., & Barnes, G. M. (1988). Similarities and differences in correlates of alcohol consumption and problem behaviors among male and female adolescents. *International Journal of Addiction, 23,* 707–728.

Yim, G. K., & Lowy, M. T. (1984). Opioids, feeding, and anorexias. *Federation Proceedings, 43,* 2893–2897.

Zuckerman, M., Ball, S., & Black, J. (1990). Influences of sensation-seeking, gender, risk appraisal, and situational motivation on smoking. *Addictive Behaviors, 15,* 209–220.

14

Sensitization as a Process Underlying the Progression of Drug Use via Gateway Drugs

Susan Schenk

Both cross-sectional and longitudinal studies have demonstrated that use of illicit drugs, like cocaine, is reliably preceded by use of other drugs, like nicotine and alcohol (Yamaguchi & Kandel, 1984; Kandel & Davies, 1991; Kandel et al., 1992; Kandel & Yamaguchi, 1993; Merrill et al., 1999). The Gateway Hypothesis of drug abuse posits that the use of some drugs (Gateway drugs) increases the risk of subsequent drug abuse. If so, identification of factors that predispose to Gateway drug use may lead to early identification of those at risk for other drug use.

Several hypotheses have focused on either personality characteristics or environmental circumstances in the use of drugs and the progression of drug use (Jessor et al., 1980; Donovan et al., 1985; Donovan & Jessor, 1985; Wood et al., 1995; Costa et al., 1989; Donovan & Jesser, 1983; Swadi, 1999). For example, sensation seeking traits have been hypothesized to predict the initial foray into experimentation with psychoactive drugs (Wills et al., 1994). Because of the relative ease of procurement of nicotine and alcohol, these drugs would be most likely to be the ones used first. Initial use of other, more difficult to obtain and illicit drugs may follow as a result of a continuing search for new sensations and exposure to environmental circumstances that are more amenable to obtaining of these drugs. Thus, the Gateway progression may be viewed as a "progression of convenience" for those individuals who are predisposed to an elevated need to experience novel forms of stimulation; the prevailing

The hypotheses generated in this chapter were derived from results of animal experiments funded by research Grant DA 10084 from the National Institute on Drug Abuse. The methylphenidate data were collected with partial support from the Drug Enforcement Agency (DEA).

psychosocial climate may determine which drugs are more easily obtained and are therefore most likely to be experimented with first.

A critical component of the Gateway Hypothesis is the attempt to explain the progression of drug use on the basis of individual and/or environmental factors. The reliability of the progression has been cited as evidence that use of tobacco, alcohol, and/or marijuana should be considered a risk factor for *use* of other drugs. A question remains as to whether use of some drugs also increases the risk of subsequent *abuse* of illicit drugs. It is important to differentiate *use* and *abuse* because they may imply different causes. *Abuse* refers to compulsive drug use and can be characterized by a lack of control (WHO, 1992). The probability of initial use may be predicted on the basis of a variety of personality or environmental factors, but the probability of continued use and abuse is likely dependent on additional factors related to the pharmacological effects of the drug itself.

The purpose of the present chapter is to explore the possibility that those individuals for whom drug use develops into a pattern that is consistent with abuse are those that exhibit enhanced sensitivity to some of the pharmacological properties of the drug. The possibility that repeated consumption of Gateway drugs may produce changes in the response of central reward relevant circuitry is examined. The thesis that these changes enhance the positive reinforcing effects of other drugs of abuse, thereby rendering the individual at risk for continued use of the drug, is evaluated.

Animal studies are ideally suited to address questions concerning the influence of prior drug experience on subsequent drug responses. An obvious advantage is that drug self-administration by laboratory animals is not influenced by the social issues that may influence human drug use (religious, financial, legal, moral). Additionally, drug exposure parameters can be reliably manipulated and controlled, thereby providing the opportunity to examine the influence of exposure to various drugs on the response to other drugs.

This chapter presents data from laboratory animal studies that have examined the effect of preexposure to some drugs on the subsequent behavioral response to either the same or different drugs. An initial question considered is whether exposure to drugs that are currently considered Gateway drugs (nicotine, alcohol, and marijuana) alters the behavioral response to cocaine, a drug that commonly is used later in the progression. A second question concerns whether additional drugs should be considered potential Gateway drugs because exposure also renders laboratory animals more sensitive to the effects of cocaine. Finally, the possibility that the exposure to drugs at the higher end of the progression may render subjects more sensitive to the effects of drugs at the lower end is explored.

Many of the drugs of interest for this chapter are psychostimulants that share the effect of producing hyperlocomotion. Changes in the magnitude of this behavioral response as a function of prior exposure to the same or different drugs have been used as an index of drug sensitivity in many of the studies. This is an easily and reliably quantified response that can reflect changes in drug potency and/or efficacy. However, changes in drug produced hyperactivity are not necessarily relevant to the subsequent consumption of drugs. Accordingly, other studies have examined changes in the propensity to self-administer drugs as a function of preexposure. Additionally, studies have examined the ability of acute exposure to one drug to alter the effects of another drug as indicated by drug produced changes in self-administration of a drug or in the discriminative stimulus properties of a self-administered drug.

The Pharmacological Characteristics of Drug Abuse

A number of factors may underlie the initial approach and consumption of drugs of abuse. Their continued use, however, is generally attributed to the ability of the drugs to produce positive effects. Drugs that are self-administered by humans are, with few exceptions, self-administered by laboratory animals. Accordingly, laboratory studies of self-administration have been exploited to determine the pharmacological features of drug abuse.

Many drugs of abuse have different primary pharmacological effects, but they share the effect of enhancing transmission in central dopaminergic pathways. For the purposes of this chapter, the discussion is restricted to those drugs that have been proposed to be Gateway drugs, nicotine, alcohol, and marijuana. However, dopaminergic mechanisms have been identified in self-administration of virtually all drugs of abuse (see Chapter 15).

Nicotinic receptors, located on dopaminergic cell bodies (Clarke & Pert, 1985), increase dopaminergic cell firing when activated by nicotine (Calabresi et al., 1989), thereby increasing mesolimbic dopamine release (Di Chiara & Imperato, 1988). Alcohol decreases the activity of gamma–aminobutynic acid–ergic (GABAergic) neurons in the ventral tegmental area, thereby leading to a disinhibition of mesolimbic dopamine neurons (Kohl et al., 1998) and increased extracellular concentrations of dopamine within the mesolimbic system (Imperato & Di Chiara, 1986). The interaction between cannabinoids and dopamine has been less intensely investigated. There is evidence, however, that Δ^9-tetrahydrocannabinol (Δ^9-THC) produces an increase in spontaneous firing of dopamine neurons within the ventral tegmental area (French, 1997; French et al., 1997; Gessa et al., 1998) and increases extracellular concentrations of dopamine in the nucleus accumbens (Chen et al., 1990).

There is an impressive accumulation of data that have indicated the importance of dopaminergic systems in drug self-administration. Microdialysis measurements of nucleus accumbens dopamine levels have indicated that during self-administration, each infusion of cocaine produces a transient increase in dopamine levels (Wise et al., 1995; Hemby et al., 1997; Pettit & Justice 1989; 1991) and that lever pressing is initiated when synaptic dopamine returns to preinjection levels (Wise et al., 1995). Pharmacological manipulations have indicated that these drug produced increases in dopamine are critical to the maintenance of self-administration. Thus, pretreatment with dopamine antagonists or neurotoxic lesions to central dopamine pathways decrease self-administration of cocaine (Roberts & Koob, 1982; Roberts et al., 1977, 1980; Caine & Koob, 1994), ethanol (Pfeffer & Samson, 1988; Samson et al., 1993; Rassnick et al., 1993), and nicotine (Rose & Corrigal., 1997; Corrigal & Coen, 1991; Corrigal et al., 1992). Further, some drugs of abuse are self-administered intracranially directly into dopamine terminal areas and self-administration is blocked by coadministration of dopamine antagonists (Phillips et al., 1994; Hoebel et al., 1983); these findings highlight the importance of dopaminergic mechanisms in the maintenance of drug self-administration.

Of interest, repeated, intermittent exposure to a variety of psychostimulants produces a sensitized behavioral and neurochemical response to subsequent exposures. Thus, repeated exposure to cocaine enhances the ability of the drug to increase locomotor activation and shifts the dose effect curve for this behavioral effect to the left (Partridge & Schenk, 1999). This behavioral sensitization is accompanied by a neurochemical sensitization such that the ability of cocaine to increase synaptic dopamine is enhanced in sensitized rats (Kalivas et al., 1993). Sensitization has been hypothesized to be critical in the initiation, maintenance, and relapse to drug abuse and to be the correlate of a switch from drug *use* to drug *abuse* (Robinson & Berridge, 1993; Schenk & Partridge, 1997). It is possible that sensitization also provides a mechanism for the progression of drug use both within and across drugs.

Effect of Repeated Drug Exposure on Drug Sensitivity

A number of studies have documented that exposure to some Gateway drugs produces a sensitized behavioral response to the drug in addition to neuroadaptations in dopamine neurotransmission. Behavioral studies have primarily examined the ability of drug injections to enhance locomotor activity after acute or repeated administration.

The acute effect of nicotine on locomotor activity is dependent on dose. High doses tend to produce a suppression of activity (Morrison & Stephenson, 1972), but low doses primarily produced increases in activity (Clarke et al., 1988). With repeated low-dose exposures, a sensitized response was produced and the dose effect curve for nicotine produced activation shifted upward (Ksir et al., 1987; Schenk et al., 1991). This sensitized behavioral response was accompanied by a sensitized neurochemical response; nicotine produced increases in synaptic dopamine became sensitized after preexposure (Balfour et al., 1998). Pretreatment with nicotine also decreased the latency to subsequent acquisition of nicotine self-administration (Shoaib et al., 1997), suggesting that prior exposure to nicotine increased the initial reinforcing effect of the drug and predisposed rats to the positive reinforcing effects. These findings strengthen the contention that drug exposure, through neurochemical sensitization, increases the propensity of rats to self-administer nicotine.

Repeated exposure to ethanol also produced a sensitized response to the locomotor activating effects of subsequent exposures (Roberts et al., 1995; Lessov & Phillips, 1998). This sensitized behavioral response was accompanied by a sensitized neurochemical response; forced choice or self-administered ethanol exposure increased the response of dopamine neurons to electrical or K^+ induced activation (Nestby et al., 1997, 1999). Of interest, the ability of ethanol to enhance locomotion appears to be species specific because mice, but not rats, exhibit this response. However, ethanol self-administration rendered rats more sensitive to the subsequent reinforcing effects of ethanol (Brown et al., 1998); that finding also supports the idea that repeated exposure to some drugs of abuse increases the risk for increased use of the same drug.

There is a relative paucity of studies that have examined the effects of repeated exposure to marijuana. However, acute exposure to Δ^9-THC produces primarily behavioral suppression that exhibits tolerance after repeated exposures (Ameri, 1999). These effects have been attributed to actions on central cannabinoid receptors. A small number of studies have suggested that Δ^9-THC may produce positive effects in laboratory animals (Takahashi & Singer, 1979; Gardner et al., 1988; Lepore et al., 1995). Aversive effects of the drug, however, have also been reported (Chaperon et al., 1998).

Cross-Sensitization

As indicated previously, repeated exposure to some Gateway drugs produces sensitized neurochemical responses in dopaminergic pathways that have been implicated in the self-administration of cocaine and other drugs of abuse. This finding suggests that a potential mechanism for the progression of drug use may be due to this sensitization process, which enhances the initial effects of other drugs and thereby increases the risk of continued use. This possibility has been tested in a small number of laboratory studies that have examined the effect of preexposure to one drug on the response to the effects of another drug.

Pretreatment with subchronic doses of nicotine (0.2 mg/kg) sensitized mice to ethanol produced hyperlocomotion, and this sensitized behavioral response was accompanied by an elevation of dopamine turnover (Johnson et al., 1995). In tests of the ability of nicotine preexposure to sensitize rats to the effects of cocaine, rats were first exposed to nicotine or saline, during a 9-day pretreatment phase. The ability of cocaine to produce hyperactivity was then measured. This pretreatment regimen sensitized rats to the motor activating effect of nicotine, as indicated by a progressive increase in activity with repeated exposures (Schenk et al., 1991). After the pretreatment phase, an acute injection of cocaine to the saline pretreated rats increased locomotor activity in a dose dependent manner. However, the nicotine pretreated rats did not respond to any dose of cocaine tested (5.0–20.0 mg/kg) (Schenk et al., 1991; Horger et al., 1992), suggesting that they were tolerant, rather than sensitized, to cocaine's motor activating effect. Similar results were reported after pretreatment with nicotine to mice; there was no indication of sensitization to cocaine's motor activating effects in these subjects (Itzhak & Martin, 1999).

The effect of the same nicotine pretreatment regimen on cocaine self-administration was measured in other groups of rats. In contrast to the rats that exhibited a decreased response to cocaine's motor activating effect, nicotine pretreated rats acquired cocaine self-administration with shorter latencies than saline pretreated control subjects (Horger et al., 1992).

A decreased latency to acquisition of cocaine self-administration is a characteristic effect produced by increasing the dose of cocaine available for self-administration (Schenk et al., 1991, 1993). Therefore, these data suggested that nicotine pretreatment sensitized rats to cocaine's reinforcing effects and predisposed them to self-administer cocaine.

Subsequent studies determined whether the behavioral sensitization to the reinforcing effects of cocaine produced by nicotine pretreatment was accompanied by sensitization of neurochemical systems that had been implicated in cocaine self-administration. Rats received the 9-day nicotine pretreatment regimen, as in the behavioral studies. On the test day, a dialysis probe was placed through a previously implanted guide cannula into either the nucleus accumbens or the medial prefrontal cortex, terminal areas of the mesocorticolimbic dopamine system. The effect of a systemic injection of cocaine on dopamine overflow in these two dopamine terminal areas was then measured (Horger et al., 1994). Basal levels of dopamine did not differ as a function of pretreatment. An acute injection of cocaine (20.0 mg/kg) produced comparable increases in dopamine levels regardless of pretreatment condition. Thus, nicotine pretreatment rendered rats more sensitive to the reinforcing effects of cocaine, but this behavioral sensitization was not correlated with an increased response to the ability of cocaine to increase synaptic dopamine. The mechanisms underlying the capacity of nicotine preexposure to sensitize rats to the reinforcing effects of cocaine are currently poorly understood, but the behavioral data are consistent with the idea that nicotine pretreatment produces a sensitized response in reward relevant central pathways. This sensitized response may be the reason that nicotine is a Gateway drug that renders subjects, once initiated, at risk for subsequent continued use of other drugs.

In a test of cross-sensitization after pretreatment with ethanol, mice that had prior exposure to ethanol were sensitized to the motor activating effects of cocaine (Wise et al., 1996; Itzhak & Martin, 1999) and morphine (Netsby et al., 1997; Itzhak & Martin, 1999) but not amphetamine (Netsby et al., 1997). Pretreatment with amphetamine, however, increased the voluntary consumption of ethanol (Fahlke et al., 1994), suggesting that the reinforcing effects of this drug can be sensitized by preexposure to another self-administered drug. These data also raise the intriguing possibility that exposure to drugs at the higher end of the progression (amphetamine) may sensitize rats to the reinforcing effects of drugs at the lower end (ethanol). This possibility, which has not been investigated to a great extent, is discussed later in the chapter.

Alcohol preferring and alcohol avoiding rats have been produced by bidirectional breeding for high and low voluntary alcohol drinking, respectively (Eriksson, 1968). In addition to their different levels of ethanol consumption, these rats exhibit different sensitivities to the ability of repeated injections of other self-administered drugs to produce sensitized behavioral responses. Alcohol preferring rats were more prone to self-administer solutions of cocaine or etonitazene orally (Hyytia & Sinclair, 1993) or to self-administer heroin intravenously (Hyytia et al., 1996). The alcohol preferring rats also became more readily sensitized to the activating effects of either cocaine or morphine (Honkanen et al., 1999). These data suggest that a genetic predisposition for ethanol self-administration may reflect changes in general reward circuitry that also mediate the reinforcing effects of other drugs of abuse. Taken together, these findings support the idea that voluntary ethanol intake, or a genetic predisposition to enhanced ethanol self-administration, may change the response of central systems to other drugs of abuse, thereby rendering the subject more susceptible to self-administration of other drugs. The enhanced sensitivity to cocaine and other drugs may explain why ethanol is a Gateway drug that renders individuals, once initiated, at risk for progression to the continued use of other drugs of abuse.

To my knowledge, studies that examine the influence of prior exposure to marijuana have not been conducted, possibly because of the relative difficulty in producing self-administration in laboratory animals.

Other Potential Gateway Drugs?

If Gateway drugs are those drugs that sensitize subjects to the behavioral and neurochemical effects of other drugs, there are a number of candidates in addition to nicotine and ethanol. Some potential Gateway drugs have been identified in animal laboratory studies the basis of on their pharmacological and behavioral effects.

Caffeine?

One such candidate is the methylxanthine caffeine. Caffeine does not directly stimulate dopaminergic systems, but it has indirect dopamine agonist effects through its ability to antagonize adenosine receptors. Blockade of adenosine receptors, particularly adenosine (A_{2a}) receptors located on GABAergic neurons innervating the nucleus accumbens, disinhibits dopamine D_2 receptors (Ferre et al., 1992). The acute administration of caffeine produces hyperactivity that is antagonized by pretreatment with dopaminergic antagonists (Garrett & Holtzman, 1994), suggesting that some of the behavioral effects of caffeine are due to dopaminergic mechanisms.

After repeated exposure to caffeine rats showed no indication of a sensitized behavioral response (Schenk et al., 1990); caffeine produced motor activation neither increased nor decreased during a 9-day treatment regimen. However, repeated prior exposure to caffeine sensitized rats to the behavioral effects of other drugs. After pretreatment with caffeine, cocaine induced motor activation was enhanced (Schenk et al., 1990). Other studies have shown that the behavioral effects of cocaine are enhanced by coadministration of caffeine. For example, there was a leftward shift in the dose effect curve for the locomotor activating effects of cocaine (Schenk et al., 1990), as well as in the dose effect curve for cocaine self-administration (Schenk et al., 1994). Additionally, for rats that are trained to discriminate caffeine from saline injections, cocaine generalized to the caffeine cue (Holtzman, 1986), suggesting that the two drugs produce similar subjective effects. Caffeine pretreatment also shifted the dose effect curve for cocaine generalization to the left (Harland et al., 1989; Gauvin et al., 1990); that shift also suggests that the two drugs produce similar subjective effects. However, the interaction between cocaine and caffeine may be unidirectional because caffeine failed to generalize to a cocaine cue for rats that were trained to discriminate cocaine from saline (Gauvin et al., 1990).

The most compelling evidence that caffeine may be a Gateway drug for harder drug use is derived from self-administration studies. Rats that were pretreated with caffeine for 9 days were subsequently sensitized to the positively reinforcing effects of cocaine (Horger et al., 1991). There was a decreased latency to acquisition of cocaine self-administration, and this sensitized behavioral response was accompanied by a sensitized neurochemical response. The ability of an acute injection of cocaine to increase dopamine overflow in the nucleus accumbens was also increased in rats that were pretreated with caffeine (Horger et al., 1991). Unfortunately, caffeine is poorly self-administered by laboratory animals, rendering tests of the influence of cocaine exposure on the reinforcing effects of caffeine untestable in these subjects.

Methylphenidate?

The pharmacological profile of methylphenidate (Ritalin) compares favorably to that of cocaine and amphetamine in terms of the ability to block the reuptake of dopamine (Sonders et al., 1997) and to stimulate dopamine release (Clemens & Fuller, 1979). Imaging studies in humans in 1995 indicated that methylphenidate binds to cocaine sites in the brain (Volkow et al., 1995). Laboratory studies indicated that in rats trained to discriminate cocaine from saline, methylphenidate generalized well to the cocaine cue, suggesting that the two drugs produce comparable subjective effects. Further, methylphenidate produces conditioned as well as primary reinforcing effects, as indicated by its ability to elicit approach behavior to environments that have been paired with its administration (Martin-Iverson et al., 1985) and to maintain operant responding (Wilson & Schuster, 1971; Bergman et al., 1989).

Given that methylphenidate is comparable both behaviorally and neurochemically to cocaine, it was expected that repeated exposure to methylphenidate would produce sensitized responses and cross-sensitization to cocaine's effects. The acute effects of methylphenidate appear to mirror some of the effects of other dopaminergic agonists, but repeated administration of methylphenidate failed to produce a sensitized locomotor activating response (McNamara et al., 1993). Rather, repeated treatment with 20.0 mg/kg/day methylphenidate resulted in tolerance to the motor activating effect of the drug.

In a subsequent study, rats received 21 daily injections of a subchronic dose of methylphenidate (1.0 mg/kg/day). Three days after the last pretreatment, cocaine produced hyperactivity was measured. Acute or repeated administration of this low dose of methylphenidate failed to alter either horizontal or vertical activity. When the effect of cocaine was subsequently measured, the rats that were pretreated with methylphenidate were less sensitive to cocaine than the saline pretreated rats (see Figure 14.1). These preliminary data were comparable to the decreased sensitivity to cocaine-produced hyperlocomotion after pretreatment with nicotine discussed previously.

As occurred after nicotine pretreatment, repeated exposure to methylphenidate produced a sensitized response when the reinforcing effects of cocaine were measured after preexposure. For these tests, rats received nine daily pretreatment injections of methylphenidate (0.0, 5.0, or 20.0 mg/kg) and, 3 days after the last of the injections, latency to acquisition of cocaine self-administration (0.25 mg/kg/infusion) was measured. The latency to acquisition was significantly reduced for rats that received the high-dose methylphenidate pretreatment (see Figure 14.2).

These data suggest that methylphenidate sensitized rats to the reinforcing effects of cocaine. Accordingly, it is possible that this drug is

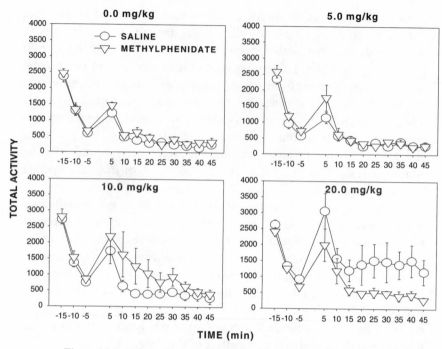

Figure 14.1. Effect of pretreatment with methylphenidate (1.0 mg/kg/day) on cocaine produced motor activation (0.0–2.0 mg/kg). Rats received methylphenidate during a 22-day pretreatment regimen, and the effect of cocaine was measured 3 days following the last injection. A significant increase in activity was produced by 20.0 mg/kg cocaine, but this effect was reduced in methylphenidate pretreated rats.

also a potential Gateway drug that renders individuals who have been initiated into cocaine use at greater risk for continued use of the drug.

Can "Hard" Drugs Be Gateway Drugs?

The previous sections have been devoted to examining the possibility that "soft" drugs like nicotine, ethanol, caffeine, or methylphenidate can be considered Gateway drugs because of their ability to produce sensitization to the reinforcing effects of "hard" drugs like cocaine. The data suggest that repeated exposure to Gateway drugs produces a neurochemical sensitization so that the initial response to cocaine is increased. Because of this enhanced response it is suggested that the probability of continued drug-taking will be increased.

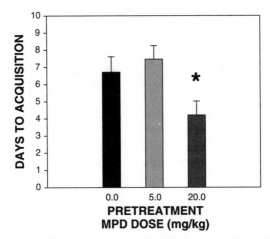

Figure 14.2. Number of days required to meet the criteria for acquisition of cocaine self-administration for rats that received prior treatment with methylphenidate. Pretreatment with 20.0 mg/kg methylphenidate for 9 days decreased the latency to acquisition of cocaine self-administration.

This process by which repeated exposure to some drugs increases the response to other drugs suggests that a common neuroadaptation is a consequence of repeated exposure. If so, the order of drug exposure should *not* be a determining factor in how the drug use progresses. That is, exposure to "hard" drugs would be expected to produce sensitization to the effects of "soft" drugs as a result of the drug induced sensitization of neurochemical systems. Although is not common for humans to initiate drug use with hard drugs, like cocaine, the sensitization hypothesis presented in this chapter suggests that this infrequent occurrence may be due to factors that limit availability or access to cocaine when drug use is being initiated.

A small number of laboratory studies have supported the idea that exposure to hard drugs can produce sensitization to the effects of soft drugs. It should be noted that these studies are less commonly conducted than the reverse sequence. However, pretreatment with cocaine enhanced the motor activating effect of ethanol (Itzhak & Martin, 1999), and pretreatment with amphetamine increased the voluntary consumption of ethanol (Fahlke et al., 1994). In laboratory studies of self-administration it is not uncommon for rats to be trained initially to self-administer cocaine in order to facilitate the acquisition of self-administration of other drugs. This anecdotal finding suggests that cocaine exposure may sensitize rats to the reinforcing effects of other drugs. If so, it is possible that the progression of drug use is a progression of convenience, as suggested in the introduction to this chapter, and that the notion of a Gateway drug may require expansion to include drugs that sensitize subjects to the reinforcing effects of other self-administered drugs.

References

Ameri, A. (1999). The effects of cannabinoids on the brain. *Progress in Neurobiology, 58*, 315–348.

Balfour, D.J.K., Benwell, M.E.M., Birrell, C. E., Kelly, R. J., & Al-Aloul, M. (1998). Sensitization of the mesoaccumbens dopamine response to nicotine. *Pharmacology Biochemistry and Behavior, 59*, 1021–1030.

Bergman, J., Madras, B. K., Johnson, S. E., & Spealman, R. D. (1989). Effects of cocaine and related drugs in nonhuman primates: 3. Self-administration by squirrel monkeys. *Journal of Pharmocology and Experimental Therapeutics, 251*, 150–155.

Brown, G., Jackson, A., & Stephens, D. N. (1998). Effects of repeated withdrawal from chronic ethanol on oral self-administration of ethanol on a progressive ratio schedule. *Behavioural Pharmacology, 9*, 149–161.

Caine, S. B., & Koob, G. F. (1994). Effects of dopamine D-1 and D-2 antagonists on cocaine self-administration under different schedules of reinforcement in the rat. *Journal of Pharmacology and Experimental Therapeutics, 270*, 209–218.

Calabresi, P., Lacey, M. G., & North, R. A. (1989). Nicotinic excitation of rat ventral tegmental neurons in vitro studied by intracellular recording. *British Journal of Pharmacology, 98*, 135–140.

Chaperon, F., Soubrie, P., Puech, A. J., & Thiebot, M.-H. (1998). Involvement of central cannabinoid (CB1) receptors in the establishment of place conditioning in rats. *Psychopharmacology, 135*, 324–332.

Chen, J. P., Paredes, W., Li, J., Smith, D., Lowinson, J., & Gardner, E.L. (1990). Delta 9-tetrahydrocannabinol produces naloxone blockable enhancement of presynaptic basal dopamine efflux in nucleus accumbens of conscious, freely-moving rats as measured by intracerebral microdialysis. *Psychopharmacology, 102*, 156–162.

Clarke, P.B.S., Fu, D. S., Jakubovic, A., & Fibiger, H. C. (1988). Evidence that mesolimbic dopaminergic activation underlies the locomotor stimulant action of nicotine in rats. *Journal of Pharmacology and Experimental Therapeutics, 246*, 701–708.

Clarke, P.B.S., & Pert, A. (1985). Autoradiographic evidence for nicotine receptors in nigrostriatal and mesolimbic dopaminergic neurons. *Brain Research, 348*, 355–358.

Clemens, J. A., & Fuller, R. W. (1979). Differences in the effects of amphetamine and methylphenidate on brain dopamine turnover and serum prolactin concentration in reserpine-treated rats. *Life Sciences, 24,* 2077–2081.

Corrigal, W. A., & Coen, K. M. (1991). Selective dopamine antagonists reduce nicotine self-administration. *Psychopharmacology, 104,* 171–176.

Corrigal, W. A., Franklin, K.B.J., Coen, K. M., & Clarke, P.B.S. (1992). The mesolimbic dopamine system is implicated in the reinforcing effects of nicotine. *Psychopharmacology, 107,* 285–289.

Costa, F. M., Jessor, R., & Donovan, J. E. (1989). Value on health and adolescent conventionality: A construct validation of a new measure in problem-behavior therapy. *Journal of Applied Psychology, 19,* 841–861.

Di Chiara, G., & Imperato, A. (1988). Drugs abused by humans preferentially increase synaptic dopamine concentrations in the mesolimbic system of freely moving rats. *Proceedings of the National Academy of Science USA, 85,* 5274–5278.

Donovan, J. E., & Jessor, R. (1983). Problem drinking and the dimension of involvement with drugs: A Guttman scalogram analysis. *American Journal of Public Health, 73,* 543–552.

Donovan, J. E., & Jessor, R. (1985). Structure of problem behavior in adolescence and young adulthood. *Journal of Consulting and Clinial Psychology, 53,* 890–904.

Donovan, J. E., Jessor, R., & Costa, F. M. (1985). Syndrome of problem behavior in adolescence: A replication. *Journal of Consulting and Clinical Psychology, 56,* 890–904.

Eriksson, K. (1968). Genetic selection for voluntary alcohol consumption in the albino rat. *Science, 159,* 739–741.

Fahlke, C., Hanson, S., Engel, J. A., & Hard, E. (1994). Effects of striatal 6-OHDA lesions or amphetamine sensitization on ethanol consumption in the rat. *Pharmacology Biochemistry and Behavior, 47,* 345–349.

Ferre, S., von Euler, G., Johansson, B., Fredholm, B. B., & Fuxe, K. (1992). Adenosine-dopamine interactions in the brain. *Neuroscience, 51,* 501–512.

French, E. D. (1997). Δ^9-Tetrahydrocannabinol excites rat VTA dopamine neurons through activation of cannabinoid CB1 but not opioid receptors. *Neuroscience Letters, 226,* 159–162.

French, E. D., Dillon, K., & Wu, X. (1997). Cannabinoids excite dopamine neurons in the ventral tegmentum and substantia nigra. *Neuroreport, 8,* 649–652.

Gardner, E., Paredes, W., Smith, D., Donner, A., Milling, C., Cohen, D., & Morrison, D. (1988). Facilitation of brain stimulation reward by delta-9-tetrahydrocannabinol. *Psychopharmacology, 96,* 142–144.

Garrett, B. E., & Holtzman, S. G. (1994). D1 and D2 dopamine receptor antagonists block caffeine-induced stimulation of locomotor activity in rats. *Pharmacology Biochemistry and Behavior, 47,* 89–94.

Gauvin, D. V., Craido, J. R., Moore, K. R., & Holloway, F. A. (1990). Potentiation of cocaine's discriminative effects by caffeine: A time-effect analysis. *Pharmacology Biochemistry and Behavior, 36,* 195–197.

Gessa, G., Melis, L., Muntoni, A. L., & Diana, M. (1998). Cannabinoids activate mesolimbic dopamine neurons by an action on cannabinoid CB1 receptors. *European Journal of Pharmacology, 341,* 39–44.

Harland, R. D., Gauvin, D. V., Michaelis, R. C., Carney, J. M., Seale, T. W., & Holloway, F. A. (1989). Behavioral interaction between cocaine and caffeine: A drug discrimination analysis in rats. *Pharmacology Biochemistry and Behavior, 32,* 1017–1023.

Hemby, S. E., Co, C., Koves, T. R., Smith, J. E., & Dworkin, S. I. (1997). Differences in extracellular dopamine concentrations in the nucleus accumbens during response-dependent and response-independent cocaine administration in the rat. *Psychopharmacology, 133,* 7–16.

Hoebel, B. G., Monaco, A. P., Hernandez, L., A. E., Aulissi, E., Stanley, B. G., & Lenard, L. (1983). Self-injection of amphetamine directly into the brain. *Psychopharmacology, 81,* 158–163.

Holtzman, S. G. (1986). Discriminative stimulus properties of caffeine in the rat: Noradrenergic mediation. *Journal Pharmacology and Experimental Therapeutics, 239,* 706–714.

Honkanen, A., Mikkola, J., Korpi, E. R., Hyytia, P., Seppala, T., & Ahtee, L. (1999). Enhanced morphine- and cocaine–induced behavioral sensitization in alcohol–preferring AA rats. *Psychopharmacology, 142,* 244–252.

Horger, B. A., Giles, M., & Schenk, S. (1992). Preexposure to amphetamine and nicotine predisposes rats to self-administer a low dose of cocaine. *Psychopharmacology, 107,* 271–276.

Horger, B. A., Valadez, A., Wellman, P. J., & Schenk, S. (1994). Augmentation of the neurochemical effects of cocaine in the ventral striatum and prefrontal cortex following preexposure to amphetamine but not nicotine: An in vivo microdialysis study. *Life Science, 55,* 1245–1251.

Horger, B. A., Wellman, P. J., Morien, A., Davies, B. T., & Schenk, S. (1991). Caffeine exposure sensitizes rats to the reinforcing effects of cocaine. *NeuroReport, 2,* 53–56.

Hyytia, P., & Sinclair, J. D. (1993). Oral etonitazene and cocaine consumption by AA, ANA and Wistar rats. *Psychopharmacology, 111,* 409–414.

Hyytia, P., Schulteis, G., & Koob, G. F. (1996). Intravenous heroin and ethanol self-administration by alcohol-preferring AA and alcohol-avoiding ANA rats. *Psychopharmacology, 125,* 248–254.

Imperato, A., & Di Chiara, G. (1986). Preferential stimulation of dopamine release in the nucleus accumbens of freely moving rats by ethanol. *Journal of Pharmacology and Experimental Therapeutics, 239,* 219–228.

Itzhak, Y., & Martin, J. L. (1999). Effects of cocaine, nicotine, dizocipline and alcohol on mice locomotor activity: Cocaine-alcohol cross-sensitization involves up-regulation of striatal dopamine transporter binding sites. *Brain Research, 818,* 204–211.

Jessor, R., Chase, J. A., & Donovan, J. E. (1980). Psychosocial correlates of marijuana use and problem drinking in a national sample of adolescents. *American Journal of Public Health, 70,* 604–613.

Johnson, D. H., Blomqvist, O., Engel, J. A., & Soderpalm, B. (1995). Subchronic intermittent nicotine treatment enhances ethanol-induced locomotor stimulation and dopamine turnover in mice. *Behavioral Pharmacology, 6,* 203–207.

Kalivas, P. W., Sorg, B. A., & Hooks, M. S. (1993). The pharmacology and neural circuitry of sensitization to psychostimulants. *Behavioral of Pharmacology, 4,* 315–334.

Kandel, D. B., & Davies, M. (1991). Cocaine use in a national sample of U.S. youth (NLSY): Ethnic patterns, progression and predictors. In S. Schober & C. Schade (Eds.), *The epidemiology of cocaine use and abuse.* NIDA Research Monograph 110 (pp. 151–188). Washington, DC, U.S. Department of Health and Human Services.

Kandel, D. B., Yamaguchi, K., & Chen, K. (1992). Stages of progression in drug involvement from adolescence to adulthood: Further evidence for the Gateway Theory. *Journal of Studies in Alcohol, 53,* 447–457.

Kandel, D. B., & Yamaguchi, K. (1993). From beer to crack: Developmental patterns of drug involvement. *American Journal of Public Health, 83,* 851–855.

Kohl, R. R., Katner, J. S., Chernet, E., & McBride, W. J. (1998). Ethanol and negative feedback regulation of mesolimbic dopamine release in rats. *Psychopharmacology, 139,* 79–85.

Ksir, C. J., Hakan, R. L., & Kellar, K. J. (1987). Chronic nicotine and locomotor activity: Influences of exposure dose and test dose. *Psychopharmacology, 92,* 25–29.

Lepore, M., Worel, S. R., Lowinson, J., & Gardner, E. (1995). Cannabinoid place preference induced by Δ^9-tetrahydrocannabinol: Comparison with cocaine, morphine and food reward. *Life Sciences, 56,* 2073–2080.

Lessov, C. N., & Phillips, T. J. (1998). Duration of sensitization to the locomotor stimulant effects of ethanol in mice. *Psychopharmacology, 4,* 374–382.

McNamara, C. G., Davidson, E. S., & Schenk, S. (1993). A comparison of the motor activating effects of acute and chronic exposure to amphetamine and methylphenidate. *Pharmacology Biochemistry Behavior, 45,* 729–732.

Martin-Iverson, M. T., Ortmann, R., & Fibiger, H. C. (1985). Place preference conditioning with methylphenidate and nomifensine. *Brain Research, 332,* 59–67.

Merrill, J. C., Kleber, H. D., Shwartz, M., Liu, H., & Lewis, S. R. (1999). Cigarettes, alcohol, marijuana, other risk behaviors, and American youth. *Drug and Alcohol Dependence, 56,* 205–212.

Morrison, C. F., & Stephenson, J. A. (1972). The occurrence of tolerance to a central depressant effect of nicotine. *British Journal of Pharmacology, 46,* 151–156.

Netsby, P., Vanderschuren, L.J.M.J., De Vries, T. J., Hogenboom, F., Wardeh, G., Mulder, A. H., & Schoffelmeer, A.N.M. (1997). Ethanol, like psychostimulants and morphine, causes long-lasting hyperreactivity of dopamine and acetylcholine neurons of rat nucleus accumbens: Possible role in behavioural sensitization. *Psychopharmacology, 133,* 69–76.

Netsby, P., Vanderschuren, L.J.M.J., De Vries, T. J., Mulder, A. H., Wardeh, G., Hogenboom, F., & Schoffelmeer, A.N.M. (1999). Unrestricted free-choice ethanol self-administration in rats causes long-term neuroadaptations in the nucleus accumbens and caudate putamen. *Psychopharmacology, 141,* 307–314.

Partridge, B., & Schenk, S. (1999). Context-independent sensitization to the locomotor activating effects of cocaine. *Pharmacology Biochemistry and Behavior, 63,* 543–548.

Pettit, H. O., & Justice, J. B., Jr. (1989). Dopamine in the nucleus accumbens during cocaine self-administration as studies by in vivo microdialysis. *Pharamcology Biochemistry and Behavior, 34,* 899–904.

Pettit, H. O., & Justice, J. B. Jr. (1991). Effect of dose on cocaine self-administration behavior and dopamine levels in the nucleus accumbens. *Brain Research, 539,* 94–102.

Pfeffer, A. O., & Samson, H. H. (1988). Haloperidol and apomorphine effects on ethanol reinforcement in free-feeding rats. *Pharmacology Biochemistry and Behavior, 29,* 343–350.

Phillips, G. D., Robbins, T. W., & Everitt, B. J. (1994). Bilateral intra-accumbens self-administration of D-amphetamine: Antagonism with intra-accumbens SCH-23390 and sulpiride. *Psychopharmacology, 114,* 477–485.

Rassnick, S., Pulvirenti, L., & Koob, G. F. (1993). SDZ-205,152, a novel dopamine receptor agonist, reduces oral ethanol self-administration in rats. *Alcohol, 10*: 127–132.

Roberts, A. J., Lessov, C. N., & Phillips, T. J. (1995). Critical role for gluco-corticoid receptors in stress- and ethanol-induced locomotor sensitization. *Journal of Pharmacology and Experimental Therapeutics, 275,* 790–797.

Roberts, D.C.S., Corcoran, M. E., & Fibiger, H. C. (1977). On the role of ascending catecholaminergic systems in intravenous self-administration of cocaine. *Pharmacology Biochemistry Behavior, 6,* 615–620.

Roberts, D.C.S., & Koob, G. F. (1982). Disruption of cocaine self-administration following 6-hyroxydopamine lesions of the ventral tegmental area in rats. *Pharmacology Biochemistry and Behavior, 17,* 901–904.

Roberts, D.C.S., Koob, G. F., Klonoff, P., & Fibiger, H. C. (1980). Extinction and recovery of cocaine self-administration following 6-hydroxydopamine lesions of the nucleus accumbens. *Pharmacology Biochemistry and Behavior, 12,* 781–787.

Robinson, T. E., & Berridge, K. C. (1993). The neural basis of drug craving: An incentive-sensitization theory of addiction. *Brain Research Review, 18,* 247–291.

Rose, J. E., & Corrigal, W. A. (1997). Nicotine self-administration in animals and humans: similarities and differences. *Psychopharmacology, 130,* 28–40.

Samson, H. H., Hodge, C. W., Tolliver, G. A., & Haraguchi, M. (1993). Effects of dopamine agonists and antagonists on ethanol-reinforced behavior: The involvement of the nucleus accumbens. *Brain Research Bulletin, 30,* 133–141.

Schenk, S., Horger, B. A., Peltier, R., & Shelton, K. (1991). Supersensitivity to the reinforcing effects of cocaine following 6-hydroxydopamine lesions to the medial prefrontal cortex in rats. *Brain Research, 543,* 227–235.

Schenk, S., Horger, B. A., & Snow, S. (1990). Caffeine preexposure sensitizes rats to the motor activating effects of cocaine. *Behavioral Pharmacology, 1,* 447–451.

Schenk, S., & Partridge, B. (1997). Sensitization and tolerance in psychostimulant self-administration. *Pharmacology Biochemistry and Behavior, 57* 543–550.

Schenk, S., Snow, S., & Horger, B. A. (1991). Preexposure to amphetamine but not nicotine sensitizes rats to the motor activating effects of cocaine. *Psychopharmacology, 103,* 62–66.

Schenk, S.,Valadez, A., McNamara, C., House, D., Higley, D., Bankson, M. T., Gibbs, S., & Horger, B. A. (1993). Development and expression of sensitization to cocaine's reinforcing properties: Role of NMDA receptors. *Psychopharmacology, 111,* 332–338.

Schenk, S., Valadez, A., Horger, B. A., Snow, S., & Wellman, P. J. (1994). Interactions between caffeine and cocaine in tests of self-administration. *Behavioural Pharmacology, 5,* 153–158.

Shoaib, M., Schindler, C. W., & Goldberg, S. R. (1997). Nicotine self-administration in rats: Strain and nicotine pre-exposure effects on self-administration. *Psychopharmacology, 129,* 35–43.

Sonders, M. S., Zhu, S.-J., Zahniser, N. R., Kavanaugh, M. P., & Amara, S. G. (1997). Multiple ionic conductances of the human dopamine transporter: The actions of dopamine and psychostimulants. *Journal of Neuroscience, 17,* 960–974.

Swadi, H. (1999). Individual risk factors for adolescent substance use. *Drug and Alcohol Dependence, 55,* 209–224.

Takahashi, R. N., & Singer, G. (1979). Self-administration of delta-9—tetrahydrocannabinol by rats. *Pharmacology Biochemistry Behavior, 11,* 737–740.

Volkow, N. D., Ding, Y. S., Fowler, J. S., Wang, G. J., Logan, J. Gatley, J. S., Dewey, S., Ashby, C., Lieberman, J., Hitzemann, R., & Wolf, A. P. (1995). Is methylphenidate like cocaine? Studies on the pharmacokinetics and distribution in the human brain. *Archives of General Psychiatry, 52,* 456–463.

Wills, T. A., Vaccaro, D., & McNamara, G. (1994). Novelty-seeking, risk-taking and related constructs as predictors of adolescent substance use: An application of Cloninger's theory. *Journal of Substance Abuse, 6,* 1–20.

Wilson, M. C., & Schuster, C. R. (1971). The effects of chlorpromazine on psychomotor stimulant self-administration in the rhesus monkey. *Psychopharmacologia, 26*, 115–126.

Wise, R. A., Gingras, M. A., & Amit, Z. (1996). Influence of novel and habituated testing conditions on cocaine sensitization. *European Journal of Pharmacology, 307*, 15–19.

Wise, R. A., Newton, P., Leeb, K., Burnette, B., Pocock, D., & Justice, J. B. Jr. (1995). Fluctuations in nucleus accumbens dopamine concentration during intravenous cocaine self-administration in rats. *Psychopharmacology, 120*, 10–20.

Wood, P. B., Cochran, J. K., Pfefferbau, B., & Arneklev, B. J. (1995). Sensation-seeking and delinquent substance use: An extension of learning theory. *Journal of Drug Issues, 25*, 173–193.

World Health Organization (1992). *The ICD-10 classification of mental and behavioral disorders*. Geneva: Author.

Yamaguchi, K., & Kandel, D. B. (1984). Patterns of drug use from adolescence to young adulthood: 3. Predictors of progression. *American Journal of Public Health, 74*, 673–681.

15

Neurobiology of Drug Addiction

George F. Koob

Major advances in our understanding of the neurobiology of addiction have been made and have important implications for a biological component of a Gateway Hypothesis of drug addiction vulnerability. The present chapter explores the conceptual framework and animal models that guide neurobiological research in addiction and reviews these neurobiological mechanisms for different components of the addiction process. Neurobiological mechanisms for the positive reinforcing effects of drugs of abuse, the negative reinforcement associated with drug dependence, and the neurobiological substates of craving are discussed. The focus is on neurobiological elements common to all major drugs of abuse that inform the Gateway Hypothesis from a biological perspective. Activation of certain neurochemical systems contributing to the acute reinforcing effects of drugs of abuse and activation of brain stress systems during acute withdrawal, in a common brain circuitry, may be common neurobiological mechanisms that have implications for the Gateway Hypothesis of the development of drug addiction.

Drug Addiction and Animal Models

Drug addiction is a chronically relapsing disorder that can be defined as a compulsion to take a drug with loss of control over drug

This is publication number 11295-NP from The Scripps Research Institute. This work was supported by National Institutes of Health Grants AA06420 and AA08459 from the National Institute on Alcohol Abuse and Alcoholism and DA04043, DA04398, and DA08467 from the National Institute on Drug Abuse. The author would like to thank Mike Arends for his assistance with the preparation of this chapter.

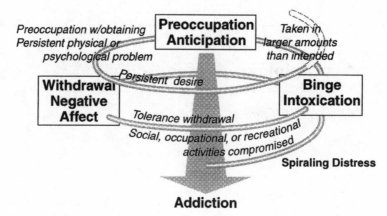

Figure 15.1. Diagram of the spiraling distress/addiction cycle from a psychiatric/addiction perspective: Three major components of the addiction cycle with DSM-IV criteria for substance dependence incorporated. (Taken with permission from Koob & Le Moal, 1997.)

intake (Figure 15.1). Important challenges for neurobiological research are to understand not only how drug use proceeds to drug addiction but why some individuals have a vulnerability for the transition that occurs between controlled substance or drug use and the loss of control that defines addiction or substance dependence.

Progress in understanding the neurobiology of drug dependence has depended not only on the development of molecular, neurobiological, and neuropharmacological tools for understanding the neuropharmacological mechanisms of action of drugs of abuse, but also the development of animal models of drug dependence that allow interpretation of neuropharmacological advances in the context of the disorder under study. An important issue in such a multidisciplinary pursuit is that an operational framework from which to derive animal models is needed (see Table 15.1).

The motivating factors for the development, maintenance, and persistence of drug addiction can be broken down into four major sources of reinforcement in drug dependence: positive reinforcement, negative reinforcement, conditioned positive reinforcement, and conditioned negative reinforcement (Wikler, 1973) (Table 15.1). Clearly, positive reinforcing effects are critical for establishing self-administration behavior, and some have argued the hypothesis that positive reinforcement is the key to drug dependence (Wise, 1988). However, although alleviation of withdrawal symptoms (negative reinforcement) may not be a major

Table 15.1. *Relationship of Addiction Components and Behavioral Constructs of Reinforcement*

Addiction Component	Behavioral Construct
Pleasure	Positive reinforcement
Self-medication	Negative reinforcement
Habit	Conditioned positive reinforcement
Habit	Conditioned negative reinforcement

motivating factor in the *initiation* of compulsive drug use, a compelling case can be made for compromises in hedonic processing associated with drug abstinence as a driving force of addiction (Solomon, 1977; Koob & Le Moal, 1997). Clearly, the construct of negative reinforcement plays an important role in the *maintenance* of drug use after the development of dependence. Largely unexplored has been the issue of individual differences in vulnerability to this transition to drug dependence. Thus, although initial drug use may be motivated by the positive affective state produced by the drug, continued use leads to neuroadaptation to the presence of drug and to another source of reinforcement, the negative reinforcement associated with relieving negative affective consequences of drug termination. Indeed, the defining feature of drug dependence has been argued to be the establishment of a negative affective state (Russell, 1976). However, an even more compelling motivational force is the hypothesis that negative affective states, even during protracted abstinence, can contribute to the reinforcement associated with drug-taking by changing the "set point" for hedonic processing (Koob & Le Moal, 1997). Much progress has been made in identifying the neuronal substrates for the acute positive reinforcing effects of drugs of abuse. A more recent focus has been on the neuronal substrates for negative reinforcement and the conditioned reinforcing effects that contribute to relapse. The present chapter only briefly addresses the neurobiological substrates for the acute positive reinforcing effects of drugs of abuse as these data have been reviewed extensively elsewhere (Koob et al., 1999; Koob & Nestler, 1997; Koob, Sanna, & Bloom, 1998). Instead, the focus of the present review is on how the neurobiological substrates involved in the acute positive reinforcing effects of drugs of abuse change with the development of addiction, and which neurochemical changes that are set in motion may explain vulnerability to relapse and individual differences in vulnerability to addiction.

Neurological Mechanisms for the Positive Reinforcing Effects of Drugs

The neural substrates of reward have long been hypothesized to involve the neuronal circuits forming the medial forebrain bundle. The medial forebrain bundle contains both ascending and descending pathways that include most of the brain's monoamine systems (Olds & Milner, 1954; Stein, 1968; Nauta & Haymaker, 1969), and the structures involved include those that support intracranial self-stimulation: the ventral tegmental area, the basal forebrain, and the medial forebrain bundle, which connects these two areas (Olds & Milner, 1954; Stein, 1968; Liebman & Cooper, 1989; Valenstein & Campbell, 1966) (Figure 15.2). Significant insights into the neurochemical and neuroanatomical components of the medial forebrain bundle have provided the key not only to drug reward but also to natural rewards.

The principal focus of research on the neurobiology of drug addiction has been the origins and terminal areas of the mesocorticolimbic dopamine system, and there is now compelling evidence for the importance of this system in drug reward. The major components of this drug reward circuit are the ventral tegmental area (the site of dopaminergic cell bodies), the basal forebrain (the nucleus accumbens, olfactory tubercle, frontal cortex, and amygdala), and the dopaminergic connection between the ventral tegmental area and the basal forebrain. Other components are the opioid peptide, gamma-aminobutyric acid (GABA), glutamate, serotonin, and presumably many other neural inputs that interact with the ventral tegmental area and the basal forebrain (Koob, 1992) (see Figure 15.2). The neuronal components of this circuitry involved in the positive reinforcement associated with different drugs are discussed briefly, and a construct called the *extended amygdala* that provides important insights into the relationship of drug reward to natural reward systems is introduced.

Psychomotor stimulants of high abuse potential interact initially with monoamine transporter proteins that have been cloned and characterized (Kilty, Lorang, & Amara, 1991; Blakely et al., 1991; Giros, El Mestikawy, Bertrand, & Caron, 1991) and are located on monoaminergic nerve terminals. These transporters terminate a monoamine signal by transporting the monoamine from the synaptic cleft back into the terminals. Cocaine inhibits all three monoamine transporters – dopamine, serotonin, and norepinephrine – thereby potentiating monoaminergic transmission. Amphetamine and its derivatives also potentiate

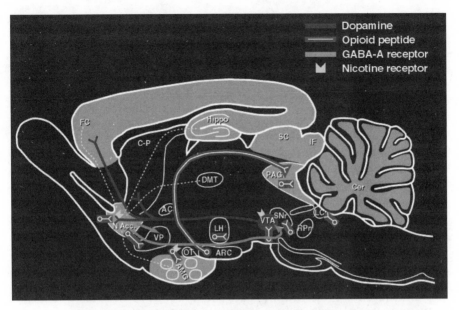

Figure 15.2. Sagittal rat brain section illustrating a drug (cocaine, amphetamine, opiate, nicotine, and alcohol) neural reward circuit that includes a limbic-extrapyramidal motor interface. The bold projection from the VTA indicates a projection of the mesocorticolimbic dopamine system thought to be a critical substrate for psychomotor stimulant reward. This system originates in the A10 cell group of the ventral tegmental area and projects to the N. Acc., olfactory tubercle, ventral striatal domains of the C-P, and amygdala. The white-within-bold lines indicate opioid peptide-containing neurons, systems that may be involved in opiate, ethanol, and possibly nicotine reward. These opioid peptide systems include the local enkephalin circuits (short segments) and the hypothalamic midbrain beta-endorphin circuit (long segment). Shaded gray regions indicate the approximate distribution of GABA$_A$ receptor complexes, some of which may mediate sedative/hypnotic (ethanol) reward, determined by both tritiated flumazenil binding and expression of the alpha, beta, and gamma subunits of the GABA$_A$ receptor. Notched, bold, solid structures indicate nicotinic acetylcholine receptors hypothesized to be located on dopaminergic and opioid peptidergic systems. Dotted lines indicate limbic afferents to the N Acc. The light gray projection from the N Acc. to the VTA represents efferents from the nucleus accumbens thought to be involved in psychomotor stimulant reward. N Acc., nucleus accumbens; VTA, ventral tegmental area; C-P, caudate putamen; GABA, gamma-aminobutyric acid; VP, ventral pallidum; LH, lateral hypothalamus; SNr, substantia nigra pars reticulata; DMT, dorsomedial thalamus; PAG, periaqueductal gray; OT, olfactory tract; AC, anterior commissure; LC, locus coeruleus; AMG, amygdala; Hippo, hippocampus; Cer, cerebellum, FC, frontal cortex. (Modified with permission from Koob, 1992.)

monoaminergic transmission, but by increasing monoamine release. Amphetamine itself is transported by all three transporters into monoaminergic nerve terminals, where it disrupts the storage of the monoamine transmitters. This leads to an increase in extravascular levels of the monoamines and to the reverse transport of the monoamine into the synaptic cleft via the monoamine transporters (Rudnick & Clark, 1993). The mesocorticolimbic dopamine system appears to be the critical substrate for both the psychomotor stimulant effects of amphetamine and cocaine (Kelly, Seviour, & Iversen, 1975; Kelly & Iversen, 1976; Pijnenburg, Honig, & Van Rossum, 1975) and their reinforcing actions (Yokel & Wise, 1975; Ettenberg, Pettit, Bloom, & Koob, 1982). The most direct evidence implicating dopamine in the reinforcing actions of cocaine is from studies of intravenous self-administration and of conditioned place preference. Dopamine receptor antagonists, when injected systemically, reliably decrease the reinforcing effects of cocaine and amphetamine self-administration in rats and block conditioned place preferences for these drugs (Yokel and Wise, 1975; Ettenberg, Petit, Bloom, & Koob, 1982; Phillips & Fibiger, 1987; Beninger & Hahn, 1983; Beninger & Herz, 1986; Morency & Beninger, 1986). All three dopamine receptor subtypes have been implicated in the reinforcing actions of cocaine as measured by intravenous self-administration, including the D_1 (Koob, Le, & Creese, 1987), D_2 (Woolverton & Virus, 1989; Bergman, Kamien, & Spealman, 1990), and D_3 receptors (Caine & Koob, 1993). Dopamine D_1 and D_2 antagonists also block the place conditioning produced by amphetamine (Leone & Di Chiara, 1987; Beninger, Hoffman, & Mazurski, 1989).

Opiate drugs such as heroin also have acute reinforcing properties (Schuster & Thompson, 1969), and if they are provided in limited access situations, rats and primates (Deneau, Yanagita, & Seevers, 1969) maintain stable levels of opiate intake on a daily basis without obvious signs of physical dependence (Koob, Pettit, Ettenberg, & Bloom, 1984). Systemic and central administration of competitive opiate antagonists decrease this acute opiate reinforcement (Goldberg, Woods, & Schuster, 1971; Weeks & Collins, 1976; Ettenberg et al., 1982; Koob, Pettit, Ettenberg, & Bloom, 1984; Vaccarino, Pettit, Bloom, & Koob, 1985). The mu opioid receptor subtype appears to be particularly important for the reinforcing actions of heroin and morphine (Negus et al., 1993). Also, knock-out mice without the mu receptor do not show morphine induced analgesia or morphine induced conditioned place preferences (Matthes et al., 1996).

The sites of action for opioid antagonists to block the reinforcing effects of opiates appear to be associated with the same neural circuitry associated with psychomotor stimulant reward (see Figure 15.2). Many data suggest that neural elements in the region of the ventral tegmental area *and* the nucleus accumbens are responsible for the reinforcing properties of opiates and that there are both dopamine dependent and dopamine independent mechanisms of opiate action (Pettit, Ettenberg, Bloom, & Koob, 1984; Stinus et al., 1989; Spyraki, Fibiger, & Phillips, 1983; Shippenberg, Herz, Spanagel, Bals-Kubik, & Stein, 1992).

Sedative-hypnotics, such as barbiturates, benzodiazepines, and ethanol, all produce a characteristic euphoria, disinhibition, anxiety reduction, sedation, and hypnosis. The sedative and antipunishment (anxiolytic) effects of sedative-hypnotics are associated with facilitation of the $GABA_A$ receptor (Richards, Schoch, & Haefely, 1991). Studies of the neuropharmacological basis for the anxiolytic properties of sedative-hypnotics also provided some of the first clues to their reinforcing properties and abuse potential (Koob & Britton, 1996). The finding that GABAergic antagonists reverse many of the behavioral effects of ethanol led to the hypothesis that GABA has a role in the intoxicating effects of ethanol (Frye & Breese, 1982; Liljequist & Engel, 1982). The partial inverse benzodiazepine agonist R0 15-4513, which has been shown to reverse some of the behavioral effects of ethanol (Suzdak et al., 1986), produces a dose dependent reduction of oral ethanol (10%) self-administration in rats (Samson, Tolliver, Pfeffer, Sadeghi, & Mills, 1987; Rassnick et al., 1992; June et al., 1992). More recent studies have shown similar effects with potent GABA antagonists microinjected into the brain, where the most effective site to date has been the central nucleus of the amygdala (Institute of Medicine, 1996).

Ethanol antagonism of the N-methyl-D-aspartate (NMDA) receptor also appears to contribute to the intoxicating effects of ethanol (Hoffman, Rabe, Moses, & Tabakoff, 1989; Lovinger, White, & Weight, 1989). Possibly via its initial effects on the $GABA_A$ and NMDA glutamate receptors, ethanol influences several additional neurotransmitter systems in the brain that are believed to be involved in its reinforcing properties. There is much evidence implicating dopamine in the reinforcing actions of low, non-dependence inducing doses of ethanol. Dopamine receptor antagonists have been shown to reduce lever pressing for ethanol in nondeprived rats (Pfeffer & Samson, 1988), and extracellular dopamine levels also have been shown to increase in nondependent rats orally self-administering low doses of ethanol (Weiss et al., 1992). However, virtually complete 6–hydroxydopamine denervation of the nucleus accumbens did not alter voluntary responding for ethanol (Rassnick, Stinus, & Koob, 1993). Thus, as with opiates, these results suggest that activation of mesocorticolimbic dopamine transmission may be associated with important aspects of ethanol reinforcement, but this activation may not be critical. In fact, evidence suggests that other sedative-hypnotics such as benzodiazepines decrease mesocorticolimbic activity (Murai et al., 1994). Other dopamine independent neurochemical systems likely contribute to the mediation of ethanol's reinforcing actions, and a view that multiple neurotransmitters combine to "orchestrate" the reward profile of ethanol is emerging (Engel et al., 1992). Reinforcing actions include actions on serotonergic and opioid peptide systems.

Nicotine has an initial molecular site of action as a direct agonist at nicotinic acetylcholine receptors. Although brain nicotinic acetylcholine receptors are widely distributed throughout the brain, to date it is the receptors specifically in the brain mesolimbic dopamine system that have been implicated in its reinforcing actions (Malin, Lake, Carter, Cunningham, & Wilson, 1993; Malin et al., 1994). Interestingly, nicotinic acetylcholine receptor antagonists and opioid peptide antagonists can precipitate a physical withdrawal syndrome in rats (Malin et al., 1994; Malin et al., 1993). Thus, nicotine may alter function in both the mesocorticolimbic dopamine system and opioid peptide systems in the same neural circuitry associated with other drugs of abuse (Corrigall, Franklin, Coen, & Clarke, 1992) (see Figure 15.2).

Tetrahydrocannabinol (THC) is a drug of abuse and dependence (Anthony, Warner, & Kessler, 1994). THC binds to the cannabinoid-1 receptor, which is widely distributed throughout the brain but is particularly concentrated in the extrapyramidal motor system of the rat (Herkenham et al., 1990). THC has been shown to decrease reward thresholds in rats in acute administration (Lepore, Liu, Savage, Matalon, & Gardner, 1996; Gardner et al., 1988) and produce a place preference (Lepore, Vorel, Lowinson, & Gardner, 1995). In addition, a 1997 study in mice showed intravenous self-administration of a synthetic THC analog (Fratta, Martellotta, Cossu, & Fattore, 1997). THC activates the mesocorticolimbic dopamine system (Chen, Paredes, Lowinson, & Gardner, 1991), and recent data suggest that it can selectively increase the release of dopamine in the shell of the nucleus accumbens as do other drugs of abuse (Tanda, Pontieri, & Di Chiara, 1997).

Neurobiological Substrates for Negative Reinforcement Associated With Drug Addiction

Acute withdrawal from drugs of abuse has long been associated with physical signs, the manifestation of which varies with each drug of abuse. Recent conceptualizations of addiction have considered the manifestation of physical signs of withdrawal as only one of a constellation of symptoms associated with addiction (American Psychiatric Association, 1994). However, there are several common actions associated with acute withdrawal that may have motivational significance in contributing to the maintenance of drug addiction. Acute withdrawal is associated with a negative affective state, including various negative emotions such as dysphoria, depression, irritability, and anxiety. For example, cocaine withdrawal in humans in the outpatient setting is characterized by severe depressive symptoms combined with irritability, anxiety, and anhedonia lasting several hours to several days (i.e., the "crash") and may be one of the motivating factors in the maintenance of the cocaine dependence cycle (Gawin & Kleber, 1986). Inpatient studies have shown similar changes in mood and anxiety states, but they generally are much less severe (Weddington et al., 1991). Opiate withdrawal is characterized by severe dysphoria, and ethanol withdrawal produces dysphoria and anxiety.

The neural substrates and neuropharmacological mechanisms of the motivational effects of drug withdrawal may involve the same neural systems implicated in the positive reinforcing effects of drugs of abuse. Recent studies, using the technique of intracranial self-stimulation to measure reward thresholds throughout the course of drug dependence, have shown that reward thresholds are increased (reflecting a decrease in reward) after chronic administration of all major drugs of abuse, including opiates, psychostimulants, alcohol, and nicotine. These effects reflect changes in the activity of the same mesocorticolimbic system (midbrain–forebrain system) implicated in the positive reinforcing effects of drugs and can last up to 72 hours, depending on the drug and dose administered (see Figure 15.3) (Markou & Koob, 1991; Schulteis, Markou, Gold, Stinus, & Koob, 1994; Leith & Barrett, 1976; Parsons, Koob & Weiss, 1995; Markou, & Koob, 1992; Legault & Wise, 1994).

The neurochemical basis for neuroadaptive mechanisms that reflect changes in reward function has been hypothesized to be neurochemical changes associated with the same neurotransmitters implicated in the acute reinforcing effects of drugs (Koob & Bloom, 1988) (see Figure 15.4).

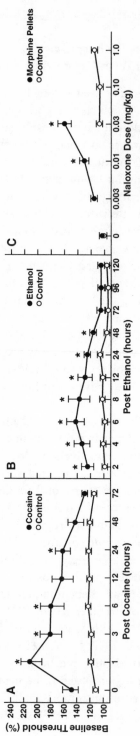

Figure 15.3. Changes in reward threshold associated with chronic administration of three major drugs of abuse. Reward thresholds were determined using a rate independent discrete trials threshold procedure for intracranial self-stimulation (ICSS) of the medial forebrain bundle. (A) Rats equipped with intravenous catheters were allowed to self-administer cocaine for 12 straight hours before withdrawal and reward threshold determinations. Elevations in threshold were dose dependent where longer bouts of cocaine self-administration yielded larger and longer lasting elevations in reward thresholds. (Redrawn with permission from Markou & Koob, 1991.) (B) Elevations in reward thresholds with the same ICSS technique after chronic exposure to ethanol of approximately 200 mg% in ethanol vapor chambers. (Redrawn with permission from Schulteis et al., 1995.) (C) Elevations in reward thresholds using the same ICSS technique after administration of very low doses of the opiate antagonist naloxone to animals made dependent on morphine by using two 75-mg morphine (base) pellets implanted subcutaneously. (Redrawn with permission from Schulteis et al., 1994.) Asterisks refer to significant differences between treatment and control values. Values are mean + S.E.M.

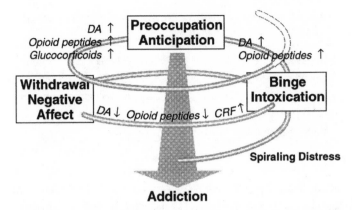

Figure 15.4. Diagram of the spiraling distress/addiction cycle from a neuro-chemical perspective: The figure shows the three major components of the addiction cycle with the changes in different neurotransmitters incorporated at different stages of the addiction cycle (see text for details). (Taken with permission from Koob & Le Moal, 1997.)

Examples of such homeostatic, within system adaptive neurochemical events include decreases in dopaminergic and serotonergic transmission in the nucleus accumbens during drug withdrawal as measured by *in vivo* microdialysis (Weiss, Markou, Lorang, & Koob, 1992; Parsons et al., 1995), increased sensitivity of opioid receptor transduction mechanisms in the nucleus accumbens during opiate withdrawal (Stinus, Le Moal, & Koob, 1990), decreased GABAergic and increased NMDA glutamatergic transmission during ethanol withdrawal (Roberts, Cole, & Koob 1996; Weiss et al., 1996; Fitzgerald & Nestler, 1995), and differential regional changes in nicotine receptor function (Collins, Bhat, Pauly, & Marks, 1990; Dani & Heinemann, 1996) (Table 15.2).

Recruitment of other neurotransmitter systems in the adaptive responses to drugs of abuse may involve neurotransmitter systems not linked to the acute reinforcing effects of the drug (Koob & Bloom, 1988) (see Figure 15.4). Another common adaptation to repeated administration of drugs of abuse that may not be involved in the acute reinforcing effects of the drugs may be the activation of brain and pituitary stress systems (Table 15.2). Pituitary adrenal function is activated during drug dependence, and acute withdrawal from drugs of abuse in humans and dysregulation can persist even past acute withdrawal (Kreek, 1987; Kreek et al., 1984). Corticotropin-releasing factor (CRF) function, outside the pituitary adrenal axis, also appears to be activated during acute

Table 15.2. *Neurotransmitters Implicated in the Motivational Effects of Withdrawal From Drugs of Abuse*

↓ Dopamine	Dysphoria
↓ Opioid peptides	Pain, dysphoria
↓ Serotonin	Pain, dysphoria, depression
↓ GABA	Anxiety, panic attacks
↑ Corticotropin-releasing factor	Stress

withdrawal from cocaine, alcohol, opiates, and THC and thus may mediate behavioral aspects of stress associated with abstinence (Koob, Heinrichs, Menzaghi, Merlo-Pich, & Britton, 1994; Heinrichs, Menzaghi, Schulteis, Koob, & Stinus, 1995; Rodriguez de Fonseca, Carrera, Navarro, Koob, & Weiss, 1997; Richter & Weiss, 1999). Rats treated repeatedly with cocaine, nicotine, and ethanol show significant anxiogenic like responses after cessation of chronic drug administration that are reversed with intracerebroventricular administration of a CRF antagonist (Rassnick, Heinrichs, Britton, & Koob, 1993; Sarnyai et al., 1995). Microinjections into the central nucleus of the amygdala of lower doses of the CRF antagonist also reversed the anxiogenic like effects of ethanol withdrawal (Rassnick et al., 1993), and similar doses of the CRF antagonist injected into the amygdala were active in reversing the aversive effects of opiate withdrawal (Heinrichs et al., 1995).

Neurobiological Substrates for Craving

The persistence of changes in drug reinforcement mechanisms that characterize drug addiction suggests that the underlying mechanisms are long-lasting, and indeed considerable attention is being directed at drug regulation of molecular mechanisms such as gene expression. Two types of transcription factors, cyclic aminophosphate response-element binding protein (CREB) and novel Fos-like proteins (termed *chronic Fos-related antigens* [FRAs]) have been hypothesized to be possible mediators of chronic drug action (Hope et al., 1994; Hyman, 1996; Widnell et al., 1996). The challenge for the future will be to relate regulation of a specific transcription factor to specific neuropharmacological features of drug reinforcement associated with specific histories of drug administration (vulnerability to acute challenges versus changes in set point associated with protracted abstinence).

Animal models for the study of relapse have been limited and are currently under development (Koob, 1995). Neuropharmacological probes that activate the mesocorticolimbic dopamine system have been shown to reinstate self-administration in animals trained and then extinguished on intravenous drug self-administration rapidly (deWit & Stewart, 1981; Stewart & deWit, 1987). There are a limited number of observations using other models. Acamprosate, a drug being marketed in Europe to prevent relapse in alcoholics that has potential glutamate modulatory action (O'Brien, Eckardt, & Linnoila, 1995), blocks the increase in drinking observed in rodents after forced abstinence, again in nondependent rats (Heyser, Schulteis, Durbin, & Koob, 1998). Similarly, opioid antagonists were shown to prevent the increase in drinking of ethanol in animals post stress (Volpicelli, Davis, & Olgin, 1986), and subsequently, naltrexone was shown to have efficacy in preventing relapse in detoxified human alcoholics as mentioned previously (O'Malley et al., 1992; Volpicelli, Alterman, Hayashida, & O'Brien, 1992). Also, a 1996 study reports that agonists selective for D1 dopamine receptors, but not for D2-like receptors, can block reinstatement of lever pressing inferred to represent cocaine seeking behavior (Self, Barnhart, Lehman, & Nestler, 1996).

Extended Amygdala: A Common Substrate for Drug Reinforcement

Recent neuroanatomical data and new functional observations have provided support for the hypothesis that the neuroanatomical substrates for the reinforcing actions of drugs may involve a common neural circuitry that forms a separate entity within the basal forebrain, termed the *extended amygdala* (Alheid & Heimer, 1988). As originally described by Johnston (Johnston, 1923), the term *extended amygdala* represents a macrostructure that is composed of several basal forebrain structures: the bed nucleus of the stria terminalis, the central medial amygdala, the posterior medial part of the nucleus accumbens (e.g., posterior shell) (Heimer & Alheid, 1991), and the area termed the *sublenticular substantia innominata*. There are similarities in morphological and immuno-histochemical characteristics, and connectivity in these structures (Alheid & Heimer, 1988). They receive afferent connections from limbic cortices, hippocampus, basolateral amygdala, midbrain, and lateral hypothalamus. The efferent connections from this complex include the posterior medial (sublenticular) ventral pallidum, medial ventral tegmental area, various brain stem projections, and, perhaps most intriguing from a functional point of view, a considerable projection to the lateral hypothalamus (Heimer, Zahm, Churchill, Kalivas, & Wohltmann, 1991).

Recent studies have demonstrated selective neurochemical and neuropharmacological actions in specific components of the extended amygdala both in the acute reinforcing effects of drugs of abuse and in the negative reinforcement associated with drug dependence. D1 dopamine antagonists are effective in blocking cocaine self-administration when the antagonist is administered directly into the shell of the nucleus accumbens, the central nucleus of the amygdala (Caine, Heinrichs, Coffin, & Koob, 1995), and the bed nucleus of the stria terminalis (Epping-Jordan, Markou, & Koob, 1998). Moreover, selective activation of dopaminergic transmission occurs in the shell of the nucleus accumbens in response to acute administration of virtually all major drugs of abuse (Pontieri, Tanda, & Di Chiara, 1995; Tanda, Pontieri, & Di Chiara, 1997; Pontieri, Tanda, Orzi, & Di Chiara, 1996). In addition, the central nucleus of the amygdala has been implicated in the GABAergic and opioidergic influences on the acute reinforcing effects of ethanol (Hyytia & Koob, 1995; Heyser, Roberts, Schulteis, Hyytia, & Koob, 1995).

Evidence that parts of the extended amygdala are involved in the aversive stimulus effects of drug withdrawal includes activation of CRF systems in the central nucleus of the amygdala (Merlo-Pich et al., 1995). Also, changes in sensitivity to opiate antagonists occur in opiate dependent rats in the nucleus accumbens and central nucleus of the amygdala (Stinus et al., 1990; Koob, Wall, & Bloom, 1989). The concept of the extended amygdala may ultimately link the recent developments in the neurobiology of drug reward with existing knowledge of the substrates for emotional behavior (Davis, 1997), essentially bridging what have been largely independent research pursuits. Perhaps more importantly, this neuronal circuit is well situated to form a heuristic model for exploring the mechanisms associated with vulnerability to relapse and concepts such as craving, both of which may involve secondary conditioned reinforcement constructs.

Drug dependence not only involves acquisition of drug-taking and maintenance of drug-taking, but also functions as a chronic relapsing disorder with reinstatement of drug-taking after detoxification and abstinence. Both the positive and negative affective states can become associated with stimuli in the drug-taking environment or even internal cues through classical conditioning processes (Wikler, 1973). Reexposure to these conditioned stimuli can provide the motivation for continued drug use and relapse after abstention. There is evidence in humans that the positive reinforcing effects of drugs such as heroin and cocaine, as measured by subjective reports of euphoria or "high," can become conditioned to previously neutral stimuli. Patients being treated for heroin addiction and allowed to self-administer either saline solution or heroin reported that both saline solution and heroin injections were pleasurable, particularly in the patient's usual injection environment (Soloman, 1980). Alternatively, patients, even detoxified subjects, can report negative affective symptoms like those associated with drug abstinence when returning to environments similar to those associated with drug dependence (O'Brien, 1975).

In addition, there is increasing evidence that chronic exposure to drugs of abuse can change the "set point" for drug reward. Animals with prolonged access to cocaine continue to increase their cocaine intake on a daily basis and show enhanced intake of cocaine at all doses tested. Indeed, the dose effect function appears to shift upward instead of to the right (tolerance) or to the left (sensitization) (Ahmed & Koob, 1998). Such a change in drug reward set point may reflect an allostatic rather than homeostatic adaptation. Here, all the parameters of the internal milieu must be marshaled to match perceived and anticipated environmental demands in order to maintain stability. Maintenance of this stability at a new pathological set point can provide the basis by which a small challenge can lead to breakdown, or, in drug addiction, relapse (Koob & Le Moal, 1997). The hypothesis suggested here is that the neurobiological bases for this complex syndrome of protracted abstinence may involve subtle molecular and cellular changes in the circuitry associated with the extended amygdala. Elucidation of these changes will be the challenge of future research on the neurobiology of addiction.

Implications of Neurobiological Findings for the Gateway Hypothesis

Significant neurobiological evidence can be identified in our understanding of drug addiction that may have implications for a Gateway Hypothesis of development of addiction whereby experience with one psychoactive substance contributes to the vulnerability to addiction to other psychoactive substances. These neurobiological elements can be found in different components of the addiction process as conceptualized as a chronically relapsing disorder of compulsive drug use. At a global level, the brain reward system is activated by all major drugs of abuse and becomes dysregulated with chronic administration of all major drugs of abuse. The neurochemical basis for these changes is currently under intense investigation, but most drugs of abuse acutely activate the mesolimbic dopamine system; the stimulant drugs have the most dramatic effects and the sedative-hypnotics have less dramatic effects. This activation clearly is most critical for the positive reinforcing effects of drugs of abuse when the drugs are first self-administered and presumably plays a role in vulnerability to relapse. In addition, the dysphoria associated with acute withdrawal clearly appears to be linked to decreases in dopaminergic function with many, if not all, major drugs of abuse. Another common element associated with addiction is the activation of nonreward, or even antireward, systems during acute abstinence. Much evidence suggests that acute withdrawal from all drugs of abuse studied to date is an activation of pituitary adrenal and central nervous system stress systems, notably corticotropin-releasing factor. Whether such changes extend to the realm of protracted abstinence and vulnerability to relapse and whether other stress systems are similarly activated are areas of current investigation. Thus, the neurobiological characteristic of drug dependence provide a rich substrate whereby multiple drugs contribute to brain reward dysregulation that sets the stage for the transition from drug use to drug addiction and could be conceptualized as lending a biological basis to a Gateway Hypothesis.

References

Ahmed, S. H., & Koob, G. F. (1998). Transition from moderate to excessive drug intake: Change in hedonic set point. *Science, 282*, 298–300.

Alheid, G. F., & Heimer, L. (1998). New perspectives in basal forebrain organization of special relevance for neuropsychiatric disorders: The striatopallidal, amygdaloid, and corticopetal components of substantia innominata. *Neuroscience, 27*, 1–39.

American Psychiatric Association. (1994). *Diagnostic and statistical manual of mental disorders* (4th ed.). Washington, DC: American Psychiatric Press.

Anthony, J. C., Warner, L. A., & Kessler, R. C. (1994). Comparative epidemiology of dependence on tobacco, alcohol, controlled substances, and inhalants: Basic findings from the National Comorbidity Survey. *Experimental and Clinical Psychopharmacology, 2*, 244–268.

Beninger, R. J., & Hahn, B. L. (1983). Pimozide blocks establishment but not expression of amphetamine-produced environment-specific conditioning. *Science, 220*, 1304–1306.

Beninger, R. J., & Herz, R. S. (1986). Pimozide blocks establishment but not expression of cocaine-produced environment-specific conditioning. *Life Sciences, 38*, 1425–1431.

Beninger, R. J., Hoffman, D. C., & Mazurski, E. J. (1989). Receptor subtype-specific dopaminergic agents and conditioned behavior. *Neuroscience and Biobehavioral Reviews, 13*, 113–122.

Bergman, J., Kamien, J. B., & Spealman, R. D. (1990). Antagonism of cocaine self-administration by selective dopamine D1 and D2 antagonists. *Behavioural Pharmacology, 1*, 355–363.

Blakely, R. D., Berson, H. E., Fremeau, R. T., Jr., Caron, M. G., Peek, M. M., Prince, H. K., & Bradley, C. C. (1991). Cloning and expression of a functional serotonin transporter from rat brain. *Nature, 354*, 66–70.

Caine, S. B., Heinrichs, S. C., Coffin, V. L., & Koob, G. F. (1995). Effects of the dopamine D1 antagonist SCH 23390 microinjected into the accumbens, amygdala or striatum on cocaine self-administration in the rat. *Brain Research, 692*, 47–56.

Caine, S. B., & Koob, G. F. (1993). Modulation of cocaine self-administration in the rat through D-3 dopamine receptors. *Science, 260*, 1814–1816.

Chen, J. P., Paredes, W., Lowinson, J. H., & Gardner, E. L. (1991). Strain-specific facilitation of dopamine efflux by delta 9-tetrahydrocannabinol in the nucleus accumbens of rat: An in vivo microdialysis study. *Neuroscience Letters, 129*, 136–180.

Collins, A. C., Bhat, R. V., Pauly, J. R., & Marks, M. J. (1990). Modulation of nicotine receptors by chronic exposure to nicotinic agonists and antagonists. In G. Bock & J. Marsh (Eds.), *The biology of nicotine dependence.* Ciba Foundation Symposium (Vol. 152, pp. 68–82). New York: John Wiley.

Corrigall, W. A., Franklin, K.B.J., Coen, K. M., & Clarke, P.B.S. (1992). The mesolimbic dopaminergic system is implicated in the reinforcing effects of nicotine. *Psychopharmacology, 107*, 285–289.

Dani, J. A., & Heinemann, S. (1996). Molecular and cellular aspects of nicotine abuse. *Neuron, 16*, 905–908.

Davis, M. (1997). Neurobiology of fear responses: The role of the amygdala. *Journal of Neuropsychiatry and Clinical Neurosciences, 9*, 382–402.

Deneau, G., Yanagita, T., & Seevers, M. H. (1969). Self-administration of psychoactive substances by the monkey. *Psychopharmacologia, 16*, 30–48.

deWit, H., & Stewart, J. (1981). Reinstatement of cocaine-reinforced responding in the rat. *Psychopharmacology, 75*, 134–143.

Engel, J. A., Enerback, C., Fahlke, C., Hulthe, P., Hard, E., Johannessen, K., Svensson, L., & Soderpalm, B. (1992). Serotonergic and dopaminergic involvement in ethanol intake. In C. A. Naranjo & E. M. Sellers (Eds.), *Novel pharmacological interventions for alcoholism* (pp. 68–82). New York: Springer.

Epping-Jordan, M. P., Markou, A., & Koob, G. F. (1998). The dopamine D-1 receptor antagonist SCH 23390 injected into the dorsolateral bed nucleus of the stria terminalis decreased cocaine reinforcement in the rat. *Brain Research, 784,* 105–115.

Ettenberg, A., Pettit, H. O., Bloom, F. E., & Koob, G. F. (1982). Heroin and cocaine intravenous self-administration in rats: Mediation by separate neural systems. *Psychopharmacology, 78,* 204–209.

Fitzgerald, L. W., & Nestler, E. J. (1995). Molecular and cellular adaptations in signal transduction pathways following ethanol exposure. *Clinical Neuroscience, 3,* 165–173.

Fratta, W., Martellotta, M. C., Cossu, G., & Fattore, L. (1997). WIN 55, 212-2 induces intravenous self-administration in drug-naive mice (abstract). *Society for Neuroscience Abstracts, 23,* 1869.

Frye, G. D., & Breese, G. R. (1982). GABAergic modulation of ethanol-induced motor impairment. *Journal of Pharmacology and Experimental Therapeutics, 223,* 750–756.

Gardner, E. L., Paredes, W., Smith, D., Donner, A., Milling, C., Cohen, D., & Morrison, D. (1988). Facilitation of brain stimulation reward by delta-9-tetrahydrocannabinol. *Psychopharmacology, 96,* 142–144.

Gawin, F. H., & Kleber, H. D. (1986). Abstinence symptomatology and psychiatric diagnosis in cocaine abusers: Clinical observations. *Archives of General Psychiatry, 43,* 107–113.

Giros, B., El Mestikawy, S., Bertrand, L., & Caron, M. G. (1991). Cloning and functional characterization of a cocaine-sensitive dopamine transporter. *FEBS Letters, 295,* 149–154.

Goldberg, S. R., Woods, J. H., & Schuster, C. R. (1971). Nalorphine-induced changes in morphine self-administration in rhesus monkeys. *Journal of Pharmacology and Experimental Therapeutics, 176,* 464–471.

Heimer, L., & Alheid, G. (1991). Piercing together the puzzle of basal forebrain anatomy. In T. C. Napier, P. W. Kalivas, & I. Hanin (Eds.), *The basal forebrain: Anatomy to function: Advances in experimental medicine and biology* (Vol. 295, 1–42). New York: Plenum Press.

Heimer, L., Zahm, D. S., Churchill, L., Kalivas, P. W., & Wohltmann, C. (1991). Specificity in the projection patterns of accumbal core and shell in the rat. *Neuroscience, 41,* 89–125.

Heinrichs, S. C., Menzaghi, F., Schulteis, G., Koob, G. F., & Stinus, L. (1995). Suppression of corticotropin-releasing factor in the amygdala attenuates aversive consequences of morphine withdrawal. *Behavioural Pharmacology, 6,* 74–80.

Herkenham, M., Lynn, A. B., Little, M. D., Johnson, M. R., Melvin, L. S., de Costa, B. R., & Rice, K. C. (1990). Cannabinoid receptor localization in brain. *Proceeding of the National Academy of Sciences of the United States of America, 87,* 1932–1936.

Heyser, C. J., Roberts, A. J., Schulteis, G., Hyytia, P., & Koob, G. F. (1995). Central administration of an opiate antagonist decreases oral ethanol self-administration in rats (abstract). *Society for Neuroscience Abstracts, 21*, 1698.

Heyser, C. J., Schulteis, G., Durbin, P., & Koob, G. F. (1998). Chronic acamprosate eliminates the alcohol deprivation effect while having limited effects on baseline responding for ethanol in rats. *Neuropsychopharmacology, 18*, 125–133.

Hoffman, P. L., Rabe, C., Moses, F., & Tabakoff, B. (1989). N-methyl-D-aspartate receptors and ethanol: Inhibition of calcium flux and cyclic GMP production. *Journal of Neurochemistry, 52*, 1937–1940.

Hope, B. T., Nye, H. E., Kelz, M. B., Self, D. W., Iadarola, M. J., Nakabeppu, Y., Duman, R. S., & Nestler, E. J. (1994). Induction of a long-lasting AP-1 complex composed of altered Fos-like proteins in brain by chronic cocaine and other chronic treatments. *Neuron, 13*, 1235–1244.

Hyman, S. E. (1996). Addiction to cocaine and amphetamine. *Neuron, 16*, 901–904.

Hyytia, P., & Koob, G. F. (1995). $GABA_A$ receptor antagonism in the extended amygdala decreases ethanol self-administration in rats. *European Journal of Pharmacology, 283*, 151–159.

Institute of Medicine. (1996). *Pathways of addiction: Opportunities in drug abuse research*. Washington, DC: National Academy Press.

Johnston, J. B. (1923). Further contributions to the study of the evolution of the forebrain. *Journal of Comparative Neurology, 35*, 337–481.

June, H. L., Colker, R. E., Domangue, K. R., Perry, L. E., Hicks, L. H., June, P. L., & Lewis, M. J. (1992). Ethanol self-administration in deprived rats: Effects of Ro15-4513 alone, and in combination with flumazenil (Ro15-1788). *Alcoholism, Clinical and Experimental Research, 16*, 11–16.

Kelly, P. H., & Iversen, S. D. (1976). Selective 6-OHDA-induced destruction of mesolimbic dopamine neurons: Abolition of psychostimulant-induced locomotor activity in rats. *European Journal of Pharmacology, 40*, 45–56.

Kelly, P. H., Seviour, P. W., & Iversen, S. D. (1975). Amphetamine and apomorphine responses in the rat following 6-OHDA lesions of the nucleus accumbens septi and corpus striatum. *Brain Research, 94*, 507–522.

Kilty, J. E., Lorang, D., & Amara, S. G. (1991). Cloning and expression of a cocaine-sensitive rat dopamine transporter. *Science, 254*, 578–579.

Koob, G. F. (1992). Drugs of abuse: Anatomy, pharmacology, and function of reward pathways. *Trends in Pharmacological Sciences, 13*, 177–184.

Koob, G. F. (1995). Animal models of drug addiction. In F. E. Bloom & D. J. Kupfer (Eds.), *Psychopharmacology: The fourth generation of progress* (pp. 759–772). New York: Raven Press.

Koob, G. F., & Bloom, F. E. (1988). Cellular and molecular mechanisms of drug dependence. *Science, 242*, 715–723.

Koob, G. F., & Britton, K. T. (1996). Neurobiological substrates for the anti-anxiety effects of ethanol. In H. Begleiter & B. Kissin (Eds.), *The pharmacology of alcohol and alcohol dependence* (pp. 477–506). New York: Oxford University Press.

Koob, G. F., Caine, S. B., Hyytia, P., Markou, A., Parsons, L., Roberts, A., Schulteis, G., & Weiss, F. (1999). Neurobiology of drug addiction. In M. D. Glantz & C. R. Hartel (Eds.), *Drug abuse: Origins and interventions*, (pp. 161–190). Washington, DC: American Psychological Association.

Koob, G. F., Heinrichs, S. C., Menzaghi, F., Merlo-Pich, E., & Britton, K. T. (1994). Corticotropin-releasing factor, stress and behavior. *Seminars in the Neurosciences, 6*, 221–229.

Koob, G. F., & Le, Moal, M. (1997). Drug abuse: Hedonic homeostatic dysregulation. *Science, 278*, 52–58.

Koob, G. F., Le, H. T., & Creese, I. (1987). The D-1 dopamine receptor antagonist SCH 23390 increases cocaine self-administration in the rat. *Neuroscience Letters, 79*, 315–320.

Koob, G. F., & Nestler, E. J. (1997). The neurobiology of drug addiction. *Journal of Neuropsychiatry and Clinical Neurosciences, 9*, 482–497.

Koob, G. F., Pettit, H. O., Ettenberg, A., & Bloom, F. E. (1984). Effects of opiate antagonists and their quaternary derivatives on heroin self-administration in the rat. *Journal of Pharmacology and Experimental Therapeutics, 229*, 481–486.

Koob, G. F., Sanna, P. P., & Bloom, F. E. (1998). Neuroscience of addiction. *Neuron, 21*, 467–476.

Koob, G. F., Wall, T. L., & Bloom, F. E. (1989). Nucleus accumbens as a substrate for the aversive stimulus effects of opiate withdrawal. *Psychopharmacology, 98*, 530–534.

Kreek, M. J. (1987). Multiple drug abuse patterns and medical consequences. In H. Y. Meltzer (Ed.), *Psychopharmacology: The third generation of progress* (pp. 1597–1604). New York: Raven Press.

Kreek, M. J., Ragunath, J., Plevy S., Hamer, D., Schneider, B., & Hartman, N. (1984). ACTH, cortisol and beta-endorphin response to metyrapone testing during chronic methadone maintenance treatment in humans. *Neuropeptides, 5*, 277–278.

Legault, M., & Wise, R. A. (1994). Effects of withdrawal from nicotine on intracranial self-stimulation (abstract). *Society for Neuroscience Abstracts, 20*, 1032.

Leith, N. J., & Barrett, R. J. (1976). Amphetamine and the reward system: Evidence for tolerance and post-drug depression. *Psychopharmacologia, 46*, 19–25.

Leone, P., & Di Chiara, G. (1987). Blockade of D1 receptors by SCH 23390 antagonizes morphine- and amphetamine-induced place preference conditioning. *European Journal of Pharmacology, 135*, 251–254.

Lepore, M., Liu, X., Savage, V., Matalon, D., & Gardner, E. L. (1996). Genetic differences in delta 9-tetrahydrocannabinol-induced facilitation of brain stimulation reward as measured by a rate-frequency curve-shift electrical brain stimulation paradigm in three different rat strains. *Life Science, 58*, PL365–PL372.

Lepore, M., Vorel, S. R., Lowinson, J., & Gardner, E. L. (1995). Conditioned place preference induced by delta 9-tetrahydrocannabinol: Comparison with cocaine, morphine, and food reward. *Life Sciences, 56*, 2073–2080.

Liebman, J. M., & Cooper, S. J. (1989). The neuropharmacological basis of reward. Oxford: Clarendon Press.

Liljequist, S., & Engel, J. (1982). Effects of GABAergic agonists and antagonists on various ethanol-induced behavioral changes. *Psychopharmacology, 78*, 71–75.

Lovinger, D. M., White, G., & Weight, F. F. (1989). Ethanol inhibits NMDA-activated ion current in hippocampal neurons. *Science, 243*, 1721–1724.

Malin, D. H., Lake, J. R., Carter, V. A., Cunningham, J. S., Hebert, K. M., Conrad, D. L., & Wilson, O. B. (1994). The nicotine antagonist mecamylamine precipitates nicotine abstinence syndrome in the rat. *Psychopharmacology, 115*, 180–184.

Malin, D. H., Lake, J. R., Carter, V. A., Cunningham, J. S., & Wilson, O. B. (1993). Naloxone precipitates abstinence syndrome in the rat. *Psychopharmacology, 112*, 339–342.

Markou, A., & Koob, G. F. (1991). Postcocaine anhedonia: An animal model of cocaine withdrawal. *Neuropsychopharmacology, 4*, 17–26.

Markou, A., Koob, G. F. (1992). Construct validity of a self-stimulation threshold paradigm: Effects of reward and performance manipulations. *Physiology and Behavior, 51*, 111–119.

Matthes, H. W., Maldonado, R., Simonin, F., Valverde, O., Slowe, S., Kitchen, I., Befort, K., Dierich, A., Le Meur, M., Dolle, P., Tzavara, E., Hanoune, J., Roques, B., & Kieffer, B. L. (1996). Loss of morphine-induced analgesia, reward effect and withdrawal symptoms in mice lacking the mu-opioid-receptor gene. *Nature, 383*, 819–823.

Merlo-Pich, E., Lorang, M., Yeganeh, M., Rodriguez de Fonseca, F., Raber, J., Koob, G. F., & Weiss, F. (1995). Increase of extracellular corticotropin-releasing factor-like immunoreactivity levels in the amygdala of awake rats during restraint stress and ethanol withdrawal as measured by microdialysis. *Journal of Neuroscience, 15*, 5439–5447.

Morency, M. A., & Beninger, R. J. (1986) Dopaminergic substrates of cocaine-induced place conditioning. *Brain Research, 399*, 33–41.

Murai, T., Koshikawa, N., Kanayama, T., Takada, K., Tomiyama, K., & Kobayashi, M. (1994). Opposite effects of midazolam and beta-carboline-3-carboxylate ethyl ester on the release of dopamine from rat nucleus accumbens measured by in vivo microdialysis. *European Journal of Pharmacology, 261*, 65–71.

Nauta, J. H., & Haymaker, W. (1969). Hypothalamic nuclei and fiber connections. In W. Haymaker, E. Anderson, & W.J.H. Nauta (Eds.), *The hypothalamus* (pp. 136–209). Springfield, IL: Charles C. Thomas.

Negus, S. S., Henriksen, S. J., Mattox, A., Pasternak, G. W., Portoghese, P. S., Takemori, A. E., Weinger, M. B., & Koob, G. F. (1993). Effect of antagonists selective for mu, delta and kappa opioid receptors on the reinforcing effects of heroin in rats. *Journal of Pharmacology and Experimental Therapeutics, 265,* 1245–1252.

O'Brien, C. P. (1975). Experimental analysis of conditioning factors in human narcotic addiction. *Pharmacological Reviews, 27,* 533–543.

O'Brien, C. P., Eckardt, M. J., & Linnoila, V.M.I. (1995). Pharmacotherapy of alcoholism. In F. E. Blood, D. J. Kupfer (Eds.), *Psychopharmacology: the fourth generation of progress* (pp. 1745–1755). New York: Raven Press.

O'Malley, S. S., Jaffe, A. J., Chang, G., Schottenfeld, R. S., Meyer, R. E., & Rounsaville, B. (1992). Naltrexone and coping skills therapy for alcohol dependence: A controlled study. *Archives of General Psychiatry, 49,* 881–887.

Olds, J., & Milner, P. (1954). Positive reinforcement produced by electrical stimulation of septal area and other regions of rat brain. *Journal of Comparative and Physiological Psychology, 47,* 419–427.

Parsons, L. H., Koob, G. F., & Weiss, F. (1995). Serotonin dysfunction in the nucleus accumbens of rats during withdrawal after unlimited access to intra-venous cocaine. *Journal of Pharmacology and Experimental Therapeutics, 274,* 1182–1191.

Pettit, H. O., Ettenberg, A., Bloom, F. E., & Koob, G. F. (1984). Destruction of dopamine in the nucleus accumbens selectively attenuates cocaine but not heroin self-administration in rats. *Psychopharmacology, 84,* 167–173.

Pfeffer, A. O., & Samson, H. H. (1988). Haloperidol and apomorphine effects on ethanol reinforcement in free-feeding rats. *Pharmacology, Biochemistry and Behavior, 29,* 343–350.

Phillips, A. G., & Fibiger, H. C. (1987). Anatomical and neurochemical sub-strates of drug reward determined by the conditioned place preference tech-nique. In M. A. Bozarth (Ed.), *Methods of assessing the reinforcing properties of abused drugs* (pp. 275–290). New York: Springer-Verlag.

Pijnenburg, A.J.J., Honig, W.M.M., & Van Rossum, J. M. (1975). Inhibition of d-amphetamine-induced locomotor activity by injection of haloperidol into the nucleus accumbens of the rat. *Psychopharmacologia, 41,* 87–95.

Pontieri, F. E., Tanda, G., & Di Chiara, G. (1995). Intravenous cocaine, mor-phine, and amphetamine preferentially increase extracellular dopamine in the "shell" as compared with the "core" of the rat nucleus accumbens. *Proceedings of the National Academy of Sciences of the United States of America, 92,* 12304–12308.

Pontieri, F. E., Tanda, G., Orzi, F., & Di Chiara, G. (1996). Effects of nicotine on the nucleus accumbens and similarity to those of addictive drugs. *Nature, 382,* 255–257.

Rassnick, S., D'Amico, E., Riley, E., Pulvirenti, L., Zieglgansberger, W., & Koob, G. F. (1992). GABA and nucleus accumbens glutamate neurotrans-mission modulate ethanol self-administration in rats. In P. W. Kalivas & H. H. Samson (Eds.), *The neurobiology of drug and alcohol addiction.* Annals of the New York Academy of Sciences (Vol. 654, pp. 502–505). New York: The New York Academy of Sciences.

Rassnick, S., Heinrichs, S. C., Britton, K. T., & Koob, G. F. (1993). Microinjection of a corticotropin-releasing factor antagonist into the central nucleus of the amygdala reverses anxiogenic-like effects of ethanol withdrawal. *Brain Research, 605,* 25–32.

Rassnick, S., Stinus, L., & Koob, G. F. (1993). The effects of 6-hydroxydopamine lesions of the nucleus accumbens and the mesolimbic dopamine system on oral self-administration of ethanol in the rat. *Brain Research, 623,* 16–24.

Richards, G., Schoch, P., & Haefely, W. (1991). Benzodiazepine receptors: New vistas. *Seminars in Neuroscience, 3,* 191–203.

Richter, R. M., & Weiss, F. (1999). In vivo CRF release in rat amygdala is increased during cocaine withdrawal in self-administering rats. *Synapse, 32,* 254–261.

Roberts, A. J., Cole, M., & Koob, G. F. (1996). Intra-amygdala muscimol decreases operant ethanol self-administration in dependent rats. *Alcoholism, Clinical and Experimental Research, 20,* 1289–1298.

Rodriguez de Fonseca, F., Carrera, M.R.A., Navarro, M., Koob, G. F., & Weiss, F. (1997). Activation of corticotropin-releasing factor in the limbic system during cannabinoid withdrawal. *Science, 276,* 2050–2054.

Rudnick, G., & Clark, J. (1993). From synapse to vesicle: The reuptake and storage of biogenic amine neurotransmitters. *Biochimica et Biophysica Acta, 1144,* 249–263.

Russell, M.A.H. (1976). What is dependence? In G. Edwards, M.A.H. Russell, D. Hawks, & M. MacCafferty (Eds.), *Drugs and drug dependence* (pp. 182–187). Lexington, MA: Lexington Books.

Samson, H. H., Tolliver, G. A., Pfeffer, A. O., Sadeghi, K. G., & Mills, F. G. (1987). Oral ethanol reinforcement in the rat: Effect of the partial inverse benzodiazepine agonist RO15-4513. *Pharmacology, Biochemistry and Behavior, 27,* 517–519.

Sarnyai, Z., Biro, E., Gardi, J., Vecsernyes, M., Julesz, J., & Telegdy, G. (1995). Brain corticotropin-releasing factor mediates "anxiety-like" behavior induced by cocaine withdrawal in rats. *Brain Research, 675,* 89–97.

Schulteis, G., Markou, A., Cole, M., & Koob, G. F. (1995). Decreased brain reward produced by ethanol withdrawal. *Proceedings of the National Academy of Sciences of the United States of America, 92,* 5880–5884.

Schulteis, G., Markou, A., Gold, L. H., Stinus, L., & Koob, G. F. (1994). Relative sensitivity to naloxone of multiple indices of opiate withdrawal: A quantitative dose-response analysis. *Journal of Pharmacology and Experimental Therapeutics, 271,* 1391–1398.

Schuster, C. R., & Thompson, T. (1969). Self-administration and behavioral dependence on drugs. *Annual Review of Pharmacology and Toxicology, 9,* 483–502.

Self, D. W., Barnhart, W. J., Lehman, D. A., & Nestler, E. J. (1996). Opposite modulation of cocaine-seeking behavior by D1- and D2-like dopamine receptor agonists. *Science, 271*, 1586–1589.

Shippenberg, T. S., Herz, A., Spanagel, R., Bals-Kubik, R., & Stein, C. (1992). Conditioning of opioid reinforcement: Neuroanatomical and neurochemical substrates. In P. W. Kalivas & H. H. Samson (Eds.), *The neurobiology of drug and alcohol addiction*. Annals of the New York Academy of Sciences (Vol. 654, pp. 347–356). New York: The New York Academy of Sciences.

Solomon, R. L. (1977). The opponent-process theory of acquired motivation: The affective dynamics of addiction. In J. D. Maser & M.E.P. Seligman (Eds.), *Psychopathology: Experimental models* (pp. 124–145). San Francisco: W.H. Freeman.

Solomon, R. L. (1980). The opponent process theory of acquired motivation: The costs of pleasure and the benefits of pain. *American Journal of Psychology, 35*, 691–712.

Spyraki, C., Fibiger, H. C., & Phillips, A. G. (1983). Attenuation of heroin reward in rats by disruption of the mesolimbic dopamine system. *Psychopharmacology, 79*, 278–283.

Stein, L. (1968). Chemistry of reward and punishment. In D. H. Efron (Ed.), Psychopharmacology, a review of progress (1957–1967) (pp. 105–123). Washington, DC: U.S. Government Printing Office.

Stewart, J., & deWit, H. (1987). Reinstatement of drug-taking behavior as a method of assessing incentive motivational properties of drugs. In M. A. Bozarth (Ed.), *Methods of assessing the reinforcing properties of abused drugs*. New York: Springer-Verlag.

Stinus, L., Le Moal, M., & Koob, G. F. (1990). Nucleus accumbens and amygdala are possible substrates for the aversive stimulus effects of opiate withdrawal. *Neuroscience, 37*, 767–773.

Stinus, L., Nadaud, D., Deminiere, J. M., Jauregui, J., Hand, T. T., & Le Moal, M. (1989). Chronic flupentixol treatment potentiates the reinforcing properties of systemic heroin administration. *Biological Psychiatry, 26*, 363–371.

Suzdak, P. D., Glowa, J. R., Crawley, J. N., Schwartz, R. D., Skolnick, P., & Paul, S. M. (1986). A selective imidazobenzodiazepine antagonist of ethanol in the rat. *Science, 234*, 1243–1247.

Tanda, G., Pontieri, F. E., & Di Chiara, G. (1997). Cannabinoid and heroin activation of mesolimbic dopamine transmission by a common mu1 opioid receptor mechanism. *Science, 276*, 2048–2050.

Vaccarino, F. J., Pettit, H. O., Bloom, F. E., & Koob, G. F. (1985). Effects of intracerebroventricular administration of methyl naloxonium chloride on heroin self-administration in the rat. *Pharmacology Biochemistry and Behavior, 23*, 495–498.

Valenstein, E. S., & Campbell, J. F. (1966). Medial forebrain bundle-lateral hypothalmic area and reinforcing brain stimulation. *American Journal Physiology, 210,* 270–274.

Volpicelli, J. R., Alterman, A. I., Hayashida, M., & O'Brien, C. P. (1992). Naltrexone in the treatment of alcohol dependence. *Archives of General Psaychiatry, 49,* 876–880.

Volpicelli, J. R., Davis, M. A., & Olgin, J. E. (1986). Naltrexone blocks the post-shock increase of ethanol consumption. *Life Science, 38,* 841–847.

Weddington, W. W., Jr., Brown, B. S., Haertzen, C. A., Hess, J. M., Mahaffey, J. R., Kolar, A. F., & Jaffe, J. H. (1991). Comparison of amantadine and desipramine combined with psychotherapy for treatment of cocaine dependence. *American Journal of Drug and Alcohol Abuse, 17,* 137–152.

Weeks, J. R., & Collins, R. J. (1976). Changes in morphine self-administration in rats induced by prostaglandin E1 and naloxone. *Prostaglandins, 12,* 11–19.

Weiss, F., Hurd, Y. L., Ungerstedt, U., Markou, A., Plotsky, P. M., & Koob, G. F. (1992). Neurochemical correlates of cocaine and ethanol self-administration. In P. W. Kalivas & H. H. Samson (Eds.), *The neurobiology of drug and alcohol addiction.* Annals of the New York Academy of Sciences (Vol. 654, pp. 220–241). New York: The New York Academy of Sciences.

Weiss, F., Markou, A., Lorang, M. T., & Koob, G. F. (1992). Basal extracellular dopamine levels in the nucleus accumbens are decreased during cocaine withdrawal after unlimited access self-administration. *Brain Research, 593,* 314–318.

Weiss, F., Parsons, L. H., Schulteis, G., Hyytia, P., Lorang, M. T., Blood, F. E., & Koob, G. F. (1996). Ethanol self-administration restores withdrawal-associated deficiencies in accumbal dopamine and 5-hydroxytryptamine release in dependent rats. *Journal of Neuroscience, 16,* 3474–3485.

Widnell, K., Self, D. W., Lane, S. B., Russell, D. S., Vaidya, V. A., Miserendino, M.J.D., Rubin, C. S., Duman, R. S., & Nestler, E. J. (1996). Regulation of CREB expression: In vivo evidence for a functional role in morphine action in the nucleus accumbens. *Jorunal of Pharmacology and Experimental Therapeutics, 276,* 306–315.

Wikler, A. (1973). Dynamics of drug dependence: Implications of a conditioning theory for research and treatment. *Archives of General Psychiatry, 28,* 611–616.

Wise, R. A. (1988). The neurobiology of craving: Implications for the understanding and treatment of addiction. *Journal of Abnormal Psychology, 97,* 118–132.

Woolverton, W. L., & Virus, R. M. (1989). The effects of a D1 and a D2 dopamine antagonist on behavior maintained by cocaine or food. *Pharmacology, Biochemistry and Behavior, 32,* 691–697.

Yokel, R. A., & Wise, R. A. (1975). Increased lever pressing for amphetamine after pimozide in rats: Implications for a dopamine theory of reward. *Science, 187,* 547–549.

Part VI

Conclusion

16

The Gateway Hypothesis Revisited

Denise B. Kandel and Richard Jessor

The chapters in this volume present what is currently known about the Gateway Hypothesis. Their authors have explored the hypothesis from various perspectives ranging from developmental social psychology to prevention and intervention science, and from animal models and neurobiology to analytical methodology. The presentations have elaborated the nature and extent of the empirical support for the Gateway Hypothesis at this point in time. They have also revealed the complexities embedded in the formulation of the Gateway Hypothesis. In this brief Afterword, we revisit the hypothesis in light of what our colleagues have reported, and we discuss several conclusions that derive from their presentations.

Parsing the Gateway Hypothesis

Advancing understanding of the Gateway Hypothesis requires that it be parsed into three interrelated, component propositions. All three have emerged from the research and the reviews reported in the preceding chapters.

The first proposition embedded in the Gateway Hypothesis is that among adolescents *there is a developmental sequence of involvement with different classes or categories of drugs*, such that initiation into drug use begins with the drugs earlier in the sequence, namely, the legal drugs, alcohol and tobacco. Involvement with illicit drugs occurs later in the developmental sequence; and marijuana is the bridge in the sequence between the licit and the other illicit drugs. Although there are further refinements to be made about the sequence of drug progression (especially about differentiation within the licit and illicit categories of drugs), the central assertion of the sequence proposition is that drug progression among adolescents proceeds sequentially, or in ordered stages, from licit drugs through marijuana to other illicit drugs. The evidence for this proposition and this particular sequence is quite robust across the last two decades in American society. There is also supporting evidence from other Western nations.

The second proposition embedded in the Gateway Hypothesis is that *the use of a drug earlier in the sequence is associated with an increased risk or likelihood of use of a drug later in the sequence.* The evidence in support of the proposition about association is also strong and derives both from etiological and prevention/intervention studies, including those presented in this volume.

The third proposition encompassed by the Gateway Hypothesis is that *the use of a drug earlier in the sequence, such as alcohol or tobacco, causes the use of a drug later in the sequence, for instance, marijuana.* This is the Gateway Hypothesis proposition that is most widely invoked in public discourse and in policy debates. Even among interventionists, it is often part of the rationale for a focus on programs to prevent initiation of drugs early in the sequence. The research reported in this volume and that reviewed in the various chapters provide no support for the proposition about causality. There is no compelling evidence that the use of a drug earlier in the sequence, in and of itself, causes the use of a drug later in the sequence or, for that matter, that it causes the use of any other drug or, indeed, any other behavior. The difficulty of establishing causality is, of course, intrinsic to much of social science. Making a causal claim is difficult in the absence of carefully controlled experimental designs. Even more important, perhaps, is the difficulty of ruling out alternative inferences that can explain the association between the initiation of an earlier drug and the initiation of a later drug in the developmental sequence. At this time, the causal interpretation of the Gateway Hypothesis is still without scientific foundation.

In the discussion that follows, we examine each of the three propositions in light of what has been learned from the chapters in this volume. Our discussion is framed within a perspective about adolescent development as a whole, a perspective in which drug initiation and progression must be seen as only one aspect of the larger process of development and change in both person and social context that characterizes this period of the life course. A full understanding of drug use in the life of an adolescent can only be achieved by understanding as well the rest of the adolescent's life and the everyday social world in which the adolescent is situated.

The Sequence Proposition

As noted earlier, the evidence for a prototypical developmental sequence of drug use from alcohol or tobacco, to marijuana, to other illicit drugs is well established in the United States and in other selected countries. From the larger perspective on adolescent development, a developmental sequence within a domain of behavior is not unusual and is even to be expected. Sexual development, for example, has well established developmental staging from autoerotic initiation, to so-called "necking" to "petting above the waist," to "petting below the waist," to "going all the way." The same is true for delinquent behavior, which begins with minor transgressions and status offenses and progresses to misdemeanors and then to felonies. In these other domains, it is perhaps more easily seen that the developmental sequence is socially organized and involves processes of exploration and learning, and of social opportunity and access. The normative regulation of developmental sequences in these domains applies just as well to drug use development, as do the issues of differential social opportunity and differential access. Indeed, it is clear that the developmental sequence of drug involvement is socially and historically determined and that it may vary over time and in different groups. The first drug that an individual will use is likely to be that which is most readily available and which is also legally and normatively acceptable.

A more penetrating consideration of the drug progression sequence raises a number of important issues. First, although well established, the sequence cannot be considered invariant. There are variations in the extent to which the basic pattern is observed in different groups and at different historical periods. Racial minorities are somewhat less likely to follow the orderly progression than Whites; younger cohorts, born after 1965, are less likely to exhibit that pattern than older cohorts born earlier; a higher proportion of heavy users have started their drug career with an illicit drug compared with individuals in the general population; and there is evidence of subgroups of individuals who initiate their drug use with drugs later in the sequence, or who skip stages, or who initiate drugs from different stages in the sequence, for example, alcohol and marijuana, simultaneously. What this means is that sequential progression is not inherent in the nature of the drugs themselves but emerges from the social organization of their availability and the social and personal definitions of their use.

Second, initiation of a drug early in the sequence does not entail the beginning of an inexorable progression through the remainder of the sequence. Only a very small minority of youth progress to late-stage illicit drug use. It is only for this small segment of drug users that the sequence of drug progression as a whole is relevant.

Third, the sequence is based entirely on the use of different drugs or classes of drugs rather than on differential use of a given drug. Yet, there is progression within the use of a drug, from initiation and exploration to more regular use to daily use to heavy use to dependence. How this within drug progression maps onto the between drug progression has not been well explored.

Fourth, the sequence of drug progression reflects a developmental order based on drug use behavior alone, as if drug use were independent of the adolescent's involvement in other, non–drug use behavior occurring during the very same period of the life course. It is more useful to see the drug progression sequence as having been extirpated from a much richer and more complex developmental sequence that includes other key behaviors and experiences, such as sexual initiation, dropping out of school, starting a part-time job, joining a gang, experiencing psychiatric problems, or getting involved in church activities. Establishing the location of non–drug use experiences within the drug progression sequence would not only provide a deeper understanding of the sequence itself, but would embed drug progression within the course of adolescent development as a whole.

Finally, there is the issue of whether additional drugs need to be considered in the drug progression sequence. The potential importance of caffeine as an earlier licit drug that might well precede alcohol and tobacco in any sequence of drug progression has been raised. Similarly, prescribed psychotropic drugs may represent the last stage in the progression. Studies of the drug progression sequence will need to give more attention to these possibilities.

In sum, although the sequence is well established, its meaning and significance for understanding drug use careers and adolescent development as a whole, are not yet obvious. The issues we have touched on constitute part of an agenda for future research to achieve a deeper understanding of the larger significance of the sequence of drug progression.

The Association Proposition

The association proposition assumes that the use of an earlier stage drug is correlated with an increment in the risk of using a drug next in the sequence. For example, those who have used alcohol or tobacco are shown to be at increased risk of using marijuana compared with those who have never used alcohol or tobacco. Said otherwise, it is less likely that an adolescent will use a drug later in the sequence if he or she has not already used a drug earlier in the sequence.

The research reported in the chapters in this volume, both the studies concerned with etiology and those concerned with prevention, have provided strong evidence in support of the association proposition. The likelihood of initiating a drug later in the sequence is enhanced among those who have initiated use of an earlier drug, and prevention of the initiation of a drug earlier in the sequence has been shown to be associated with a reduced likelihood of initiation of a drug later in the sequence.

What emerges most compellingly about the association proposition from the preceding chapters is that increased risk of transition through the drug sequence is associated far more strongly with *intensity* of use than it is with use per se. This is a critical contribution to a deeper understanding of the Gateway Hypothesis. The key antecedent to risk of progression to a later drug is heavy or frequent involvement with a drug earlier in the sequence. This conclusion has implications for both etiological and prevention research. For the former, it calls for greater understanding of variation in the risk and protective factors that generate a pervasive commitment to or enduring reliance on a drug so that its use is central to daily life and warrants characterization as abuse or dependence; for prevention it raises at least an additional agenda, the prevention of abuse or heavy involvement rather than of use alone.

The Causal Proposition

The association between the use of an earlier drug and the increased risk of use of one later in the sequence is often interpreted as demonstrating causal influence. Such an interpretation is untenable because association does not establish causation. The latter requires that all reasonable alternative inferences be rejected and that there be an understanding of the processes underlying association. The most obvious alternative inference is that those factors that influenced the use of the initial drug are also responsible for the use of the subsequent drug. There is a set of etiological "third variables" that underlie and explain the relationship between the two observed variables, the use of the initial drug and the increased risk of use of a subsequent drug. It is this important distinction that led us to parse the proposition of association from that of causation.

Several issues regarding the causal proposition have been clarified by the chapters in the volume. Consideration of causal influence needs to be concerned with intensity of use rather than use per se, because intensity appears to be more strongly associated than use with transition in the drug sequence. Moreover, any effort to establish causality will have to resolve the fundamental issue that the antecedent risk and protective factors that influenced earlier drug use, especially intense drug use, may also be the factors that influenced transition or progression to a later stage drug. Analyses that control for relevant antecedent influences in longitudinal designs are well represented in the chapters in this volume. Such efforts advance understanding by articulating the network of factors relevant to variation in adolescent drug use or intensity of use. They also have shown that the association between a lower-stage and a higher-stage drug can be reduced substantially by instituting such controls. The reduction in the magnitude of the association reflects the explanatory role played by the antecedent or control variables, and it reveals the success of the authors in achieving a substantial explanatory account of drug use and drug progression.

When an association remains after controlling a large variety of relevant variables, that residual association has sometimes been imputed to drug use itself, or to intensity of use, as representing its direct causal influence. However, such claims need to be tempered by the limitations of the existing evidence. First, all the relevant variables cannot be controlled in any single study. Even the most rigorous investigation can gain control over only a subset of the influences at work in an adolescent behavior as complex as drug use. Second, most investigators have given greater attention to assessing the adolescent than to assessing the larger social ecological factors and the immediate context of drug use behavior. The social environment is often summarized by a handful of sociodemographic attributes that are relatively remote from behavior, or by perceived models and pressure for drug use. Much less attention has been paid to assessment of the models themselves, to social norms, to cultural and subcultural values, to the social organization of access and availability of supplies, and to ethnographic assessments of the social meaning of adolescent drug use behavior in the various contexts of daily life. This is a key lacuna of uncontrolled variation in contemporary research on adolescent drug use.

Third, the domain of relevant variables under consideration should be broadened to include biological and genetic factors, and may benefit from the use of genetically informative samples, such as twins or adoptees.

Fourth, the research on delineating the factors that can account for variation in drug use has focused almost exclusively on establishing risk factors and, until very recently, has tended to ignore protective factors, factors that promote positive, prosocial behavior and that buffer the impact of exposure to risk. Clearly, variation in involvement with drugs, whether use or heavy use, is a joint outcome of the pattern of risk and protection that characterizes any sample of youth.

Fifth, it will be important to identify factors that may be differentially relevant at different stages of drug involvement, and for different subgroups of young people.

Finally, a more systematic approach to controlling the factors relevant to variation in drug involvement is to rely on theory to specify those variables. Greater reliance on theory would increase the likelihood of exhausting the multiple sources of variance involved.

Thus, it remains possible that uncontrolled sources of influence underlie whatever residual association obtains between earlier- and later-stage drug use. To reject that possibility, research that is comprehensive across all domains of influence from genetics to culture would be required. This is the reason why causal claims in the Gateway Hypothesis – the causal proposition – are still beyond reach.

Conclusion

The chapters in this volume demonstrate the understanding that contemporary behavioral science has achieved about how adolescents become involved in drug use and progress to the use of different drugs or drug classes. A major objective of the volume, to expand the range of approaches to the Gateway Hypothesis and to examine their convergence, has been achieved. The more common etiological studies were supplemented by prevention/intervention studies, by state-of-the-art analytic methodology, and by the contributions of animal models and neurobiology. These different approaches were all brought to bear on a single issue of broad societal concern – the Gateway Hypothesis. In this regard the enterprise is unique and its accomplishments are provocative.

Clearly, much remains to be done. Our parsing of the Gateway Hypothesis into propositions about sequence, association, and causality has suggested a research agenda that derives from each of those topics. Perhaps the overriding challenge for the future is to achieve a better understanding of heavy involvement with drugs and of the role of heavy involvement and of other factors in the transitions along the sequence of drug development. This challenge can be met by engaging new domains of knowledge and by more systematically articulating the domains we are already familiar with. With respect to new domains of knowledge, the work on animal models is promising. The pursuit of such models can capture some of the critical processes involved in drug use behavior and progression, such as the effects of prior exposure to drugs and the impact of stress. However, the limitations of these models for representing the personal meanings and the social aspects of drug use behavior will test the ingenuity of animal modelers in their future research. The work in neurobiology and the new developments in behavioral genetics represent other areas of increasing relevance to understanding processes underlying drug intensification and drug progression.

With regard to the more familiar domains of inquiry, there is a need for more penetrating assessments of the contexts of daily adolescent life, that is, for better contextual models. Greater attention also needs to be paid to protective factors in the adolescent, in the social context, and in the culture. Such efforts will expand our understanding of the factors relevant to variation in drug initiation as well as drug intensification and drug progression. The more exhaustive the explanatory account, the less likely there will be residual association to permit inferences about cause to be attached to drug use per se, or even to intensity of drug use.

We conclude that interpretations of the Gateway Hypothesis should be restricted to the propositions about sequencing and association. The causation proposition is without evidential support at this time. A research agenda that can help clarify where in the overall nomological network the causal vector should be located is what is clearly called for if we are to advance the science of drug initiation and drug progression. Implementing that agenda is the task before all of us.

Index